Proving Grounds

PROVING

GROUNDS

Militarized Landscapes, Weapons Testing, and the Environmental Impact of U.S. Bases

EDITED BY

Edwin A. Martini

UNIVERSITY OF WASHINGTON PRESS

Seattle and London

This publication is supported in part by a grant from the Burnham-Macmillan Endowment of the Department of History at Western Michigan University, and by the Donald R. Ellegood International Publications Endowment.

© 2015 by the University of Washington Press
Printed and bound in the United States of America
Design by Thomas Eykemans
Composed in Chaparral, typeface designed by Carol Twombly
18 17 16 15   5 4 3 2 1

UNIVERSITY OF WASHINGTON PRESS
www.washington.edu/uwpress

LIBRARY OF CONGRESS CATALOGING-IN-PUBLICATION DATA
Proving grounds : militarized landscapes, weapons testing, and the environmental impact of U.S. bases / edited by Edwin A. Martini. — 1st edition.
    p.   cm.
  Includes bibliographical references and index.
  ISBN 978-0-295-99465-9 (hardcover : alk. paper)
1. Military bases—United States—Environmental aspects.   2. Military bases, American—Environmental aspects.   3. Nuclear weapons—Testing—Environmental aspects.   4. United States—Military policy—Environmental aspects.   I. Martini, Edwin A., 1975–, editor.
II. Title: Militarized landscapes, weapons testing, and the environmental impact of U.S. bases.
  UC403.P76   2015
  355.7028'6—dc23   2014035526

FRONTISPIECE: The atomic cloud during the "Baker" nuclear test at the Bikini Atoll. Date: July 25, 1946. Source: commons.wikimedia.org.

For Alex, Sydney, and Ellie.

May you grow up in a cleaner,
safer, and more peaceful world.

Contents

Acknowledgments

THIS edited volume began with a number of conversations about military bases, weapons testing, environmental history, and the desire to broaden the approaches scholars were bringing to these topics. Having initially planned to produce a monograph, I discovered a network of colleagues working on similar projects. In conference sessions and in hallways at the annual meetings of the American Society for Environmental History and the Society of Historians of American Foreign Relations, that monograph turned into a collection of essays, and this book began to take shape. I am grateful to the organizers of those conferences for providing spaces for intellectual engagement that cross disciplinary, geographic, and even generational divides.

All of the contributors have been a joy to work with—incredibly responsive in turning their pieces around for publication. Although it startled me to learn that I had become a "senior" scholar in the eyes of many graduate students, I am pleased to have met so many wonderful, talented, up-and-coming scholars throughout this project. Their work represents promising new directions for scholarship in multiple fields, and I look forward to following their careers. At my own institution, I am appreciative of the ongoing support of my colleagues in the Department of History at Western Michigan University (WMU), especially after I took on a full-time administrative assignment. Several graduate assistants—particularly Bill Watson, Skylar Bre'z, and Leland Hart—helped with various stages of this work. My thanks go to them as well as to Joe Brandão, Mitch Kachun, and Dorilee Schieble for making those arrangements possible. I am especially grateful to Lynne Heasley, who introduced me to the wonderful world of environmental history and the many amazing scholars who populate it.

At WMU, I am incredibly fortunate to work with a wonderful group of people in the College of Arts and Sciences (CAS) who support my ongoing scholarly work. Dean Alex Enyedi has provided me the time and resources to research and write; my treasured colleague Cathryn Bailey has taught me so much about so many things; my partner in crime and fellow Minnesotan Kevin Knutson is a joy to work, play, and conspire with; and Kim Hunt and the rest of the CAS team make coming to work everyday fun and rewarding.

Having long admired the University of Washington Press, particularly its offerings in environmental studies, I am pleased that they agreed to publish this manuscript. My sincere appreciation goes to Ranjit Arab, Tim Zimmermann, Jacqueline Volin, and the rest of the wonderful staff at the press for all their hard work and support throughout every stage of this project.

Finally, as always, none of this would have been possible without my family. With this book completed, I hope to find more time to visit and, in some cases to meet, my beautiful nieces, to whom this book is dedicated. To my boys, Gracen and Kyan, and most important, to Genanne Zeller: I do not know what I could possibly have done to deserve to share my life with three such amazing people, but I live every day in profound appreciation for each of you.

Proving Grounds

INTRODUCTION

Bases, Places, and the Layered Landscapes of American Empire

EDWIN A. MARTINI

THROUGHOUT the southeastern United States today, the longleaf pine ecosystem is a shadow of its former self. It used to dominate the landscapes of this region, but years of economic development and population growth have taken a significant toll, drastically reducing the reach of this species. One area in rural Georgia is an exception to this rule. Here, the pines continue to grow thick and tall, protected by a local organization deeply invested in maintaining the natural environment. That unlikely conservationist is the U.S. Army.[1]

Fort Stewart, home to the Third Infantry Division, has long been a testing ground for military hardware and tactics. It also has become a testing ground for the twenty-first-century "greening" of the military, in which ecosystem conservation—long assumed to be antithetical to militarized landscapes—is seen as a means of supporting and training U.S. forces while the army provides a form of environmental steward-ship to the land under its control. As is to be expected, such a relation-ship is not without its contradictions. The defense and protection of this forest of old-growth, largely fire-resistant trees has provided an ideal training ground for the troops, who have been deployed exten-sively in the war in Iraq.[2] Fort Stewart and the longleaf pine are among a surprisingly large number of complex intersections between the U.S. military and the landscapes—natural, human, and cultural—in which it operates. Yet these interactions remain surprisingly little studied by both military and environmental studies scholars. This book seeks to fill that gap.

Proving Grounds brings together an international and interdisciplinary group of scholars to explore the ways in which the natural environment has both shaped and been shaped by the proliferation of U.S. military bases and weapons testing during the second half of the twentieth century. Featuring the work of historians, political scientists, geographers, and environmental studies scholars, this collection moves beyond the limits of previous approaches to the subject by integrating diplomatic, military, and political history with perspectives from environmental studies that take nonhuman elements and actors as central subjects with historical agency. The result is a complex and nuanced view that embraces the ironies, contradictions, and unintended consequences of U.S. militarism around the world. Far from the seemingly monolithic style offered in other edited volumes, these essays survey the environmental damage caused by weapons testing and military bases but also reveal how the natural environment has shaped and, in some cases, limited the power of the U.S. military. In certain instances, military bases have served as unintended protectorates for flora and fauna that might have otherwise been destroyed. Taken as a whole, the contributions in this book demonstrate exciting approaches by scholars currently working at the intersections of these fields. Also explored are possible future directions for interdisciplinary research on a range of topics.

The expansion of U.S. military bases after the 1950s has produced a somewhat limited range of scholarly studies, particularly since the end of the Cold War in the early 1990s. As politicians, policy makers, and their constituents grappled with the problems posed by America's "empire of bases" and the economies and communities that have grown up around them, scholars sought to make sense of questions that had been largely ignored during the Cold War. Recent scholarship examining military bases has generally fallen into one of two schools: a "policy" approach, largely rooted in political science and international relations, and a "resistance" school, rooted largely in anthropology and history. Within these schools are two somewhat overlapping waves.

EDWIN A. MARTINI

The first wave of scholarship, appearing in the late 1990s and early 2000s, attempted to accomplish two things: first, it sought to document and name the empire, to make visible that which had remained largely invisible to American citizens for so long; second, it examined the political and economic problems posed by these bases after the Cold War in terms of what it would mean both for local communities threatened with the closure of bases on which they relied and for the United States to maintain its extensive network of overseas bases now that the Cold War was over. Such books as David Sorenson's *Shutting Down the Cold War: The Politics of Military Base Closure*, Anni Baker's *American Soldiers Overseas*, and Kent Calder's *Embattled Garrisons: Comparative Base Politics and American Globalism* represented the policy school of this initial wave, documenting the network of bases and detailing the surrounding politics from a detached perspective and largely leaving aside value judgments about American militarism and imperialism.[3]

An alternative trend during the same period took a much more critical stance. Led by Chalmers Johnson's *Blowback: The Costs and Consequences of American Empire*, this scholarship provided the framework for the resistance school that would emerge in the second wave. The pioneering interdisciplinary work of Cynthia Enloe laid the foundation for a feminist critique of bases and militarism. In such books as *The Morning After: Sexual Politics at the End of the Cold War* and *Bananas, Beaches, and Bases: Making Feminist Sense of International Politics*, Enloe provided a more sophisticated social and political map of the empire of bases and its impact on the everyday life of its many diverse subjects.[4] Although many of these early policy studies contained material on resistance to U.S. bases overseas by citizens of the nations in which they were located, this issue came to dominate the second wave of scholarship, which followed closely on the heels of the first. Combining the efforts of the policy school to document and catalog the empire with the more critical approaches of Enloe and Johnson, this next movement focused almost exclusively on the question of resistance and adopted a more focused, case study approach on particular bases. Some investigations within this school, exemplified by Alexander Cooley's *Base Politics: Democratic Change and the U.S. Military Overseas*, built on the more detached policy perspectives rooted in political sciences and international relations. These studies explored, for example, the negotiations of status-of-forces agreements (SOFAs).

Other scholarship, largely rooted in anthropology—most notably Catherine Lutz's edited collection *Bases of Empire: The Global Struggle against U.S. Military Outposts*—enlisted activists and academics alike to document the multifaceted resistance among local residents to U.S. bases around the world. This wave provided a number of monograph-length case studies, but the overwhelming majority focused on the largest and most well-known U.S. bases: those in Germany, Japan, Puerto Rico, and South Korea. Katherine McCaffrey's *Military Power and Popular Protest: The U.S. Navy in Vieques, Puerto Rico*, Masamichi Inoue's *Okinawa and the U.S. Military: Identity Making in the Age of Globalization*, and Maria Höhn and Seungsook Moon's *Over There: Living with the U.S. Military Empire from World War Two to the Present* all built on the work of Enloe and the resistance school to offer increasingly complex views of the impact U.S. bases have had on local communities, economies, and identities around the world.[5]

Although these bodies of literature have grown more sophisticated over time, they continue to be limited in fundamental ways. They remain largely bound by disciplines and fields. Even the rich collections of essays in *Bases of Empire* and *Over There* are rooted almost exclusively in social science approaches from anthropology, history, and sociology, which limit the questions asked. Most notably, these perspectives have focused only on the human actors involved, paying little if any attention to the environmental consequences of the bases and to the role played at and around the sites by nonhuman actors. By bringing environmental studies scholars into the mix, *Proving Grounds* addresses a broader range of questions from an expanded set of approaches. The resistance school, furthermore, has exclusively explored *overseas* bases, ignoring the issues surrounding U.S. installations regardless of location. One of the major benefits of embracing methods from environmental studies is that scholars are encouraged to transcend national, geographic, and disciplinary boundaries.

Proving Grounds offers a global study from multiple perspectives, providing a multifaceted analysis of the impact of U.S. military installations at home and around the world. This collection seeks to build on more recent work from such scholars as J. R. McNeil, David Painter, Chris Pearson, Peter Coates, and Tim Cole—all of whom have moved the examination of militarized landscapes in richly interdisciplinary and transnational directions. The book seeks not only to fill a gap in the existing literature but also to serve as a model for future exploration in multiple fields. The contributors, largely junior scholars working on the cutting edge, have constructed essays that will shape the conversations at the intersection of these fields for years to come.[6] This volume grew in part out of related panels at both the American Society for Environmental History and the Society for Historians of American Foreign Relations, which suggests the power of the recent convergence in these fields. The intersection of military and environmental history is indeed powerful and growing, demonstrated by special issues of such journals as *Diplomatic History* that have been devoted to environmental approaches, the growing presence of pieces related to military history in the flagship journal *Environmental History*, and the parallel trend of environmentally focused essays appearing in the *Journal of Military History* and *War and Society*.[7]

THE ESSAYS

The chapters in *Proving Grounds* are organized chronologically and thematically, exploring the changes and evolution in weapons testing, base politics, and environmentalist thinking in the second half of the twentieth century. The first three chapters look at the militarization of landscapes, largely in the North American West, after the Second World War. Brandon C. Davis's chapter 1, "Defending the Nation, Protecting the Land: Emergency Powers and the Militarization of American Public Lands," lays the foundation. Contrary to many interpretations, the mid-century militarization of public lands in the United States was not an inevitable response to a wartime crisis beyond the control of policy makers. In fact, the U.S. military's initial legal claims to public lands were temporary, tenuous, and controversial. These claims relied on an extralegal, overreaching system of executive military land withdrawal that became formalized during the transition from world war to Cold War. Despite this shift, the military's land use policies remained ad hoc, which led to widespread abuse, inefficiency, and mismanagement that proved detrimental to public land users. Drawing on numerous examples from executive orders and legal cases, Davis's chapter provides a foundational understanding into the broader federal land claim authority upon which all subsequent developments at U.S. bases established during and after World War II are predicated.

The defining tool tested in, on, above, and around these increasingly militarized landscapes was, of course, nuclear weaponry. Countless scholarship has explored the history, culture, and impact of the atomic bomb, but few have taken into account the role that natural and environmental forces have played in testing and development. Neil Oatsvall, in chapter 2, "Weather, Otters, and Bombs: Policy Making, Environmental Science, and U.S. Nuclear Weapons Testing, 1945–1958," probes the relationship between U.S. nuclear testing and the environment from 1945 to 1960 to demonstrate nature's integral role in the development of U.S. tests. Policy makers of the era deeply understood the importance of the natural world, even if they would not have articulated their thoughts as such. There was an intense relationship between testing and natural phenomena such as the weather, local testing environs, and animals in the area.

Decision makers certainly did not set out to protect the environment with nuclear tests, but their choices in many instances demonstrated a deep sensitivity to the natural world. Oatsvall uses multiple case studies, including tests on Pacific islands and underground testing, to show that far greater attention was paid to the impact on water and wildlife than has previously been appreciated. The natural world structured the range of choices and decisions available to policy makers. From the landscape and geology of islands, to the weather patterns in the Pacific, to the local sea otter population, Oatsvall makes a convincing case that the nexus of nuclear weapons and the natural world operated as a two-way street: scientific conceptions of the environment affected atomic tests just as much (or more) as tests altered the natural world.

In chapter 3, Leisl Carr Childers explores shifts in the mind-sets of those in communities directly affected by weapons testing. By the mid-1950s the military-industrial complex, in particular its nuclear components, had become part of everyday life for many living in the American West. In "Incident at Galisteo: The 1955 Teapot Series and the Mental Landscape of Contamination," Childers shows how the U.S. military, the Atomic Energy Commission (AEC), and ranchers in central Nevada negotiated agreements as to where and when to run bombing missions, conduct atomic tests, and graze cattle. Rather than deem these activities incompatible on the same geography, government officials and ranchers in Nevada worked out informal arrangements. Using a variety of sources to reconstruct the varied reactions to expanded nuclear testing,

EDWIN A. MARTINI

Childers examines how the rapid growth in knowledge about the effects and risks of radiation radically altered not only the relationship between many ranchers and the federal government but also the mental maps that the ranchers used to make sense of their surrounding landscape. An investigation of cattle deaths believed by the ranchers to be caused by radioactive fallout highlights Childers's central point. In many cases the ranchers were heavily invested in, and benefited directly from, the military-industrial complex. The possibility and eventual likelihood that their cattle had been killed by radiation (although they never got definitive proof) shook the confidence that many had in the nuclear program, the military, and the federal government.

As weapons testing and the American empire of bases expanded during the Cold War, the landscapes of contamination and the reach of the U.S. military expanded well beyond the American West. Chapter 4, my own, "'This Is Really Bad Stuff Buried Here': Agent Orange, Johnston Atoll, and the Rise of Military Environmentalism," looks at the remote outpost of Johnston Atoll, about eight hundred miles southeast of Hawaii, to demonstrate the reach of these landscapes and the growth in "military environmentalism" that became increasingly prevalent into the 1970s. During the late 1950s and early 1960s, Johnston became a primary location for atmospheric nuclear testing, and after the United States returned control of Okinawa to Japan in 1970, the military moved large quantities of chemical munitions from Okinawa to Johnston. The atoll base became best known for its role in the final destruction of U.S. stockpiles of Agent Orange after the use of the herbicide was discontinued in the Vietnam War. Johnston became a test site for hazardous military operations in the age of environmentalist thinking.

Forced to grapple with the Environmental Protection Agency (EPA) and other new regulatory and statutory developments, the same U.S. military that continued to deny that Agent Orange was harmful to soldiers and civilians was now required to write lengthy, detailed environmental impact statements documenting the safety procedures to be used in the operations, the hazards posed by the chemicals themselves, and the overall potential impact of the procedures on everything from drinking water and air quality to coral reef growth and the migratory patterns of rare birds. By exploring what these efforts meant for the air force and for the soldiers and airmen who participated in them, this chapter shows how the U.S. military, albeit unintentionally and somewhat reluctantly, made significant contributions to the rise of environmentalist thinking in the 1970s.

The use of unconventional weapons such as herbicides, most commonly associated with the Vietnam War, remains a grossly understudied area of U.S. Cold War history. Daniel Weimer, in chapter 5, "The War on Plants: Drug Control, Militarization, and the Rehabilitation of Herbicides in U.S. Foreign Policy from Operation Ranch Hand to Plan Colombia," examines the Operation Ranch Hand controversy and how U.S drug control officials successfully negotiated a strong environmental movement. The result was a new role for herbicides within U.S. foreign policy. In 1971, U.S. aerial defoliation operations in Vietnam ceased, and in 1975 the Ford administration ratified the 1925 Geneva Protocol prohibiting the use of chemical or biological weapons.

Yet during this same period the U.S. government—the State Department, the Drug Enforcement Administration (DEA), and the U.S. Department of Agriculture (USDA)—conducted testing of herbicides on drug crops in Jamaica (1974) and Mexico (1974–75). By 1983, U.S. environmental legislation afforded no barriers to American financial and material support of herbicide spraying in the service of the drug war. Because the U.S. officials charged with prosecuting the war on drugs firmly believed that source control of drug crops (opium poppies, coca, and marijuana) was vital to reducing drug abuse and drug-related crime in the United States, American policy makers encouraged Latin American governments to enact defoliation programs within their borders. The drug war and the American military bases supporting the war on drugs constituted a new geography of U.S. empire that enabled the annual spraying of tens of thousands of acres of drug crops in Central and South America with a variety of defoliants. In the end, the war on drugs (and the U.S. military bases undergirding it) resulted—directly and indirectly—in environmental effects ranging from soil infertility, water contamination, erosion, deforestation, and damage to nontarget flora and fauna as well as negative impacts on human health.

The later years of the Cold War brought a growing set of concerns from communities surrounding U.S. military bases both at home and abroad. Jennifer Liss Ohayon, in chapter 6, "Addressing Environmental Risks and Mobilizing Democracy? Policy on Public Participation in U.S. Military Superfund Sites," explores the promise and peril of community efforts to become more directly engaged with the cleanup of former military installations. Several government initiatives have led public participation to be widely implemented in decommissioned military bases in the form of citizen advisory boards, workshops, site tours, and technical assistance grants to communities. While significant resources and legislative and social support surround these programs, institutional, political, and cultural barriers have often constrained influence from public participants over remedial decisions in former military sites.

Cleanup strategies and schedules are largely influenced by private contractors and redevelopers, for example, yet most participation programs are limited in discussing site reuse. Other barriers include the distribution of resources in cleanup decisions and an agency emphasis on trust building rather than constructive forms of political conflict in communities with historically strained relationships with government agencies. Despite procedural barriers, participation programs have been sites of active contestation over potential health and ecological risks from military contamination and appropriate remedial strategies. Using specific case studies and participant research, Ohayon offers an assessment of whether these initiatives can address the substantive reasons forwarded by the public for participation, including improved accountability and responsiveness in cleanup and monitoring activities and reduced risk exposures.

Exploring similar developments at overseas U.S. bases, Heejin Han and Yooil Bae examine the complex interactions surrounding the environmental effects of American bases in South Korea. Chapter 7, "Reality Revealed: U.S. Military Bases, Environmental Impact, and Civil Society in South Korea," looks at the history of the SOFA that largely governs the role of the U.S. military in the country. With expanded democratic rights and a growing middle class in the 1980s, South Korean activists began to express their discontent with the SOFA, especially regarding its unequal and unfair treatment of crimes committed by U.S. soldiers inflicted upon Korean civilians. South Korean nongovernmental organizations have begun to pay attention to environmental pollution at the U.S. military bases and the impact on neighboring communities. These concerns have emerged as more U.S. bases are returned to Korea, and the SOFA has been revised accordingly. Case studies illustrate how the South Korean people's increasing awareness of environmental risks and impacts has led to their call for civilian participation in the investigation process and the public release of information and data. This chapter offers useful lessons for policy makers and citizens alike interested in improving these processes in the future.

The final two chapters return to some of the unintended consequences that have sprung from the intersection of military bases and environmental policy in the late twentieth century. As the Cold War wound down, the U.S. military found itself increasingly engaged with environmental laws and regulations and in a position to repurpose some of its lands for other, more environmentally friendly purposes. These developments raise interesting questions about the intention of leaders in developing a more "environmentally friendly" or "green" military and the ways in which the repurposing of bases can serve as an erasure to the history that came before it. In chapter 8, "A Wildlife Insurgency: The Endangered Species Act, Citizen-Initiated Lawsuits, and the Department of Defense at the End of the Cold War," Katherine M. Keirns looks at the cause of endangered wildlife and reveals changes in attitudes and actions by the services. A useful tool for analyzing how this relationship evolved, the Endangered Species Act (ESA) is the most prominent environmental law for which there is no direct link between the goals of the law and the health or well-being of the military and its people. Yet this is the environmental law that the Defense Department has gone out of its way to associate with itself. Throughout the late 1970s and early 1980s, military leaders learned that the ESA is the single environmental law they cannot avoid. The process under which the U.S. military has shifted from bad environmental actor to complicated conservationist is critical to understanding how environmentalism has penetrated American culture far beyond its traditional left/right polarization.

David G. Havlick's concluding chapter, "Restoration and Meaning on Former Military Lands in the United States," brings the collection full circle, back to the shifting landscapes, both natural and cognitive, that shape and were shaped by the Cold War and the empire of bases at home and abroad. Former military lands in the United States have been converted to many new uses, including more than a million acres designated since the late 1980s as national wildlife refuges. But this potentially positive development is far more complicated than it appears. Restoration and remediation often privilege an ecological focus informed by pre-European reference conditions. New names and land use missions can serve to further obscure the prior histories and cultural significance of these lands. Against this tendency toward erasure, which is often seen as an inherent and positive attribute of restoration projects that remove prior degradation, Havlick considers how cultural meanings can be retained and integrated with ecological restoration efforts. Based on more than fifty interviews, hundreds of visitor surveys, and research visits to more than a dozen sites of recent military-to-wildlife conversion in the United States, this chapter demonstrates the importance of considering these sites as layered geographies with significant cultural and ecological features. At the same time, simple categories or narratives must be resisted; the complexity of history and ecology, restoration and meaning, must be confronted.

EXCAVATING MULTILAYERED LANDSCAPES

Taken as a whole, this collection demonstrates a number of themes that emerge from an interdisciplinary, globally engaged approach to the study of U.S. military bases, weapons testing, and the natural environment. Building on the framework described in Havlick's chapter, we might think about these themes as "layers" of complex landscapes that have been reconstructed and deconstructed through a variety of disciplinary and methodological approaches. They suggest common threads as well as a number of intellectual landscapes that future scholarship might explore, excavate, and interpret.

This book addresses the need to take the landscape itself as a central subject and offers specific ways of thinking about the militarization and demilitarization of landscapes that reinforce the inherent connections between physical sites and various frameworks through which that site is understood. Davis's chapter demonstrates the ways in which both world wars and the Cold War provided new ways of seeing and altering the landscape. In reconstructing historical debates over the rights, needs, and dangers of the military, the state, and the land itself, Davis articulates larger narratives engendered by these conflicts.

Childers reminds us that these lands were far from empty, populated by, among others, ranchers and their cattle. As knowledge about radiation and fallout grew, the lens through which many communities in the American West had come to understand their heavily militarized surroundings was fundamentally altered, reshaping the cultural, political, and policy landscapes of the region and period. Weimer's chapter demonstrates the powerful narrative of the "war on drugs" in reshaping imagined and physical landscapes. The narrative helped policy makers negotiate a political landscape in which the militarization of herbicides had been marginalized. This new "war story," like that of the Cold War before it, helped remake Latin America as a battleground.

These essays illuminate the history of what has recently come to be known as "military environmentalism," best understood as the complex ways, both intentional and accidental, in which militaries have responded to, shaped, and promoted a range of environmentalist policies. Oatsvall's chapter shows that the history of military environmentalism predates the emergence of the modern environmental movement in the 1960s and 1970s. The natural environment shaped approaches to, and understandings of, nuclear testing in the postwar world; even while conceiving of them as potential targets and sources, animals, water supplies, and ecosystems were shown concern by the military, which often manifested in surprising ways. This complicated traditional conceptions of militarism and the environment. My chapter on the destruction of Agent Orange at and around Johnston Atoll takes place at a pivotal moment in the emergence of military environmentalism: the mid- to late 1970s. In the wake of the Vietnam War and charges of ecocide, the U.S. military was forced to deal with a newly created regulatory system. Although the military's environmental record is decidedly mixed, the examples in this chapter make the argument for moving beyond representations in which the military simply reacts to ostensibly external environmental, cultural, and political forces.

Keirns's essay on the Endangered Species Act reminds us that the act changed not only the landscape of environmental law in the United States but also the way in which the U.S. military came to understand the landscapes in which it operated. Keirns reveals a world in which citizens had been emboldened by a long decade of protest, a growing environmental consciousness, and a legal apparatus to enforce ecological protection. The military could no longer hide under the banner of national security; reluctantly or not, it began to alter some of its practices and paved the way for the military-to-wildlife conversion projects like those described in Havlick's chapter.

Han and Bae's chapter, like Ohayon's, offers an important reminder that the military's environmental policies are not enacted in a vacuum; they are constructed in real landscapes and have real impact on the surrounding areas, including the local population. Han and Bae explore how

EDWIN A. MARTINI

South Korean civil society has shaped public response to, and participation in, public debates over the environmental impact of U.S. bases. The complexities of international law, diplomacy, and status-of-forces agreements between nations have made it much more difficult for non-U.S. citizens living around U.S. military bases to pursue democratic remedies and achieve just results.

Several chapters point to the uncertainty that surrounds the past, present, and future of U.S. military bases, particularly regarding the long-term impact on human and environmental health. This adds to a rich and growing body of work on uncertainty and risk assessment in modern societies.[8] Ohayon examines these forces, looking at public and official responses to several contaminated sites. These sites deal with the scientific uncertainty that underlies remediation and educational efforts, and they grapple with complex and divisive histories of environmental racism, poverty, and economic dependency that too often accompany military bases. Feelings of betrayal and distrust about the U.S. military around these sites, at home and abroad, further complicate genuine efforts at transparent and cooperative remediation. Havlick's chapter on restoration and meaning serves as a useful bookend. Capturing the uncertainty and the ambivalence inherent in military environmentalism, he notes that lands owned today by the Department of Defense "are both the most biologically diverse and the most contaminated of any category of federal land in the United States." Even more powerful than this contradiction is his demonstration of the ways in which efforts to "green" these sites can serve as an erasure of the history of the places themselves, obscuring "deeper and more far reaching impacts of militarization."

Havlick's description of the unintended consequences that surround U.S. military bases seems an appropriately ambivalent end to this introduction. As the United States continues to struggle to define a coherent global strategy in the wake of the Cold War and the "war on terror," the question of what to do with the empire of bases that continue to litter the planet is unavoidable. Diverse communities around the world deal with the problems and potential surrounding former military sites. What will be the militarized landscapes of the future? What types of materials, memories, and waste will they leave behind? What will become of places like Eglin Air Force Base in Florida? What will the soil surrounding the former air base in Kandahar, Afghanistan, look like in twenty or thirty years? What will the cancer rates be in Fallujah, Iraq, two generations from now? What might be the unforeseen environmental consequences of drone warfare, or of weapons that have yet to be invented? The answer, of course, and the point in many ways, is that we do not know.

NOTES

1   Bruce Dorminey, "Military Bases Provide Unlikely Refuge for South's Longleaf Pine," *Environment 360*, available at http://e360.yale.edu/feature/military_bases_ provide_unlikely_refuge_for_longleaf_pine_in_us_south/2463/, originally posted November 10, 2011. Dorminey describes the research on several current and former military sites, led by John Orrock, a conservation biologist at the University of Wisconsin.

2   Ibid. Dorminey quotes army biologist Tim Beaty: "The openness of the longleaf pine and the thin stands provides [*sic*] visibility and maneuverability that is very consistent with what a mechanized force like the Third Infantry division likes to fight in." The longleaf pine has long been valorized throughout the American Southeast, serving as the state tree for Alabama and immortalized in many songs over the years, most recently in Jason Isbell's "Alabama Pines" on his 2011 release *Here We Rest* (from Lightning Rod Records).

3   David Sorenson, *Shutting Down the Cold War: The Politics of Military Base Closure* (New York: Palgrave MacMillan, 1998); Anni Baker, *American Soldiers Overseas* (Westport, CT: Praeger, 2004); and Kent Calder, *Embattled Garrisons: Comparative Base Politics and American Globalism* (Princeton, NJ: Princeton University Press, 2007).

4   Chalmers Johnson, *Blowback: The Costs and Consequences of American Empire* (New York: Metropolitan Books, 2000); and Cynthia Enloe, *The Morning After: Sexual Politics at the End of the Cold War* (Berkeley: University of California Press, 1993), and *Bananas, Beaches, and Bases: Making Feminist Sense of International Politics* (Berkeley: University of California Press, 2000).

5   Alexander Cooley, *Base Politics: Democratic Change and the U.S. Military Overseas* (Ithaca, NY: Cornell University Press, 2008); Catherine Lutz, ed., *Bases of Empire: The Global Struggle against U.S. Military Outposts* (New York: New York University Press, 2009); Katherine McCaffrey, *Military Power and Popular Protest: The U.S. Navy in Vieques, Puerto Rico* (New Brunswick, NJ: Rutgers University Press, 2004); Masamichi Inoue, *Okinawa and the U.S. Military: Identity Making in the Age of Globalization* (New York: Columbia University Press, 2007); and Maria Höhn and Seungsook Moon, eds., *Over There: Living with the U.S. Military Empire from World War Two to the Present* (Durham, NC: Duke University Press, 2010).

6   J. R. McNeill and David Painter, "The Global Environmental Footprint of the U.S. Military, 1789–2003," in Charles E. Closmann, ed., *War and the Environment: Military Destruction in the Modern Age* (Lubbock: Texas A&M Press, 2009); and Chris

Pearson, Peter Coates, and Tim Cole, eds., *Militarized Landscapes: From Gettysburg to Salisbury Plain* (New York: Continuum, 2010). Among a flood of other work over the past several years situated at the intersection of military and environmental history, see the foundational Edmund Russell, *War and Nature: Fighting Humans and Insects with Chemicals from World War I to Silent Spring* (Cambridge: Cambridge University Press, 2001); and Richard P. Tucker and Edmund Russell, eds., *Natural Enemy, Natural Ally: Toward an Environmental History of War* (Corvallis: Oregon State University Press, 2004). Also see David Zierler, *The Invention of Ecocide: Agent Orange, Vietnam, and the Scientists Who Changed the Way We Think about the Environment* (Athens: University of Georgia Press, 2011); and David Biggs, *Quagmire: Nation-Building and Nature in the Mekong Delta* (Seattle: University of Washington Press, 2011).

7   For examples, see the special edition of *Diplomatic History* edited by Kurk Dorsey and Mark Lytle, "Special Forum with Environmental History," *Diplomatic History* 32, no. 4 (September 2008), 515–651. An especially relevant piece in that issue is Lisa M. Brady, "Life in the DMZ: Turning a Diplomatic Failure into an Environmental Success," *Diplomatic History* 32, no. 3 (2008): 585–611; Matt Evenden, "Aluminum, Commodity Chains, and the Environmental History of the Second World War," *Environmental History* 16, no. 1 (2011): 69–93; and Edwin Martini, "Incinerating Agent Orange: Operations Pacer HO, Pacer IVY, and the Global Legacies of the Chemical War," *Journal of Military History* 76, no. 3 (July 2012): 809–36.

8   Among many excellent works in these areas, see Ulrich Beck's *Risk Society: Toward a New Modernity* (1982; reprint, Thousand Oaks, CA: Sage Publications, 1992) and his *Ecological Enlightenment: Essays on the Politics of the Risk Society* (New York: Humanity Books, 1995). Also see J. Stephen Kroll-Smith, Phil Brown, and Valerie Gunter, eds., *Illness and the Environment: A Reader in Contested Medicine* (New York: New York University Press, 2000). Jane Franklin, ed., *The Politics of Risk Society* (Malden, MA: Blackwell Publishers, 1998); and Bruno Latour, *Pandora's Hope: Essays on the Reality of Science Studies* (Cambridge, MA: Harvard University Press, 1999). More recently, these theories have been updated and applied by, among others, Christopher Sellers, *Hazards of the Job: From Industrial Disease to Environmental Health Science* (Chapel Hill: University of North Carolina Press, 1997); Joe Thornton, *Pandora's Poison: Chlorine, Health, and a New Environmental Strategy* (Cambridge: Massachusetts Institute of Technology Press, 2000); and Greg Mittman, Michelle Murphy, and Christopher Sellers, eds., *Landscapes of Exposure: Knowledge and Illness in Modern Environments* (Chicago: University of Chicago Press, 2004). A very useful overview can be found in J. Stephen Kroll-Smith's and Worth Lancaster's article "Bodies, Environments, and a New Style of Reasoning," *Annals of the American Academy of Political and Social Science* 584 (2002): 203–12. For excellent applications of all of these ideas in specific case studies of particular environments and chemicals, see Kristin Shrader-Frechette, *Burying Uncertainty: Risk and the Case against Geological Disposal of Nuclear Waste* (Berkeley: University of California Press, 1993); Michelle Murphy, *Sick Building Syndrome and the Problem of Uncertainty: Environmental Politics, Technoscience, and Women Workers* (Durham,

NC: Duke University Press, 2006); Linda Nash, *Inescapable Ecologies: A History of Environment, Disease, and Knowledge* (Berkeley: University of California Press, 2007); and Nancy Langston's outstanding study, *Toxic Bodies: Hormone Disruptors and the Legacy of DES* (New Haven, CT: Yale University Press, 2009).

CHAPTER 1

DEFENDING THE NATION, PROTECTING THE LAND

Emergency Powers and the Militarization of American Public Lands

BRANDON C. DAVIS

THE rapid advances in warfare technologies that occurred during and after World War II depended on a corresponding increase in the military's demand for new training, gunnery, bombing, rocketry, missile, aircraft, and chemical, biological, and nuclear weapons proving grounds. Speaking to Congress in 1957, Representative William Dawson of Utah observed that "the greatest military machine the world has ever known now holds more than 43,000 square miles of American soil and is still enlarging its area of occupation." Today these lands, which were largely drawn from the public domain, form the "cornerstone" of the Department of Defense's operations.[1]

Nearly all aspects of America's condition of permanent war are predicated on the military's ongoing occupation of public land.[2] But the question of how the U.S. military came to occupy so much land has remained elusive to historians.[3] As cultural critic John Beck evocatively puts it, the "land itself is withdrawn from public usage and annihilating weapons exploded upon it, and nowhere is there any sense of an explanatory narrative or evidence of the agents of this transformation."[4] Instead, the military's claims to land are "defined by invisible rules," or through the "control of information," or simply through "the rhetoric of defence and national security."[5] More common is the sense that the military's expansive presence is an inevitable outgrowth, or unavoidable response, to events and forces beyond our control.[6] Such explanations may have merit, but they do little to help us understand the policies and procedures that legitimized the military's acquisition and continuing control of public lands.

The U.S. military's initial claims to public lands at the outset of World War II attracted significant controversy within Franklin Roosevelt's administration. In order to withdraw lands to the War Department's expectations, executive officials had to circumvent a number of legal controls. To explain how the U.S. military seemingly bypassed these obstacles, it is necessary to understand not only the history of executive emergency war powers but also the history of emergency land withdrawal powers. Since the early 2000s, scholars have increasingly examined how the state of perpetual war has given rise to a permanent state of emergency, in which the use of temporary emergency powers has become, as philosopher Giorgio Agamben has written, "the dominant paradigm of government." Studies on emergency wartime powers in the United States have looked into how such powers have eroded democratic controls and civil liberties, allowing executive agencies to, among other things, spy on, denounce, intimidate, or intern their own citizens and deport, detain, torture, or execute their alleged enemies.[7]

Times of war and crisis have undoubtedly enhanced independent executive powers, but so has the practice of executive land withdrawal. The powers to defend the nation and the powers to protect public lands stem from the same indeterminate sources of emergency executive power. For too long, scholars have not fully recognized how a variety of independent executive powers, including those for contemporary war efforts and security programs, are rooted in the executive power to manage public lands. This chapter reveals how the U.S. military relied not only upon the president's prerogative to defend the nation to legitimize land claims but also upon the president's duty to protect America's public lands. In particular, the legal precedents that have ensued from the long-standing and frequent use of the president's emergency withdrawal powers have played an important role in allowing calls for the exclusive use of public lands for military purposes to take hold.

This assertion of withdrawal power at the outset of World War II redefined the executive's ability to acquire federal lands and shaped the general trajectory of U.S. military development. Once the military's land claims took hold, an unbound, independent system of executive military land withdrawals was quickly established. This system—originally intended to respond to a temporary wartime emergency—gradually became formalized as World War II ended and the military and political climate shifted to the Cold War. Despite this, land withdrawal powers remained ad hoc and uncircumscribed, which led to widespread abuse, inefficiency, and mismanagement. Subsequent efforts to reign in and reform executive military land withdrawal powers were highly effective at detailing the abuse of power but less effective at rectifying its consequences. This chapter demystifies the policies and procedures behind the executive assertion of power over public land that accompanied the mid-twentieth-century buildup of U.S. military forces. It provides a foundational look at the broader federal land claim authority upon which all subsequent developments at military bases established during and after World War II are predicated.

THE PRESIDENT'S DUTY TO PROTECT THE LAND

Concerns about the relationship between war, abuses of power, and American democracy are not new. The framers of the U.S. Constitution recognized the inherent problems involved in granting specific constitutional powers to defend against threats that are "impossible to foresee or define." They left the president with indeterminate powers to act in states of war and other national emergencies. These emergency powers, as attorney general Frank Murphy noted in 1939, "have never been specifically defined, and in fact cannot be, since their extent and limitations are largely dependent upon conditions and circumstances."[8]

Emergency powers provide the U.S. government with the flexibility to respond to unforeseen crises that its regular, more restrictive form of government could not handle, with the ultimate goal being a return to constitutional normalcy. In addition to providing practical advantages to the executive, emergency powers enhance opportunities for abuse of political power and authority. Of larger significance is the fact that war and other types of emergencies increasingly do not have clear beginnings or endings, making a return to normalcy all the more difficult. Constitutional expert Clinton Rossiter was one of the first scholars to recognize that, with the continuing threat of global war and weapons of mass destruction after World War II, the United States could not "go home again; the positive state is here to stay, and from now on the accent will be on power, not limitations."[9]

Investigations on the use of emergency powers have tended to focus on the tensions between liberty and security and the ways in which, as Supreme Court justice Robert H. Jackson noted in 1951, "passion, intolerance and suspicions of wartime . . . reduce our liberties to a shadow, often in answer to exaggerated claims of security."[10] The American vision of freedom, however, is historically premised not only on the idea of inalienable rights but also on the idea that "the lands are initially infused with public not private rights." The free use of land, in other words, has always been essential to understandings of American freedom and liberty, just as the nation's security has continually depended on the welfare of its public lands and resources. Americans' political, spiritual, moral, and material values are all wrapped up in shifting understandings and governance of public lands.[11]

The use of emergency powers is typically understood as being justified only as a response to situations of great urgency that threaten the nation, such as wartime. Yet the area of governance in which presidents have most often and most liberally exercised powers reaching beyond accepted constitutional norms has arguably been in their efforts to protect the nation's public lands. In cases where, as the interior secretary E. A. Hitchcock described to the Senate in 1902, "emergencies appeared to demand such action in furtherance of public interest," presidents have been compelled to independently withdraw lands from private exploitation or to reserve them for specific public uses.[12] Not only were such withdrawals made without any clear legislative or other legal authority; they were sometimes made in direct violation of existing land laws.[13]

The best-known examples of independent withdrawals are those President Theodore Roosevelt famously made for conservation purposes in the early twentieth century. Conservationists of all stripes have championed Roosevelt's style of conservation, characterizing the practice of seizing "the initiative without pointing to any statutory authority" as an important element of the bold, visionary executive leadership style that contributed to "one of the great success stories of American government."[14] While the end result may indeed be praiseworthy, such standard assessments do not fully consider some of the broader consequences of natural resource policies. In challenging these triumphalist interpretations, environmental historians have highlighted the ways federally driven conservation policies have not only disempowered and dispossessed local peoples from land and resources but also heralded "the rise of the modern administrative state."[15]

Conservation polices also had significant influence in expanding presidential power. Roosevelt's theory of presidential stewardship, which represents one of the most far-reaching constructions of executive power ever put forward, was originally formulated as a defense for independent executive land withdrawals. Interior secretary James Garfield went as far as claiming that the "stewardship duty of the Executive is most concretely manifest in the care of the specific property known as the public lands and their resources."[16] By themselves, theories of executive stewardship, and similar constructions of independent executive authority, generally attract controversy and do not hold up well to legal scrutiny, particularly in the courts. Yet whenever the courts have been asked to review cases in which stewardship-like powers were used for withdrawing public lands, the executive assertion of power has almost always prevailed.[17] Such rulings, moreover, have played an important role in expanding the boundaries of presidential powers.

The land law case that has had the most influence in shaping presidential power is *United States v. Midwest Oil Company,* in which the Supreme Court upheld President William Taft's 1909 emergency withdrawals of extensive oil reserves from private exploitation.[18] In this case, the court argued that when emergencies and other conditions not anticipated by legislation occurred, the executive, as the active agent of government, was the only person in "a position to know when the public interest required particular portions of the people's lands to be withdrawn." The court recognized that independent executive withdrawals had taken place relatively frequently in the nation's history, and in not a single instance did Congress "repudiate the power claimed or the withdrawal orders made" but rather "uniformly and repeatedly acquiesced in the practice." This acquiescence, the court further argued, "was equivalent to consent" and "operated as an implied grant of power."[19]

Out of this ruling emerged a more tangible construction of executive power in which, as constitutional historian Edward Corwin noted, "the President was recognized as being able to acquire authority from the silences of Congress as well as from its positive enactments, provided only the silences were sufficiently prolonged."[20] To be clear, the justices in the *Midwest Oil* case emphasized that their decision did not "mean that the Executive can, by his course of action, create a power"; nonetheless, the decision legitimized and set the boundaries to the exercise of certain types of independent executive powers. Under *Midwest Oil* a long-standing, historical executive practice of governance, known by and acquiesced to by Congress, could now be, as Taft put it, considered "legal as if there had been an express act of Congress authorizing it."[21]

This construction of implied executive power gained wider influence after the Supreme Court justices Felix Frankfurter and Robert H. Jackson relied on it in their highly influential opinions in the 1952 *Youngstown Sheet and Tube Co. v. Sawyer* case. Here the court struck down President Harry Truman's effort to seize steel mills to avert a strike during the Korean War.[22] Justice Jackson's rationale for recognizing certain types of independent executive powers was based on the realization that "while the Constitution diffuses power the better to secure liberty, it also contemplates that practice will integrate the dispersed powers into a workable government."[23] The model for such a workable government is perhaps most clearly seen in the unique land management practices developed between the executive and legislative branches during the nineteenth and early twentieth century, as recognized in the *Midwest Oil* decision.[24]

Today *Youngstown* is recognized as a landmark case that forms "the current dominant paradigm through which most important constitutional questions of war, foreign affairs, and separation-of-powers issues in general are understood and evaluated by Congress, the President, and the courts."[25] Ironically, the "executive construction of the Constitution revealed in *Midwest Oil* case" and recognized in *Youngstown* has become the "gold standard," not necessarily because of how it promotes a workable government in times of crisis but, as the former solicitor general Neal Katyal noted, "because its all-things-to-all-people quality can provide arguments favoring any branch of government under many circumstances."[26]

In his 2006 testimony to Congress, Mike Dean, a former legal counselor for President Richard Nixon, observed that the *Midwest Oil* decision is too vague to serve as the "leading case on Congressional acquiescence." It does not hold up particularly well against "executive attorney generals who take the most aggressive reading possible in all situations that favor executive power."[27] A case in point is deputy assistant attorney general John Yoo's notorious September 25, 2001, memorandum on the president's authority to use military force. Yoo relied upon *Midwest Oil*, *Youngstown*, and Jackson's language of integrating "the dispersed powers into a workable government" to support the Bush administration's claims of having "inherent executive power" to use military force to retaliate and act "preemptively against terrorist organizations."[28] While the memorandum itself remains controversial, Yoo's arguments about the "independent authority" recognized in *Midwest Oil* and *Youngstown* have been adopted to help justify a wide variety of contemporary executive war powers and security programs, including the detainment of enemies in Afghanistan, the George W. Bush administration's warrantless surveillance program, and President Barack Obama's 2011 interventions in Libya.[29] The powers to defend the nation and the powers to protect public lands are entangled together in ways that Constitutional, natural resource, and other historians have not fully appreciated. Not only is the stewardship duty of the president most concretely manifest in the care of the public lands, but the care of the public lands has provided an important arena for the expansion of the stewardship presidency.

WARTIME URGENCY AND THE EXPANSION OF EXECUTIVE WITHDRAWAL POWERS

Strands of independent executive power first recognized in court rulings upholding presidential withdrawal powers are linked to a variety of contemporary war powers and security programs in unexpected and underappreciated ways. The interconnections between land, executive power, and wartime security are more pronounced in the period during and after World War II, when both the exercise of executive emergency powers and the need for massive military reserves reached peak levels. On May 27, 1941, well before the Japanese attack on Pearl Harbor, President Franklin Delano Roosevelt declared that "an unlimited national emergency" existed in America that required "the strengthening of our defense to the extreme limit of our national power and authority." FDR was no stranger to using executive emergency powers, having declared a national economic emergency two days after assuming office in 1933. In the early 1940s he made it clear to Congress and the American people that he was willing to ignore statutory legal provisions and "not hesitate to use every power vested in me to accomplish the defeat of our enemies."[30]

To assure victory, FDR issued hundreds of executive orders, with perhaps the most controversial one being Executive Order 9066, which gave the U.S. military the power to relocate and intern more than seventy thousand American citizens of Japanese descent. The overwhelming majority of executive orders issued during the "unlimited" wartime emergency were orders to withdraw public lands for military purposes.[31] Contrary to popular understandings, the issuance of such withdrawal orders did not come without resistance at the federal level. During the early stages of the war, there was significant controversy within the administration over the question of whether the president held the power to acquire exclusive control of public lands for governmental uses. The confidential, cabinet-level decisions made during this time of military urgency redefined the president's ability to acquire federal lands and shaped the trajectory of U.S. military development.

At the center of this controversy stood Robert H. Jackson, then serving as Roosevelt's attorney general. Part of Jackson's responsibilities included approving all of FDR's executive orders.[32] In July of 1940, Jackson made the unprecedented move of rejecting a withdrawal order. While the withdrawal was only for a small parcel of land in Oregon, Jackson's rejection destabilized an important presidential power at the very time this power was set to be liberally employed for the war effort. The crux of Jackson's concerns rested on how the 1910 Withdrawal Act limited the president's ability to establish reservations over which the federal government would have complete jurisdiction and control, and not be subject to public land laws.[33] The act itself had authorized, for the first time, nearly all of the withdrawal powers that had long been practiced by presidents. The catch was that all withdrawals under the act had to be open to private mining interests.[34] Perhaps of even larger significance was how the act restricted the president's preexisting implied withdrawal authority. Under *Midwest Oil*, congressional acquiescence is equivalent to consent until the power is "revoked by some subsequent action by Congress."[35] Notably, one of the main purposes of the 1910 Withdrawal Act was, as the chairman on the Senate Committee of Public Lands stated, "to put this power in direct and express statutory form rather than the common law of the courts, and limit it."[36]

Emergency powers are far easier to institute than they are to retract, and presidents' notions of holding both stewardship and implied powers toward public lands did not die easily. Much like the period before the 1910 Withdrawal Act, the administrative practices of executive officials continued to have bearing on the nature of executive withdrawal authority. After 1910, most executive withdrawals were made in accordance with the terms of the act. Yet when the conditions "appeared to demand such action in furtherance of public interest," executive officials continued to withdraw lands independently without clear legal authority and in direct violation of existing land laws, just as they had done before 1910. Congress's supposed acquiescence to such unauthorized withdrawals emboldened executive officials to believe they held some type of independent withdrawal powers, and also, paradoxically, allowed claims of implied withdrawal power to resurface and gain legitimacy.[37]

In response to Jackson's rejection of FDR's 1940 withdrawal order, the secretary of interior, Harold Ickes, contended that the repeated, consistent, and uncontested practice of independent executive withdrawals since the issuance of 1910 act were "eloquently persuasive" in confirming the president's "presumed inherent general withdrawal power."[38] By themselves, such claims did not fully resolve the legal questions concerning the 1910 act's restrictions. That lands "vital to the national security" could be "subject at any and all time . . . to entry and exploration" from private mining interests was a mandate that few officials in the War and Interior Departments were willing to accept. To obtain what war secretary Harold Stimson described as "the free and unrestricted use of its military reservations," leading members of the Roosevelt administration did not ignore the legislative mandates limiting presidential withdrawal power, as conservationists had done at the turn of the century. Nor did they follow through with Stimson's and others' suggestion to ask Congress for clarification. Rather, they chose to act internally and reinterpret the 1910 act as only applying to "temporary" executive withdrawals and not affecting "in any way the inherent authority of the President" to make permanent reservations.[39]

In 1884 interior secretary L.Q.C. Lamar observed if presidents held inherent power to withdrawal public lands for military purposes, they "might in violation of law put in reservation for military purposes any amount of lands and thus take them out of operation of the general laws. To assert such a principle is to claim for the executive the power to repeal or alter the Acts of Congress at will." Interestingly, such Constitutional issues were raised at time when a relatively minuscule portion of America's public lands were devoted to military use.[40] When far greater amounts of land were reserved for military purposes during and after World War II, similar questions about the extent of executive power or the ultimate authority to control the public domain were addressed confidentially by presidential officials without input from Congress, the courts, or the public. Jackson appears to have been the only person in Roosevelt's administration concerned with these broader Constitutional questions.

Despite significant opposition from some of the most powerful members of Roosevelt's administration, Jackson maintained his position, noting that he found "nothing in the language of the act or in its administration to support" such viewpoints. "The plain, unambiguous provisions of the act," he continued, "are to the contrary."[41] His influential 1952 opinion in *Youngstown*—described "as the greatest single opinion ever written by a Supreme Court justice"—is just one of many reasons Jackson is widely considered America's foremost authority on wartime security and law.[42] Standing up to presidential assertions of inherent withdrawal powers during a time of military urgency is not among these reasons. For within eight days of FDR's declaration of an unlimited emergency, Jackson made a complete reversal. Relying on the same basic points and evidence that he had forcefully rejected less than two months earlier, Jackson contended that Congress's 1910 Withdrawal Act and the Supreme Court's decision in *Midwest Oil* confirmed, beyond a doubt, the president's powers to reserve lands for the exclusive government use.[43]

Although Jackson's initial opinions were kept secret until the late 1960s, and largely remain in obscurity today, his revised published opinion affirming presidential withdrawal authority is well known. Commentators have noted how Jackson "strained to find authority," indulged in "tortured interpretation," and "rendered the [Withdrawal] Act virtually meaningless."[44] Despite these possible shortcomings, his reversal appears to have cleared up, at least to the satisfaction of the agencies within the executive office, any ambivalence held toward presidential withdrawal powers. Even though Jackson is commonly remembered for the numerous times he stood up to claims of inherent executive authority throughout his career, his revised opinion came to serve as the de facto authorization to a presidential power that would, over the next thirty years, increasingly be understood as not only inherent and unfettered but also applicable to all executive land management practices.[45] Most important, Jackson's authorization and Roosevelt's declaration of an unlimited national emergency set in motion an aggressive, independent assertion of executive military land withdrawal powers that reshaped the U.S. military's relationship to America's public lands.

THE MID-TWENTIETH-CENTURY MILITARIZATION
OF AMERICA'S PUBLIC LANDS

Unilateral presidential actions to lock up public lands have almost always been met with stiff opposition, especially from Congress and state governments. At the same time, the imperative of responding to wartime emergencies has enabled presidents to assert powers that would, under normal circumstances, be unthinkable. From the start of World War II to the mid-1950s, the unthinkable became an accepted reality, as nearly twenty million acres of "jealously guarded" public land was rapidly withdrawn from the public domain and put under the control of military interests.[46] The numerous war and security crises of this period greatly enhanced the executive branch's control over public lands. This was especially the case during World War II.

Throughout his presidency FDR had readily relied upon declarations of national emergencies to justify controversial actions. So it is not surprising that his claims to more than thirteen million acres of public land for military purposes rested upon "the findings of necessity for the emergency use of such lands" for "purposes incident to the national emergency and the prosecution of the war."[47] While the imperatives of responding to wartime threats are undoubtedly important, in practice the legitimacy of executive emergency powers often depends on claims of necessity as well as some type of Constitutional or legislative underpinning. Roosevelt's unlimited emergency, along with Jackson's authorization of withdrawal authority, seemingly worked together to provide the administration with ample grounds to justify its extensive World War II military land claims.

Relying explicitly on emergency powers instead of Jackson's authorization did make these land withdrawals contingent upon the wartime emergency. Consequently, most withdrawal orders issued during the war stated that the lands would be returned to their former "jurisdiction, uses, and administration" six months after the termination of the unlimited emergency. To remove all doubt that this would occur, FDR, shortly before his death in 1945, issued an executive order that amended all World War II military land withdrawals to include the six-month termination requirement.[48] Beyond the administration's understanding of the war as a temporary crisis, there were additional strategic advantages in treating the withdrawals as provisional. Permanently removing thirteen million acres of public lands from federal land laws under the terms of Jackson's authorization would have likely upset the many public land users with long-standing interests in these lands, as well as the congressional members who represented them.

Notably, when the Interior Department did explicitly rely on Jackson's authorization to permanently withdrawal millions of acres of public lands in Utah containing strategically important minerals in 1943, "immediate and violent protest on the part of the officials and citizens of the State of Utah" ensued, prompting congressional investigations and hearings. In their 1945 report on the withdrawal, Congress accused Interior Department officials of using subterfuge, obfuscation, and distorted interpretations to circumvent the 1910 Withdrawal Act and "thwart the laws and will of the Congress." They strongly condemned the "the many hasty, ill-considered and needless, though highly disturbing, withdrawal orders" made under the "broad powers of the President" and suggested that "the time has arrived for Congress to recapture and exercise its control over public land withdrawals."[49] Congress's numerous reproaches in this investigation ended up being merely cautionary, as legislation restricting the so-called "broad withdrawal powers of the President" did not come until many years later. The incident illustrates the volatile conditions under which certain executive withdrawals were made during the war and why such withdrawals required careful handling. FDR's assurance that World War II military withdrawals would be "restored" to how they "existed prior to the withdrawal" can be understood as a measure to avoid potentially disruptive situations detrimental to the war effort. This may help explain part of the reason why protests against the military use of public lands were significantly less active during the war compared with the early to mid-1950s.[50]

Incidentally, Roosevelt's unlimited emergency did not officially end until April of 1952, when the United States signed a peace treaty with Japan. By this time, it was clear to defense officials that the World War II withdrawals would still "be needed for an indefinite period" beyond the expiration date. Instead of taking transparent, authorized legal actions to handle the problem, Truman's administration relied entirely on internal administrative measures. One day before the withdrawals were set to revert to their former jurisdiction, a representative from the Interior Department sent letters to army and navy officials saying they could continue to occupy the lands under the assumption that an official order revoking the six-month termination requirement would soon be made.[51] Four years after this date, 85 percent of the original World War II withdrawals, representing forty-nine individual withdrawals covering 11.8 million acres of land, were still under the control of the Defense Department (formerly known as the War Department), and no additional legal measures had been taken. Instead, the military's legal claims to the public lands taken during the war would continue to rely on the largely symbolic legitimacy of inter-cabinet correspondence for years to come.[52]

With the end of the unlimited emergency came an end to understanding military land withdrawals as being contingent upon wartime or emergency conditions. Land management powers once carefully justified as necessary responses to temporary emergency conditions became routine functions. By the mid-1950s executive officials based their legal claims to public lands entirely upon the presumed "express power" authorized in "the 1941 letter of the Attorney General, as supported by the Supreme Court in the *Midwest Oil* decision."[53] The one thing that did not change after the end of the unlimited national emergency was the need for military land. During the 1950s demands for new military proving grounds rivaled World War II demands. Between 1954 and 1955 alone, the Defense Department made requests amounting to nearly thirteen million additional acres of public land.[54]

The actual process by which these lands were withdrawn was fairly straightforward. After receiving clearance from the Defense Department, the heads of the requesting military agency—from either the navy, army, or air force—would file an application with the local land office of the Interior Department. In their applications they would need to provide a statement describing the general purpose for which the lands would be used (except when such purposes were classified) and a statement indicating whether the withdrawal should preclude grazing, mineral leasing, and mining locations.[55]

The secretary of the interior, who had been delegated by the president to handle all military land withdrawals, had at his discretion the option to afford the public an opportunity to object to an application. He could also object on his own behalf, in which case the matter would be turned over the Bureau of Budget for settlement. If the Interior Department decided the withdrawal should be made, an executive withdrawal order would be issued and passed on to the director of the Bureau of the Budget and the attorney general for final review and approval.[56]

In practice, defense officials appear to have fully taken advantage of this largely unrestricted and purely cabinet-level approach to land withdrawals. Filing applications, for example, largely consisted of the requesting military agencies, as the chairmen of a two-year congressional investigation into military withdrawals noted in 1957, simply taking "out a slip of paper in the nature of the application . . . for an area perhaps one hundred miles long and fifty miles wide" and claiming that "it was absolutely necessary to their operations."[57]

The Defense Department, which was initially in charge of clearing these requests, had no procedures in place for assessing defense agencies' actual need for new lands or for determining how current holdings were being utilized.[58] In 1956 testimony to Congress, a witness representing the Defense Department further noted that requests for new military lands come "signed by the Secretary of the military department involved. It has been approved by him. . . . and the figures have been approved by his staff, and by his expert. In the Office of the Secretary of Defense, we are not expert in that field and while we may question and ask them to restudy and recheck, in the final analysis we must accept their figures in those records."[59] The end result was that, as was concluded in the 1957 congressional report, the Defense Department "cleared without question applications for the withdrawal of millions of acres of additional lands solely on the basis of an asserted need by the requesting" military agency.[60]

The Defense Department was not alone in deferring to a higher expertise, as the Interior Department also had, it was concluded, "for years approved application after application on the basis of Defense Department request, since the Interior was without authority or the technical data needed to challenge them."[61] In their congressional testimonies, defense officials acknowledged that they had in fact never been held up nor "had a turndown from the Department of Interior."[62] This streamlined, administrative approach to land withdrawals allowed U.S. defense agencies to quickly amass the tracts of property deemed essen-

BRANDON C. DAVIS

tial to their mission of defending the nation. As an apparent show of confidence in the way executive withdrawals were being carried out, Truman removed the requirement in 1952 that the director of the Bureau of the Budget and the attorney general must screen and approve withdrawal orders before they become effective, which is what originally brought the issue of executive withdrawal authority to the attention of Robert Jackson in the early 1940s.[63]

The lack of procedures for assessing how current landholdings were being used led to predictable problems of inefficiency, yet the severity of these problems is surprising even today. It was revealed in 1957, for example, that for fifteen years the air force had held a three-hundred-thousand-acre area west of Salt Lake City, which they had never used and did not even know they actually controlled.[64]

The Defense Department's inconsistent (and frequently nonexistent) land use policies led to what Congress described as "a recitation of incalculable wastefulness—of taxpayers' dollars, of resources within the reservations marked 'closed' for so many years to public multiple use and enjoyment, and of unquestionable but immeasurable damaging effect to the local economies from which each unneeded or unused acre was carved."[65]

Although grazers may have suffered the most severe economic hardships, the military's most vocal opponents were conservation advocates and officials. Far from being "khaki conservationists," they accused the military of unnecessarily locking up land, disregarding conservation laws and programs, and obstructing federal and state officials charged with managing the fish, game, wildlife, and other natural resources located on military reserves.[66]

Author Seth Shulman has noted how during the 1970s and 1980s the military relied on their supposed "unique status" within society to resist environmental "regulations and oversight at every chance." The story was no different in the 1940s and 1950s. The military's understanding of holding complete jurisdiction over their reserves conflicted with conservationists who argued that the military's control did not extend to the wildlife and other natural resources located within the reserves. Despite the many concerns of conservationists, military leaders made it clear to legislators that conservation and recreational needs "must be subordinate to the primary mission" of defending the nation, and that they "would violently object to any . . . legislation" interfering with their exclusive jurisdiction.[67] That the powers conservationists and the military held over public lands were at least partly derived from some of the same indeterminate sources of executive power was irony lost on most of the individuals caught up in these disputes.

Conservationists' opposition likely represents the most direct and prevalent challenge made to the military's land claim authority since the military began aggressively asserting control over public lands in the early 1940s. This is not to say that there were not innumerable protests and legal challenges made against the military's rapid acquisition of tens of millions of acres of public land. Yet the vast majority of these challenges did not directly question the "authority vested in the President" that was tied to national defense and, at least according to administrative interpretations, sanctioned by the Supreme Court and congressional legislation. Instead, opponents of the military largely focused on, as was the case with grazers, questions of compensation or whether the military actually required the lands they claimed to need or, correspondingly, if the current use of the land outweighed the importance of the military's proposed use of it.[68]

RECAPTURING EXECUTIVE POWERS AND THE CHALLENGES OF RETURNING TO NORMALCY

After nearly twenty years of being put into practice, the executive branch's independent approach to military land withdrawals received external examination. The major goal of Congress's investigation was the recapture "of those powers which the executive branch of the Government has acquired over a long period of years with respect to the utilization of this Nation's most valuable assets, the human and natural resources of the public lands."[69] Despite such doubts, Congress acknowledged that they had "perhaps, since 1941 remained silent" and therefore "indulged in a practice 'equivalent to acquiescence and consent.'" In actuality, the question of whether Congress had indeed acquiesced was not pursued in much depth, since recapturing the withdrawal authority from the president under the terms of *Midwest Oil* merely required Congress to end its alleged silence—and the bill it drafted was "specifically aimed at breaking that silence—if silence it be."[70] The Engle Act also contained general rules for the management of wildlife and other natural resources on military reserves. After the Engle Act, conservation efforts at military reserves would be as much the product of legislative mandate as an unintended or ironic consequence of locking up land. Based on Congress's recommendations, the Defense Department agreed to adopt centralized procedures for the oversight and management of their existing landholdings.[71] Its most noteworthy impact may be with how it appears to have tempered new claims to public lands for defense purposes.[72]

It is clear that during this period nobody wanted to deal with the troubling question of how temporary emergency powers exercised without clear legislative, judicial, or popular consent allowed military interests to gain seemingly permanent, exclusive control to millions of acres of public land. A quarter century after the passage of the Engle Act, Defense Department legal advisers were seemingly surprised to find "serious questions about the current legal adequacy of land withdrawals for some DOD installations" and predicted that ongoing "crisis reactions" were likely to occur within the department as "continuing discoveries of inadequate or illegal public land control by the various armed forces" were made. Around the same time these findings were made, the cultural critic Paul Virilio made the highly provocative claim that World War II did not conclude with Allied victory in 1945 but had, in fact, never ended. Regarding the administration of U.S. military lands, Virilio's seemingly unconventional views could not be truer.[73]

Perhaps of even larger significance, the Engle Act focused only on limiting the president's implied withdrawal powers and did nothing to address the use of executive emergency powers, specifically noting that in the event of war or national emergency, all provisions in the act could be waived. With such language, it is unlikely that the Engle Act, if it had been in place in 1941, would have made much difference in preventing the 800 percent increase in military real property holding that came within three years after the outbreak of World War II.[74]

Giorgio Agamben and others have warned that the increasingly common assertion of emergency wartime powers threatens to unravel the rule of law and other democratic institutions. In the case of mid-twentieth-century military land claims, however, the downward spiral into absolutism was not a free-fall descent. The need for legitimacy introduced the possibility of political and legal deliberation. Interestingly, the person at the center of this deliberation was one of twentieth century's top authorities on executive power in wartime. In retrospect, Robert Jackson's eventual authorization of withdrawal powers may seem like an inevitable outcome; yet treating processes like these with a preordained certainty, or as unavoidable responses to overpowering events beyond our control, can serve as an excuse to not ask basic questions about the exercise of military and other forms of governmental power.[75]

NOTES

1   103 Cong. Rec. 5520 (1957); and Jack Utter et al., "Military Land Withdrawals: Some Legal History and a Case Study," *University of Arizona College of Agriculture Paper* no. 541 (1985): 48.

2   Rachel Woodward, *Military Geographies* (Malden, MA: Blackwell Publishing, 2004), 12, 35.

3   In following Gerald Nash's lead, western historians have treated the federal government's power to acquire and occupy public lands for military purposes as a given, repeatedly noting how the West's old liabilities of remoteness and isolation suddenly became "virtues that provided a magnet" for vast new defense installations. See Gerald Nash's *The American West Transformed: The Impact of the Second World War* (Bloomington: Indiana University Press, 1985), 23, 158.

4   John Beck, *Dirty Wars: Landscape, Power, and Waste in Western American Literature* (Lincoln: University of Nebraska Press, 2009), 135.

5   Ibid., 129; and Woodward, *Military Geographies*, 153.

6   On the sense of determinism during war, see Mary L. Dudziak, *War Time: An Idea, Its History, Its Consequences* (New York: Oxford University Press, 2012), 3–9, 23, 117–18.

7   Giorgio Agamben, *State of Exception* (Chicago: University of Chicago Press, 2005), 2.

8   Alexander Hamilton, "Federalist Paper No. 23: The Necessity of a Government as Energetic as the One Proposed to the Preservation of the Union," December 18, 1787, available at www.constitution.org/fed/federa23.htm; and Request of the Senate for an Opinion as to the Powers of the President, "In Emergency or State of War," 39 *Opinion of the Attorney General*, 343, 347–48 (1939).

9   John Brenkman, *The Cultural Contradictions of Democracy: Political Thought since September 11* (Princeton, NJ: Princeton University Press, 2007), 60; Oren Gross and Fionnuala Ní Aoláin, *Law in Times of Crisis: Emergency Powers in Theory and Practice* (New York: Cambridge University Press, 2006), 8; and Clinton L. Rossiter, *Constitutional Dictatorship: Crisis Government in the Modern Democracies* (Princeton, NJ: Princeton University Press, 1948), 313.

10   Robert H. Jackson, "Wartime Security and Liberty under Law," *Buffalo Law Review* 1 (1951): 13.

11   Harold H. Bruff, "Executive Power and the Public Lands," *University of Colorado Law Review* 76 (2005): 503–20, 508.

12   Senate Doc. 232, 57th Cong. 1st Sess., Vol. 17, March 3, 1902.

13   The U.S. Constitution's Property Clause gives Congress complete, unlimited
      control over the territory and other property of the United States, including
      the nation's public lands. Through the enactment of land laws, Congress has
      delegated a variety of land management powers to the executive branch. For
      further details on land law history, see Charles F. Wheatley, "Study of Withdraw-
      als and Reservations of Public Domain Lands," *Public Land Law Review Commission*
      1 (1969): 47–88; and George C. Coggins, Charles F. Wilkinson, and John D. Leshy,
      Federal Public Land and Resource Law, 5th ed. (New York: Foundation Press, 2002).
      Legal investigations revealed that from the early eighteenth century up until
      1910, presidents had independently made 252 withdrawals that were not clearly
      based on any statutory authority, see *United States v. Midwest Oil Co.*, 236 U.S. 459
      at 471 (1915).

14   John D. Leshy, "Shaping the Modern West: The Role of the Executive Branch,"
      Colorado Law Review 72, no. 2 (2001): 287–310, 295, 301, 304, 309.

15   Karl Jacoby, *Crimes against Nature: Squatters, Poachers, Thieves, and the Hidden
      History of American Conservation* (Berkeley: University of California Press, 2001), 5
      (quotation), 49, 195.

16   Secretary of the Interior, *Department of Interior Annual Report, Administrative
      Reports*, vol. 1 (Washington, D.C.: Government Printing Office: 1908), 12. Theo-
      dore Roosevelt's belief that it "was not only his right but his duty to do anything
      that the needs of the nation demanded" perhaps represents the most controver-
      sial aspect of his stewardship theory. See Theodore Roosevelt, *Theodore Roosevelt,
      an Autobiography* (Cambridge, MA: Da Capo Press, 1985), 372.

17   Leshy, "Shaping the Modern West," 94; Bruff, "Executive Power and the Public
      Lands," 505–8; and David H. Getches, "Managing the Public Lands: The Authority
      of the Executive to Withdraw Lands" *National Resources Journal* 22 (1982): 280,
      288–300.

18   *United States v. Midwest Oil Co.*, 236 U.S. at 459; and *Grisar v. McDowell*, 73 U.S. 363
      at 381 (1869).

19   *United States v. Midwest Oil Co.*, 236 U.S. at 471, 481, 475; and Brief for Appellant,
      United States v. Midwest Oil Co., 236 U.S. at 459 (1915).

20   Edward S. Corwin, *The President: Office and Powers, 1787–1984: History and Analysis
      of Practice and Opinion* (New York: New York University Press, 1984), 143.

21   *United States v. Midwest Oil Co.*, 236 U.S. at 474; and William Howard Taft, *William
      Howard Taft: Essential Writings and Addresses* (Hackensack, NJ: Fairleigh Dickin-
      son, 2009), 198.

22   *Youngstown Sheet and Tube Co. v. Sawyer*, 343 U.S. 579 at 610–13 (1952) (Frank-
      furter, F., concurring); and *Youngstown Sheet*, 343 U.S. at 637 (Jackson, J., concur-
      ring). For a closer examination of the justices' views toward implied powers,
      see Patricia Bellia, "Executive Powers in Youngstown's Shadows," *Constitutional
      Commentary* 19 (2002): 101–6; and Henry P. Monaghan, "The Protective Power of
      the Presidency," *Columbia Law Review* 93, no. 1 (January 1993): 35–38.

23   *Youngstown Sheet*, 343 U.S. at 635 (Jackson, J., concurring); and *Mistretta v. United
      States*, 488 U.S. 361 at 381, 386 (1989).

24   Brief for Appellant, *United States v. Midwest Oil Co.*, 236 U.S. at 459 (1915); and *United States v. Midwest Oil Co.*, 236 U.S. at 472–73. For additional commentary on the unique land management practices developed between the executive and legislative branches, see Getches, "Managing the Public Lands," 288–300; Bruff, "Executive Power and the Public Lands," 503–12; Coggins, Wilkinson, and Leshy, *Federal Public Land and Resource Law*, 126; and Monaghan, "Protective Power of the Presidency," 44–47.

25   Michael Stokes Paulsen, "Youngstown Goes to War," *Constitutional Commentary* 19, no. 87 (2002): 215–16, 220.

26   *Youngstown Sheet* 343 U.S. at 613 (Frankfurter, F., concurring); and Neal Kumar Katyal, "The Supreme Court, 2005 Term—Hamdan v. Rumsfeld: The Legal Academy Goes to Practice," *Harvard Law Review* 120 (2006): 99.

27   An Examination of the Call to Censure the President: Hearings before the Senate Committee on the Judiciary, 109th Cong. 78–79 (March 31, 2006).

28   John Yoo, "The President's Constitutional Authority to Conduct Military Operations against Terrorists and Nations Supporting Them," September 25, 2001, available at www.justice.gov/sites/default/files/olc/opinions/2001/09/31/op-olc -v025-p0188.pdf. For *Midwest Oil*'s possible influence on presidential war powers, see Louis Fisher and Gordon Silverstein, *Presidential War Power* (Lawrence: University Press of Kansas, 1998), 21, 190–201; and Francis Dunham Wormuth, *To Chain the Dog of War: The War Power of Congress in History and Law* (Champaign: University of Illinois Press, 1989), 133–44, 165–76.

29   See *Hamdi v. Rumsfeld*, 542 U.S. at 507, 519 (2004); Attorney General Alberto R. Gonzales to Senator William H. Frist, January 19, 2006, available at www. justice.gov/ag/readingroom/surveillance9.pdf; and Memorandum Opinion from Caroline D. Krass, Principal Deputy Assistant Attorney General, Office of Legal Counsel to the Attorney General, Authority to Use Military Force in Libya, April 1, 2011, available at www.justice.gov/sites/default/files/olc/opinions/2011/04/31/ authority-military-use-in-libya.pdf. For a counter ruling, see *Hamdan v. Rumsfeld*, 548 U.S. at 557 (2006).

30   Franklin D. Roosevelt, "Announcing Unlimited National Emergency," May 27, 1941, available at http://docs.fdrlibrary.marist.edu/052741.html; "War Powers Act," 48 Stat. 1689 (1933); and Committee on Government Operations, *Executive Orders and Proclamations: A Study of a Use of Presidential Powers*, H.R. 89166, 15 (1957).

31   In June 1942 the power to make executive orders for the withdrawal of public lands was delegated to the secretary of the interior. Thereafter, all withdrawal orders became known as Public Land Orders; see Exec. Order No. 9146, 7 FR 3067, April 28, 1942. For compilations of both executive and public land orders, see U.S. Department of the Interior, Bureau of Land Management, "Land and Realty: Table of Public Land Orders, 1942–2012," available at www.blm.gov/wo/st/en/ prog/more/lands/public_land_orders.html; and National Archives, Federal Register, "Executive Orders Disposition Tables Index," available at www.archives.gov/ federal-register/executive-orders/disposition.html.

32   Exec. Order No. 6247, January 10, 1932; and *The Administration and Use of Public Lands: Hearings Before a Senate Subcommittee on Public Lands and Surveys*, 78th Cong., pt. 11, 3524–27 (1943).

33   Unpublished Opinion of Attorney General, July 25, 1940, reprinted in Wheatley, "Study of Withdrawals," B-6–B-11; and A. J. Wirtz to Robert H. Jackson, August 21, 1940, reprinted in Wheatley, "Study of Withdrawals," B-12.

34   Considered a "compromise" with mining interests at the time, this restriction reaffirmed the long-standing congressional mandate to open public lands to private interests, see Act of June 25, 1910, Ch. 421, § 1, 36 Stat. 847 (43 USC § 141); and 45 Cong. Rec. No. 7475 (1910).

35   *United States v. Midwest Oil*, 236 U.S. at 481.

36   45 Cong. Rec. No. 7475 (1910); and Wheatley, "Study of Withdrawals," 90–103.

37   Charles F. Wheatley Jr., "Withdrawals under the Federal Land Policy Management Act of 1976," *Arizona Law Review* 21 (1979): 311–27, 315; and Getches, "Managing the Public Lands," 292–98.

38   Harold L. Ickes to Robert H. Jackson, February 13, 1941, reprinted Wheatley, "Study of Withdrawals," B-30.

39   Thomas T. Emerson, Memorandum for Mr. Fahy, May 9, 1941; W. B. Woodson to Robert H. Jackson, November 29, 1940; Henry L. Stimson to Robert H. Jackson, December 21, 1940; J. Wayne C. Taylor to Robert H. Jackson, December 30, 1940; and Ickes to Jackson, February 13, 1941, all reprinted in Wheatley, "Study of Withdrawals," B-50, B-21, B-24, B-25, B-30.

40   The withdrawal order in question in the 1884 case embraced 638 acres of land; see U.S. Department of the Interior, *Decisions*, vol. 6 (1888), 16, 19 (quotation).

41   Robert H. Jackson to Harold L. Ickes, April 11, 1941, reprinted in Wheatley, "Study of Withdrawals," B35–B37.

42   Sanford Levinson, "Why the Canon Should Be Expanded to Include the Insular Cases and the Saga of American Expansionism," *Constitutional Comment* 17, no. 2 (2000): 242; Edward T. Swaine, "Political Economy of Youngstown," *Southern California Law Review* 83, no. 2 (2010): 2–6; and Mary L. Dudziak, "Law, Power, and 'Rumors of War': Robert Jackson Confronts Law and Security after Nuremberg," *Emory University School of Law Legal Studies Research Paper Series*, no. 12–191 (2012): 366–85.

43   Committee on Interior and Insular Affairs, "Military Public Land Withdrawals," S. Rep. No. 857, 12 (1957).

44   Getches, "Managing the Public Lands," 295, 297; and Wheatley, "Study of Withdrawals," 124–25.

45   Wheatley, "Withdrawals under the Federal Land Policy Management Act of 1976," 317; Wheatley, "Study of Withdrawals," 108; U.S. Public Land Law Review Commission, "One Third of the Nation's Land" (1970), 43–44; and Getches, "Managing the Public Lands," 97–100.

46   103 Cong. Rec. 5521 (1957). For figures, see S. Rep. No. 857, at 15, 18, 28–30, 40, 62, 67 (1957); and Wheatley, "Study of Withdrawals," 299–300. Private lands acquired through condemnation, purchase, transfer, donation, lease, or temporary use

agreements between private owners or federal officials under the Second War Powers Act 56 Stat. 176 (1942) or similar authorities are not included in this figure.

47   Executive Order 9526, 10 FR 2423, March 2, 1945; and S. Rep. No. 857 at 19–20 (1957).

48   Executive Order 9526.

49   Committee on Public Lands and Surveys, "Some Public Land Withdrawals in Utah: Their Relation to Oil, Potash, and Magnesium Resources, and to Executive Authority to Make Withdrawals," S. Rep. No. 908, at 8–9, 24, 48–58 (1945).

50   Darrin Hostetler, "Wrong War, with the Wrong Enemy, at the Wrong Time: The Coming Battle over the Military Land Withdrawal Act and an Experiment in Privatizing the Regulation of Public Lands," *Environmental Law Review* 29 (1999): 309–10.

51   Joel D. Wolfsohn to Thomas E Finletter, October 27, 1952, reprinted in Utter et al., "Military Land Withdrawals," 50; and S. Rep. No. 857 at 21–23 (1957).

52   S. Rep. No. 857 at 19–20 (1957); Hearings on H.R. 627, H.R. 575, H.R. 608, H.R. 931, H.R. 1148, H.R. 3403, H.R. 3661, H.R. 3788, H.R. 3799, H.R. 3869, Before the Committee on Interior and Insular Affairs, 85th Congress, 244–46 (1957), (hereafter cited as "Hearings on H.R. 627 [1957]"). For legitimacy of presidential assertions of power, see Kenneth R. Mayer, *With the Stroke of a Pen: Executive Orders and Presidential Power* (Princeton, NJ: Princeton University Press, 2002), 17–22.

53   S. Rep. No. 857 at 12 (1957). Truman also declared his own national wartime emergency in December 1950, but his administration never appears to have connected these emergency powers with military land withdrawal powers, see Proclamation No. 2914, 15 Fed. Reg. 9029 (December 19, 1950).

54   S. Rep. No. 857 at 15–19, 29 (1957).

55   Hearings on H.R. 627, 84–85 (1957); and S. Rep. No. 857 at 20–21 (1957).

56   S. Rep. No. 857 at 20 (1957).

57   103 Cong. Rec. 5512 (1957).

58   Hearings on H.R. 627, 58 (1957); and S. Rep. No. 857 at 62 (1957).

59   S. Rep. No. 857 at 36–37 (1957).

60   S. Rep. No. 857 at 62 (1957).

61   S. Rep. No. 857 at 62 (1957); and Hearings on H.R. 627, 234–237 (1957).

62   Hearings on H.R. 627, 94 (1957).

63   S. Rep. No. 857 at 2–3, 22 (1957); and 103 Cong. Rec. 5526 (1957).

64   S. Rep. No. 857 at 53, 65–66 (1957); and Hearings on H.R. 627, 90, 100–101, 112 (1957).

65   Taylor Grazing Act, 43 U.S.C. 315 et seq. Section 315q. For history of this amendment, see Committee on the Judiciary, *Compensation for Cancellation of Grazing Permits*, S. Rep No. 1045, 15 (quotations), 12–18 (1966). For prominent legal cases related to compensation due to lost grazing leases, see *Osborne v. United States*, 145 F.2d 892 (9 Cir., 1944); *United States v. Cox et al (United States v. Beasley et al.)*, 190 F.2d 293 (10th Cir., 1951); and *United States, v. Jaramillo et al.*, 190 F.2d 300 1 (10th Cir., 1951).

66 Hearings on H.R. 627, 81 (1957); S. Rep. No. 857 at 50 (1957); and 103 Cong. Rec. 5521 (1957).

67 S. Rep. No. 857 at 50, 48 (1957).

68 Hearings on H.R. 627 at 59–60 (1957).

69 S. Rep. No. 908 at 8–9, 24, 48–58 (1945); and Hearings on H.R. 627, 64–66 (1957).

70 103 Cong. Rec. 5521 (1957).

71 For the Engle Act's influence on subsequent military land withdrawals, see Hearings on H.R. 5426, 5470, 4932, 5965, and S. 837 (1984); Military Land Withdrawal Act of 1986, Public Law No. 99–606, 100 Stat. 3457 (1986); Committee on Interior and Insular Affairs, Military Land Reform and Reassessment Act of 1992, H.R. 1031 (1992); Military Land Reform: Hearings on H.R. 2080 Before the Subcommittee on National Parks, Forests, and Public Lands of the House Committee on Natural Resources, 103d Cong. (1994); and Military Land Withdrawal Act of 1999, Public Law 106–65, 113 Stat. 885.

72 Hearings on H.R. 627, 59, 60, 64 (1957); and 103 Cong. Rec. 5526 (1957).

73 Committee on Interior and Insular Affairs, Non Military Land Withdrawals, S. Rep No. 1669 (1960); Federal Land Policy and Management Act of 1976, Public Law No. 94–579, § 704(a), 90 Stat. 2744; and Wheatley, "Withdrawals under the Federal Land Policy Management Act," 317.

74 Jules Lobel, "Emergency Power and the Decline of Liberalism," *Yale Law Journal* 9 (1989): 1414–18; and Coggins, *Federal Public Land and Resource Law*, 352–53.

75 Robert H. Jackson, "Is Our Constitutional Government in Danger?" *Town Meeting* 4, no. 5 (November 1939): 15–16.

CHAPTER 2

WEATHER, OTTERS, AND BOMBS

Policy Making, Environmental Science, and U.S. Nuclear Weapons Testing, 1945–1958

NEIL OATSVALL

At the appointed time, there was a blinding flash lighting up the whole area brighter than the brightest daylight. A mountain range three miles from the observation point stood out in bold relief. Then came a tremendous sustained roar and a heavy pressure wave which knocked down two men outside the control center. Immediately thereafter, a huge multi-colored surging cloud boiled to an altitude of over 40,000 feet. Clouds in its patch disappeared. Soon the shifting substratosphere winds dispersed the now grey mass.

> —U.S. War Department description
> of the first atomic bomb detonation

A T 5:30 in the morning on July 16, 1945, humans first unleashed the power of the atom in the form of a bomb. The test occurred at a "remote section" of the Alamogordo Air Base in New Mexico, far from the public. One U.S. War Department press release described how, before the

2.1 The world's first detonation of a nuclear weapon at Trinity, on July 16, 1945. This photo shows the blast sixteen milliseconds after detonation. At this point the fireball is about six hundred feet wide. Image courtesy of the U.S. Department of Energy.

test, "darkening heavens, pouring forth rain and lightning immediately up to the zero hour, heightened the drama." The press release explained: "Ominous weather which had dogged the assembly of the bomb had a very sobering effect on the assembled experts whose work was accomplished amid lightning flashes and peals of thunder. The weather, unusual and upsetting, blocked out aerial observation of the test." However, even though there was no "assurance of favorable weather," the first atomic detonation occurred as scheduled.[1] The actual test itself presented a terrifyingly striking and yet fascinatingly horrible spectacle, as the War Department's description attested.[2]

From the outset, natural forces played a considerable role in U.S. nuclear testing. Historian Ferenc M. Szasz claimed that scientists turned the entire Los Alamos Trinity site into "a sprawling, open-air scientific laboratory," melding science and the environment into an indistinguish-

NEIL OATSVALL

2.2 The Trinity blast a second or so later. After this test Robert Oppenheimer proclaimed, quoting from the Bhagavad Gita: "I am become Death, the shatterer of worlds." Image courtesy of the U.S. Department of Energy.

able mass.[3] The official War Department press release described the blast in relation to the natural world, particularly the weather and the mountains. Weather had been a significant factor in the test's preparations, because summer thunderstorms could come upon the site quickly and unexpectedly. Jack M. Hubbard, the chief meteorologist for the project, explained the operation date was "set from above"; it was necessary to tailor the experiment to the expected wind and weather conditions. Questions also existed about whether a blast would produce rain or affect the winds.[4] Future nuclear tests would similarly influence and be influenced by the natural world, as the United States continued nuclear weapons testing to maintain and increase its nuclear superiority over the rest of the world, particularly the Soviet Union. The Soviets tested their first nuclear bomb in 1949, and after that, from a military perspective U.S. testing became even more imperative.[5]

This chapter probes the connections between nuclear weapons testing, executive policy making, and environmental science. When the United States conducted atomic bomb trials, environmental conditions affected how those tests transpired and the conclusions drawn from them. Geology, geography, prevailing winds, and other natural features played a role in site selection, and the evidence of the different ways bombs affected the lithosphere, hydrosphere, and atmosphere influenced not only knowledge production but also how military and political policy makers perceived and processed that information. Weather and prevailing winds proved particularly crucial and affected determinations about when and how tests could take place. Testing also created anxieties that the tests themselves might affect meteorological phenomena. Other concerns centered around what the tests might do to the surrounding flora and fauna, particularly mammals and fish in the area. In short, the history of how the Atomic Energy Commission (AEC) tested the United States's nuclear arsenal demonstrates a connection between policy makers' conceptions of the environment and of nuclear bombs.

To investigate the interplay between environment, science, nuclear weapons testing, and executive decision making, this chapter examines three cases of U.S. nuclear weapons testing during the early Cold War: Operation Crossroads in 1946 (the first two postwar nuclear tests), the case of testing (or not) on Amchitka Island in the early 1950s, and the interaction between testing, meteorological conditions, and radioactive fallout. The testing process inculcated a greater awareness among policy makers of the interconnection between the environment and nuclear weapons testing, forcing them to think more deeply about natural factors in the context of testing nuclear bombs. This awareness did not morph into a modern environmentalist ethos among executive decision makers, particularly in the White House and the AEC. However, the interplay between the environment (defined here broadly as the nonhuman natural world, including not only biotic entities such as plants and animals but also abiotic elements such as winds, weather, and rocks), scientific research, and national security coalesced into a program of nuclear research and development that forced policy makers to consider the natural world when making their plans. Two terms, as used in this chapter, are worth defining: environmental science and policy makers (or decision makers). "Environmental science" refers to a broad range of disciplines that includes, but is not limited to, ecology, biology, chemistry, geology, and meteorology. Physics is also important, but in the studied tests this discipline played a very different role, used more to find better ways to harness nuclear energy than to understand the surrounding world. "Policy makers" (or "decision makers") refers to the executive branch of the federal government, principally the AEC commissioners (the commission's top-level administrators) and White House officials. This definition excludes other important policy makers in the United States, especially in the legislative branch, but focusing on the executive branch allows for a fuller consideration of the day-to-day administration of nuclear weapons testing.

Historical scholarship on the interaction between nuclear weapons and the environment has typically focused on how these tests have damaged environmental health. These works have portrayed the relationship of U.S. atomic weapons testing to the natural world as little more than an environmental menace, largely because important work by critics of atomic weapons testing showed the world exactly how dangerous nuclear weapons tests could be to human and environmental health. Barry Commoner is the best known of these critics. He wrote in 1958: "In part, our present troubles derive from the unequal pace of the development of physics and biology. We understand nuclear energy well enough to explode great quantities of radioactive materials into the atmosphere. But our present knowledge of biology and its attendant sciences is not adequate for contending with the difficulties that follow when the radioactive dust settles back to earth."[6] Commoner led the charge for scientists to become more involved in politics and use their knowledge to help end nuclear testing. His work helped make the world a safer, healthier place.

Scholars have frequently mistaken policy makers' lack of concern for environmental well-being as a lack of attention paid to the natural world.[7] For example, historians Mark D. Merlin and Ricardo M. Gonzalez have claimed that "most, if not all, [U.S. tests in the Pacific Ocean] were initiated with explicit political intention, often with little regard for the ecological consequences."[8] But such assertions run contrary to the significant attention paid—through meteorology, geology, ecology, and biology—to the environmental aspects of areas in which testing occurred. Historian Mark Fiege has demonstrated that before the United States ever detonated its first atomic bomb, atomic scientists held an "intense fascination with nature" that helped inspire them to produce the prerequisite knowledge necessary for creating the bomb. This knowledge production was not merely "heartless men in white coats calculating on chalkboards and experimenting in laboratories," he claimed. Instead, the scientists who worked on the Manhattan Project held a reverence for nature and frequently spent time out in the natural world hiking and reflecting. Fiege chronicled how these men's childhoods and adult experiences in the natural world heavily influenced and inspired their scientific research. "The nation's atomic project, especially the bomb," he wrote, "was deeply embedded in the human relationship to nature."[9]

Most previous scholarship has not fully appreciated the crucial relationship between the environment and U.S. nuclear weapons testing. In an otherwise excellent article, Merlin and Gonzalez, like many historians before them, proceeded from the assumption that U.S. officials did not share their values about how policy makers should have protected the natural world from nuclear tests. It is not that the United States, in their words, had "little regard for the ecological consequences" of nuclear weapons testing. U.S. policy makers certainly did care about how tests might affect local and global ecology; they just did not prioritize environmental or ecological health in their decision making. Fiege took an important step toward recognizing a more nuanced, two-way interaction between nuclear weapons and the environment. This chapter follows his lead by demonstrating that connections between the bomb, nuclear weapons testing, and the environment continued after the Manhattan Project.[10]

OPERATION CROSSROADS

Somewhat of a paradox exists in the history of nuclear weapons: although the most well-known nuclear blasts occurred during World War II, the vast majority of atomic weapon detonations occurred as tests during times of relative peace. By the time World War II ended, the United States had detonated the world's second and third nuclear bombs.[11] President Truman learned of the first wartime use of an atomic bomb from a telegram, which informed him: "Big bomb dropped on Hiroshima . . . First reports indicate complete success which was even more conspicuous than earlier test."[12] Such language implied that the bombing of Hiroshima was a test just like the bomb detonation at the Los Alamos Trinity site had been.[13] Whether bombs dropped as acts of war can be considered tests is beyond the scope of this chapter, but the mere comparison implicit in the telegram demonstrates the entangled nature of testing and scientific knowledge. After the war, U.S. nuclear tests occurred primarily at two locations, in the Southwest and at Pacific Ocean locations near the Marshall Islands (about two thousand miles southwest of Hawaii). The United States's first postwar tests occurred in July 1946 in the Pacific as part of Operation Crossroads.

During the operation the United States detonated two bombs on the Bikini Atoll, a small lagoon in the Marshall Island chain.[14] Testers intended for Operation Crossroads to show what a nuclear blast would do to ships and their crews; therefore, they had ships moored in the atoll's lagoon at various predetermined distances. In addition to allowing the United States to conduct oceanic tests, Bikini also had the advantage of being several thousand miles from the mainland. The first test of the series, detonated on July 1, was code-named Able. By all accounts, the detonation went mostly as planned, other than going off fifteen hundred to two thousand feet west of the assigned target. Able's intensity "approached the best of the three previous atomic bombs," and it detonated at the planned altitude, a few hundred feet above the sea.

Many of the ships surrounding the blast showed considerable damage. Exposed personnel (had there been any) would have experienced high casualties. Those sheltered "would not have been immediately incapacitated by burns alone," although they would have received lethal doses of radiation. "In general," the report said, "no significant unexpected phenomenon occurred, although the test was designed to cope with considerable variation from predictions. There was no large water wave formed. The radioactive residue dissipated in the manner expected. No damage occurred on Bikini Island, about three miles from the explosion center." The test went well enough that evaluators claimed, "The importance of large-scale research has been dramatically demonstrated."[15]

The second test, held on July 25 and code-named Baker, did have unexpected environmental phenomena. An underwater detonation, Baker caused gigantic waves that, even one thousand feet from the center of the detonation, were eighty to one hundred feet high. The bigger problem was the incredible radiation and the unexpected form it took. The preliminary report to President Truman said, "Great quantities of radioactive water descended upon the ships from the column or were thrown over them by waves." This "highly lethal radioactive water" made

2.3 Operation Crossroads, the Baker shot, detonated on July 25, 1946. In this photograph both the moored ships and nuclear test (at the time, the height of technology) combine with the palm trees (reminiscent of a tropical paradise) to create an almost paradoxical scene. Image courtesy of the U.S. Department of Energy.

it unsafe for any inspection teams to board the moored ships for days. Beyond the ships that were physically destroyed by Baker (testers used a similar setup for Able), the surviving ships were effectively scuttled while still afloat. Although it was "impossible to evaluate an atomic burst in terms of conventional explosives," the report described Baker as incredibly destructive. The contaminated ships "became radioactive stoves, and would have burned all living things aboard them with invisible and painless but deadly radiation."[16]

The Able and Baker blasts show an evolving understanding about the relationship between testing atomic bombs and scientific knowledge about the environment. Atomic bomb tests were, at their core, scientific experiments. While Able likely spewed radioactive material into the air, airborne contamination went mostly unmentioned in reports because the experiment was not designed to measure for it. The radioactive water

NEIL OATSVALL

from Baker, however, occupied a central place in analyses because its effects were readily detected within the existing experimental framework attempting to measure radioactive contamination of the moored ships. Thus the different reactions to Able and Baker reveal the importance of environmental science to test evaluations. Evaluators might have been able to avoid talking about a radioactive column of air or minimize its effects in their reports because they did not detect it, but a tidal wave of radioactive water proved too much to ignore: the Committee to Observe the Atomic Bomb Tests estimated the radioactive spray covered 90 percent of the target array (moored ships and submarines surrounding the blast). This was the equivalent to exposing the area to "many hundred tons of radium," the committee asserted.

Weather also played an important role in judging experimental results. When evaluators deemed weather conditions for the Baker blast "perfect," they demonstrated that nuclear tests changed testers' evaluation criteria; these tests caused experimenters to view meteorological reports through their aims and desires for nuclear testing. Had weather conditions not been "perfect," any test results would have been mediated through that evaluation. After Operation Crossroads concluded, the committee looked at the possible effects of nuclear bombs, especially the nuclear tidal wave Baker had produced, and concluded: "The Bikini tests strongly indicate that future wars employing atomic bombs may well destroy nations and change present standards of civilization."[17] Weather, water, and air were not merely the settings for nuclear weapons testing; instead, they became the experimental mediums through which humans understood and evaluated tests' successes and failures and possible impacts on civilization.

Although the importance of environmental knowledge to nuclear weapons testing is clear in hindsight, it does not mean that evaluators thought of either the tests or their reports in environmentalist terms. The assessments judged Baker's incredible waves of radioactive water to be an "impressive result" and not necessarily an environmental phenomenon—the wave was considered more as a scientific product than part of the natural world. The final report of the Joint Chiefs of Staff declared that the tests at Bikini "provided data essential to future military planning, giving bases for the calculation of the conditions under which the maximum destructive effects of an atomic explosion will be obtained against various types of land and water targets and against living organisms." Testers had used live animals as subjects on the moored ships, but even if effects on animal biology comprised an essential aspect of the tests, evaluators thought of the affected animals purely in military terms.[18]

The animals were important to testers because they represented hypothetical future bomb targets, not because their lives had any inherent value or worth. Just as bombing pilots frequently talk about "the hit" without any reference to the destructive aftermath of their bombs, test evaluators proved more concerned with the effects their bombs might have on targets than with the natural world and its creatures.[19] Among the more than thirty thousand pages of "detailed technical reports" were "the data relating to nuclear physics, medical phases of radiation, including military aspects of radiological safety, and those relating to oceanography, meteorology, and marine and island biology and geology."[20] To evaluators, nuclear testing sites were not spaces where nuclear technology interacted with the environment. Rather, as Szasz suggested, they were open-air testing laboratories.

Operation Crossroads also revealed that Alamogordo, New Mexico, was not a suitable site for all U.S. nuclear weapons tests. The AEC's late 1940s establishment of "a proving ground in the Pacific for routine experiments and tests of atomic weapons" showed the importance of testing to the commission and demonstrated how policy makers increasingly involved environmental knowledge in their decisions. The commission declared that tests "must be a routine part of any weapons program," and the president later approved that statement for inclusion in an AEC report.[21] The required characteristics for test locations melded geopolitical and environmental considerations. One summary listed those nine requirements: (1) protected anchorage six miles in diameter; (2) at least three hundred miles from urban areas; (3) less than one thousand miles from a B-29 base; (4) a region without "violent storms"; (5) "predictable currents of known and great lateral and vertical dispersion. Good fast surface currents which avoid fishing areas, steamer lines and inhabited shores"; (6) a certain minimum distance from the continental United States; (7) an unpopulated area; (8) an area owned or controlled by the United States; and (9) a temperate tropical climate. Bikini best fit these qualifications. The resident "population [was] less than 200 and can be readily moved to another atoll" (whether they wanted to or not). In respect of the Department of Interior's wishes, the AEC studied the location regarding the effects tests would have on fisheries.[22] Thus long

NEIL OATSVALL

before any tests ever occurred, without any real concern for environmental health or protection of the natural environment, in choosing their ideal site policy makers explicitly considered the natural world.

For larger tests, AEC leaders used environmental and scientific reasoning and eschewed Bikini Atoll in favor of establishing a permanent Pacific Proving Grounds at Eniwetok Atoll. The two locations are around a hundred miles apart, both in the Marshall Islands chain. Eniwetok gained the nod because Bikini did not have the sufficient land surface to accommodate the instrumentation for proper scientific observations. Also, only 145 residents called Eniwetok home and, "very important from a radiological standpoint, it is isolated and there are hundreds of miles of open seas in the direction in which winds might carry radioactive particles." Eniwetok's natural features proved crucial for its selection. The atoll also held the geographic advantage of being far away from other people (its residents and their connection to their homeland were not considered in this health and safety calculus). A press release on Eniwetok's selection declared: "All test operations will be under laboratory control conditions." Eniwetok, in the minds of U.S. policy makers, was thereafter turned into a laboratory.[23]

AMCHITKA ISLAND

In the fall of 1950, U.S. policy makers discussed conducting underground tests at Amchitka Island, located in the Aleutian chain. Planning reached a critical stage and on October 30, 1950, Truman approved testing there for the next fall.[24] What makes the case of Amchitka worth studying is that, even with presidential approval, the test series was eventually scuttled because of environmental considerations. The environmental factors that came into play reflect the mind-sets of policy makers at the time and the connections between environmental science and nuclear weapons testing.

Evaluations of the eight atomic bomb tests to date had provided the United States with a great deal of information on the effects of bombs detonated at heights up to two thousand feet and, in the case of Baker, even under water. Yet no information existed on the effects of a nuclear bomb detonated underground. If the United States needed a penetrating atomic weapon—for example, to attack "particularly well constructed or deep underground targets"—the data at hand would not be sufficient to construct such a device.[25] U.S. decision makers needed tests that would help them better understand the relationship between nuclear weapons detonations and the lithosphere.

Site selection held particular importance in underground testing; the choice hinged on nine factors that combined issues of environment, politics, and logistics: safety, sovereignty, security, public relations, climate, geology, cost, accessibility, and size. Although testers did not think that underground nuclear testing would be particularly dangerous (at least in comparison to other atomic tests), they still believed it should be done not in the United States. Instead, "certain remote areas in Canada and other areas within the Commonwealth, such as Australia, offered some advantages." Remote Canadian sites made the cut over other locations; the Caribbean had too many people, the Pacific Proving Grounds at Eniwetok did not have the correct size or geology, and evaluators discarded many Alaskan sites "because of inaccessibility, extreme climate, unsatisfactory geology and the considerable number of trappers and prospectors."[26] A combination of human factors, natural features, and geography thus intermingled to create the determining criteria for site selection: "Careful consideration of the several isolated, uninhabited islands toward the outer end of the Aleutian Chain led to the determination that Amchitka Island is the only site that satisfies all of the established criteria to an acceptable degree." Even though Amchitka was completely uninhabited (because the U.S. government had removed Native inhabitants during World War II), the island had the infrastructure necessary for testing, leftover from the war.

Some natural factors worked against the site, though, such as the island's mostly "bad" climate and the Department of the Interior's strong desire to preserve indigenous wildlife. A selection memo explained: "Rain and fog predominate in the summer and snow and high winds in the winter." Such concerns could be worked around, because "for a short period in May and in a longer period in September and October, the weather can be expected to be moderate." Even with a few environmental problems (and some security concerns: the island was so close to the Soviet Union), policy makers deemed Amchitka Island "the only site presently available that reasonably satisfies all the criteria established for the safe conduct of an underground and surface atomic test." Another report noted that prevailing winds from west to east meant that the USSR would not be able to detect the tests by radiological means. In this case, national security was deemed more important than reducing radiation exposure of U.S. and allied citizens.[27]

Site selection at Amchitka was challenged by significant criticism emerging from the Department of Interior because of concerns about wildlife protection. Dale E. Doty, assistant secretary of the interior, wrote that he and his department protested using the island for testing because it represented "the principal concentration center for the total existing population of sea otter which had been brought to near extinction during Russian occupation of Alaska and which is now being restored and re-colonized over a part of its former range under the close protection by the Fish and Wildlife Service." U.S. officials used the Amchitka herd for stock as part of a transplanting and management program, and although there were otters elsewhere, the herd had only increased on Amchitka. This is not to say that Doty believed in purely preservationist ideals—he also argued that the value of each otter pelt would average around one thousand dollars, with some topping twenty-five hundred dollars. Keeping the site viable for otters would produce "revenue to the Government, once the resource is restored to a production basis, [of] hundreds of thousands of dollars annually."[28] Like nuclear weapons testing in general, concern for the environment did not necessarily mean a desire to protect flora and fauna from harm in any absolute sense.

In Doty's opinion, testing personnel entering the site "would undoubtedly provide opportunity for the molesting and killing of animals." Also because the island's beaches were situated within the danger area of the test, the blast itself, along with "falling debris, flash, and possibly direct radiation," would likely harm the animals. The potential for long-lived radiation was also worrisome. From the department's perspective, "it would hardly have been possible to have chosen a more objectionable area than Amchitka." Doty argued that certain provisions needed to be incorporated into test programs if the operations were to proceed. Laws needed to be followed to ensure "the maximum possible protection of the sea otter from poaching or from any unnecessary disturbance or molestation." Also, the Fish and Wildlife Service would need money to trap and transfer many otters over the winter to safer areas, which would be costly and require "considerable logistic support" from the U.S. military. Even considering all of these precautions, Doty believed that the testing should happen elsewhere, as Amchitka was the only place that otters had recovered as well as they had.[29] Policy makers noted these objections but decided to go on with the test and to work with the Department of the Interior "to preserve the indigenous wild life [sic] inhabiting the island."[30]

While otter populations could not deter those wanting to test on Amchitka, the area's natural formations could. Sometime before the proposed fall 1951 testing date, reports surfaced that "detailed exploration of [Amchitka Island] has revealed geological conditions less favorable than preliminary surveys had indicated." Analysis of the newly discovered "geological conditions" indicated that any data gained from tests on Amchitka would be less accurate than initially believed. This caused policy makers to rethink their plans; perhaps a continental site might be better, as more "favorable geological and meteorological conditions are known to exist at several possible continental test sites than at Amchitka Island." Ultimately Amchitka was jettisoned in favor of the Nevada Test Site, with the recognition that a continental site would clear up many logistical problems.[31]

The case of Amchitka demonstrates the selective inclusion of environmental science into planning and how some environmental factors simply mattered more to policy makers than others. Factors like the survival of sea otters or what might be perceived today as environmental health were deemed less important, at least in terms of what could be worked around and what could not. What proved crucial were aspects, both geological and broadly environmental, that might have influenced the accuracy of data gained during U.S. nuclear tests. Certain environmental concerns could be decisive to U.S. policy makers, even if they might not have used the explicitly environmentally conscious language that this chapter does.

WEATHER AND FALLOUT

After the Amchitka discussion, the AEC and other executive policy makers settled into a pattern where the most talked about environmental issues surrounding testing, recognized as environmental in nature or not, were radiation from blasts and interactions with the weather. In the early 1950s, both the AEC and the White House paid significant attention to how weather influenced atomic bomb testing and how those tests might affect the weather. Before and after any nuclear blast, testers made significant meteorological measurements to ensure that proper conditions existed. After one test, an Air Force "group of 2,400 made

2.4 Weather balloons used for stratospheric fallout monitoring. Balloons like these marked the confluence of U.S. nuclear weapons advancement and the interests of U.S. scientific advancement. The National Archives at College Park, MD (NACP), RG 326, P Entry 73, Folder: Stratospheric Biology and Medicine, Photo: Balloon Photo in back of folder, Box 3. Location: 650/8/30/01.

weather observations, and operated experimental aircraft including radar-directed 'drones' to collect observations in and near the radioactive clouds that follow atomic explosions."[32] In one March 1952 memo, an AEC representative said that precautions for preventing excessive radiation included "cloud tracking and sampling" by the air force and cooperation with around a hundred Weather Service stations.[33] Considering meteorological effects was becoming ever more important.

The January 1953 semiannual AEC report to Congress focused on weather and atomic bomb testing. The report explained the precautions taken during weapons tests to prevent "hazard to the public from blast or fall-out." The AEC constructed a national system to monitor "fall-out radioactivity." One of the best ways to limit the spread of fallout and to gain accurate test results was to make sure that proper weather conditions existed before tests. Predetonation forecasts began seventy-two hours in advance. If those predictions were still favorable twenty-four hours before a scheduled test, the operational sequence began. If weather proved unfavorable, the test might be canceled. Because wind and rain

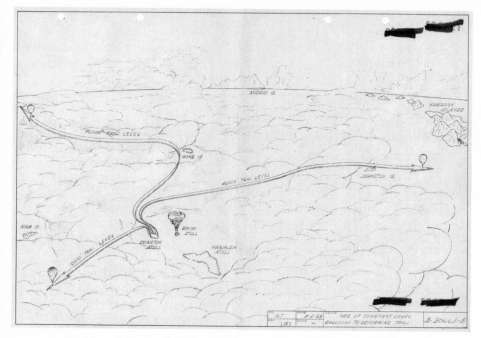

2.5 Drawing of the use of weather balloons to monitor stratospheric fallout in the Pacific. This drawing conveniently hides most of Micronesia under cloud cover, including heavily populated downwind locales like most of the Marshall Islands. Perhaps most notably, strategic U.S. interests—like Midway and Hawaii—feature most prominently on the map. NACP, RG 326, P Entry 73, Folder: Stratospheric Biology and Medicine, Oversized Balloon Illustration, Box 3. Location: 650/8/30/01.

were known to dramatically affect fallout distribution, the weather formed a crucial part of ensuring a test was as safe as possible. The report claimed that the "intensity of blast waves at any locality depends more upon various weather phenomena than upon the energy yield of the detonation."[34] Weather was not merely a secondary concern; it mattered a great deal to planners for both public safety and accuracy of data.

For a time, significant concerns existed about whether atomic detonations themselves might affect the weather.[35] AEC commissioners discussed this at the May 26, 1953, meeting. Gordon Dean, then chairman of the AEC, questioned whether adverse weather conditions following detonations at Eniwetok could be attributed to those tests, as a report had claimed the bad weather "appeared to have been caused by the shots." Photographs showed that heavy clouds and squalls developed after the blasts, along with a series of high-altitude storms (around forty thousand feet high). The committee eventually concluded that "weather conditions prior to the shot time were favorable to rain, and the large vertical disturbances caused by the blast seemed to have 'triggered' the storms which began at Eniwetok and spread north and west over an area of 250,000 square miles." However, "meteorological experts" had not discerned "any relationship between the recent weather conditions throughout the U.S. and the Nevada tests."[36]

On June 10, 1953, the AEC commissioners again met to discuss the effects of nuclear weapons testing on weather, particularly because of "numerous charges" in the press saying that tests at Nevada Proving Grounds had caused "unusual weather conditions in parts of the United States."[37] During previous tests at Eniwetok, weather conditions after tests had been in accord with pretest meteorological predictions. With the evidence presented, the commissioners reckoned that the disturbances, which included "rain squalls over the ocean [and] small storms, but no winds of hurricane force," might have been caused by blasts. A military representative, along with a UCLA-based scientist, claimed that there had been similar air circulations following tests in Nevada as at the Pacific Proving Grounds, but the continental tests caused disturbances for only a few minutes and lacked sufficient moisture in the desert to create storm conditions. "No material in the bomb debris could cause rain or a tornado," they concluded. "It was possible for a tornado to be 'triggered' by external conditions, but it needed moisture as a fuel to become selfsustaining [sic]."

Instead, the high number of tornadoes that spring "could be attributed to an unusual pressure condition forcing moist Gulf air across the U.S. at a high level until it came in contact with a cold air mass coming down from Canada, and that by no mechanism known was it possible for the tornadoes to have been caused by the Nevada tests." The commissioners needed to respond to public views, especially the charges that tests at the Nevada Proving Grounds had caused tornadoes.[38] The issue of weather and nuclear fallout continued to be prominent for several years, as the AEC held a conference in 1956 on "Possible Effects of Nuclear Explosions on Weather."[39] After the development of the massively powerful hydrogen bomb, however, issues surrounding testing and fallout changed dramatically.

2.6 Operation Castle, the Bravo test, detonated on March 1, 1954. This bomb, one of the first thermonuclear weapons detonated, caused the *Lucky Dragon* controversy and showered the Marshall Islanders with radioactive fallout. Image courtesy of the U.S. Department of Energy.

The hydrogen bomb, a weapon that incorporated the fusion of atoms (not principally fission like previous atomic bombs), launched the world into the thermonuclear age and radically altered the scale of potential environmental change. Lewis Strauss, chairman of the AEC, explained the thermonuclear tests at President Eisenhower's March 31, 1954, official press conference. Strauss had recently visited the Pacific Proving Grounds to view the second part of a series of tests of thermonuclear weapons. After the Soviets had detonated their first atomic bomb in August 1949, Strauss explained, the United States could only maintain its nuclear superiority with either a significant quantitative edge in bombs or by developing something greater than existing fission weapons "by a degree of magnitude comparable to the difference between fission bombs and conventional bombs." Therefore in 1950, President Truman had asked the AEC to start making a hydrogen fusion bomb—a

NEIL OATSVALL

thermonuclear bomb. The United States tested a prototype at Eniwetok in November 1952, and the Soviets tested one in August 1953. On March 1, 1954, as part of Operation Castle, the United States tested what was easily the biggest nuclear device the world had seen to date.[40]

That March blast, code-named Bravo, ended up being several times more destructive than expected and produced significantly more fallout than anticipated. The test had not spun out of control, Strauss stressed. When badgered by the media about whether other tests might, he responded, "I am informed by the scientists that [a test getting out of control] is impossible."[41] Strauss argued that the AEC "has conducted the tests of its larger weapons away from the mainland so that the fall-out would occur in the ocean where it would be quickly dissipated both by dilution and by the rapid decay of most of the radioactivity which is of short duration." This is why the United States had conducted previous tests at Bikini in the Marshall Islands—its "good winds" from February to April would blow any fallout away from inhabited atolls. The biggest problem with the Castle Bravo blast was that it far exceeded any estimates of its power; it did indeed smother with fallout Marshall Island inhabitants and a passing Japanese fishing vessel, the *Lucky Dragon 5* (misidentified as the "Fortunate Dragon" by Strauss).[42]

Strauss defended U.S. actions and downplayed any problems, environmental or otherwise, with Bravo. The public and press had the wrong idea about what these Pacific atolls were like, he explained. "Each of these atolls is a large necklace of coral reef surrounding a lagoon two to three hundreds of square miles in area, and at various points on the reef like beads on a string appear a multitude of little islands, some a few score acres in extent—others no more than sandpits," and the United States used the "small, uninhabited, treeless sand bars" for experiments. "The impression that an entire atoll or even large islands have been destroyed in these tests is erroneous," he stressed. "It would be more accurate to say a large sandspit or reef."[43]

With his statement, Strauss noted several other environmental phenomena worth mentioning. First, he reinforced the importance of meteorology to testing when he discussed how, before each blast, testers carefully surveyed the winds at all elevations up to many thousands of feet (because winds are not the same at every elevation). Testers conducted long-range weather forecasts because it takes days to do such measurements. Even though there was a warning area set before tests, he admitted that sometimes humans did get caught in the danger zone of fallout. This of course included the crew of the *Lucky Dragon*, the "natives," and some weather personnel. Although the tests caused some increase in "background" radiation, this decreased rapidly and the stories about widespread contamination of tuna or other fish could not be substantiated. Instead, the only place anyone had found contaminated fish was in the hold of the *Lucky Dragon* and, of course, near the test site. The fish near the site should not have concerned anyone, according to Strauss, because "at certain seasons of the year, almost all fish caught are normally poisonous as a result of feeding on certain seasonally prevalent micro-organisms, and the natives and our Task Force personnel do not eat them at such times."[44] Because the only fish contaminated by radiation were not fit for human consumption, Strauss believed they were worthless by any measurement. Even after the negative consequences from the 1954 hydrogen bomb tests, the United States continued to test in the Pacific.

After 1954 the issue of fallout and the radiation effects of weapons testing became more important to the public, particularly after the *Lucky Dragon* incident. Commissioner Strauss sent a letter to President Eisenhower in March 1955 about an upcoming test that would be conducted around forty thousand feet high. He included an article titled "Atomic Blast Six Miles Up To Test New Air Defense: Nuclear Warhead for Missiles Use To Be Tried Out Soon in Nevada." Strauss thought the article was necessary because it would "prevent apprehension by observers of the high altitude test (40,000 feet) which will be seen for long distances." The piece told its readers that even humans standing at ground level directly underneath the blast would only receive 1/100th of a normal x-ray dose because the test would be so high.[45] But even with such assurances, many civilians felt nervous.

In the spring of 1956, a reporter questioned the president about why the United States continued to research the hydrogen bomb, prompting Eisenhower to discuss the interconnectedness of environmental science and atomic weapons research. The nation had gone ahead with testing, he responded, "not to make a bigger 'bang,' not to cause more destruction, [but instead] to find out ways and means in which you can limit it, make it useful in the defensive purposes of shooting against a fleet of airplanes coming over, to reduce 'fall-out,' to make it more a military weapon and less one just of mass destruction." The country knew how to make atomic bombs big, he explained, but that did not interest the United States anymore—making smaller bombs of reduced fallout did.[46] Reducing fallout required improving scientific knowledge, especially about the environment.

This argument was common. The July 1956 semiannual AEC report discussed Operation Redwing, which had occurred a few months prior. Redwing had been a full-scale test series at Eniwetok aimed "toward development of defensive weapons." In the interest of safety, these tests had been postponed because of unfavorable weather, especially after the 1954 Operation Castle Bravo blast. Monitoring the weather functioned as a safety precaution for the shot itself and for control of the resulting fallout. Other tests in the Pacific Ocean had mechanisms in place "to make measurement of radioactivity in sea water and in marine organisms." Testers sampled water on the surface and at various depths, along with plankton and fish, with sampling extending "as far westward as radioactivity is detectable." Radioactivity sampling also occurred in the form of land and marine biological surveys on Eniwetok and Bikini Atolls and lagoons.[47]

A public statement by the president in October 1956 furthered the U.S. government's position that the nation's citizenry should not worry about nuclear fallout from tests. As Eisenhower reminded the public, fallout had been a known issue since the first atomic test at Trinity, and the AEC had been "continuously engaged in the study of the biological effect of radiation." Reports were publicly available, and a 1956 finding of the National Academy of Sciences called biological damage from tests "essentially negligible." Moreover, the Committee on Meteorology of the National Academy of Sciences had determined "there was no evidence to indicate that climate has been in any way altered by past atomic and thermonuclear explosions."[48]

One series of tests, Operation Plumbbob, illustrates how significant the interaction between environmental science and nuclear detonations had become by the end of Eisenhower's presidency. Plumbbob's primary purpose was to increase scientific knowledge about nuclear tests, especially concerning fallout and biomedical effects. While the operation did not focus exclusively on improving knowledge on nuclear testing and the environment, a great many subprojects did. The proposal claimed that the Plumbbob blasts would "contribute significantly to the knowledge necessary for the improvement of our self-defense against enemy action in the event of war and the establishment of proper safeguards in peacetime applications of nuclear energy." Among other projects, the series included research on "radio-ecological aspects of nuclear fallout," intended to study "persistence of gross fission products" in the environment after fallout; "biophysical aspects of fallout phenomenology," which looked at "the physical and chemical characteristics of fallout materials"; and an inquiry into "the physical and chemical characteristics of fallout materials," which made "fallout studies on raw agricultural products, such as exposed wheat dumps, corn and sugar cane stalks, and dried-fruit flats, to determine whether cleanup is possible, to recommend methods of protection, and to evaluate types of agricultural packaging."[49]

Plumbbob showed a concern for how the test site environment might affect and be affected by a nuclear detonation. The April 17, 1957, AEC commissioners meeting included discussion of a "Special Shot" for Plumbbob that would be underground. This test presented two major problems—containment of the radiation and accurate measurement of the yield. The Nevada Test Site had geological conditions that would help ensure that the test blast did not cause an earthquake. Fears existed that if an earthquake happened at the same time, the AEC might be blamed for the natural occurrence; if an earthquake took place, seismic readings could tell from where it originated. The commissioners discussed what the likely effects of an underground firing would be, and "the extent of absorption of energy at a given geologic fault." They reached the conclusion that very little energy could be transferred "through a fault from one structure to another."[50]

When that underground blast eventually occurred, it seemed to be a resounding success. Policy makers had explicitly incorporated natural features into their tests. The Rainier Shot of Operation Plumbbob, fired on September 19, 1957, was a 1.7-kiloton blast in a tunnel in a mesa at the Nevada Test Site. Intended to "eliminate fall-out, be independent of weather, and eliminate other offsite effects," evaluators declared after the test "practically all radioactive fission products were trapped in highly insoluble fused silica, indicating very little likelihood of ground water contamination." Three months later the test site still had elevated temperatures from the radiation (up to 194 degrees Fahrenheit), but evaluators thought the shot had gone so well "that devices 100 times as powerful as Rainier could be safely fired underground at the Site."[51] The setting for the Rainier Shot had been incorporated as a crucial element in planning the blast.

Once the dust settled on Plumbbob, the AEC had detonated twenty-four nuclear devices and conducted six "safety experiments" on reducing fallout in the natural world at the Nevada Test Site, from March 15 to October 12, 1957. Two new testing techniques proved worthwhile—suspending bombs from balloons and detonating bombs deep underground. Using balloons prevented the atomic bomb's resulting fireball from touching the ground, which supposedly dramatically lowered the amount of radioactive fallout. The January 1958 semiannual AEC report claimed that of the tests that had used this method, "none resulted in significant fallout in the test region." For the underground tests "a tunnel was dug horizontally into a mesa and at its end was bent in almost a complete circle." The testers placed a "device of known low yield" at the end of the tunnel, as this formation would seal off the main tunnel with rocks during the detonation so that no radiation might escape. "The experiment's objective of containing all radiation was achieved," the AEC declared.[52] The underground nuclear tests reveal a seeming paradox in U.S. nuclear testing and the environment. Even though nuclear weapons created dangerous fallout radiation, the U.S. government continued to test nuclear weapons with the expressed goal of creating less fallout radiation. Although one of the greatest benefits of underground tests was that they produced little to no atmospheric radioactive contamination or fallout, the more valuable part to policy makers was that such tests often enhanced environmental scientific knowledge. AEC policy makers privileged certain understandings of the natural world more than others, especially depending on how these did or did not support what the AEC perceived to be its mission and purpose (certainly not environmental protection).

Despite an international lawsuit trying to end nuclear testing, a hunger strike by citizen activists at the AEC headquarters, and one man claiming that nuclear testing during a full moon might cause flooding, the U.S. government expressed few public reservations about its tests.[53] The AEC claimed that weapons testing had the major objectives of "improved weapons; smaller, more efficient, and more rugged strategic, tactical and defensive weapons; development of strategic, tactical and defensive weapons with greatly reduced radioactive fallout."[54] The implication of this statement is clear: nuclear testing had only gotten safer and produced less fallout, so the public should not worry about it. Nonetheless, when asked about seeing an actual atomic bomb test, President Eisenhower replied at one press conference, "They won't allow me." After the laughter died down, he elaborated: "I have seen all the weapons, I just haven't been allowed to go to the tests."[55] Hypothetically speaking, the bombs may have been safe but weren't safe enough when the president's well-being was on the line.

Of course, the tests never were entirely safe, even with precautions. After Operation Hardtack, a memo stated: "The land area of the Bikini and Eniwetok Atolls, the water area of their lagoons, and the adjacent areas within three miles to seaward of the atolls and the overlying airspace will remain closed to vessels and aircraft which do not have specific clearance."[56] The craft with clearance focused on conducting surveys "to measure radioactivity in sea water and marine organisms."[57] Tests produced significant worldwide radioactive fallout, which increased as more nations detonated more bombs over time, leading to environmental concern at the highest levels of government.

On October 31, 1958, the United States, the United Kingdom, and the Soviet Union entered into nuclear test cessation talks in an attempt to achieve a full ban on all nuclear weapons tests by signing nations. This marked a pivotal moment for the entire world, but the talks began only after the United States finished its large Hardtack test series. Initially planned to end in July 1958, the tests did not end until much later because of weather concerns.[58] U.S. tests ceased for a time as part of an agreement to work toward a treaty ban (these early talks never produced a signed treaty, and the United States started testing again during the Kennedy administration). But before tests stopped that Halloween, scientific knowledge about the environment had weighed heavily on the minds of policy makers, so much so that decision makers often labeled individual test shots and sometimes entire test series with names that explicitly evoked environmental imagery.[59]

Whether it was concern for how the weather might affect a test (or be affected by a test) or for the sea otters and geology of a specific site, decision makers showed time and again that scientific conceptions of the natural world mattered. Of course, this is not to say that consideration meant environmentalist sentiment—far from it. Policy makers saw little paradox in dismissing concern for Amchitka's otters while at the same time canceling the test series because other environmental factors—geological features—did not fit their requirements. Even with a frequent lack of concern for environmental welfare, the actions and decisions of policy makers reflect that they proved deeply conscious of the interconnections between environmental science and testing nuclear weapons.

Policy makers understood the ramifications of their choices on the environment and how those spaces and their inhabitants might change plans for nuclear testing. As time passed, the tests helped policy makers in both the White House and the AEC develop an increasing awareness about the natural world. Simply put, the environment and environmental science mattered in U.S. nuclear weapons testing. Those in power understood a connection and worked scientific understanding into decisions and policies. The nexus of nuclear weapons and the natural world operated as a two-way street, with scientific conceptions of the environment affecting atomic tests just as much (or more) as tests altered the natural world.

NOTES

Epigraph: Harry S. Truman Presidential Library (HSTL), Papers of Truman, President's Secretary's Files, Box 174, Folder Atomic Bomb, Press Releases [1 of 3], War Department Press Release on New Mexico Test Site, 3.

1 Ferenc Szasz went so far to say, "If one examines the list of desired ideal weather conditions gathered from the group leaders and compares them with the actual conditions at the time of the July 16 shot, the contrast is striking." Ferenc M. Szasz, *The Day the Sun Rose Twice: The Story of the Trinity Nuclear Explosion, July 16, 1945* (Albuquerque: University of New Mexico Press, 1985), 77–78.

2 HSTL, Papers of Truman, President's Secretary's Files, Box 174, Folder Atomic Bomb, Press Releases [1 of 3], War Department Press Release on New Mexico Test Site, 1–3.

3 Szasz, *Day the Sun Rose Twice*, 5.

4 Ibid., 67–74.

5 As scholar Marek Thee has argued, "The history of the nuclear arms race is intimately interrelated with the systematic testing of nuclear weapons." Marek Thee, "The Pursuit of a Comprehensive Nuclear Test Ban," *Journal of Peace Research* 25, no. 1 (March 1988): 15.

6 Barry Commoner, "The Fallout Problem," *Science* 127, no. 3305 (May 1958): 1023–26.

7 This chapter does not consider many of the human elements of testing, but there is no shortage of historians who are critical of nuclear weapons and the people who tested them, such as Phillip L. Fradkin in *Fallout: An American Nuclear Tragedy* (Tucson: University of Arizona Press, 1989), and Richard L. Miller in *Under*

the Cloud: The Decades of Nuclear Testing (New York: Free Press, 1986). Barton Hacker took a kinder view, claiming: "Those responsible for radiation safety in nuclear weapons testing under the auspices of the Atomic Energy Commission were competent, diligent, and cautious. They understood the hazards and took every precaution within their power to avoid injuring either test participants or bystanders. Testing, of course, meant taking risks, and safety could never be the highest priority. Those in charge sometimes made mistakes, but for the most part they managed to ensure that neither test participants nor bystanders suffered any apparent damage from fallout." Barton C. Hacker, *Elements of Controversy: The Atomic Energy Commission and Radiation Safety in Nuclear Weapons Testing, 1947–1974* (Berkeley: University of California Press, 1994), 9. Debra Rosenthal has even probed the mind-sets of those who work on nuclear weapons design in *At the Heart of the Bomb: The Dangerous Allure of Weapons Work* (Reading, PA: Addison-Wesley Publishing, 1990). A work that examines both environmental and human health effects of nuclear weapons is Arjun Makhijani, Howard Hu, and Katherine Yih, eds., *Nuclear Wastelands: A Global Guide to Nuclear Weapons Production and Its Health and Environmental Effects* (Cambridge: Massachusetts Institute of Technology Press, 1995).

8   Merlin and Gonzalez provide a catalog of both short- and long-term, "direct and indirect atmospheric, geological, and ecological effects of nuclear testing in Remote Oceania." These included obvious effects such as atmospheric fallout and large bomb craters but also lesser-known issues like how a large piece of coral reef broke off at some point between 1952 and 1958. Mark D. Merlin and Ricardo M. Gonzalez, "Environmental Impacts of Nuclear Testing in Remote Oceania, 1946–1996," in *Environmental Histories of the Cold War*, ed. J. R. McNeill and Corinna R. Unger (Cambridge: Cambridge University Press, 2010), 167.

9   Mark Fiege, "The Atomic Scientists, the Sense of Wonder, and the Bomb," *Environmental History* 12, no. 3 (July 2007): 578, 580, 584.

10   John Hersey's *Hiroshima* (1946; reprint, New York: Bantam Books, 1981) caused people in the United States to consider the effects radiation might have on biological entities. Hersey's work started as a single issue of the *New Yorker* but became a monograph. Other evidence for early understandings about the environment and the nuclear complex is provided by Hollywood movies such as *Them!* (1954), which portrayed a nightmare scenario in which radiation turned ants into mutated terrors the size of Volkswagen Beetles. *Them!* was Warner Brothers's highest grossing film of 1954 and a bona fide box office hit. William M. Tsutsui, "Looking Straight at *Them!* Understanding the Big Bug Movies of the 1950s," *Environmental History* 12, no. 2 (April 2007): 237–53. Tsutsui's argument is that these radioactive bug movies of the 1950s and early 1960s represent not so much fear over nuclear technology, the Cold War, and humanity's inability to control nature, but rather how bugs can be scary: many people were terrified of actual insect invasions, because of warnings by many entomologists of the time. Historian Ralph Lutts has suggested that Rachel Carson's influential *Silent Spring* (1962) would not have had nearly the same effect on society had citizens

not already been primed to think in distinctly ecological ways (especially about unseen forces) by concerns about radioactive fallout in the previous decade. Ralph H. Lutts, "Chemical Fallout: Rachel Carson's *Silent Spring*, Radioactive Fallout, and the Environmental Movement," *Environmental Review* 9, no. 3 (Autumn 1985): 210–25.

11   On the decision to drop nuclear bombs on Japan, see J. Samuel Walker, *Prompt and Utter Destruction: Truman and the Use of Atomic Bombs against Japan* (Chapel Hill: University of North Carolina Press, 2004). Walker argues, "In fact, however, Truman never faced a categorical choice between the bomb and an invasion that would cost hundreds of thousands of American lives." Instead, Walker claims, Truman had five fundamental considerations in using the atomic bomb in warfare: a commitment to end the war as soon as possible; the need to justify the effort and expense of making the bombs; the desire to achieve diplomatic edge in the growing rivalry with the Soviets; a lack of incentives to not use the bomb; a hatred of the Japanese and a desire for vengeance. See pages 5, 92–96.

12   HSTL, Papers of George M. Elsey, Box 113, Telegram from Secretary of War to President, August 6, 1945.

13   Some of the earliest appraisals of the atomic bombs dropped on Hiroshima and Nagasaki can be found in the Strategic Bombing Survey. Most striking are the photographs of destruction wrought. HSTL, White House Central Files, Confidential Files, Box 4, Folder Atomic Bomb and Energy, August 1945 to November 1949, 1 of 2, "The United States Strategic Bombing Survey: The Effects of Atomic Bombs on Hiroshima and Nagasaki," June 30, 1946.

14   An amusing story to come out of these tests centers around a journalist who, having seen the tests at Bikini that summer, asked if he had the security clearance to describe the mushroom cloud produced at Alamogordo as purple. After an argument ensued about the actual color of the cloud (it had been white), one of the security clearance personnel reminded the journalist that he had been wearing purple sunglasses the day of the Alamogordo test. HSTL, Dean G. Acheson Papers, Box 2, Folder Atomic Energy, 1947–1948, "Control of Atomic Energy, Address by H. Thomas Austern at New York University on March 20, 1948," Washington Square College Alumni, 1.

15   HSTL, Papers of Harry S. Truman, Official File, Box 1533, Folder 692-F, "The President's Committee to Observe the Atomic Bomb Tests, Press Release of Preliminary Report on July 1, 1946, Bikini Atoll tests," July 11, 1946. Animals exposed in ships during the tests (which many people later protested) proved paramount in determining the radiation damage that would have been suffered by any crews: "Measurements of radiation intensity and a study of animals exposed in ships show that the initial flash of principal lethal radiations, which are gamma-rays and neutrons, would have killed almost all personnel normally stationed aboard the ships centered around the air burst and many others at greater distances." HSTL, Papers of Harry S. Truman, Official File, Box 1527, Folder OF 692-A Atomic Bomb, "Preliminary Report Following the Second Atomic Bomb Test," July 30, 1946, 1.

16 HSTL, Papers of Harry S. Truman, Official File, Box 1527, Folder OF 692-A Atomic Bomb, "Preliminary Report Following the Second Atomic Bomb Test," July 30, 1946, 2–3.

17 HSTL, Papers of Harry S. Truman, Official File, Box 1533, Folder 692-F, "The President's Committee to Observe the Atomic Bomb Tests, Report Carl Hatch to President," July 29, 1946, 1–3. On the Crossroads tests, also see HSTL, Papers of Harry S. Truman, Official File, Box 1533, Folder 692-G Joint Chiefs of Staff Evaluation Board, "Preliminary Report Following the Second Atomic Bomb Test."

18 Of course, this does not mean that civilians thought of such animals in military terms. For criticism of the decision to use animals as test subjects during Crossroads tests, see HSTL, Papers of Harry S. Truman, Official File, Box 1528, Folder 692-A Miscellaneous (May–December 1946) Letter Vaughn Gary to President, June 17, 1946; Letter R. Maxwell Bradner to President, July 2, 1946; Letter Rolf Kreitz to President, July 2, 1946; and Letter Walter G. Gleassen to President, July 9, 1946. Several of these letters, all in HSTL, used explicitly religious reasoning for being against the use of animals during nuclear weapons testing. Similar protestations occurred during the Eisenhower presidency. In particular, an article in the *Denver Post* about the AEC Division of Biology and Medicine using dogs for experiments elicited a great many telegrams from Colorado residents. Dwight D. Eisenhower Presidential Library (DDEL), White House Central Files, General File, Box 1213, Folder 155 1955, Various Telegrams, April 26, 1955.

19 More concern about the effects of Crossroads tests on the environment can be found in HSTL, Papers of Harry S. Truman, Official File, Box 1527, Folder 692-A Miscellaneous (April–October 1945), Letter Schuyler Otis Bland to Truman, November 24, 1945; Papers of Clark Clifford, Subject File, 1945–54, Box 1, Folder Atomic Energy—Newspaper clippings and Releases, "Smoke From Vesuvius," *Dayton News*, April 20, 1948; Papers of Harry S. Truman, Official File, Box 1528, 692-A Miscellaneous (January–April 1946), Letter Mrs. M. Conan to Truman, April 3, 1946, Mrs. Conan's letter also contained vicious anti-Communist sentiment, saying, "America you can't make a pet out of communism. You will get badly stung if you try it! Communism is the anti-Christ." She held up God as the best way to defeat Communist threats.

20 Citations from the entire paragraph can be found in HSTL, Papers of Truman, President's Secretary's Files, Box 176, Folder Atomic Testing, Crossroads, "The Evaluation of the Atomic Bomb as a Military Weapon: The Final Report of the Joint Chief's of Staff Evaluation Board for Operation Crossroads," June 30, 1947, 16, 19–21.

21 HSTL, White House Central Files, Confidential Files, Box 4, Folder Atomic Bomb and Energy August 1945 to November 1949, 2 of 2, Memo from D. E. Lilienthal to President, July 18, 1947; and HSTL, White House Central Files, Confidential Files, Box 60, Folder Atomic Energy Commission, "Cross Reference Sheet, re establishing a Proving Ground in the Pacific for routine experiments and tests of atomic weapons," July 19, 1947.

22 HSTL, Papers of Truman, President's Secretary's Files, Box 176, Folder Atomic

Testing, Crossroads, "Proposed Plan for Atomic Bomb Test against Naval Targets."

23 HSTL, Papers of Clark Clifford, Subject File, 1945–54, Box 1, Folder Atomic Energy—Newspaper Clippings and Releases, "Press Release on the Establishment of Pacific Experimental Installations," December 1, 1947.

24 HSTL, Papers of Truman, President's Secretary's Files, Box 176, Folder Atomic Energy, Superbomb Data, Memo from James S. Lay Jr. to Secretary of State, Secretary of Defense, and Chairman of the Atomic Energy Commission, Subj: Underground and Surface Atomic Bomb Tests, October 30, 1950.

25 HSTL, Papers of Truman, President's Secretary's Files, Box 176, Folder Atomic Energy, Superbomb Data, Memo from James S. Lay Jr. to President, October 27, 1950, 1–2.

26 Ibid., 3.

27 Ibid., 4.

28 HSTL, Papers of Truman, President's Secretary's Files, Box 176, Folder Atomic Energy, Superbomb Data, Letter from Dale E. Doty to James S. Lay Jr., October 13, 1950, 1.

29 Ibid., 2–3.

30 HSTL, Papers of Truman, President's Secretary's Files, Box 176, Folder Atomic Energy, Superbomb Data, Memo from James S. Lay Jr. to President, October 27, 1950, 7.

31 Amchitka was later used in a different test series. HSTL, Papers of Truman, President's Secretary's Files, Box 176, Folder Atomic Testing, Windstorm, Memo from G. C. Marshall to Executive Secretary, National Security Council, Subj: Operation Windstorm, May 21, 1951.

32 *Tenth Semiannual Report of the Atomic Energy Commission to Congress, July 1951* (Washington, D.C.: U.S. Government Printing Office), 6.

33 HSTL, Papers of Truman, President's Secretary's Files, Box 176, Folder Atomic Energy, Superbomb Data, Letter Morse Salisbury to Joseph Short, Subj: Draft Press Release on New Tests, March 19, 1952, 3–4.

34 *Thirteenth Semiannual Report of the Atomic Energy Commission to Congress, January 1953* (Washington, D.C.: U.S. Government Printing Office), 77–97. These atomic bomb tests fundamentally were about producing data for scientists to analyze. Take, for example, the massive data sets on such subjects as subsurface temperature of the bomb range in Las Vegas, Nevada, in June of 1951, or seismological readings at Amchitka. See the National Archives at College Park, MD (NACP), RG 374 Records of the Defense Threat Reduction Agency, Box 6, Folder Original Field Notes, Proj 1(8)a, Opn B-J or NACP, RG 374 Records of the Defense Threat Reduction Agency, Box 6, Folder Records from the Seismic Survey of Amchitka Island. Reference Program 8.1 of Windstorm Operation. Classified Information.

35 The notion that human activities, especially explosions and detonations, might have an affect on the weather is nothing new. See James Rodger Fleming, *Fixing the Sky: The Checkered History of Weather and Climate Control* (New York: Columbia University Press, 2010).

36   NACP, RG 326 Records of the Atomic Energy Commission, Entry A1 19, Minutes of
       the Meetings of the AEC, Box 6, Meeting No. 869, May 26, 1953, 325.

37   Though this chapter does not cite anything specifically, also see *Fourteenth Semi-
       annual Report of the Atomic Energy Commission to Congress, July 1953* (Washington,
       D.C.: U.S. Government Printing Office), 53. One of the more intriguing resources
       for studying the 1,350-square-mile (860,000 acres) Nevada Proving Ground has
       to be *The Nevada Test Site*. As the book claims in the preface, "While the nuclear
       genie popped out of his bottle at White Sands Proving Ground on July 16, 1945, it
       may be said that he learned to dance at the Nevada Test Site." *The Nevada Test Site:
       A Guide to America's Nuclear Proving Ground* (Culver City, CA: Center for Land Use
       Interpretation, 1996), 7, 9.

38   NACP, RG 326 Records of the Atomic Energy Commission, Entry A1 19, Minutes of
       the Meetings of the AEC, Box 6, Meeting No. 875, June 10, 1953, 357–58.

39   NACP, 326 Records of the Atomic Energy Commission, Entry 73, Division of
       Biology and Medicine, Records Relating to Fallout Studies, 1953–6, Box 2, Folder
       Conference—Effect of Atomic Weapons on Weather.

40   DDEL, Dwight D. Eisenhower Papers as President, Ann Whitman File, Press Con-
       ference Series, Box 2, Folder Press Conference March 31, 1954, Statement by Lewis
       L. Strauss, 1. Also see *Seventeenth Semiannual Report of the Atomic Energy Commission
       to Congress, January 1955* (Washington, D.C.: U.S. Government Printing Office), 14.

41   DDEL, Dwight D. Eisenhower Papers as President, Ann Whitman File, Press
       Conference Series, Box 2, Folder Press Conference March 31, 1954, Official White
       House Transcript of President Eisenhower's Press and Radio Conference #33, 13.

42   DDEL, Dwight D. Eisenhower Papers as President, Ann Whitman File, Press
       Conference Series, Box 2, Folder Press Conference March 31, 1954, Statement
       by Lewis L. Strauss, 2–3.

43   Ibid., 2.

44   Ibid., 2–4.

45   DDEL, Dwight D. Eisenhower Papers as President, Ann Whitman File, Adminis-
       trative Series, Box 4, Folder Atomic Energy Commission 1955–56 (7), Letter from
       Lewis L. Strauss to Eisenhower, March 28, 1955.

46   DDEL, Dwight D. Eisenhower Papers as President, Ann Whitman File, Press
       Conference Series, Box 4, Press Conference April 24, 1956, Official White House
       Transcript of President Eisenhower's Press and Radio Conference #85, 8.

47   *Twentieth Semiannual Report of the Atomic Energy Commission, July 1956*, 8, 115. Also
       see *Twenty-First Semiannual Report of the Atomic Energy Commission to Congress,
       January 1957* (Washington, D.C.: U.S. Government Printing Office), 9–11.

48   DDEL, Dwight D. Eisenhower Papers as President, Ann Whitman File, Adminis-
       trative Series, Box 4, Folder Atomic Energy Commission 1955–56 (2), Statement by
       the President, October 24, 1956.

49   Other projects had a distinctly environmental or biological component. DDEL,
       John Stewart Bragdon Records, Miscellaneous File, Box 1, Folder Atomic Energy
       Commission, Operation Plumbbob Civil Effects Test Group Project Summaries,
       1957, ii, 42, 43, 47.

50 NACP, RG 326 Records of the Atomic Energy Commission, Entry A1 19, Minutes of the Meetings of the AEC, Box 10, Meeting No. 1277, April 17, 1957, 193–95.

51 *Twenty-fourth Semiannual Report of the Atomic Energy Commission to Congress, July 1958* (Washington, D.C.: U.S. Government Printing Office), 14.

52 *Twenty-third Semiannual Report of the Atomic Energy Commission to Congress, January 1958* (Washington, D.C.: U.S. Government Printing Office), 274–75.

53 The "Suit to Enjoin Nuclear Tests," filed by a group of fourteen people from five different countries, used environmental reasoning. It asked "to enjoin the Atomic Energy Commissioners and the Secretary of Defense from detonating any nuclear weapons that produce radiation, and specifically the tests scheduled this month at Eniwetok. The plaintiffs claim that these tests will produce radioactive fallout which will produce harmful mutations in their progeny and will probably give them leukemia and bone cancer. The four Japanese also claim that they are fishermen who will be barred from the Eniwetok area." DDEL, White House Central Files, Official File, Box 451, Folder OF 108-A Atomic Weapons, Atomic and Hydrogen Bombs (9), Letter from George Cochran Doub to H. Roemer McPhee, April 23, 1958. The hunger strike at AEC headquarters occurred in May 1958. NACP, RG 326 Records of the Atomic Energy Commission, Entry A1 19, Minutes of the Meetings of the AEC, Box 11, Meeting No. 1372, May 9, 1958. The citizen worried about the moon, James H. Ouzts, was quite serious, even though it appears comical now, when he claimed, "Urgently request that under no circumstances you permit any type of hydrogen or atomic war head [*sic*] be exploded any where near the moon most especially when it is new because the margin of balance between the Earth and moon at this time is so small and the attraction between them is so great that it will move billions of gallons of water on Earth and cause flood tides. If this balance should be interrupted and cause the dark side of the moon to swing toward Earth then you have a situation the same as a positive atom and a negative electron. In the name of God and humanity I urgently request that you pass this information to the rest of the world." DDEL, White House Central Files, General File, Box 1216, Folder 155-B, April–June 1959, Telegram, James H. Ouzts to President, March 23, 1959.

54 *Twenty-fourth Semiannual Report of the Atomic Energy Commission to Congress, July 1958* (Washington, D.C.: U.S. Government Printing Office), 13.

55 DDEL, Dwight D. Eisenhower Papers as President, Ann Whitman File, Press Conference Series, Box 8, Press Conference June 17, 1959, Official White House Transcript of President Eisenhower's Press and Radio Conference, #161, 4–5.

56 DDEL, White House Office, Office of the Special Assistant, OCB Series, Subject Subseries, Box 5, Folder Nuclear Energy Matters (5) [Apr–Oct 1958], Pacific Nuclear Tests Concluded, September 3, 1958

57 The pretest estimations claimed that "the detonations are not expected to add enough radioactive material to natural levels of radioactivity in the ocean to be harmful to marine life." Either way, testing of the waters and marine life occurred, as well as studies into the "ultimate destination and behavior of radioactivity in the sea water and in marine organisms." *Twenty-fourth Semiannual*

Report of the Atomic Energy Commission to Congress, July 1958 (Washington, D.C.: U.S. Government Printing Office), 348–50.

58   Robert A. Divine, "Eisenhower, Dulles, and the Nuclear Test Ban Issue: Memorandum of a White House Conference, 24 March 1958," *Diplomatic History* 2, no. 1 (October 1978): 321–30.

59   Perhaps the best example of this is the Hardtack I test series from April 28 to August 18, 1958. The names of its individual blasts, in order of testing date, were Yucca, Cactus, Fir, Butternut, Koa, Wahoo, Holly, Nutmeg, Yellowwood, Magnolia, Tobacco, Sycamore, Rose, Umbrella, Maple, Aspen, Walnut, Linden, Redwood, Elder, Oak, Hickory, Sequoia, Cedar, Dogwood, Poplar, Scaevola, Pisonia, Juniper, Olive, Pine, Teak, Quince, Orange, and Fig.

CHAPTER 3

INCIDENT AT GALISTEO

The 1955 Teapot Series and the Mental Landscape of Contamination

LEISL CARR CHILDERS

I N July 1955, Los Alamos Scientific Laboratory and the Atomic Energy Commission (AEC) marked the tenth anniversary of the initial atomic test by opening the secret New Mexico installation for the first time to a select group of visitors. Media personnel eagerly gathered on the Pajarito Plateau to tour Los Alamos's facilities and travel to the enigmatic Trinity site, the original atomic ground zero—an area, according to *New York Times* science reporter Robert K. Plumb, "still marked by slight radioactivity and by the presence of a peculiar man-made mineral named trinitite." Located in the Jornada del Muerto desert 250 miles south of the laboratory, ground zero featured a slight, but clearly perceptible, crater in an expanse of desolate rock and sand abandoned in the decade after the blast. The enthralled Plumb found that in contrast Los Alamos had become a hub of activity, its personnel dedicated to researching the "mysteries surrounding nuclear forces." According to the promotional brochure given to those fortunate enough to tour the "forbidden city," reported Plumb, the lab was solely responsible for "every successful thermonuclear weapon that exists today in the free world."[1]

Not everything at Los Alamos was as impressive as the official AEC brochure portrayed, however. Behind the scenes of the high-profile tour and media event, program officials grappled with a flurry of memos pertaining to an ongoing investigation of cattle that had purportedly been damaged throughout northern New Mexico by radioactive fallout. A few months earlier, in May, Claude P. Williams, a uranium prospector in the Black Lake area of the Sangre de Christo Mountains northeast of Los Alamos, had written John C. Burgher, director of the AEC's Division of Biology and Medicine, about unusual Geiger counter readings, cattle with redness on their udders and blistering on their noses, local children with severe eye irritation, and weirdly blue snow. Burgher, responding to Williams's letter the week before the big event at Los Alamos, corroborated the prospector's radiation level readings but indicated that the radioactivity "could not possibly produce these effects." The matter might have passed relatively unnoticed if not for a series of potentially related cattle fatalities near Galisteo, a small traditional Spanish village nestled in a quaint valley twenty miles south of Santa Fe (figure 3.1). Several ranches in that area, including the historic José Ortiz y Pino Ranch owned by Los Alamos general contractor Robert E. McKee, had experienced "mass sickness" in their herds beginning in early April. By early July over one hundred cattle, both young and mature animals, had died.[2]

McKee had purchased the twenty-seven-thousand-acre ranch in the verdant Galisteo Basin, about sixty miles from the Los Alamos lab, in early 1955. He had bought the ranch as a starter operation for his son, Philip S. McKee, who had a degree in animal husbandry and range management from the New Mexico College of Agriculture and Mechanic Arts (today known as New Mexico State University), in Las Cruces. The McKee Ranch ran a herd of around two hundred head between the José Ortiz y Pino Ranch and several other properties totaling forty thousand acres. In addition to cattle, the McKees raised a few Quarter Horses for ranch work, rodeo competition, and short-track horse racing; they grew alfalfa to supplement their grazing ranges. Although their herd was relatively small, it meant everything to the next to youngest McKee son and his family. By the time the press toured Los Alamos in July, the McKee Ranch had lost more than thirty cattle to unexplained circumstances.[3]

It is highly likely that those individuals at Los Alamos and within the AEC who worked with Robert E. McKee, particularly in the AEC's Santa Fe and Albuquerque offices, knew of the McKee family's nascent venture into ranching. McKee's Robert E. McKee and Zia companies, headquartered in El Paso, Texas, had built and now maintained the laboratory

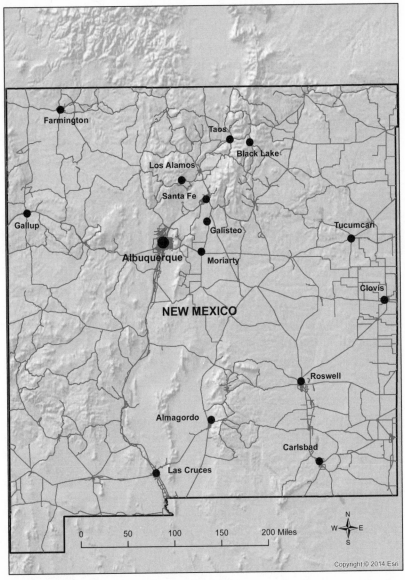

3.1 Northern New Mexico, featuring Los Alamos, Santa Fe, Black Lake, and Galisteo. Map courtesy of the GeoTree Center at the University of Northern Iowa.

and support facilities on the Pajarito Plateau so essential to the nation's atomic testing program. Given this relationship, the level of concern AEC officials exhibited about the cattle deaths in Galisteo and in other parts of northern New Mexico manifested as near panic by September of that year.

Thomas L. Shipman, the head of Los Alamos Scientific Laboratory's Health Division—the group charged with overseeing radiation safety for employees—penned a letter to James E. Reeves, the director of the Test Division in the AEC's Santa Fe Operations Office, about an eminent public relations catastrophe coalescing mere miles from their offices. Shipman explained that a "significant number of cows have died," exhibiting blistering and peeling on their udders and noses. The collected samples, including cow manure, showed signs of fission products, he wrote, and the precipitation readings made during the spring test series, dubbed Operation Teapot, had been significantly radioactive. He indicated that "there is enough circumstantial evidence to be quite impressive to a newspaper reporter, a rancher or a jury," to make them believe that the cattle had died from exposure to radioactive fallout. "Frankly," Shipman wrote, "we feel rather alarmed about the situation and feel that a program must be undertaken by someone in the near future which will establish convincing proof as to what actually did happen and why these animals died."[4]

Shipman recommended to Reeves that Los Alamos maintain some distance from the investigation of the New Mexico cattle fatalities, since, as he put it, "we don't know nothin' about cows and would prefer not to get involved in that aspect." The Health Division leader suggested that the AEC's Division of Biology and Medicine (DBM) conduct the investigation instead. Shipman hoped the DBM would settle this "grave problem" to the satisfaction of Los Alamos, the AEC, and "the press, the ranchers and the public at large." In a postscript to Reeves, he mentioned that as of the writing of his letter, the ranchers felt that the lab was making a sincere attempt to investigate the problem, but that "the attitude of a man who has lost 30 head of cattle, however, could change fairly rapidly if he questioned the sincerity of our interest in his problem."[5] The deaths of McKee's cattle and those of other ranchers near Galisteo and Black Lake was a delicate matter for Los Alamos and the AEC. Weighing on Shipman's mind was the importance of the relationship the atomic testing program had with Robert E. McKee and McKee's perception of the causes of the fatalities.

MENTALLY MAPPING ATOMIC TESTING

The tenor of Robert E. McKee's attitude toward and beliefs about the cattle losses in and around Galisteo was tied directly to his confidence in Los Alamos and the AEC. He believed in their ability to conduct continental atomic tests in such a manner as to produce no damage to human or animal bodies outside the physical testing area. His response to the AEC's investigation of fatalities in his son's cattle herd directly and very publicly demonstrated how much confidence he had in the testing program and how he felt about radioactive fallout. The ripple effects of McKee's reaction threatened to negatively impact the entire atomic testing program, reaching well beyond New Mexico to the primary site of atomic testing in Nevada. McKee's mental geography of the testing program included Los Alamos and the Nevada Proving Ground and perhaps even the areas adjacent to the atomic test site, but in no way did it include the McKee Ranch or his family.

McKee's perception of atomic testing consisted of a mental map totally separate from cattle ranching. Mental maps, constructed from both the physical navigation of space and the mental perception of what occupies that space, allow for activities conducted in close geographic proximity to be perceived as widely separated and for those conducted across a wide physical distance to be perceived as closely associated. McKee placed the ranch and atomic testing in two separate landscapes within his mental map: Los Alamos and the Nevada Proving Ground, where atomic testing took place, were part of the military-industrial complex; Galisteo and the McKee Ranch were part of his family's ranching operation. Los Alamos and Galisteo were not really adjacent in his mind, despite their proximate geographic locations and the fact that McKee moved fluidly between them, spending his workweeks in Los Alamos overseeing construction projects and his time off with his eldest son and family at the McKee Ranch. He understood the atomic testing program to be distant psychologically from the activities at the ranch even more than he understood them to be distant geographically.[6]

McKee's construction of this mental map was in large part due to how the AEC had portrayed its primary site of atomic testing. The Nevada Proving Ground, established in 1951 just sixty-five miles north of Las Vegas, was the linchpin of the testing program in 1955, providing scientists an accessible and necessary outdoor laboratory for their

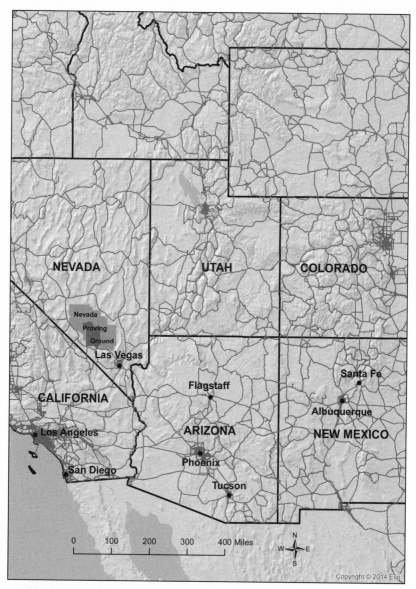

3.2 The American West, featuring the Nevada Proving Ground, Albuquerque, Las Vegas, and Los Angeles. Map courtesy of the GeoTree Center at the University of Northern Iowa.

experiments (figure 3.2). The AEC had chosen this location because of its distance from major urban centers and because it was upwind of a fairly large swath of relatively unpopulated public land. According to the AEC, scientists, engineers, and administrators planned atomic tests such that the area immediately surrounding the test site experienced no impact from blast effects, and in the area to the east, downwind of the tests, residents had minimal contact with radioactive fallout.[7]

By physically confining denotations and their residual effects to a geographic area covering only fourteen hundred square miles, officials created a mental map for themselves and the general public that placed distinct boundaries around the atomic testing program. But radioactive fallout and the potential damage many Americans were coming to believe it caused was creating a much, much larger mental map of atomic testing. This posed a threat to the program and caused the AEC an enormous amount of concern. In the mid-twentieth-century American West, residents were comfortably familiar with the presence of military personnel and the impact of training practice and weapons testing. By the end of World War II and the advent of the Cold War, as Kevin Fernlund, scholar of the American West, has explained, the region "bristled with airfields, army bases, naval yards, marine camps, missile fields, nuclear test sites, proving grounds, bombing ranges, weapons plants, military reservations, training schools, toxic waste dumps, strategic mines, transportation routes, lines of communication, laboratories, command centers, and arsenals."[8] The military-industrial complex, a term coined by President Dwight D. Eisenhower in his 1961 farewell address to explain the "conjunction of an immense military establishment and a large arms industry," had been an engine for the region's economic growth, a driver of its urbanization process, and a major use of unclaimed public land. According to Eisenhower, the total economic, political, and cultural influence of the military-industrial complex could be felt "in every city, every State house, every office of the Federal government." Historian Gerald Nash has likewise noted that the "large military establishment became a permanent fixture, a way of life" for residents of the American West, in both urban areas and the rural hinterlands.[9]

The military-industrial complex consisted of the U.S. military establishment itself and a host of other affiliated government agencies, private defense contractors, manufacturers, and support services. The pervasiveness throughout the American West of this highly intricate web of participants created a distinct physical landscape in both the region's urban centers and more isolated locations within the Great Basin, Mojave, and Chihuahua Deserts. The military chose the remotest bases to contain the most dangerous activities such as atomic testing. The Las Vegas Bombing and Gunnery Range, which encompassed the Nevada Proving Ground, felt to AEC officials as though it was in the middle of nowhere. Even the Jornada del Muerto desert between Albuquerque and El Paso that contained the Trinity site was a vast enough stretch of desert that its name invoked fear in the hearts of travelers well into the twentieth century. The remoteness and isolation of these places communicated both the secret and alarming nature of atomic testing and the extent to which testing officials had to go to keep the general population safe. The physical distance of atomic testing sites from such important urban centers as Albuquerque, Las Vegas, and Los Angeles, where most personnel operated, to the remote test installations only enhanced that perception.

Yet these testing facilities developed local populations of their own in gateway communities that existed in closer proximity to those same dangerous activities. In California, military historian Roger Lotchin has explained, aerospace contractors who manufactured aircraft (e.g., Hughes, Boeing, Lockheed Martin, and Northrop Grumman), which fueled the economic growth of Los Angeles, worked closely with military operations at several remote desert air bases and test ranges to prove new aircraft. Faced with greater restrictions on testing near Los Angeles, these contractors often pressured the federal government for greater geographic territory in which to conduct defense industry research and testing. Each military base and testing and training facility further attracted workers to the immediate region around the installations, which relied on the support services of gateway communities and supplied a ready consumer market to those businesses. The army's Fort Irwin training facility, the naval weapons testing range at China Lake, and Edwards Air Force Base (the primary experimental aircraft test flight facility) in the Mojave Desert provided the necessary space for defense contractors located in and around the Los Angeles area. These military installations drew residents to towns in close proximity—such as Barstow, Lancaster, Mojave, Ridgecrest, and Rosamond—to provide support services.[10]

Similar landscapes developed in other states. In Nevada the Nevada Proving Ground and the Las Vegas Bombing and Gunnery Range were connected to distant laboratories and firms such as Los Alamos Scientific Laboratory; Lawrence Radiation Laboratory; Reynolds Electrical and Engineering Company; Edgerton, Germeshausen, and Grier, Inc.; and Holmes and Narver, Inc. Some of these companies had a presence in Mercury and Las Vegas in Nevada, but others operated in Livermore and Los Angeles, California, and Santa Fe and Albuquerque in New Mexico. Smaller towns near Las Vegas in closer proximity to the test site (such as Indian Springs, Beatty, and Tonopah) benefited commercially from the increasing number of workers at the Nevada Proving Ground who often stopped for a drink on the way home or stayed overnight during the week. The growth of Los Alamos even affected similar small towns in New Mexico, including Galisteo, where the McKee family chose to purchase their ranch in proximity to the family's primary site of business operations. This situation created fluidity between the atomic testing program and small communities near its various installations that had nothing to do with the actual work of testing and instead stemmed from the relationship these communities had with the people who worked in the program.

The interconnected nature of the human relationships to the military-industrial complex spoke to the most worrisome aspect of the environmental relationships it produced in the American West. Maria E. Montoya, describing the impact of defense industry activities, wrote: "The desert land, its flora, its fauna, and its human inhabitants have been sacrificed so that the federal government could test its weapons and Americans could sleep safer knowing their country's potential to protect itself." According to Montoya, increased defense production during the Cold War made places deemed "empty" or "wasted" valuable for all the activities the military-industrial complex required: test sites, proving grounds, bombing ranges, secret bases, and laboratories. The places had arid and isolated environments in common, she noted, and federal officials chose them "precisely because of their landscape."[11] Environmental historian Richard White explained that in the process of their selection, "all the old liabilities of the West suddenly became virtues," including "vast distances, low population density, and arid climate." Instead, he wrote, "remoteness, isolation, and a climate that allowed people to work outdoors much of the time became major assets."[12]

But the very isolation of the land chosen for military installations and the implication of its worthlessness suggested the possibility of damage resulting from the activities conducted there. Presumably these damages would primarily affect the installations, with any residual impact influencing the relatively unpopulated surrounding areas. This physical damage would mostly touch those in close proximity, but certainly psychological damage could include anyone who experienced the effects from exposure and who doubted the ability of the military and defense contractors to conduct these activities safely. McKee, whose construction company took care of the building and maintenance of Los Alamos, was far enough away geographically from atomic testing in Nevada to make radioactive fallout the furthest thing from his mind. But he knew more than most about radiation exposure because of his work at Los Alamos; he understood that the AEC worked diligently to prevent fallout during tests. His confidence in the AEC's ability would change, however, if he thought his cattle had been exposed and damaged as a result. The cattle deaths pushed the entire atomic testing program, particularly Los Alamos and the Nevada Proving Ground, onto his mental map.

The weapons testing activities that began in Los Alamos but actually occurred some seven hundred or more miles distant at the Nevada Proving Ground would feel a lot closer if McKee believed his cattle had been damaged because of their exposure to radioactive fallout. Exposure would place atomic testing in direct proximity to his son's ranch and family. In addition, McKee's work at Los Alamos would directly affect the operations of the McKee Ranch and his son's future. Atomic testing remained distant from Galisteo so long as McKee and his family experienced no direct effects. Regardless of physical distance, McKee and others who suffered similar encounters with fallout would perceive, because of the effects of radiation exposure, that the activities that took place at the Nevada Proving Ground could have negative effects *anywhere* under the shadow of the fallout cloud.

It is no surprise then that Thomas Shipman and James Reeves cared deeply about the opinion of Robert E. McKee, a defense contractor helping his son build a ranching operation. To them, McKee's level of confidence in the AEC's ability to safely conduct the nation's atomic testing program served as a bellwether for the program's future and a reflection of the nation's confidence in atomic testing. McKee's perception of fallout and confidence in the program came from what he learned firsthand at Los Alamos, working in a limited capacity with lab administrators and other personnel and from contact with AEC officials. Of course, McKee was not involved directly with the testing program, so some of his understanding also came from what he heard in the national news and from what other ranchers told him. Unfortunately, the AEC struggled with the type and amount of information to release to the general public about atomic testing and the effects of exposure to radioactive fallout. What AEC officials chose to publicize often highlighted the uncertainty and inconsistency inherent in the atomic testing program.

OPERATION TEAPOT AND BAD WEATHER

Both Shipman and Reeves had several reasons to be concerned about radioactive fallout in the summer of 1955. Los Alamos and the AEC had concluded Operation Teapot that spring, and the testing had cost more time and energy than any continental operation to date. So named for the small devices that created a "tempest" in a "teapot," the operation was an aggressive series of twelve atomic tests conducted between mid-February and early May. Teapot had included a massive public relations campaign before the series began—the AEC's first conscious effort to proactively disclose information about atomic testing. During the operation bad weather caused multiple tests to be postponed, which tried the patience of government officials, the military, civil defense representatives, and the press. In addition, an unprecedented number of workers, sixty-six in all, suffered radiation exposure above the permissible limit, and in an unfortunate accident after one detonation, a security guard received an accidental overdose ten times that limit. The series featured the famous Apple-2 civil defense test called Operation Cue, facetiously called Operation Miscue for all the problems associated with its production. Nevertheless, AEC officials did their best to ensure that Operation Teapot guaranteed the future of the continental testing site and recovered some of the public confidence lost.[13]

The 1953 Upshot-Knothole series had created a great deal of public concern about radioactive fallout. Saint George, Utah, and the surrounding environs in Nevada had received an unexpected dusting of radioactive fallout after the Harry test; hundreds of sheep had died, wiping out several flocks. The AEC was particularly interested in avoiding more controversy while the investigation into the official cause of the massive number of sheep deaths in the area continued. Beginning in January of 1955, AEC representatives provided press releases to major national newspapers and conducted a goodwill tour across five hundred miles of the western states, assuring residents that they need not fear radioactive fallout from any of the forthcoming nuclear explosions. Just before the series began, the AEC distributed the information pamphlet "Atomic Test Effects in the Nevada Test Site Region" and released the educational film *Atomic Tests in Nevada*. The film debuted in Saint George and provided the press with unprecedented access to upbeat stories about the testing program, including an in-depth piece on the hub of testing operations in Mercury, Nevada.[14] Both the pamphlet and the film portrayed Nevadans and Utahans as used to the routine of atomic testing. The film's narrator announced that tests were "old stuff to Saint George," and residents had "seen a lot of them, ever since 1951"; supposedly, the tone of the film expressed, the tests were "nothing to get excited about anymore."[15] The message the AEC was sending to the American public was clear. The Teapot test series fell well within the normal parameters of the nation's atomic testing program. If residents had concerns, the materials implied, they probably had not done enough to understand the safety measures and routine procedures that governed the testing process.

In a rare public announcement, on February 14, 1955, the AEC broadcast that the testing series would begin the following day. Operation Teapot was designed to be similar to Upshot-Knothole, with an emphasis on smaller devices, new weapons development, understanding fission, and preparing for military and civil defense. The tests had been planned, the AEC explained, so that "the maximum radiation anyone in the country conceivably could experience from them would be 3.9 roentgens a year." This was the same dose allowed test site workers and a quarter of that which the agency considered safe. In New Mexico the *Albuquerque Journal* reported the AEC hoped that the Teapot series would not require a repetition of the warning it had given residents in Saint George two years earlier. In the previous tests of 1951 and 1953, agency officials reiterated, no persons had been injured, some small damage had been done to structures, and "some cattle and horses suffered radiation burns," but "the damage had no effect on their breeding value or the beef quality of the cattle."[16]

Despite all the preparations, Operation Teapot got off to a rough start. Slated to begin on February 15, the AEC postponed the first test three times because of unfavorable weather conditions, including high winds. To avoid creating a large cloud of radioactive debris, they ended up detonating the device on February 18 at high altitude instead of the originally planned tower shot.[17] The other twelve detonations that comprised Operation Teapot suffered similar delays due to high winds and generally unfavorable weather conditions that could carry mushroom clouds filled with radioactive debris in dangerous directions. Erring on the side of caution, the AEC rescheduled tests day to day, for at least three days each from the originally planned date. Two of the tests, Bee and Apple-2, occurred more than a week past their originally scheduled dates at the end of March and April, respectively, much to the frustration of federal officials, civilian observers, and the military personnel slated to participate in them.[18] A repetition of the events of 1953 was the last thing the AEC wanted. However, the frequency of publicly announced delays created some self-consciousness among those involved in the operation's public relations.

At the end of February, after the delays, Gladwin Hill of the *New York Times* and other journalists met with AEC commissioner Lewis L. Strauss in a press conference meant to explain Operation Teapot. Strauss stressed the important intent and ramifications of the tests to the media. Hill, taking advantage of the rare amount of disclosure from the AEC, announced to readers: "This year, for the first time, the public is getting virtually the full publishable story from officials about the Nevada Atomic tests." A senior official within the atomic testing program provided Hill with the agency's rationale behind this change in policy; within the organization "there had been a gradual realization that the 'tell-nothing' policy conceived originally for the remote Pacific tests, was unworkable on the populated continent." The American public knew a lot more about atomic matters in 1955 than it had in 1951, Hill reported, and mounting public apprehension about radiological hazards from continental testing required a more open discussion. The *New York Times* applauded the AEC's decision to "open up" and filled their daily issues with articles on the testing process, the effects of testing, and the reason for every single test delay.[19]

Information released by the AEC that addressed the delays usually included an explanation of how carefully Los Alamos and the test operations group watched the weather to prevent unnecessary complications with radioactive fallout (figure 3.3). In late April, Alvin C. Graves, the head of the Los Alamos Test Division and a renowned physicist, explained the most recent delay: "Atomic researchers were perpetually up against chances as poor as one in fourteen of getting suitable weather

3.3 Test organization officials and advisers are shown the weather evaluation, which resulted in a second twenty-four-hour postponement on February 15, 1955. The map shows the forecast fallout pattern. Photo courtesy of the National Nuclear Security Administration, Nevada Field Office.

for a shot."[20] Graves meant to reassure the American public of the caution with which those involved with the testing process approached the decision to detonate an atomic bomb. Yet equally compelling was the unintended message Graves sent that there were very few favorable moments in which to conduct atomic tests.

In early May, in the midst of the longest delay, the AEC clarified the process by which the decision was made to actually detonate a device and complete a test. Beginning twenty-four hours before the scheduled shot, the test director or manager conducted a number of conferences with top testing personnel, including the head of the lab's Test Division, up to thirty minutes prior detonating the device. The test manager, in this case James E. Reeves, was "the one man with the ultimate responsibility for anything that happens in the tests" (figure 3.4). Hill described Reeves as a "48-year-old bespectacled civilian alumnus of the United States Corps of Engineers" who could and had decided to delay tests when weather conditions were clearly unsuitable without consulting other testing personnel. Graves and Reeves were Teapot's gatekeepers, cautious men who worked at Los Alamos and at the AEC's Santa Fe Operations Office to prevent accidents on the test site and radiation exposure in the area surrounding the Nevada Proving Ground. Despite their best efforts, however, the one element neither man could control was the weather itself.[21]

Just before the detonation of the long-awaited Apple-2 test, Hill wrote in jest that if the number of test delays were any indication of Nevada's weather, "southern Nevada must have about the worst weather in the world." He clarified that actually the opposite was true; the region was known for its perfect weather for flying and sunbathing. "For atomic tests to be conducted productively and safely," he explained, "it isn't enough for the weather just to be clear." The winds had to be blowing in the right direction, at the right strength, at the right altitude so that fallout patterns would occur along an acceptable corridor north, east-northeast, southwest, or southeast up to 150 miles. Despite the AEC's concern over fallout patterns, Hill reminded readers, "there was "very little danger of anyone's getting hurt from this." Beyond the 150-mile limit, "fall-out is no consideration at all for humans."[22] The uncertainty embedded in the cautious decision making of Reeves and Graves was further reified by the AEC's tacit acknowledgment of how rare it was to find the perfect weather pattern in which to conduct atomic tests. The 150-mile limit suggested that Saint George, at 170 miles from the Nevada Proving Ground, was safe and that Los Alamos itself, at more than 700 miles distant, was clearly safe. But as some of the tests during the Upshot-Knothole series

3.4 James E. Reeves, test manager during Operation Teapot, at his desk in Camp Mercury on March 7, 1955. Photo courtesy of the National Nuclear Security Administration, Nevada Field Office.

had demonstrated in 1953, safe areas were not always immune to contamination.

THE PERCEPTION OF CONTAMINATION FROM FALLOUT

The issue of radioactive fallout loomed large in the minds of Americans and within the AEC in 1955. The tasteless, odorless, nearly invisible stuff was the most frightening effect of atomic testing, and there were many scientists who understood the nuances of radiation exposure as well as the long-term effects of low-level exposure. During the Teapot series, the AEC managed to communicate two conflicting narratives about radioactive fallout. The first was that it was a normal result from atomic testing in the Nevada desert and that AEC officials worked diligently to minimize and confine it to the test site so that Americans downwind of ground zero would never experience fallout. The second was that it was a dangerous effect of atomic warfare and the nation should prepare itself accordingly by building fallout shelters and other structures to protect Americans from the worst of it.

Part of the agency's nascent open relations policy during Teapot included publication of a report on the agency's understanding of radiation exposure effects, which filled an entire page of the *New York Times* in February 1955. AEC officials emphasized that "the hazard" from the tests in Nevada to date had been "successfully confined to the controlled area of the test site."[23] The definition of "hazard"—a word often used by the AEC to describe the harm that could be done to human life if exposed to a radiation dose significantly higher than 3.9 roentgens—did not include lesser exposures from which most people could easily recover or exposure to animals. Yet the ongoing discussion of the sheep deaths that had occurred in Utah during the Upshot-Knothole series of 1953 demonstrated the public's continued fear of exposure to radioactive fallout despite the AEC's assurances.[24]

Operation Teapot was not without its own incidents of fallout clouds and radiation exposures. Los Alamos worked to make up lost time because of the compressed firing sequences; not a week went by in the early period of the operation that some level of radioactive fallout did not dust the regions downwind. The second test in the series, dubbed Moth, detonated on February 22, produced "slight radioactive fall-out" that blew southeast across northern Arizona and the Grand Canyon toward Silver City, New Mexico.[25] After the subsequent Tesla shot fired a week later, security guard Eugene D. Haynes accidentally drove into a dangerously radioactive area on the test site and sustained "the heaviest dose of radiation ever received by any employee at its atomic proving ground." The guard was not hospitalized and the dose, while over the allowable thirteen-week limit and well over the ideal annual limit, was "not expected to cause any serious or permanent injury."[26]

During the Turk test on March 7, military troops conducting training exercises during the event had to quit their maneuvers to avoid the "potentially dangerous dust" the winds blew in their path.[27] Two weeks later, the Bee detonation actually dusted Las Vegas with radioactive fallout for the first time since testing began, although the AEC assured the public there was no danger to civilians.[28] An underground test called Ess, detonated the day after Bee, produced a large amount of radioactive dust from the tons of material it excavated.[29] And at the end of March, two devices detonated in the same day produced "the highest offsite radiation of the current test series" in Alamo, Nevada, just fifty miles from Yucca Flat and ground zero, although the reading was less than half the thirteen-week dose considered safe.[30]

The nuances of safe versus dangerous dosage levels were lost on most Americans. In a series of hearings on the government's secrecy policies, George LeRoy, a University of Chicago researcher who had spent time with radiation victims in Hiroshima, Nagasaki, and in the Marshall Islands, accused the AEC of refusing to allow the release of research data that pertained to radiation exposure. LeRoy made this accusation believing that the agency knew even more than it had disclosed and was deliberately withholding information. The AEC denied LeRoy's claims, but reports of the inability of the medical community to cope with the consequences of an attack that produced radioactive fallout belied their denial and prompted a special civil defense program to grapple with the problem.[31] In early April the Department of Defense announced that four military personnel had received eye injuries during the 1952 and 1953 tests. This news, according to national outlets, "reversed previous flat assertions by the Government that no participant or observer had been injured during Nevada tests"—a statement that had appeared in the widely distributed information booklet *Atomic Tests in Nevada*. The AEC denied the admission, calling any public discussion of harm incurred from exposure to radioactive fallout "irresponsible." AEC chairman

Lewis L. Strauss emphatically stated that the Nevada tests had "brought no injuries to anyone."[32] Despite these protests, injury from exposure became a real possibility in the public's mind.

In conjunction with these smaller reports, the agency's summary of the previous test series in the Pacific Proving Ground, released concomitant with the Teapot operation, highlighted the dangers of radioactive fallout and the uncertainties inherent in the testing process. Operation Castle, conducted between February and May of 1954 and comprised of one thermonuclear device dubbed Bravo, had modeled a devastating fallout pattern from which civil defense planners were able to project what an atomic strike would look like in the United States. Officials from the AEC charged with understanding the effects of a thermonuclear bomb detonation in the United States explained that if one such device had been dropped on the nation's capital, besides destroying the city entirely, it would cover a seven-thousand-square-mile area with radioactive fallout. Experts agreed that the population between Washington, D.C., and Philadelphia would be decimated, and only some percentage of the population between Philadelphia and New York would survive to an increasing degree further away from ground zero.[33]

Not long after, the AEC quietly revealed that the Bravo test had *actually* contaminated seven thousand square miles. Beyond the blast effects of an atomic bomb, the AEC acknowledged, the greater danger to national defense was in the exposure American populations would receive from radioactive fallout. The severe exposure of a small group of Japanese fishermen to fallout during the Bravo test provided the public with tangible evidence. But rather than motivate the construction of fallout shelters in preparation for an atomic strike, this revelation prompted public concern about testing in Nevada. In addition, in a seemingly unrelated event, two Colorado University scientists in Boulder released a statement in early March warning of the long-term effects of radiation exposure to the general population because of continental atomic testing. By the middle of the month, a former Brookhaven National Laboratory employee who headed the Atomic Center, Inc., in New York, complained to the *New York Times* that public uneasiness about radioactive fallout had intensified since report of the unfortunate Japanese fishermen was made public. In his opinion, the damage done to these men exaggerated the radiological hazard in the minds of Americans, creating a steady stream of phone calls to his office every time the AEC detonated a test in Nevada.[34]

The AEC was sending the American public mixed messages. Cases of severe radiation exposure appeared in the national press, but cases of low-level exposure usually did not; and when they did get press attention, the AEC leadership consistently denied that such exposure had caused any damage. The only report made public during Teapot about low-level radiation exposure indicated that the individual (the security guard who had accidentally ventured into a restricted area) did not go to the doctor, presumably because he did not need any medical treatment. It did not describe what the consequences of low-level exposure looked like or explain how the security guard felt.[35] Understanding the differences between the levels of radiation exposure received by the Japanese fisherman, who became very ill and suffered severe burns, and that sustained by the security guard seemed relatively straightforward to the AEC. But in light of the warnings provided by such scientists as those at Colorado University, a lingering public fear of radioactive fallout persisted irrespective of the differences in exposure levels.

FALLOUT FROM TEAPOT

By April the Teapot series was two-thirds complete. The AEC announced that the radioactive fallout outside the Nevada testing site had thus far been "infinitesimal" and that there was "positively no hazard." Published in the *Albuquerque Tribune*, the AEC's press release specifically mentioned that the radiation levels near Albuquerque were well within the safe tolerance levels for humans and that cattle were in no danger either. The only caution the AEC provided was that "atomic dust could be passed to human beings eating food on which the dust has fallen," but assured readers the radioactive dust could be washed off the food items before consumption. Low-level radioactive fallout, the statement indicated, was safe to be in but not safe to eat. From a scientist's perspective this was an accurate statement, but from the general public's point of view it was difficult to know when fallout was present since it could not be seen.[36]

As Operation Teapot progressed to its culmination, several events occurred that deepened the perceptual divide between the AEC's position that radioactive fallout from the Nevada tests was harmless and the public's increasing concern. The High Altitude (HA) detonation of April 7, the first to test a missile with a warhead, produced a small amount of fallout that blew east-southeast, according to AEC radiation monitors.

After the detonation, officials in Chicago stated they did not consider the radiation levels from the test harmful. At the same time, however, several sheepherders near Cedar City and Saint George, Utah, filed five court suits against the federal government, claiming that their animals had "sickened and died as a consequence of the fall-out from the 1953 tests," indicating that harm had occurred from exposure in the not so distant past. The Upshot-Knothole series had been very similar to those in Teapot and were conducted with fewer testing delays because of bad weather. The suits claimed that some of those exposed to radioactive fall-out did not think the exposure had been harmless.[37]

After the Post test on April 9, the AEC reported in a hearing on fallout before Congress that comprehensive investigations had failed to demonstrate there had been any adverse effects from the atomic tests at the Nevada Proving Ground. But New Mexico senator Clinton P. Anderson warned there was a great deal of "public misapprehension and unwarranted concern" about the effects of the tests, especially radioactive fallout, and although the AEC had publicly reported on the thermonuclear tests in the Pacific, the agency had not reported on those in Nevada. Senator Anderson's comments, especially those that referred to fallout as a "hopeless danger," encapsulated the concern many Americans had about any exposure to radioactive fallout, regardless of degree: there appeared to be no protection against the odorless, colorless, and nearly invisible particles. Radiation scientists reassured the American public that taking shelter inside or underground if in the path of a fallout cloud, taking baths with added cornmeal if exposed to fallout, and washing food would suffice to prevent any damage from contamination. Again, the message was mixed. It was unclear how anyone would know if they were exposed, let alone to the level that required shelter, baths, or food washing.[38]

Two weeks later, the Military Effects Test (MET) blasted military equipment and sent a fallout cloud to the northeast. In the downtime between the MET and the next delayed detonation, the AEC held a press conference to prepare those civil defense officials and press, radio, and television observers chosen to witness the test for the experience of "surviving" an atomic blast. Gordon Dunning of the AEC's Division of Biology and Medicine attempted to explain some of the nuances of radiation exposure. He compared the nation's cumulative radiation dose to date from the tests so far to the amount delivered by a chest x-ray. Dunning reminded civil defense officials and media representatives that a dose of 25 roentgens, six times that of the official safe threshold across thirteen weeks, would only just produce any "detectable biological damage." It would take about 100 roentgens to produce temporary radiation sickness. Eight roentgens was the highest radiation dose received by residents from fallout in localities around the test site, he reminded them, and the highest dose for the same during the Teapot series was 1.5 roentgens. According to Dunning, small doses such as this produced either no damage at all or damage so small as to be undetectable. Even if exposure occurred over a longer period of time, he stated, the dose would still be small because of the body's ability to repair itself.[39] While technically accurate, such statement homogenized human and animal bodies and excluded other environmental factors that could affect biological life—water and food quality, nutrition levels, age, and the presence of any other sickness.

The AEC continued to communicate the subtlety and homogeneity of the different levels of radiation exposure from fallout before the second to last test of the Teapot series, designated Apple-2. Designed as a combination diagnostic weapons, military, and civil defense test, Apple-2 featured large-scale tank and infantry maneuvers, an elaborate model town, and the largest number of observers watching the detonation. The Civil Defense Administration named their component of the test Operation Cue, as in "our cue for a renewed effort." This renewed effort had much to do with educating a public that had little accurate knowledge or understanding of the effects of atomic explosions. The model town featured furnished homes, trailers, a radio station, a transformer substation, industrial buildings, fire engines, frozen and canned food items, kitchen appliances, cars, filing cabinets, fallout shelters, and mannequins. Trained rats, mice, rabbits, guinea pigs, and dogs populated cages strategically placed in various sheltered areas to gauge the odds of surviving an atomic blast.[40]

After nine days of delay because of unfavorable weather, which earned the civil defense operation the title of Operation Miscue, Los Alamos detonated Apple-2 on May 5. The mock town suffered severe damage but not as much as the scientists seemed to expect, and most of the animals survived to undergo evaluative exams after the test. *New York Times* reporter Gladwin Hill seemed relieved to report that the worst effects—such as vaporized asphalt, exploded structures, and flying debris—were confined to the test site. The AEC announced the radiation intensity at

3.5 The final test of the spring 1955 series, code-named Zucchini, detonated on May 15. Photo courtesy of the National Nuclear Security Administration, Nevada Field Office.

the houses closest to ground zero amounted to 350 roentgens, which Alvin Graves, head of the Test Division, said was not necessarily fatal. Relative to the 100 roentgen threshold discussed by Dunning, however, it would most certainly result in severe damage. The AEC announced the fallout cloud produced by the test was harmlessly migrating northeast from Yucca Flat toward the Canadian border.[41]

Los Alamos detonated the Zucchini shot, the final test of the Teapot series, on May 15. With that, the longest of the AEC's operations came to a quiet close (figure 3.5). The agency reported that the fallout cloud diverged and headed toward Salt Lake City and northeastern Arizona, in a "favorable diffusion." Soon after, the *New York Times* ran several articles that looked closely at the effects of radioactive fallout. Science writer Robert K. Plumb contributed one story, explaining the generation of radioactive material in the "ugly mushroom cloud," the dispersal of radioactive clouds, and the kinds of injury sustained from contact. "Radiation is not often if ever immediately fatal," he wrote, "but it can damage the body so that the victims weaken and die gradually." Fallout was a critical problem, he reminded readers, and the "exact pattern

LEISL CARR CHILDERS

of fall-out can be predicted only roughly." Plumb's article sat alongside journalist Anthony Leviero's on the nation's slow response to prepare for an attack that involved a thermonuclear weapon. The problem of radioactive fallout remained at the center of the discussion, but Leviero reminded readers the AEC did not allow exposures above 3.9 roentgens during the Nevada tests.[42]

For someone such as Robert E. McKee, the safety measures reported by the press were consistent with his understanding of the framework in which the AEC conducted atomic tests. The agency, and its partner Los Alamos, worked tirelessly to ensure that testing in Nevada did not adversely affect the surrounding populated areas. But by the end of the Teapot series, McKee knew that there was something wrong with his cattle and the other herds north of the Galisteo Basin.

CONTAMINATION IN GALISTEO

From the moment uranium prospector Claude Williams first reported trouble with cattle in May 1955, the AEC's investigation of the cattle fatalities in the area between Black Lake and Galisteo lagged. By the end of July, the AEC and the Food and Drug Administration (FDA), the agency responsible for monitoring food quality for both humans and animals, knew that more than 150 cattle across four herds had died but not apparently from ingesting bad commercial stock feed. Rather, the FDA and a veterinarian from the Department of Agriculture, Charles L. Davis, thought the symptoms exhibited by the animals were consistent with some poisonous plants. A month later, no clear understanding of the cattle deaths, either near Black Lake or Galisteo, had emerged.[43]

Thomas Shipman alerted James Reeves that Norris E. Bradbury, director of Los Alamos Scientific Laboratory, had approved continued collection of "data concerning the livestock in this general area primarily to evaluate the problem" and that the AEC's Division of Biology and Medicine (DBM) was getting involved. The Health Division's findings proved disturbing. The manure samples Williams had delivered to Los Alamos "showed radioactivity" the lab deemed was "probably from fission products." Shipman was concerned that a number of cows had died "with peculiar symptoms which include blisters and peeling of the udder and blistering of the nose"; most of the cattle in the area around Black Lake had been exposed to forty inches of snowfall just after the Zucchini detonation. According to Los Alamos, the precipitation in northern New Mexico—an area that included Black Lake, Galisteo, and several other small ranching communities—during that period was "significantly radioactive." It was the snowfall from this storm in the Sangre de Christo Mountains that Williams had reported as weirdly blue in hue.[44]

By the end of September, after more than a month of investigation, the DBM still had not gotten to the bottom of the problem and contacted the Department of Agriculture to assist with further investigation. With the help of additional personnel, AEC officials arrived at their penultimate conclusion only one week later. At a meeting involving Gordon Dunning, James Reeves, and several others including a representative from the general counsel's office, the group concluded that based on the readings gathered by radiation safety officials, "the external exposure and the internal radiation, including absorption, was not sufficient to have caused the death of the cattle." Nevertheless, in "the interest of good public relations," the AEC and Los Alamos arranged for Bernard F. Trum, an army veterinarian working for the agency at the University of Tennessee, to visit Black Lake again and attempt to "ascertain without too much difficulty the possible causes of cattle losses." As for the blue snow, Dunning advised the group that according to the Weather Bureau, unusual amounts of dust in the air, such as small amounts of manganese, could have colored the snow a strange blue color.[45]

The matter seemed resolved, but in early October, Richard G. Elliott, the information officer at the AEC's Santa Fe Operations Office, sent a teletype message to Alfred J. Starbird, the director of the AEC's Division of Military Applications group that oversaw the Santa Fe and Albuquerque operations offices. The memo warned them that New Mexico senator Dennis Chavez had received letters from ranchers in the Taos area concerning the "Black Lake radiation fallout incident." Elliott warned both Starbird and Dunning that the *Albuquerque Journal* was on the verge of running a story titled "100 Cattle Killed by Radiation." The whole issue of cattle deaths due to exposure to radioactive fallout threatened to blow up. Elliott advised them he had issued a clarification to the newspaper acknowledging that "the Black Lake region, like the rest of New Mexico, did experience some light radioactive fallout from the spring test series," but that all the readings taken indicated that radiation levels related to the tests were negligible. "It was likewise concluded that fallout could not have caused the reported inflammation of skin surfaces," the statement indicated, and the cattle deaths may have had more to do with the sudden amount of snow and cold. Elliott ended with the AEC's pledge to continue to help ranchers uncover the actual cause of death.[46]

Instead of running the article as they initially envisioned, the *Albuquerque Journal* ran one titled "Black Lake Area Cattle Examined by AEC Teams." The *Albuquerque Tribune* ran a similar one titled "A-Experts Renew Inquiry into NM Cattle Deaths." Both articles provided statements from Paul Davis, a Moriarty rancher who grazed cattle in the Black Lake area. Davis definitively believed his animals had suffered from contact with radioactive fallout. The rancher had lost forty-seven animals to strange symptoms, including blistering and inflammation after contact with the heavy snows in May, which Davis described as distinctly blue. Tuffy McDowell, another rancher grazing cattle near Black Lake, lost nearly one hundred head of cattle and his had exhibited similar symptoms. The articles reported, as the AEC had indicated, that the agency was sending its own veterinarian, Bernard Trum, along with another veterinarian from the Department of Agriculture's disease eradication department named Ted Rea, to investigate the deaths again. William Allaire of the AEC was to accompany the veterinarians. The *New York Times* picked up the story in a piece titled "Atom Damage Denied." In all three articles, the AEC clarified that levels of radiation recorded in the Black Lake area had been negligible during the Teapot operation and therefore radiation exposure could not have caused the cattle fatalities. As for the blue snow, the AEC scientists had never heard of such a phenomenon.[47]

Yet even after Trum, Rea, and Allaire's additional investigation at Black Lake, the cause of the livestock fatalities remained unknown. The AEC released a report within the week to the New Mexico press stating, "Radioactive fallout 'could not have contributed' to the cattle deaths." The three investigators instead attributed the deaths to "environmental conditions" caused by the ongoing drought in the region and contributing factors such as the condition of the cattle when they arrived from their winter ranges in the Black Lake area, the animals' recent transition to high altitude, and toxic vegetation such as loco weed. Despite the AEC's report, both the *Albuquerque Journal* and the *Albuquerque Tribune* reported that rancher Paul Davis planned to file a claim for compensation.[48]

It turns out that Robert E. McKee had been keeping track of the Black Lake investigation. After the release of the AEC's final report, he wrote Bernard Trum, the AEC's veterinarian, introducing himself and stating his interest in what he had read in the newspaper. "In the last year," McKee explained, "we have lost 39 head of cattle, apparently from the same cause as mentioned in the newspaper article." He wrote: "We have tried innumerable veterinarians and other sources of information to find out what was the trouble with these cattle, but no one can say." At times, McKee added, his own air sampling had indicated "strong radioactivity" over the Galisteo Basin; he noted there were no uranium deposits in the area.[49]

McKee sent a copy of this letter to Horace Henning, the executive secretary of the New Mexico Cattle Growers' Association, suggesting that ranchers who had lost livestock that spring "form some kind of organization to work together and find out just what is the trouble." McKee also sent copies to state senators Clinton Anderson and Dennis Chavez and representative Antonio M. Fernandez, indicating that he intended to contact Paul Davis in Moriarty. Trum's concerned response a week later complimented McKee on his "forceful approach" to the issue but reiterated the investigation's findings and suggested that in his experience "many deaths among cattle seem to be of unknown ecology." Trum assured McKee that any radioactivity over his ranch should not cause him any alarm and that "those responsible for radiocontamination due to atomic weapons testing are cognizant of their responsibility and are going to guard against over-exposure in the first place." Trum indicated that he felt "flattered" McKee had turned to him for assistance and recommended the contractor wait for the results of the final animal disease tests.[50]

McKee was not satisfied with Trum's response. A week after his initial letter to Trum, he wrote to Kenner F. Hertford, manager of the AEC's Santa Fe Operations Office, explaining in detail the investigations he and his son Phillip had undertaken on their own involving researchers from New Mexico College of Agriculture and Mechanic Arts, veterinarians from Santa Fe, investigators from the Department of Agriculture's Agricultural Research Service in Albuquerque and Denver, additional researchers at Colorado State College of Agriculture and Mechanic Arts and Oklahoma Agricultural and Mechanical College, as well as officials from the Food and Drug Administration. The only results any of them found after analyzing stomach contents, fecal matter, internal organs, blood samples, cattle feed, supplements, and water, McKee clarified, was a high white blood cell count and a low red blood cell count. McKee reminded Hertford that the elevation of Galisteo was only around six thousand feet, not nearly high enough to cause cattle coming from lower elevations any difficulty. In McKee's mind, the answer was not environmental conditions, loco weed, or any common killer of cattle. "No one apparently can say what the trouble is," he wrote, "although practically everyone agrees it is not a weed poisoning that has killed the cattle at Galisteo, nor anything wrong with the condition of their stomachs, nor their blood, except a high white and low red count." McKee sent copies of this letter to Trum, Rea, Allaire, the New Mexico senators, and his congressman.[51]

At the end of October, McKee wrote Trum again about the matter and backed off a little from the forceful tone of his earlier statements. "Please understand that I am not an authority enough to say that radioactivity had anything to do with the death of these cattle," he told Trum. McKee explained his twelve-year association with Los Alamos and his other ventures with AEC contractors such as Reynolds Electrical and Engineering Company and the Eberline Instrument Company, which produced radiation-monitoring equipment. McKee perhaps hoped to indicate that he understood more about radiation exposure and cattle than the average citizen, but not as much as specialists in the field. He assured Trum his intent was not "so much trying to get something from the government," as "trying to find out what the trouble is" in order to avoid it in the future.[52]

McKee's last letter caused a great deal of consternation within the AEC. Trum wrote McKee back almost immediately with information on the general blood conditions of radiated versus irradiated cattle tested in his labs. Radiation exposure, Trum explained, produced slightly elevated white blood cell counts temporarily but more often produced a drop in the same while red blood cell counts stayed constant. Rea also wrote McKee, offering further assistance if any more cattle were lost. Rea must have been a little insecure about his role in the investigation, writing the head of animal disease eradication within the Department of Agriculture in Washington, D.C., that he had only examined one of McKee's cows, not enough to make a "definite diagnosis," but that he still suspected the problem was nutritional. Reeves asked Trum and Rea to double check their analysis and decide if anything more should be done. Trum responded to Reeves that no further investigation was warranted.

He told Reeves he was willing to do "all that is necessary to protect the government's interest" and assured Trum that "no immediate radiation damage could possibly affect the cattle."[53]

The matter of the McKee cattle came to a close when Kenner Hertford, the manager of the AEC office in Albuquerque, advised Alfred Starbird of the situation. Describing Robert E. McKee as a "rather influential citizen," Hertford explained the publicity given the Black Lake investigation had caused McKee to write the AEC, New Mexico Cattle Growers' Association officials, and members of Congress. In the absence of any logical explanation, McKee had taken up the matter with the AEC. Within the context of the increasingly problematic court cases resulting from the 1953 sheep deaths in Utah having been attributed to the Upshot-Knothole tests and the continued issue of livestock losses in Nevada that also surfaced during the Teapot series, Hertford suggested that in the future the most important of these incidents be investigated to the point of "ascertaining if possible the true cause." However, since the AEC had already publicly denied that radiation exposure was a factor in the case of the McKee cattle, further investigation by the agency could be "construed as indicating that the AEC still had some doubts." Rather than continue to investigate the cause of the cattle fatalities in Galisteo, Hertford advised that the AEC drop the matter. Hertford expected the Department of Agriculture in the future to take the lead on explaining the cattle fatalities in New Mexico, writing: "It is difficult, if not impossible, to convince the cattle owners and the general public that unexplained losses following test series are not due to radiation."[54]

For Robert E. McKee, this meant that Rea had the final say on what killed his son's cattle. Rea maintained his original position: the cattle had suffered from a low nutritional diet and possible poisoning from ingesting toxic weeds. The matter seemed at an end when the *Albuquerque Journal* again reported on the Black Lake incident. Bernard Trum, Ted Rea, and William Allaire suggested that "good range management practices would have prevented other than normal death losses in the affected herds."[55] This must have been difficult for McKee to accept and certainly pitted his work with Los Alamos against the McKee ranch operations. His son's training in livestock production and range management in New Mexico would have prepared him to operate a cattle ranch. Though the younger McKee was new to ranching in 1955, it must have been hard to believe that he would be that unaware of his cattle's feeding habits and

LEISL CARR CHILDERS

nutritional needs. Between Trum and Rea, the New Mexico cattle deaths became something of a joke. Trum ribbed Rea in a letter early the following year indicating that according to Rea's last letter, northern New Mexico must have had some more "blue snow" that winter. But, wrote Trum, "you won't see beta burns in New Mexico unless the Russians set off the bomb."[56]

Robert E. McKee never did find out the actual cause of the cattle deaths on his ranch near Galisteo and neither did the ranchers near Black Lake. In the end, it did not matter whether it was environmental conditions or toxic weeds or exposure to radioactive fallout. The importance of the incident at Galisteo is that for a while McKee *thought* it might have been radiation exposure. In lieu of any other rational explanation, having explored all the options available to him, McKee had narrowed down the possibilities to just one. Contact with radioactive fallout seemed the most likely explanation, but McKee only believed that once he had exhausted all other options. The contractor had enormous confidence in the AEC's ability to test atomic weapons in Nevada safely, but once he thought that his son's cattle had been exposed to radiation, that confidence deteriorated.

The AEC responded to McKee's inquiries with genuine concern, knowing that he was a key component of their operations in New Mexico, having literally built Los Alamos and continuing to provide essential services to the lab. The agency was intent on convincing McKee that his cattle had not been damaged by radiation exposure. Of all the people that accused the AEC of exposing their livestock to radioactive fallout, Robert E. McKee could do the most damage. Whether he believed the AEC's final evaluation is unknown; in any case, he could only pursue that possibility so far. McKee was heavily invested in the military-industrial complex and had only recently purchased the ranch to get his son Philip started in the cattle business. It may be that he decided not to push the issue too far and file a claim that had the potential to jeopardize his contract with Los Alamos.

The McKee Ranch continued operations throughout the late twentieth century, though Philip and his family faced additional hardships in their first decade of operation (figure 3.6). The winter of 1955–56 was a cold one and many of the calves born then struggled with pneumonia. Several years later, an anthrax outbreak on the ranch required the

3.6 Philip S. McKee herding steers into a pen on the McKee Ranch circa 1960. Photo courtesy of Emma Jean "Jeamie" Bewley and the Robert E. and Evelyn McKee Foundation.

McKees to quarantine their cattle, leaving them unable to buy or sell any animals. No one was sure what started the rare outbreak, although the family believed that the sheep herds run on the José Ortiz y Pino Ranch in the early twentieth century had left viable anthrax spores in the area.[57] From his experience with the 1955 Teapot operation, the elder McKee could not help but see the atomic testing program, of which he was actually a part, differently. Instead of being closely confined to the boundaries of the Nevada Proving Ground, he lived with radioactive fallout in a way that made the entire American West part of the military-industrial complex. This mental map viewed the American West as a region fully militarized. The bases, test sites and training ranges, corporate offices, and storefronts of the military-industrial complex were nearly everywhere. Atomic testing and the effects of radioactive fallout were on the minds of many.

Despite the AEC's best efforts at generating positive media attention in 1955, the agency could not convince the American public that fallout was safe. It did not actually matter whether the AEC explained the subtleties of radiation exposure or definitively demonstrated that radioactive fallout did not cause the cattle deaths in Galisteo; a transformation of McKee's mental map had occurred. It was now impossible for the public to believe in the harmlessness of low levels of exposure. Reports of cattle and sheep fatalities because of testing continued to surface well into the 1960s. As for the blue snow that fell in northern New Mexico, the story of its strangeness became fodder for conspiracy theorists. Public fear of radioactive fallout continued to pose numerous public relations problems for the AEC and Los Alamos; by 1958 international public pressure prompted the United States and the Soviet Union to agree to a testing moratorium.[58]

NOTES

The author wishes to thank Louis B. McKee and the McKee Foundation, Martha DeMarre and the Nevada Nuclear Testing Archive, and John DeGroote and Geo-Tree at the University of Northern Iowa for their time and assistance researching this story.

1   Robert K. Plumb, "Los Alamos Opens Doors to Visitors," *New York Times*, July 17, 1955.

2   John C. Burgher, Letter to Claude P. Williams, July 7, 1955, National Nuclear Security Administration/Nevada Field Office, Las Vegas, Nevada (hereafter NNSA/NFO); and Ralph M. Davidson, "Memorandum: Mass Poisoning of Cattle," July 9, 1955, NNSA/NFO.

3   Phone interview with Louis McKee, McKee Foundation, September 4, 2013; Emma Jean "Jeammie" Bewley, *The McKee Ranch* (El Paso, TX: Robert E. and Evelyn McKee Foundation, 2014), 1–8; John Hunner, *Inventing Los Alamos: The Growth of an Atomic Community* (Norman: University of Oklahoma Press, 2004), 33, 102, 109–10, 129–31.

4   Hunner, *Inventing Los Alamos*, 33, 102, 109–10, 129–31; and Thomas L. Shipman to James E. Reeves, Letter, September 1, 1955, NNSA/NFO.

5   Thomas L. Shipman to James E. Reeves, Letter, September 1, 1955, Nevada Nuclear Testing Archive, Las Vegas, Nevada (emphasis added).

6   The term "mental map" as used in this context refers to the mental perception and physical navigation of a place as developed by Kevin Lynch in his *The Image of the City* (Cambridge: Massachusetts Institute of Technology Press, 1960).

7   Terrence R. Fehner and F. G. Gosling, *Atmospheric Nuclear Weapons Testing, 1951–1963* (Washington, D.C.: U.S. Department of Energy, 2006), 35–44.

8   Kevin J. Fernlund, ed., *The Cold War American West, 1945–1989* (Albuquerque: University of New Mexico Press, 1998), 1.

9   Dwight D. Eisenhower, Farewell Address, January 17, 1961; and Gerald D. Nash, *The Crucial Era: The Great Depression and World War II*, 2nd ed. (New York: St. Martin's Press, 1992), 182.

10   Roger W. Lotchin, ed., *The Martial Metropolis: U.S. Cities in War and Peace* (New York: Praeger, 1984), 223–32; Roger W. Lotchin, *Fortress California, 1910–1961: From Welfare to Warfare* (New York: Oxford University Press, 1992), 1–2; and Greg Hise, *Magnetic Los Angeles: Planning the Twentieth-Century Metropolis* (Baltimore, MD: Johns Hopkins University Press, 1999), 117–20.

11   Maria E. Montoya, "Landscapes of the Cold War West," in *The Cold War American West, 1945–1989*, ed. Kevin J. Fernlund (Albuquerque: University of New Mexico Press, 1998), 14.

12   Richard White, *"It's Your Misfortune and None of My Own": A New History of the American West* (Norman: University of Oklahoma Press, 1991), 497.

13   Hanson W. Baldwin, "The 'Teapot' Tests," *New York Times*, April 25, 1955; Barton C. Hacker, *Elements of Controversy: The Atomic Energy Commission and Radiation Safety in Nuclear Weapons Testing, 1947–1974* (Berkeley: University of California Press, 1994), 164–69; Richard Miller, *Under the Cloud: The Decades of Nuclear Testing* (New York: Free Press, 1986), 213–42; Mary Palevsky, interview with Robert Friedrichs, February 25, 2005, Nevada Test Site Oral History Project, Special Collections, University of Nevada, Las Vegas, 24; and U.S. Department of Energy, *United States Nuclear Tests July 1945 through September 1992* (Las Vegas: Nevada Operations Office, 2000), 4–7.

14   "West Reassured on Atomic Tests," *New York Times*, January 23, 1955; Gladwin Hill, "Desert 'Capital' of the A-Bomb," *New York Times*, February 13, 1955; "Atomic Test Effects in the Nevada Test Site Region," Atomic Energy Commission (AEC), 1955; *Atomic Tests in Nevada*, film produced by the Atomic Energy Commission, 1955; and Hacker, *Elements of Controversy*, 165.

15   "Atomic Test Effects in the Nevada Test Site Region," AEC, 1955; and *Atomic Tests in Nevada*, 1955.

16   Gladwin Hill, "New Atom Tests Start Tomorrow," *New York Times*, February 14, 1955; "Fifth Series of Atomic Explosions in Nevada to be Started Tuesday," *Albuquerque Journal*, February 14, 1955; and "H-Bomb Trigger May Get Test in Blast Tuesday," *Albuquerque Tribune*, February 14, 1955.

17   "1000 Soldiers Await Atomic Tests Today," *New York Times*, February 15, 1955; "First Nevada Atomic Test Is Postponed," *Albuquerque Tribune*, February 15, 1955; "Nevada Atomic Tests Postponed by Winds," *New York Times*, February 16, 1955; "Opening Atomic Tests Delayed: Time Is Doubtful," *Albuquerque Journal*, February 16, 1955; "Bomb Data Bared in Cause of Peace," *New York Times*, February 17, 1955; "Atom Unit Changes Nevada Test Plan," *New York Times*, February 18, 1955; and Gladwin Hill, "Small Blast Opens Nevada Atom Tests," *New York Times*, February 19, 1955.

18   "Atom Blast Postponed," *New York Times*, February 20, 1955; "Nuclear Test Again Delayed," *New York Times*, February 25, 1955; "'Big Shot' Atom Test Is Postponed Again," *New York Times*, February 26, 1955; "Weather Delays 'Big Shot' Test,"

Albuquerque Tribune, February 26, 1955; "Atom Tests on Tomorrow," *New York Times*, February 28, 1955; "Atomic Test Slated Today," *New York Times*, March 1, 1955; "Big Atomic Shot Postponed Again," *Albuquerque Tribune*, March 2, 1955; "Nuclear Test Postponed," *New York Times*, March 3, 1955; "Atom Blast Off Again," *New York Times*, March 4, 1955; "Big Atom Test Again Put Off," *New York Times*, March 5, 1955; "Atomic Big Boom Slated Today," *New York Times*, March 7, 1955; "Another Bomb Test Off," *New York Times*, March 9, 1955; "Nuclear Test Is Put Off," *New York Times*, March 10, 1955; "Atomic Test Called Off," *New York Times*, March 11, 1955; "Atom Test Slated Today," *New York Times*, March 15, 1955; "Atom Blast Postponed," *New York Times*, March 17, 1955; "Atomic Test Again Postponed," *New York Times*, March 18, 1955; "Nuclear Test Is Put Off," *New York Times*, March 20, 1955; "Biggest Blast Slated," *New York Times*, March 27, 1955; "Test Blast Called Off Again," *New York Times*, March 28, 1955; "Atom Test Canceled," *New York Times*, April 4, 1955; "Atom Test Postponed," *New York Times*, April 5, 1955; "Big Atom Test Set for Today," *New York Times*, April 15, 1955; Gladwin Hill, "Weather Defers Atom Bomb Test," *New York Times*, April 26, 1955; "Atomic Blast Test Is Postponed Again," *New York Times*, April 28, 1955; "Atom Test Delayed for the Third Time," *New York Times*, April 29, 1955; "Atom Blast Test Again Due Today," *New York Times*, May 1, 1955; "Atomic Test Off Again," *New York Times*, May 3, 1955; "Why Atom Blast Is Often Delayed," *New York Times*, May 5, 1955; and "Final Shot Postponed," *New York Times*, May 10, 1955.

19 Gladwin Hill, "AEC Is Lifting Curtain on Tests," *New York Times*, February 24, 1955; and "The AEC Opens Up," *New York Times*, February 25, 1955.

20 Gladwin Hill, "Weather Defers Atom Bomb Test," *New York Times*, April 26, 1955.

21 Gladwin Hill, "Team Calls Plays on Atomic Tests, *New York Times*, May 1, 1955.

22 Gladwin Hill, "Why Atom Blast Is Often Delayed, *New York Times*, May 5, 1955.

23 "Report Issued by the Atomic Energy Commission on Effects of H-Bomb Explosions," *New York Times*, February 16, 1955.

24 Fehner and Gosling, *Atmospheric Nuclear Weapons Testing*, 109–10, 112; Miller, *Under the Cloud*, 182–86; Hacker, *Elements of Controversy*, 106–30; and Philip Fradkin, *Fallout: An American Nuclear Tragedy* (Tucson: University of Arizona, 1989), 147–62.

25 "Atomic Shot in Nevada Believed Test of Prototype for Missile Warhead," *New York Times*, February 23, 1955; and "A-Missile Explosion Jars Cities," *Albuquerque Journal*, February 23, 1955.

26 "U.S. Plans to Sell Atomic Power Soon," *New York Times,* March 6, 1955.

27 "AEC Fires Big Tower Shot," *Albuquerque Tribune*, March 7, 1955; "Crews Scamper as Wind Shifts at A-Blast Site," *Albuquerque Journal*, March 8, 1955; and "4th Nuclear Shot Is Year's Biggest," *New York Times*, March 8, 1955.

28 "Atomic Fall-out Dusts Las Vegas," *New York Times*, March 23, 1955.

29 "Atomic 'Satchel' Set Off in Nevada," *New York Times*, March 24, 1955.

30 "2 Atomic Blasts Set Off in Day," *New York Times*, March 30, 1955.

31 "Public Peril Seen in Atomic Secrecy," *New York Times*, March 15, 1955; and AEC Denies Curb on Medical Data," *New York Times*, March 16, 1955.

32   "U.S. Bares Injuries from Nevada Tests," *New York Times*, April 2, 1955; and "Strauss Scouts Atomic Injuries," *New York Times*, April 4, 1955.

33   "March H-Bomb Blast Contaminated 7000 Mile Area, AEC Says," *Albuquerque Journal*, February 16, 1955; "Anderson Back from Test Site," *Albuquerque Journal*, February 17, 1955; David Dietz, "Danger of H-Bomb Fallout Requires New Evaluation of Civil Defense Plans," *Albuquerque Tribune*, February 18, 1955; Hanson W. Baldwin, "H-Bomb Fall-Out Poses New Defense Problems," *New York Times*, February 20, 1955; Anthony Leviero, "U.S. Twice Banned Data on Fall-Out," *New York Times*, February 22, 1955; and Hacker, *Elements of Controversy*, 131–58.

34   "Facing the Fallout Problem: The AEC Reports and Scientist Advises What to Do about Radiation," *Life Magazine*, February 28, 1955, 24–26; "Controversy Over Effects of A-Tests Continues," *Albuquerque Tribune*, March 14, 1955; Dwight Martin, "First Casualties of the H-Bomb," *Life Magazine*, March 29, 1954, 17, 19–20; Meyer Berger, "About New York: Expert Says Many Exaggerate the Hazards in Atomic 'Fall-Out,'" *New York Times*, March 18, 1955; Waldemar Kaempffert, "Science in Review: Information Being Withheld by the AEC Is Sought by Medical Profession," *New York Times*, March 20, 1955; "Report on H-Bomb Hidden 3 Months," *New York Times*, March 25, 1955; and Hacker, *Elements of Controversy*, 148–52.

35   Hacker, *Elements of Controversy*, 169. Also see Hacker's footnotes 78–80 for that page.

36   "No Hazard from Fallout AEC Spokesman Asserts," *Albuquerque Tribune*, April 5, 1955.

37   "Air-Fleet Killer Is Tested by AEC," *New York Times*, April 7, 1955; and "Experts to Study Atomic Radiation," *New York Times*, April 8, 1955. For more information on the Utah sheep death cases, see Fradkin, *Fallout*.

38   William M. Blair, "AEC Sees No Peril in Nevada Fall-Out," *New York Times*, April 16, 1955; and "Experts Explode Fall-Out Myths," *New York Times*, April 17, 1955.

39   "Atom Blast Rips Supplies in Test," *New York Times*, April 16, 1955; Gladwin Hill, "Atomic Test Gets Elaborate Plans," *New York Times*, April 17, 1955; "Experts Explode Fall-Out Myths," *New York Times*, April 17, 1955; and William L. Laurence, "Radiation Effect in Country Small," *New York Times*, April 24, 1955.

40   Gladwin Hill, "Atomic Test Gets Elaborate Plans," *New York Times*, April 17, 1955; Gladwin Hill, "Atom Blast To Be 'Diagnostic' Test," *New York Times*, April 24, 1955; and Mary Palevsky, interview with Robert Friedrichs, February 25, 2005, Nevada Test Site Oral History Project, Special Collections, University of Nevada, Las Vegas, 24.

41   "Atom Blast Rocks a "Capsule Town' and Tank Troops," *New York Times*, May 6, 1955; and Gladwin Hill, "'Town' Does Well in Atomic Blast," *New York Times*, May 7, 1955.

42   "Final Nevada Test of '55 Uses Supersonic Jets for the First Time," *New York Times*, May 16, 1955; Robert K. Plumb, "Fall-Out of Bomb a Defense Factor," *New York Times*, June 10, 1955; and "Anthony Leviero, "Big Bomb Blast Jolted Civil Defense Leaders; but Program Still Lags," *New York Times*, June 10, 1955.

43   R. L. Horst, Denver District Food and Drug Administration to F. L. Schneider, Cattle Sanitary Board of New Mexico, Letter, July 28, 1955, NNSA/NFO.

44   Thomas L. Shipman to James E. Reeves, Letter, August 30, 1955, NNSA/NFO; and Donald J. Leehey, Santa Fe Operations Manager, to Alfred D. Starbird, Director of Division of Military Applications, Atomic Energy Commission, "Memorandum: Investigation of Fallout in Black Lake, New Mexico Area," September 9, 1955, NNSA/NFO.

45   Paul B. Pearson, Chief of Biology, Division of Biology and Medicine, to R. J. Anderson, Chief of Animal Disease Eradication Branch, Agricultural Research Service, Department of Agriculture, Letter, September 20, 1955, NNSA/NFO; William W. Allaire, Test Division, Memorandum to Files, Meeting on Black Lake Incident, September 28, 1955, NNSA/NFO; and Donald J. Leehey to Alfred D. Starbird, "Memorandum: Investigation of Fallout in Black Lake, New Mexico, Area," September 29, 1955, NNSA/NFO.

46   Richard G. Elliott to Alfred D. Starbird, Teletype, October 1, 1955, NNSA/NFO.

47   "A-Experts Renew Inquiry into NM Cattle Deaths," *Albuquerque Tribune*, October 12, 1955; "Black Lake Area Cattle Examined by AEC Teams," *Albuquerque Journal*, October 11, 1955; and "Atom Damage Denied," *New York Times*, October 12, 1955.

48   "AEC Report Denies Cattle Deaths Result of Fallout," *Albuquerque Journal*, October 13, 1955; and "Loco Weed Seen as Cattle Killer," *Albuquerque Journal*, October 14, 1955.

49   Robert E. McKee to Bernard F. Trum, Letter, October 17, 1955, NNSA/NFO.

50   Ibid.; Robert E. McKee to Horace H. Henning, Letter, October 17, 1955, NNSA/NFO; and Bernard F. Trum to Robert E. McKee, Letter, October 24, 1955, NNSA/NFO.

51   Robert E. McKee to Kenner F. Hertford, Letter, October 25, 1955, NNSA/NFO.

52   Robert E. McKee to Bernard F. Trum, Letter, October 31, 1955, NNSA/NFO.

53   Bernard F. Trum to Robert E. McKee, Letter, November 2, 1955, NNSA/NFO; Ted Rea to Robert E. McKee, Letter, November 2, 1955, NNSA/NFO; Ted Rea to Robert J. Anderson, Letter, November 1, 1955, NNSA/NFO; James E. Reeves to Bernard F. Trum, Letter, November 7, 1955, NNSA/NFO; James E. Reeves to F.H. Sharp, Letter, November 7, 1955; NNSA/NFO; and Bernard F. Trum to James E. Reeves, Letter, November 10, 1955, NNSA/NFO.

54   Kenner F. Hertford to Alfred D. Starbird, "Memorandum: Investigation of Livestock Losses," November 17, 1955, NNSA/NFO.

55   "Black Lake Cattle Deaths Blamed on Loco Weed," *Albuquerque Journal*, December 22, 1955.

56   Ted Rea to James E. Reeves, Letter, December 31, 1955, NNSA/NFO.

57   "Anthrax Disease Is under Control," *Santa Fe New Mexican*, October 8, 1959; "Cattle Anthrax under Control," *Farmington Daily Times*, October 8, 1959; and Bewley, *McKee Ranch*, 1–8.

58   Wayne LeBaron, author of several apocalyptic books on nuclear testing, including *Preparation for Nuclear Disaster* and *The Reluctant Survivors: How To Protect Your Family against Radiation Sickness*, briefly mentions the blue snow reported as

a consequence of radioactive fallout in *America's Nuclear Legacy* (Commack, NY: Nova Science Publishers, Inc., 1998), 53. For further information on the testing moratorium, see Hacker, *Elements of Controversy*, 196–200.

CHAPTER 4

"THIS IS REALLY BAD STUFF BURIED HERE"

Agent Orange, Johnston Atoll, and the Rise of Military Environmentalism

EDWIN A. MARTINI

O N April 15, 1970, the secretaries of the U.S. Departments of Agriculture, Interior, and Health, Education, and Welfare announced at a White House press conference that the government was suspending registration of the herbicide 2,4,5-T. This decision effectively made it illegal to sell or transport products containing the compound for most domestic purposes while at the same time such products were allowed to be sprayed along roadsides and on nonagricultural ranchlands. Although known by few Americans at the time, 2,4,5-T was a common ingredient in many commercial grade and household weed killers. It was also one half of the chemical mixture constituting Agent Orange, the herbicide that throughout the 1960s the United States sprayed more than forty-five million liters of in Vietnam. In a separate press conference minutes later, the Pentagon announced that it too, despite the objections of military commanders, was suspending most uses of herbicides containing 2,4,5-T. Amid growing health concerns about the presence of dioxin in herbicides used in the United States as well as in the Republic of Vietnam (RVN), President Richard Nixon overruled his military commanders, ordering them to phase out all herbicide operations in Vietnam by the end of 1970.[1]

Although the United States continued to use other herbicides throughout central and southern Vietnam, the permanent suspension of Agent Orange missions posed a major dilemma for the military. At the time of the announcement, more than 1.5 million gallons of Agent Orange were sitting in fifty-five-gallon drums at several bases throughout Vietnam. Another 860,000 gallons were awaiting shipment to Vietnam from the Naval Construction Battalion Center in Gulfport, Mississippi (NCBC).[2] These chemical agents, which for years had been considered vital to the U.S. war in Vietnam, now became a sharp, logistical thorn in the military's side. Faced with a permanent ban on herbicide use in Vietnam, the United States Air Force (USAF) confronted its options to divest itself of the stockpiles. Every possibility, however, carried with it a set of concerns that ranged from the practical and political to the legal and environmental. While use of the chemicals during the war had been largely unregulated, the process of divestiture and disposal, in stark contrast, would be closely monitored by both the federal government and the public.

The military and the Departments of Defense (DOD) and State in three successive administrations had alternately ignored, dismissed, or explained away the environmental and human costs of the militarization of herbicides in Vietnam. Since 1961, the United States, in concert with its South Vietnamese allies, had dumped nearly 73 million liters of herbicides over 2.6 million acres of Southeast Asia despite protests from Vietnamese villagers, enemy forces, international scientists, and even some of its own troops. By the 1970s, reports from the scientific community about the situation in Vietnam, along with growing domestic concerns about the potentially harmful side effects of herbicides, forced the hand of the Nixon administration in recognizing the dangers of herbicide use both at home and abroad. Of particular concern was the 2,4,5-T present in Agent Orange, known to contain dangerous levels of dioxin—one of the deadliest substances on the planet.[3]

The pressing question was how best to deal with the vast remaining stockpile of chemicals and their residual effects on storage and production sites. While the U.S. military continued to cling to its assertions about the relative safety of Agent Orange, it was forced to deal with the newly implemented environmental regulatory apparatus in the United States, particularly the Environmental Protection Agency (EPA). Looking back at the two operations (Operations Pacer IVY and Pacer HO)

EDWIN A. MARTINI

responsible for the consolidation and eventual disposal of Agent Orange allows us to explore the shifting global environmental consciousness that took hold in the early 1970s. The American War in Vietnam contributed substantially to this moving sensibility. The bulk of this story focuses on the United States, but the disposal of Agent Orange is a global case study. From transporting the stockpiles across the Pacific, to debating if the herbicide could be reconstituted to be sold in the global marketplace, to the final incineration of reserves at sea in the South Pacific, the U.S. military was compelled to deal with an increasingly complex matrix of environmental attitudes, laws, and regulations.

During this period the USAF continued to deny that Agent Orange was harmful to soldiers and civilians. The very same body was now required to write lengthy, detailed environmental impact statements (EIS) documenting the safety procedures to be used in the operations, the hazards posed by the chemicals themselves, and the potential impact of the procedures on everything from drinking water and air quality to coral reef growth and the migratory patterns of rare birds. This chapter reconstructs these and other key moments in what has become known as "military environmentalism," showing how environmentalist thinking influenced (and was affected by) the military's response to herbicides, contamination, and waste disposal in the 1970s.[4]

OPERATION PACER IVY AND THE DILEMMAS OF DISPOSAL

Amid the swirling winds of environmentalism in the United States and the war still raging in Southeast Asia, the DOD reached its final decision on the Agent Orange inventory in September 1971. The department recommended, for both logistical and political reasons, the immediate return of all herbicides from Vietnam to the United States. In his memo, secretary of defense Melvin Laird referenced the environmental concerns about the herbicide, noting that "all stocks, both RVN and [continental United States] with unacceptable levels of impurities will be incinerated. Options for possible use of remaining stocks would be considered."[5] The entire stockpile of Agent Orange was eventually determined to be unacceptable; the immediate issue was to locate, consolidate, and relocate the remaining stocks. By this point supplies of the agent had been removed from nearly all field units and were located at four storage sites: Bien Hoa, Da Nang, Nha Trang, and Phu Cat. Bien Hoa housed the majority of

4.1 Agent Orange stocks at Da Nang Air Base in need of transfer to new drums. When President Richard Nixon discontinued the use of Agent Orange in 1970, the military was faced with the challenge of what to do with the nearly 2.4 million gallons of the herbicide still on hand. The initial task was to deal with the inventory of barrels, many of which were leaking and rusted. The massive re-drumming operation, known as Operation Pacer IVY, took place at the air bases at Bien Hoa, Nha Trang, and Da Nang. Photo courtesy of the National Archives, College Park, Maryland.

the drums.[6] Before they could be shipped, however, thousands of deteriorating, rusted, and leaking barrels needed to either be repaired or have their contents transferred to new drums—that is, re-drummed. Thus began Operation Pacer IVY.[7]

By the end of 1971, the remaining stocks of Agent Orange had been moved to three locations that would serve as the staging points for Pacer IVY: Bien Hoa, Da Nang, and Tuy Hoa. The Seventh Air Force was charged with overseeing Pacer IVY, but personnel from the Army of the Republic of Vietnam (ARVN) did the bulk of the work handling the drums. According to Richard Carmichael, a USAF engineer, hundreds of local Vietnamese women were also employed to assist with the operations. In an interview with USAF Major (retired) Alvin Young, Carmichael recounted that he "had verbally expressed concern to the contractor because the boots, aprons, and gloves issued to the Vietnamese women were too large for them to wear. As a result, many of the Vietnamese women wore sandals and handled the herbicides without gloves."[8] Their direct, repeated exposure to large amounts of herbicide raises uncertainties about potential long-term health consequences, but it also indicates the changing attitudes about exposure to the herbicides in general. In internal memos the USAF was still disputing many of the criticisms about the effects of Agent Orange, yet during Pacer IVY air force personnel were questioning the lack of protective gear among the female contractors.

According to Young and Carmichael, at least half of the inventory at the three bases was in need of re-drumming. Photographs from Da Nang reveal extensive leaking and spillage during Pacer IVY, further complicating issues about dioxin levels in the soil and surrounding area. Unusable barrels from the re-drumming operation were to be crushed and buried in local landfills, while usable ones were rinsed, cleaned, and turned over to ARVN forces. Carmichael, who was involved in the inspection of re-drumming operations, reported to Young that very little of the proposed cleanup at Da Nang was completed and that substantial contamination of the soil at the base had occurred. Warren Hull, another USAF officer, confirmed similar results from Pacer IVY operations at Tuy Hoa airbase, a site he later described as "heavily contaminated with Agent Orange."[9] All told, more than twenty-five thousand drums of Agent Orange, half of which were in their original containers and half in new drums, departed Vietnam in March and April 1972. The M/T *TransPacific* picked them up at the three ports and set sail for the U.S. military installation on Johnston Atoll in the South Pacific, where the barrels arrived on April 19, 1972.

The supplies in Vietnam are only part of the story of Pacer IVY, however. The other 860,000 gallons then in control of the United States were in storage at the NCBC in Gulfport, which had been used as a storage and shipment site since 1968. Gulfport, like Da Nang, Bien Hoa, and other bases in Vietnam, has long been a focus of environmental and health concerns. In August 1969, Hurricane Camille struck Gulfport with sustained winds of over 160 miles per hour, one of the strongest storms ever to make landfall in the United States. Much of the Gulf Coast experienced serious damage, and the NCBC was no exception. More than fourteen hundred drums of herbicides scheduled for shipment to Vietnam were blown into the water and scattered around the port by the winds. Young reported that 412 of these were located and shipped to Vietnam; most of the others were recovered from the water. But as many as 240 drums of Agent Orange and other herbicides were never located and became a focus of future inquiries and investigations about environmental contamination at Gulfport.[10]

Over the next several years, as Pacer IVY was under way, the USAF considered no fewer than thirteen options for what to do with the massive stockpile of herbicides. By the time the remaining supply of Agent Orange had been delivered to Johnston Atoll, the Air Force Logistics Command had narrowed the options and began a formal study of five primary disposal scenarios: incineration, soil biodegradation, fractionation (converting the herbicide to its acid components through distillation), chlorinolysis, and industrial reprocessing. The Scientific Advisory Board for the USAF focused on these possibilities only after eliminating such alternatives as deep ground burials, deep well disposals, microbial reduction, and return of the herbicides to the manufacturer.[11] Throughout the exploratory process, the air force encountered reservations and regulations from local governments and constituents about the possible effects of Agent Orange disposal in their areas. The similarities in these local responses show, years before the incidents at Love Canal and Three Mile Island, the public's growing anxieties about the dangers these chemicals posed to the health of humans, animals, and the natural environment—most of which revolved around the uncertainty about the effects of dioxin exposure.

When Utah was proposed as a candidate site for herbicide disposal through soil biodegradation, the state's governor, Calvin Rampton, directed the state Department of Health to investigate the issue. The department's report indicated "universal agreement" among various state agencies that the information about the disposal process was "simply too sketchy" to support the proposal. While inconclusive biodegradation studies had been completed on acidic soils, most notably in Oregon, no data were yet available on the persistence of dioxin in alkaline-laden arid landscapes like Utah's. The report further noted that the USAF's "major push" on disposal initiatives was a combination of several factors, including the ongoing cost of storage and maintenance of herbicide barrels and the "emotional problem surrounding its use in Vietnam." Local press reports described the effort as an attempt to dump dioxin in Utah, leading to public outcry. On the basis of the report's conclusions, and despite the "close and friendly" relationship between the state and the air force, Rampton felt it was his "duty to resist the proposal."[12]

Other candidate sites for disposal included Deer Park, Texas, and Sauget, Illinois—both home to the type of large-scale chemical facilities required for destroying the dioxin in Agent Orange through incineration. Texas rebuffed proposals for the Deer Park facility, owned and operated by Rollins Environmental Services, citing "possible harmful effects to the area." The primary objections raised by the Texas Air Control Board were that the additional contamination caused by the incineration of Agent Orange would compound an already serious air pollution problem in the area. The site, located just outside of Houston, was home to a number of industrial plants, including a major Shell Oil processing plant.[13]

The Sauget site was even more problematic. Originally named Monsanto, Sauget had been the home of Monsanto Chemical Company since the early twentieth century. The Sauget plant produced Agent Orange during the war as well as DDT, plastics, and other chemicals. Sauget would later be identified by the EPA as the largest producer of polychlorinated biphenyls (PCBs) in the world, eventually being declared a Superfund site. When worries over PCB contamination became an issue in the early 1970s, the unincorporated town of Monsanto changed its name to Sauget but remained squarely on the radar screen of environmental groups and regulators.[14] When the USAF named Sauget as a possible destination for the Agent Orange supply, the EPA was quick to take note. The site's appeal seemed to be its unincorporated, seemingly isolated status, although that assessment failed to take into account the town's immediate proximity to Saint Louis, Missouri.

The matter of proximity was not lost on the residents of Missouri, however. In response to an invitation to submit public comment on the 1972 draft proposal for incineration at either Deer Park or Sauget, several Missourians wrote to the USAF and Congress to protest the plan. Saint Louis resident Douglas Thornberry wrote a lengthy, detailed letter to Robert Seamans, the secretary of the air force, criticizing USAF for "the insinuation that Sauget, Illinois is just some small place, where no one has ever heard of, and probably would assure it is located out in the back country. If you would consider a 15 mile radius circle drawn about Sauget, Illinois, you would discover a metropolitan area with a population of much more than a million people."[15] Based on data provided by the USAF, the EIS anticipated the potential release of as much as five hundred pounds per day of hydrogen chloride emissions. The EPA noted that the normal wind patterns around Sauget would blow those emissions directly over downtown Saint Louis, located directly across the Mississippi River from the facility. Although it was "impossible to accurately determine the effect of these emissions on the surrounding community," the reply concluded, "it is safe to say that such an amount of emissions over such a long period of time could represent a potentially serious condition." In the end the EPA recommended pursuing the construction of a new incinerator in a "remote region."[16]

For all of the concerns about the final resting place for Agent Orange, the proposals that generated the most attention were those involving the reprocessing of the herbicide for domestic use. Although nearly identical to domestic herbicides in use at the time, technically Agent Orange was designed specifically for the military, according to specifications provided to the DOD. Because of these specifications, and because use of the agent predated the creation of the EPA, the tens of thousands of barrels of Agent Orange awaiting their fate were not registered for domestic use in the United States. Given the heightened concerns about Agent Orange, dioxin, and the recent ban on 2,4,5-T, it was unlikely that the herbicide could be successfully registered at the time. Timber and forestry interests, ranchers, and other advocates expressed a great deal of interest in the supply of Agent Orange then in storage, given the historically heavy domestic use of 2,4-D and 2,4,5-T.[17]

"We're being besieged by both sides," an EPA spokesperson told the *San Antonio Light* in April 1972: "From ranchers who want us to get it for them, and from environmentalists who object to plans to pay for it." Ranchers and many of their congressional representatives advocated that the supply of Agent Orange be declared military surplus so that it could be sold to them at greatly reduced costs. The EPA noted that this was unlikely, because of the presence of "impurities" in the supply. In fact, military procurement guidelines for contractors specifically stipulated that "any contractor inventory dangerous to public health or safety shall not be donated or otherwise disposed of unless rendered innocuous or until adequate safeguards have been provided."[18] Many advocates of domestic herbicide applications would have disputed the dangers of dioxin, but convincing the EPA and the public that 2,4-D and 2,4,5-T in any form were "innocuous" and safe for local use remained a major obstacle.

Throughout 1972 and 1973, while other constituencies balked at having Agent Orange buried or burned in their backyards, advocates of

EDWIN A. MARTINI

herbicide use lobbied the government to allow its usage at home and abroad. Michael Newton, a forest ecologist at Oregon State University, wrote to Young, then a captain in the U.S. Air Force, requesting that they work together to "shake loose the juice," as Newton put it, to allow the U.S. Forest Service or the Bureau of Land Management to use the herbicides for brush control in forests. Newton was particularly interested in comparing the effects of clean and dirty, heavily contaminated Agent Orange. Forwarding the request, Young wrote a note on the memo, calling it an "excellent proposal for the price of five drums. Recommend we send him the Agent!"[19]

Newton and Young were not the only ones who saw the destruction of Agent Orange as a waste of resources. In a letter to Congressman Robert Sikes of Florida, who represented the area surrounding Eglin Air Force Base, a major test site for military herbicide use, air force Colonel G. C. MacDonald wrote to protest "the utterly pointless destruction of 2,300,000 gallons of military herbicide Orange, which to date has cost the taxpayer about $20,000,000." Citing previous domestic use by the U.S. Forest Service and the results of long-term testing at Eglin, MacDonald dismissed the recent furor over 2,4,5-T. He claimed that "much of the scientific community has no intention of being either honest or objective as regards herbicides or the war in Vietnam, for that matter." MacDonald closed by recommending a number of potential uses, including use by the Forest Service and for "several major road building projects in Central and South America."[20]

There was indeed interest by some Central and South American constituencies, most notably the government of Brazil. Working through the United States Agency for International Development (USAID) and the Blue Spruce Chemical Company in New Jersey, the Interior Ministry of Brazil in April 1972 requested "shipment of certain chemicals for use in Brazil to update cattle grazing lands, thereby helping to increase the output of meat and milk commodities." The chemicals in question were in fact 2,4-D and 2,4,5-T, which the ministry and its advocates understood to be surplus materials, the application of which "would have a most beneficial impact on the Brazilian economy." While both USAID and Blue Spruce asserted that the herbicide formulation was legal in Brazil, Blue Spruce nevertheless planned to set up an elaborate front corporation based in the Bahamas to avoid undue regulatory difficulties and to allow for distribution not only to Brazil but also to a number of countries in the Amazon basin, including Colombia and Venezuela. The plan was eventually nixed when the air force made clear that the herbicides would not be "donated" and that it would require formal certifications from the governments in question that Agent Orange was considered legal and "safe for use in the manner intended." Other proposed uses for international development, such as "applying Orange for aquatic weed control in Africa," also failed to develop.[21]

Neither the EPA nor the military was going to allow the use of Agent Orange at home or abroad without modification of the supply to meet the existing safety and environmental regulations. Reprocessing the herbicide would require the participation of the chemical companies responsible for the presence of considerable levels of impurities in the first place. They better than anyone understood the processes, risks, and costs involved. As early as 1968, Charles Minarik of the Chemical Corps wrote in a memo to the commander of San Antonio Air Materiel Area, operated by the USAF, that excess supplies of herbicides, if necessary, could be used for a variety of domestic and international applications. The caveat was that "discussions with representatives of industry disclose that it is not feasible to sell Orange to the manufacturer even at greatly reduced prices," because the "cost of conversion to more acceptable formulations" would be prohibitive.[22]

In March 1971, before the re-drumming operations of Pacer IVY had been completed, Richard Patterson, the government relations manager for Dow Chemical, confirmed Minarik's view in a presentation he made to the Armed Forces Pest Control Board titled "Modification and/ or Destruction of Defoliants." He began: "We [Dow] have been asked, officially and unofficially, whether we would get involved in the three remaining alternatives, i.e., purchase of the inventory, destruction of it on a contractual basis, or recommend a method of destruction." But he quickly noted that Dow was "not interested in either of the first two alternatives. . . . The economics of modification or conversion are poor, i.e., this could only be done at a loss; a large portion (probably something more than 40%) of the Orange inventory is unusable because of a dioxin level higher than one part per million; the problem of getting shipping permits and the present condition of the drums would preclude shipment out of the Gulfport facility, and the condition of the drums would present a considerable environmental hazard even if they could be shipped to our manufacturing plant in Midland, Michigan."[23]

At the time of Patterson's presentation, Agent Orange produced by Dow represented just under half of the more than eight hundred thousand gallons in dock at Gulfport—a supply his company believed was too contaminated with dioxin to be worth reprocessing. Given the opportunity to consult on other options, however, Dow was more than willing to offer its services to the U.S. government. Patterson outlined Dow's long history of design, building, and maintenance of chemical disposal facilities, including the type of specially designed industrial incinerators that could be used to achieve the high-temperature incineration of Agent Orange. Representatives of the company, he urged, could be available "on short notice" to consult and offer bids on such services.[24] Over the next several years, the disposal of Agent Orange would come to signify a great deal more than environmental safety. Although by the end of the 1960s the herbicide had become a symbol of the violence inflicted on Southeast Asia by the United States, by the mid-1970s it would serve as a stubborn reminder of the mess that war left behind. As the United States extricated itself from Vietnam, the dilemma of disposal offered a poignant, if painful, reminder of the failures that war represented. Like the toxic memories of the war, the barrels, the herbicides, and the dangers they represented could not be easily washed away, so the military did the next best thing: it hauled the remaining stockpile of Agent Orange to a remote outpost, burned it, and made it disappear.[25]

JOHNSTON ATOLL AND THE INCINERATION OF AGENT ORANGE

Given the unwillingness of the chemical companies to purchase or reformulate the herbicides, the misgivings voiced by other localities about the alternative disposal methods, and the delicate politics and diplomacy involved in foreign sales of Agent Orange, the air force decided in 1972 to proceed with incineration of the remaining stock. It filed for permits with the EPA and set out to write an initial EIS. Incineration of dioxin-laded chemicals had been tested in various commercial facilities, including those operated by Dow and highlighted in Patterson's presentation. According to the EIS:

> The data accumulated, together with theoretical considerations and applied thermochemistry, clearly indicate that the production of incomplete combustion products can be minimized to insignificant

levels. Incineration will convert the Orange herbicide to its combustion products of carbon dioxide, hydrogen chloride, and water which will be released to the atmosphere. In addition, a relatively small amount of elemental carbon and carbon monoxide will be generated in the incineration process and discharged to the atmosphere. With proper concern for the environment in which such incineration will take place, incineration is an environmentally safe method of disposal of Orange herbicide.[26]

The data presented, gathered from stocks of Orange at Johnston and Gulfport, suggested that the total amount of dioxin present in the supply to be incinerated amounted to approximately fifty pounds. With test incinerations resulting in efficiencies of more than 99 percent, the USAF believed that less then 0.05 pounds of dioxin would be released along with the water and other exhaust from the combustion process.[27]

Incineration was the most proven, reliable, and politically viable option for disposal, but there were concerns. The question remained where the incineration would take place. Rejecting earlier proposals for Texas and Illinois, the EPA had urged the air force to consider incineration in a remote location—a suggestion the project leaders took to heart. In its EIS the air force described the ideal incineration site as being "as remote as possible from both residential and industrial populations centers," where "women of childbearing age" would have a low probability of coming into contact with the Orange," preferably with a "prevailing wind of nearly constant direction and velocity." The site "should be completely under the control of the Federal Government to minimize the local political controversial effects on state or other government units."[28] One ideal site presented itself: an area of the South Pacific near the tiny, isolated group of islands known as Johnston Atoll, where the bulk of the herbicides were already in storage.

Located about eight hundred miles southeast of Honolulu, Johnston had been under U.S. control since the late nineteenth century, after its annexation of Hawaii. Throughout the 1800s Johnston was a major site of guano cultivation, gathered for fertilizer from the droppings of the many seabirds that nested on the atoll. In 1926, President Calvin Coolidge issued Executive Order 4467, declaring Johnston a wildlife refuge to protect the natural bird sanctuary. During the 1930s, President Franklin Roosevelt militarized the islands, transferring control of Johnston as

EDWIN A. MARTINI

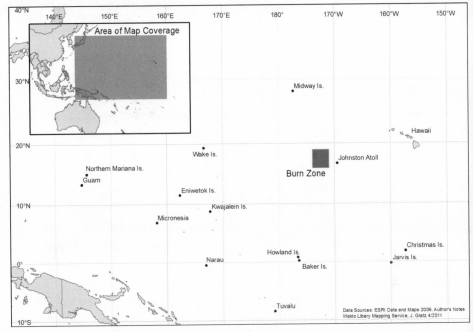

4.2 Johnston Atoll, location of Operation Pacer HO. Once the U.S. Air Force had determined that it would destroy the remaining stocks of Agent Orange, it shipped all remaining inventory to Johnston Atoll, a remote military outpost about eight hundred miles southwest of Hawaii. From there, the herbicide would be loaded onto a specially designed ship and incinerated in the designated burn zone west of the atoll. Johnston would undergo extensive environmental monitoring for several decades. Map courtesy of Western Michigan University Mapping Center, designer Jason Glatz.

well as Wake Island to the U.S. Navy. As tensions between Japan and the United States mounted, Roosevelt consolidated these areas, along with several others, as Naval Defensive Sea Areas in 1941. Originally composed of two natural islands, Johnston and Sand, the presence of the United States in the area led to coral-dredging operations that eventually resulted in the creation of two additional, human-made islands named Akau (North) and Hakina (East). Johnston and Sand Islands have also been expanded by the military from their original sizes of 60 and 13 acres to 625 and 22 acres, respectively.[29]

When the USAF assumed control over operations on Johnston after World War II, the group of islands became home to a variety of military operations, most of which centered around chemical and nuclear weapons. During the late 1950s and early 1960s, Johnston became a primary location for support of atmospheric nuclear testing. After the United States returned control of Okinawa to Japan in 1970, the military moved large quantities of chemical munitions from there to Johnston. During the most active years of nuclear testing on the atoll, which included Operation Dominic in 1962, Johnston experienced significant levels of radioactive exposure. In June 1962 a Thor missile carrying a nuclear device failed and was destroyed over Johnston, with "a substantial amount of debris" falling on and around the area. Navy teams spent the next several weeks recovering and removing radioactive debris from the water around Johnston and Sand.[30]

In July another missile failure led the radio team on the ground to destroy the missile shortly after takeoff. No nuclear explosion resulted, but the launching pad area and the lagoon on the island's northwest corner were heavily contaminated with radioactive debris, particularly plutonium. Agents with the Defense Threat Reduction Agency (DTRA) began cleanup and monitoring operations immediately, establishing a twenty-four-acre radioactive control area on the island and shipping a large volume of material off the island. The DTRA filled the resulting landfill with "240 tons of contaminated metal debris, 200 cubic meters of concrete debris, and 45,000 cubic meters of contaminated coral soil." Only about 1 percent of the weapons-grade plutonium was placed in the landfill—the vast majority of it, according to air force records, remains in the lagoon.[31]

Although extensive long-term environmental monitoring of Johnston since the 1970s has shown the atoll to be within acceptable federal limits for air, water, and soil contamination, these same reports attest that Johnston is "an unincorporated, unorganized territory of the United States" and therefore not subject to the same controls as states and other territories. The guidelines of the Clean Air Act of 1970, for example, do not apply to Johnston, and the Nuclear Regulatory Commission has no jurisdiction over the island. The military did consult with and submit multiple reports to the EPA, including the eight-hundred-page-plus final report on the at-sea incineration of Agent Orange, but the numerous references in the reports to the liminal jurisdictional and statutory status of Johnston demonstrate that much of the monitoring was left up to the military. This unclear status, along with the atoll's remarkably isolated geographic location, made it the ideal location for Operation Pacer HO.

In its final incineration plan the military decided against building an expensive incineration plant on Johnston proper. Despite the seemingly ideal location, the cost of building a facility was prohibitive, with the price of a new incinerator alone estimated at more than three million dollars. Instead, the USAF contracted with the owners of M/T *Vulcanus*, a Dutch cargo ship retrofitted in 1972 to become a specialized chemical cargo ship, complete with two incinerators located in the stern.[32] The *Vulcanus* would transport the materials to a designated "burn zone" due west of Johnston. Like Johnston, the burn area was essentially an extra-jurisdictional area—an even more remote portion of the South Pacific Ocean. Next, the air force ran into one of the operation's first major regulatory problems when confronted with the Marine Protection, Research, and Sanctuaries Act of 1972 (MPRSA). The act, signed into law while the USAF was drafting its initial EIS, was designed to prohibit "dumping of all types of materials into ocean waters and to prevent or strictly limit the dumping into ocean waters of any material which would adversely affect human health, welfare, or amenities, or the marine environment, ecological systems, or economic potentialities."[33]

When the air force submitted its initial draft of the EIS, the EPA ruled that the MPRSA did not apply because the law was unclear on the issue of air pollution at sea, which would be the primary contaminant produced by Pacer HO. By the time the air force had prepared its final EIS in 1974, however, the EPA had reversed its previous ruling and now required the USAF to go through the lengthy process of obtaining an at-sea incineration permit. This new process, which included several public hearings, forced the air force ironically to revisit the idea of reprocessing the herbicide for domestic use. It did so over the next two years, adding time and cost to the operation but resulting in the same conclusion: at-sea incineration was the safest, most politically viable way to destroy Agent Orange. In 1977 the EPA issued the permit allowing the incineration plan to proceed.[34]

The air force ran into another major hurdle when presented with new regulations passed in the early 1970s on the destruction and disposal of chemical and biological weapons. In particular, amendments to legislation covering the regulation of chemical and biological weapons (CBW) made it illegal to dispose of any chemical or biological warfare agent "unless such agent has been detoxified or made harmless to man and his environment or unless immediate disposal is clearly necessary, in an emergency, to safeguard human life."[35] The counsel's office of the USAF suggested in its recommendation that Agent Orange and other herbicides should not be considered chemical or biological agents because they were not intended as antipersonnel measures, although it did note that this was still an open question, given the growing knowledge about the effects of herbicides on "man and his environment." The debate over the legislation, the counsel's office pointed out, focused largely on agents such as VX and nerve gas, not on herbicides, but the real question was what constituted "disposal." The aim of the act, according to counsel, was to prohibit the dumping of CBW agents, especially in the ocean. The USAF, the memo went on, would not be physically dumping the herbicide in the ocean, so that provision would not apply to Pacer HO. Despite the public health and environmental concerns running throughout the memo, the ultimate justification for the recommendation to proceed was that Agent Orange, "at its present concentrations," is "*not toxic or harmful to man and his environment*, as those terms are used in the act."[36]

The explicit stance of the USAF remained that Agent Orange and its associated dioxin, even at levels well over 1 part per million (ppm), were not dangerous to human or environmental health so long as they were properly handled. This did little to assuage the growing consternation of the public as it became increasingly aware of Agent Orange over the course of the operation. Although the burn zone itself fit the ideal site criteria, the plan still required storage, transport, and shipping of the materials to and from Gulfport and Johnston—projects that involved several hundred airmen, scientists, and contractors. Just as they had throughout Pacer IVY, cries rang out from Mississippi to Johnston Atoll about how the presence of the chemicals would affect the populations and environments involved.

Many southern Mississippi residents were worried about what they viewed as another environmental disaster waiting to happen at the Naval Construction Battalion Center in Gulfport. This was far from an idle concern for a population that in many places was just beginning to recover from the devastation of Hurricane Camille. As the storage piles at the facility built up over time and became more visible from the shoreline, residents and local officials made known their anxieties over possible contamination of coastal waters and local aquatic life, both of which would have a major impact on the local fishing industry. The executive director of the Mississippi Air and Water Pollution Control

Commission requested that the herbicide "be removed immediately and without regard to the final disposition of the material. . . . It is felt this is absolutely essential because of the proximity of the material to recreational and shellfish waters, as well as large densely populated areas, and further because of the history of hurricanes and tornadoes in that particular section of the country. It is our feeling there are many other areas in the continental United States which would provide a much safer depository for this material."[37] The Chamber of Commerce in Gulfport joined the antiherbicide movement passing a resolution decrying the negative effects that "human and environmental damage" from the herbicide storage at NCBC would have on local business. Several letters from residents to local papers and to the commander of the NCBC fretted about local health issues, most of which revolved around dioxin, about which residents admitted they knew very little. As the mayor of Gulfport expressed it in his letter to the NCBC: "Like most people, I know very little about dioxin, but from what I can understand, it is one of the most deadly chemicals known to man."[38]

Senator Daniel Inouye of Hawaii was similarly troubled by the impact of the Johnston operations on his home state and its environment. In a letter to Secretary Seamans, Inouye requested clarification of the plans for the herbicide stocks in storage at Johnston, which, he noted, was located only eight hundred miles from Honolulu. "It is my understanding," the senator wrote, that the cost of the storage was currently "$11,000 a month; every day approximately 15 drums start to leak; 'herbicide orange' has been found in the local water supply; and a significant amount of the coral under the island has been killed off by these leaks." The air force responded: the senator's figures on the cost of operations and the level of leaking drums were correct, but the USAF was unaware of any damage caused to the coral or any dangers related to consumption of the drinking water. Although 2,4-D and 2,4,5-T were showing up in samples of drinking water, the air force did not "consider the levels to represent a toxic threat." Nevertheless, Seamans explained, the EPA was called in to consult and agreed that the levels did not pose a human health risk.[39]

Inouye and others had raised concerns as early as 1973, at least a year before the final decision on incineration had been made, well before the air force filed its final EIS, and more than four years before Pacer HO began in earnest, on April 29, 1977, when the military invited local and national media to a "kickoff" briefing at NCBC Gulfport.[40] Beginning with that briefing, the USAF continually stressed the safety precautions built into the program and the degree to which the personnel conducting operations at Gulfport and Johnston were protecting themselves and the surrounding environment from the potential dangers of dioxin contamination. In fact, throughout Operation Pacer HO the air force demonstrated a fairly high regard for national environmental policy and, to a degree, for the natural environment itself. This is what is so striking about this episode: the same military establishment, which in many instances insisted on the safety of these chemicals, and which continued to deny that reports of health problems among Vietnamese citizens and even among its own troops were the result of exposure to the dioxin present in Agent Orange, was now often going to extraordinary lengths to ensure the safety and protection of the landscape, seascape, wildlife, and people in the path of Operation Pacer HO.

This was no accident; it was a result of the shifting environmental awareness that had taken root in American society and the laws and regulations spawned by that awareness. Regardless of what the Pentagon, the Joint Chiefs of Staff, or USAF commanders felt about Agent Orange, they were now compelled—culturally, politically, and legally—to provide basic safeguards and levels of redundant safety precautions that soldiers and civilians could never have dreamed of during the Vietnam War. The air force could have resisted more forcefully impositions on its operations, but there is no evidence that it did. Although there is little available documentation to determine the degree to which military personnel were themselves thinking in increasingly environmental terms, the lack of a more clearly articulated opposition to such regulatory oversight suggests that the air force recognized the politics of the moment were clearly being driven by environmentalist concerns.

The Gulfport facility where the barrels would be emptied, rinsed, and crushed included a brand-new high-volume ventilation system with charcoal filters that turned over the air supply nearly once a minute.[41] Over the next month more than fifteen thousand drums went through this process at the Naval Construction Battalion Center, after which the herbicide was transferred to rail-based tankers and then pumped on to the *Vulcanus*. Young describes the working conditions of the personnel at both Gulfport and Johnston: "All of the workers were provided daily changes of freshly laundered work clothes, and the men

EDWIN A. MARTINI

4.3 Safety precautions, Operation Pacer HO, 1977. Unlike American soldiers during the war or Vietnamese civilians participating in re-drumming operations in Operation Pacer IVY, those who worked on the disposal of Agent Orange during Operation Pacer HO wore protective gear and closely followed safety regulations. Photo courtesy of the National Archives, College Park, Maryland.

working within the de-drum facility were provided protective clothing including cartridge respirators, face shields, rubber aprons, and rubber gloves. With only a few exceptions, the men rotated through all jobs involved in the dedrumming and transfer operations. All personnel were given detailed pre-operational and post-operational physical exams."[42]

The evidence from photos and motion pictures shot at Gulfport substantiate these claims. The images of Pacer HO personnel wearing aprons, gloves, protective eyewear, and ventilation masks stand in stark contrast to the images from Pacer IVY, when Vietnamese women at Da Nang Air Base wore no protective gear whatsoever while working with discarded drums, and to shirtless U.S. soldiers spraying herbicides around their base. Other instructions reinforced the basic safety precautions to be followed by Pacer HO personnel: "1. Clean clothes every day. 2. Wash before eating. 3. Rinse off any significant herbicide in contact with skin immediately and also change any saturated clothing. 4. Immediately notify Sgt. Hatch of any skin irritations or nauseous feelings. 5. Smoke in designated area near wash area after washing hands. 6. Do not discuss project with anyone off base."[43]

While similar precautions were taken at Johnston, what is most notable about the shift in environmental regulation and awareness in the documentation on Pacer HO is the concern for the natural environment surrounding these operations. In multiple versions of the EIS produced by the air force and in the voluminous data and notes compiled by its staff, hundreds of pages are devoted to the migratory, nesting, and breeding patterns of multiple bird species; several hundred more reveal the impact of herbicide storage on local coral reefs. Dozens of pages explain the intricate, multistep process for scrubbing the tanks of the *Vulcanus*. Separate volumes and appendixes describe the long-term, multiyear procedures for environmental monitoring at both Gulfport and Johnston. Even the bulky report itself notes that it was printed on recycled paper! Hundreds of thousands of man-hours over nearly a decade were committed to demonstrating the potential environmental impact of the operation.[44]

Among the voluminous records related to these efforts are eight rolls of 35-millimeter film shot at Gulfport and Johnston during Pacer HO. Made ostensibly to demonstrate the extent of safety precautions, the title card at the beginning of the sequence is actually named "Exposed With Pride"—a mantra embraced by the majority of personnel working on Operation Pacer HO in an attempt to counteract the growing claims of Vietnam veterans that Agent Orange exposure was to blame for a variety of health concerns. The men working on the draining, rinsing, and crushing of the barrels in the scenes that follow, however, are wearing multiple layers of protective gear, precisely to ensure that they were not exposed in the same manner in which troops and civilians during the war might have been.

The film goes on to trace the incineration process from start to finish, including hours of footage of the machinery and personnel involved, close shots of demonstration slides describing the "flow rates" of the herbicide as it moved through the system, and numerous shots of Pacer HO workers meticulously documenting their activities, jotting down notes, and manipulating the knobs of the complex industrial apparatuses used to process the waste. The footage also includes striking shots of the vast landscape of weathered barrels populating the beaches of Johnston before their destruction. In scenes that appear as though they might

EDWIN A. MARTINI

4.4 Documenting Operation Pacer HO, 1977. During the operation the U.S. Air Force was required to navigate the newly created environmental regulatory apparatus in the United States. As a result, the efforts to dispose of Agent Orange by incineration became arguably the most heavily documented military operation of the entire Vietnam War. Photo courtesy of the National Archives, College Park, Maryland.

have been shot by Hollywood cinematographers, endless rows of barrels fill the screen, offering some indication of what 2.3 million gallons of herbicides left behind. In the final shot of one roll, just after the Johnston personnel bid farewell to Agent Orange (holding a sign reading "Good Bye Herbie!!"), the camera traces the herbicide out to sea, as the sun sets rather beautifully over the *Vulcanus*.[45]

Not everyone on Johnston was put at ease by the precautions. USAF Staff Sergeant Jerry Firth was extremely apprehensive about the dangers of working at Johnston. In a letter to Senator William Proxmire of Wisconsin dated August 27, 1973, Firth claimed that he and other men "were literally scared to death to drink any water" on the base. "We are drinking soda pop, milk and the like," he wrote. "We are also concerned about food mixed with the water and food washed with the water." Firth's wife had seen a local news program about the presence of dioxin in Agent Orange and, he noted, was now gravely concerned about the welfare of the men stationed at Johnston.[46] Despite Firth's claim that he spoke for "a majority of the people stationed here," his letter is one of only two pieces of clear, tangible evidence expressing worries about health among the troops at Johnston, and the only one written during the operation. The other letter would not surface until 1999, when Representative Bob Stump of Arizona, chair of the House Veterans' Affairs Committee, forwarded to the USAF the suspicions of his constituent Neil Hamilton about possible dioxin exposure while stationed on Johnston.[47] These examples stand in stark contrast to the mantra "Exposed With Pride." As was true with much of Agent Orange's history, the ways in which operations were described on paper often conflicted with what happened on the ground. A closer look at the operations in Johnston and Gulfport calls into question how scrupulously the safety guidelines involving drum disposal, spillage, and waste were followed.

One of the major issues facing the USAF was what to do with the discarded drums, which totaled more than forty thousand by the end of the operation. Air force engineers working on Pacer IVY raised concerns about barrel disposal long before they knew the fate of the Agent Orange supply. "Exclusive of the method finally chosen for the disposition of herbicide Orange," a USAF memo from 1973 said, "the problem of drum disposal will remain." While the most logical, cost-effective solution was to clean and recycle the drums, "certain political and economic factors discourage this option."[48] Few wanted the herbicide in their backyards regardless of whether it was reprocessed, reused, stored, or incinerated; few communities were willing to accept the storage, reprocessing, or burial of the drums. Throughout the process the air force received mixed messages from regulatory agencies about the potential dangers and best methods of dealing with the drums. For example, in response to the revised EIS of 1972, Merlin Duval, assistant secretary of health, education, and welfare, criticized the excessive focus on drum disposal, stating that the drums could easily be cleaned and reused rather than destroyed or buried since "their contents were never that toxic." Duval criticized the USAF for suggesting that "herbicide orange must be considered a very hazardous chemical, which it actually is not." Only four days earlier, the USAF had received a formal reply from the EPA that addressed the multiple dangers of Agent Orange to the areas around the proposed incineration sites and discussed at length, as did later comments by the Department of Interior, the challenges of drum disposal.[49] Regardless of the assertions about the perils of dioxin and Agent Orange, these comments placed a high priority on finding a way to recycle, rather than bury, the remaining drums. This further demonstrated the growing reach of environmentalist thinking within the federal government.

The drums left over at the end of Pacer HO were indeed largely recycled as scrap metal, but only after extensive operations involving draining, rinsing, "weathering" (that is, allowing the barrels to dry naturally in the outside storage area on Johnston), cleaning, and finally crushing. Aside from the contentious matter of burying dioxin and general waste in a landfill, the major advantage of recycling was that while being reprocessed for steel production, the barrels would be subjected to even higher temperatures over a longer period (2900 degrees Fahrenheit over six hours) than the herbicides incinerated on the *Vulcanus* (2000 degrees Fahrenheit for just a few seconds). This ensured the destruction of the dioxin residues. The USAF seemed to grudgingly undertake the tasks involved, as was characteristic of its actions in Pacer IVY and Pacer HO as a whole. In its description of the barrel processing at Johnston, the air force noted that the extra precautions were taken to mollify worries stemming from the "controversy surrounding herbicide Orange." The final rinse and weathering, the EIS claimed, was of questionable necessity but was nevertheless "accomplished in keeping with the overall intent of minimizing the potential for adverse environmental impact."[50]

In the documentary record of Pacer HO, alongside images of protective gear and safety precautions, other pictures tell of the larger environmental fallout. The endless rows of stacked barrels at Gulfport and Johnston produced large puddles of herbicide drainage and spillage from which dioxin seeped into the soil. Other photos show the burial of waste products in small landfills in the ground. In one revealing sequence, USAF Lieutenant Colonel C. E. Thalken, who coauthored a number of internal reports and scientific publications on the persistence of TCDD (tetra-chlorodibenzo-para-dioxin, more commonly known as 2,3,7,8-TCDD) in the soil and was involved in the long-term monitoring of Gulfport and Eglin Air Force Base, inserted handwritten notes on pictures documenting disposal area sites, including that at the NCBC. A sign reads, "Keep Out: Chemicle Waste Disposal Area." Thalken initially responded to this

4.5 "Chemicle Waste Disposal Area": The other side of Operation Pacer HO. Although most personnel involved with the operation embraced the mantra of being "exposed with pride" to Agent Orange, others raised concerns about exposure to dioxin. Evidence calls into question how closely new environmental regulations were followed during the operation. Photo courtesy of the National Archives, College Park, Maryland.

with a question mark and the reply "chemical." On a close-up of the sign, he pasted a note that says, "This is really bad stuff buried here. *Chemical is spelled wrong.*"[51]

Spelling issues aside, there was indeed bad stuff buried there, and elsewhere too. Along with some of the unidentified waste disposal shown in the images, most of the waste from Gulfport, including all of the protective gear worn by personnel, was buried in a landfill in nearby Saint Louis, Mississippi.[52] Of greater concern was the dioxin residue in the soil at and around the NCBC itself. The incineration required long-term environmental monitoring studies to be conducted at both Gulfport and Johnston, studies that remained in place for years—decades in the case of Johnston. Early monitoring reports from Gulfport show that the USAF was well aware of significant soil contamination in the storage areas, but the focus of the reports tended to be on the drainage ditch

EDWIN A. MARTINI

that ran through the compound and could have transported the dioxin off the base. Some early tests at Gulfport showed TCDD levels as high as 2 parts per billion (ppb) in crayfish, mosquitoes, and fish from the drainage ditch, between seven thousand and nine thousand feet downstream from the storage area.

At the time of the studies, the federal government had placed the "permissible limit" of TCDD at 1 ppb. These initial reports showed that between two and four acres of the fifteen-acre storage site at Gulfport were contaminated with dioxin at meaningful levels, in some cases more than 200 ppb, but the consensus of the authors was that the dioxin was dissipating over time and that the drainage ditch was not moving dangerous levels of dioxin into the environment. The recommendations were to continue monitoring but also to leave the area undisturbed to allow for the natural biodegradation of Agent Orange and its associated dioxin.[53] A few years later, when soil samples from the storage area were still showing TCDD levels in the hundreds of ppb, the USAF decided to undertake a major decontamination effort through the reprocessing of the heaviest areas of contaminated soil by incineration and eventually reburial in a contained, underground cement landfill. The final stages of this operation concluded in 2001, but as of 2010 the EPA and the state of Mississippi had not certified the site as environmentally safe.[54]

Similar long-term studies were conducted on Johnston Atoll, which experienced a number of the same problems as those at Bien Hoa, Da Nang, Gulfport, and other major storage sites. Because Johnston was home to the largest number of drums for the longest period of time, and because of the effects of salty water and air on the inventory, the attention to barrel condition and re-drumming was even greater there. The EIS for Pacer HO claimed that the sandy, coral soil on and around Johnston would absorb the herbicide and TCDD and limit its passage into the surrounding area, including the water. Given the levels of herbicide in and around the storage and transfer areas, however, there was a legitimate basis for concern. One memo from 1978 noted that as many as thirty thousand gallons of Agent Orange may have been spilled over the six years of storage and re-drumming operations on the island. Still, throughout the long-term monitoring process, conducted by USAF staff as well as independent contractors and scientists, the water, air, wildlife, and soil on Johnston, outside of the storage area itself, demonstrated insignificant levels of TCDD that consistently dissipated over time. The overall impact of Pacer HO on Johnston and its surroundings appears to have been, as the initial reports claimed, negligible. By 2004 even the heavily contaminated storage area was showing levels of less than 1 ppb TCDD, allowing the USAF to proceed with its plan to terminate the mission on the atoll pending a final environmental review.[55]

The USAF handled Pacer IVY and Pacer HO efficiently, effectively, and with attention to detail. As Gulfport shows, even with stringent regulations and careful oversight, it was difficult, if not impossible, to avoid environmental contamination by TCDD when dealing with a large supply of Agent Orange. But as Johnston shows, when the safety regulations and procedures were built into the process from the outset and adhered to closely, the impact on the natural environment and the personnel involved could be effectively minimized. The point is not that the military itself had an official change of heart about the potential hazards of dioxin during the process of destroying it; it is that the latest federal regulations required the military to do so, even when they felt it was a waste of their time and energy, which was the case more often than not. Regardless of the feelings of the USAF, a new regulatory apparatus was in place by the end of the war in Vietnam, one that forced the military to deal with the herbicides and the potential dangers, real or imagined, in a wholly different manner. Air force personnel took soil samples, rinsed and weathered the barrels, and monitored the health of the coral reef and the migration patterns of birds because they *had* to.

Military personnel were not immune from the rapid rise in environmentalist thinking during this period. The mantra of Pacer HO veterans was that they, like Operation Ranch Hand veterans before them, had been "Exposed With Pride." This belies any concerns that their handling of Agent Orange caused any ill effects on their health. While sources do not exist that would help us understand how the personnel working at Johnston and Gulfport felt about their work, the overwhelming indication from the available documentation is that the majority of air force actors involved saw the safety precautions as unwelcome and superfluous. A closer reading of this evidence suggests a more complicated picture. Personnel consistently took precautions to prevent direct exposure to the herbicide, but despite claims of safety, they can never say with certainty that they are safe from the dioxin present in Agent Orange. Regardless of what science did or did not tell them, regardless of what long-term environmental impact statements reveal about the safety of Johnston's coral reefs or Gulfport's shrimp, these citizens and veterans know that "bad stuff is buried there," bad stuff that they handled closely on a regular basis.[56]

This shift in global environmental consciousness in the late twentieth century led to legal and policy formulations for which environmentalists fought. They pushed for objectively measurable scientific effects on nature over subjective and experiential effects on the body, the people themselves, including military personnel, who directly encountered environmental concerns. Although the story of Agent Orange is somewhat unique given its high profile among the legacies of the Vietnam War, the proliferation of weapons testing and overseas U.S. military bases after World War II suggest that there are many stories like Pacer IVY and Pacer HO still to be told. A full accounting of the rise of environmentalist thinking in the second half of the twentieth century must take seriously the impact and the experiences of the U.S. military. By exploring the intersections of environmental and military history, scholars in multiple fields and subfields can better explain how responses to weapons like Agent Orange contributed to growing environmental awareness and activism.

NOTES

1   "Press Release: Home Use of 2,4,5-T Suspended," Alvin L. Young Collection on Agent Orange, National Agricultural Library, Beltsville, Maryland (ALY), Series VIII, Subseries 1, no. 05170; "Final Environmental Statement: Disposition of Orange Herbicide by Incineration," Department of Air Force (November 1974), ALY, Series II, Box 3, No. 0094, page1 (hereafter cited as Final EIS); and "U.S. Curbs Sales of a Weed Killer," New York Times, April 16, 1970, A29.

2   Final EIS, 1.

3   These figures come from Jeanne Stellman et al., "The Extent and Patterns of Usage of Agent Orange and Other Herbicides in Vietnam," Nature 422 (April 2003): 681–87. Agent Orange was the most infamous of the six "rainbow herbicides" used by the United States in Southeast Asia. It was a 1:1 mixture of 2,4-D (2,4-dichlorophenoxyacetic acid) and 2,4,5-T (2,4,5-trichlorophenoxyacetic acid). The dioxin found in Agent Orange is 2,3,7,8-tetrachlorodibenzo-para-dioxin, more commonly known as 2,3,7,8-TCDD, or simply TCDD. It is one of dozens of toxins known collectively as dioxins. The name is derived from the location of the chlorine atoms on the molecule (positions 2, 3, 7, and 8) and their position relative to the benzene and oxygen atoms. The configuration of these components

on the TCDD molecule makes 2,3,7,8-TCDD by far the most toxic form of dioxin, thousands of times more toxic than other polychlorinated dioxins. TCDD can be produced by a number of processes, including the manufacture of herbicides such as 2,4,5-T. 2,4-D continues be the active ingredient in a number of widely used herbicides.

4   Among the growing list of works operating at the intersection of military and environmental history are Edmund Russell's classic *War and Nature* (Cambridge: Cambridge University Press, 2001); Mark Lytle, "An Environmental Approach to American Diplomatic History," *Diplomatic History* 20, no. 2 (March 1996): 279–300; many of the essays in the special edition "New Directions in Diplomatic and Environmental History" of *Diplomatic History* 32, no. 4 (September 2008), particularly Lisa M. Brady's fascinating piece, "Life in the DMZ: Turning a Diplomatic Failure into an Environmental Success," 585–611; Richard P. Tucker and Edmund Russell, eds., *Natural Enemy, Natural Ally: Toward an Environmental History of War* (Corvallis: Oregon State University Press, 2004); Matthew Evenden, "Aluminum, Commodity Chains, and the Environmental History of the Second World War," *Environmental History* 16 (January 2011), 69–93; and most recently, David Zierler's important book, *The Invention of Ecocide: Agent Orange, Vietnam, and the Scientists Who Changed the Way We Think about the Environment* (Athens: University of Georgia Press, 2011). For more on military environmentalism, see Jacob Darwin Hamblin, *Arming Mother Nature: The Rise of Catastrophic Environmentalism* (New York: Oxford University Press, 2013); and Peter Coates et al., "Defending Nation, Defending Nature? Militarized Landscapes and Military Environmentalism in Britain, France, and the United States," *Environmental History* 16, no. 3 (July 2011): 456–91.

As for Operations Pacer IVY and Pacer HO, they have received only the smallest amount of attention from military historians and have been completely overlooked by environmental historians. William Buckingham's official USAF history, *Operation Ranch Hand: The Air Force and Herbicides in Southeast Asia, 1961–1971* (Washington, D.C.: Office of Air Force History, 1982), mentions them in passing in his epilogue. Ranch Hand veteran and historian Paul Cecil's *Herbicidal Warfare: The Ranch Hand Project in Vietnam* (New York: Praeger, 1986) devotes less than a page to the operations. The only focused attention on Pacer IVY or Pacer HO has come from Alvin Young, a retired USAF colonel (as well as a PhD in plant physiology and environmental toxicology) who has long worked on issues related to the development, testing, and legacies of military herbicides. As the notes in this chapter make clear, I make extensive use of Young's papers at the National Agricultural Library and his book *The History, Use, Disposition, and Environmental Fate of Agent Orange* (New York: Springer, 2009), which was commissioned as an official study by the Department of Defense.

5   "Disposition of Herbicide Orange: Memorandum, SECDEF to Chair, JCS," September 13, 1971, Agent Orange Litigation Files (AOLF), National Archives, College Park, Maryland (NARA) RG 340, box 183, no. 1945–242.

6   "Fact Sheet: Status of Herbicide Orange," March 7, 1972, AOLF, box 195, no. 1971–35.

7   According to Col. Alvin Young, "pacer" is a "USAF term for logistical movements"; Pacer IVY thus referred to the movement of the inventory (InVentorY) of Orange. Pacer HO referred to the final shipment and incineration of Herbicide Orange (HO). Young, *History, Use, Disposition, and Environmental Fate*, 123.

8   Ibid., 128.

9   Quoted in ibid., 131–32.

10   Ibid., 135. For more on Hurricane Camille, see the U.S. Department of Commerce's "Preliminary Report on Hurricane Camille" (November 1969), available at www .nhc.noaa.gov/archive/storm_wallets/atlantic/atl1969-prelim/camille/TCR-1969Camille.pdf; and Ernest Zebrowski and Judith Howard, *Category Five: The Story of Camille, Lessons Learned from America's Most Violent Hurricane* (Ann Arbor: University of Michigan Press, 2005).

11   Alvin Young, "Dilemma for Disposal of Agent Orange," ALY, series VI, subseries 3, no. 03899, pages 3–4.

12   "Summary of Report on Disposal of Herbicide Orange in Utah," Lyman Olson, Director of Public Health, to Governor Rampton, April 30, 1973; Agent Orange Claims Resolution Files (AOCRF), box 1, folder 3; Young, "Dilemma for Disposal of Herbicide Orange"; "Dioxin in Utah and Vietnam," ALY, series VI, subseries 3, no. 03085; and Rampton to Billy Welch, May 7, 1973, AOCRF, NARA RG340, box 1, folder 3.

13   A concise sample of the responses to the proposed action by the state of Texas are included in the Final EIS, appendix L, especially pages L9–L20. Additional memos from a variety of state agencies can be found in "Technical Report: Incineration of Herbicide Orange by Incineration," Final EIS, appendix D5, pages 65–70. In an interesting parallel to this story, the Deer Park facility did become the final point of reprocessing and destruction of the Americans' supplies of napalm in 2001, although again not without controversy. Local residents and others in the path of the napalm inventory's transit from San Diego raised safety concerns. For more on this, see "Relegating Napalm to Its Place in History," *Los Angeles Times*, April 1, 2001.

14   William Spain, "Yes, in My Backyard: Tiny Sauget, Illinois, Likes Business Misfits," *Wall Street Journal*, October 3, 2006. According to its official, published corporate history, Monsanto (both the town and the company) was named by founder John Queeny after his wife, Olga Mendez Monsanto. Dan J. Forrestal, *The Story of Monsanto: Faith, Hope, and $5000: The Trials and Triumphs of the First 75 Years* (New York: Simon and Schuster, 1977), 13.

15   "Subject: Disposition of Orange by Incineration," Douglass Thornberry to Robert Seamans (March 1, 1972), Final EIS, appendix L, page 16.

16   "Draft Environmental Impact Statement Reply," EPA to USAF, March 8, 1972, included in appendix C, "Technical Report: Incineration of Agent Orange," USAF Environmental Health Laboratory, March July 1972, ALY, series II, no. 00179, pages 56–60. The stench in the air over the Sauget area was well known to locals and would later be immortalized in the song "Sauget Wind," by the southern Illinois–based band Uncle Tupelo ("They're poisoning the air for per-

sonal wealth") on their release *Still Feel Gone* (Rockville Records, 1991).

17   Young, "Dilemma for Disposal of Herbicide Orange," 5.

18   "Ranchers Would Use Banned Army Defoliant," *San Antonio Light*, April 17, 1972, located in AOCRF, box 1, folder 6; and Armed Services Procurement Regulation 24–101.2, page 2,407, located in AOCRF, box 1, folder 6.

19   Correspondence: Newton to Young, September 22, 1972, AOLF, box 183. For more on Newton's work, see "Oregon Reforestation Trials with Herbicide Orange, Reports, Correspondence and Pictures, 1971–1980," ALY, series VI, subseries 3, no. 03759.

20   Col. C. G. MacDonald to Bob Sikes, AOCRF, box 15, folder 9.

21   Correspondence, USAID to Blue Spruce Company; and "Memorandum for the Record, USAF Supply and Maintenance, April 28, 1972," AOCRF, box 4, folder 2. The African weed control proposal is discussed in "Domestic Use of Herbicides," Charles Minarik to Commander, San Antonio Air Material Area (SAAMA), December 6, 1968, AOCRF, box 1 folder 6.

22   "Domestic Use of Herbicides," AOCRF.

23   Richard Patterson, "Modification and/or Destruction of Defoliants," presentation to Armed Forces Pest Control Board, March 1971, AOCRF, box 1, folder 1.

24   Ibid.

25   I am indebted to David Zierler for helping me to clarify several components of this chapter, including this powerful, symbolic connection.

26   Final EIS, 2.

27   Ibid.

28   Ibid., 14.

29   This information is culled from the various drafts of the EIS issued by the air force prior to, during, and after Operation Pacer HO. The most thorough and updated summary of Johnston Atoll can be found in the draft EIS of January 2004 produced by USAF for the termination of the air force mission on Johnston. The draft EIS had been available online through the EPA (www.epa.gov) through 2004 but appears to have been removed as of early 2011. A copy of the draft can be found in the Hawaii State Library, Honolulu (call number H 623.047 EA).

30   Draft EIS, Termination of the Air Force Mission, Johnston Atoll, 3–48. The Defense Threat Reduction Agency (DTRA) was actually formally established within the Department of Defense in 1998, consolidating a number of agencies that had long worked on chemical, nuclear, and biological weapons testing and monitoring. The agency tasked with the initial inspections on Johnston would most likely have been the Defense Atomic Support Agency (DASA).

31   Draft EIS, Termination of the Air Force Mission, Johnston Atoll, 3–49.

32   For more on the ship's specifications, see "At Sea Incineration of Herbicide Orange Onboard the M/T *Vulcanus*," ALY, series 6, subseries 3, no. 03967.

33   Marine Protection, Research, and Sanctuaries Act of 1972, 33 U.S.C. §1401, text available at www.law.cornell.edu/uscode/text/33/1401.

34   *Ocean Incineration: Its Role in Managing Hazardous Waste*, U.S. Office of Technology Assessment, OTA-O-313 (Washington, D.C.: Government Printing Office, 1986),

181; and Young, *History, Use, Disposition, and Environmental Fate,* 143.

35   See 50 U.S.C. 1518, on disposal, detoxification, report to congress, and emergen-
      cies, at www.gpo.gov/fdsys/granule/USCODE-1995-title50/USCODE-1995-title50
      -chap32-sec1518.

36   "The Applicability of 50 U.S.C. 1512–1518 to the Sale or Destruction of Agent
      Orange," Memorandum for the Assistant General Counsel, Installations, USAF
      Office of General Counsel, November 26, 1974, AOCRF, box 9, folder 6 (emphasis
      in original).

37   Final EIS, appendix L, page L3.

38   "Harrison County Board of Supervisors Resolution Demands Removal of Her-
      bicides from Naval Base" (April 1974), AOCRF, box 2, folder 14; for a sample of
      similar letters and the mayor's letter, see AOCRF, box 2, folder 14.

39   Inouye to Seamans, September 6, 1973, AOCRF, box 8, folder 3; and Col. Howes to
      Inouye, September 26, 1973, AOCRF, box 8, folder 2.

40   Young, *History, Use, Disposition, and Environmental Fate,* 144.

41   "Herbicide Orange Site Treatment and Environmental Monitoring: Summary
      Report and Recommendations for Naval Construction Battalion Center, Gulfport,
      MS," November 1979, ALY, series II, no. 0187, 11.

42   Young, *History, Use, Disposition, and Environmental Fate,* 145–47. Young's source
      regarding the medical information is J. A. Calcagni, "Evaluation of Medical
      Examinations on Workers with Possible Exposure to Herbicide Orange during
      Project Pacer HO," USAF Occupational and Environmental Lab Report, November
      1979, ALY, series III, subseries 3, no. 01854.

43   Instructions included in "Gulfport, MS Survey: Notes, 1976," ALY, series VI, sub-
      series 3, no. 03932.

44   Final EIS; see also "Reports, Correspondence, Notes: Project Pacer HO, 1972–
      1982," ALY, series II, box 5, no. 03787.

45   "Herbicide Orange Motion Picture Records," NARA RG 341.5.2.

46   Firth to Proxmire, August 17, 1973, AOCRF, box 2, folder 13.

47   "A. Orange on Johnson [sic] Atoll," Virtual Vietnam Archives, Texas Tech Univer-
      sity, Bud Harton Collection, accessed electronically, no. 168300010714.

48   "Memorandum: Drum Disposal," May 1, 1973, ALY, series VI, subseries 3, no.
      03804.

49   "Comments on Draft Environmental Statement—Disposition of Orange Herbi-
      cide by Incineration," Final EIS, Appendix L, pages 21–32.

50   Ibid., 25.

51   Thalken's notes are included in three images housed in the "Miscellaneous
      Records Related to the Herbicide Orange Project" collection, NARA RG 341/190,
      box 5.

52   Young, *History, Use, Disposition, and Environmental Fate,* 150.

53   "Herbicide Orange Site Treatment and Environmental Monitoring: Summary
      Report and Recommendations," especially pages iii–iv, 27–30; and Air Force
      Engineering and Services Laboratory, "Herbicide Orange Monitoring Program:
      Interim Report," December 1982, available at handle.dtic.mil/100.2/ADA143260.

54 Young, *History, Use, Disposition, and Environmental Fate*, 296.

55 "Land Based Environmental Monitoring at Johnston Island: Disposal of Herbicide Orange: Final Report for Period 1977–1978," USAF/OEHL, ALY, series VI, subseries 3, no. 03984; "Johnston Island Herbicide Orange Storage Site Monitoring Project," USFA/OEHL, ALY, series VI, subseries 3, no. 04010; "Progress Report to USAF on Degradation of Herbicide Orange and TCDD in Herbicide Sites on Johnston Island and Gulfport, Mississippi," Flammability Research Center, University of Utah (May 17, 1979), AOLF, box 19; Young, *History, Use, Disposition, and Environmental Fate*, 272–76, 297–99; and "Draft Environmental Impact Statement, Termination of the Air Force Mission Johnston Atoll Airfield."

56 These developments are also covered by a large body of literature devoted to chemical exposure and the so-called risk society. I have been particularly informed by Ulrich Beck's foundational work in this area. Beck's *Risk Society: Toward a New Modernity* (Thousand Oaks, CA: Sage Publications, 1992) remains the foundational work in this area. A useful companion to Beck's volume is Jane Franklin, ed., *The Politics of Risk Society* (Malden, MA: Blackwell Publishers, 1998), with contributions by Beck, Anthony Giddens, and others. The shifting epistemologies and ontologies of human bodies, chemicals, and nature can be found in a number of works as well. Among the most important figures in this literature are the science studies scholar Bruno Latour, particularly his *We Have Never Been Modern* (Cambridge, MA: Harvard University Press, 1993) and *Pandora's Hope: Essays on the Reality of Science Studies* (Cambridge, MA: Harvard University Press, 1999).

Together with Latour, Donna Haraway's *Simians, Cyborgs, and Women: The Reinvention of Nature* (New York: Routledge, 1991), especially her famous essay "A Cyborg Manifesto," helped challenge the notion of individual bodies as being somehow separate from nature. These theories have been updated and applied by, among others, Christopher Sellers, *Hazards of the Job: From Industrial Disease to Environmental Health Science* (Chapel Hill: University of North Carolina Press, 1997); and Joe Thornton, *Pandora's Poison: Chlorine, Health, and a New Environmental Strategy* (Cambridge: Massachusetts Institute of Technology Press, 2000). A useful overview can be found in Steve Kroll-Smith's and Worth Lancaster's article "Bodies, Environments, and a New Style of Reasoning," *Annals of the American Academy of Political and Social Science* 584 (2002): 203–12.

For excellent applications of all of these ideas in specific case studies of particular environments and chemicals, see Michelle Murphy, *Sick Building Syndrome and the Problem of Uncertainty: Environmental Politics, Technoscience, and Women Workers* (Durham, NC: Duke University Press, 2006); Linda Nash, *Inescapable Ecologies: A History of Environment, Disease, and Knowledge* (Berkeley: University of California Press, 2007); and Nancy Langston, *Toxic Bodies: Hormone Disruptors and the Legacy of DES* (New Haven, CT: Yale University Press, 2009).

CHAPTER 5

THE WAR ON PLANTS

Drug Control, Militarization,
and the Rehabilitation of Herbicides
in U.S. Foreign Policy from Operation
Ranch Hand to Plan Colombia

DANIEL WEIMER

FLYING low above the Sinaloan landscape, Thomas Mace scrutinized
the terrain below for signs of poppy cultivation. Often piloting con-
fiscated Cessnas, and accompanied by either a Mexican pilot or a member
of the Federal Judicial Police, the airplane itself and the poppies Mace
sought spoke to the burgeoning nature of opium and heroin production
in Mexico during the 1970s. Starting in July 1976, Mace, for one year,
acted as chief of photo-interpretation for the Spectral Data Corporation, which was under contract with the United States Agency for International Development (USAID) to undertake aerial photography and
remote sensing operations to document illicit poppy cultivation in the
Sinaloan highlands and elsewhere across Mexico. He oversaw the analysis of photographs produced by cameras fitted with lenses designed to
reveal the spectral signature of opium poppies (*Papaver somniferum*).
Using the spectral data, Mace developed photomosaic maps indicating
the location of poppy fields. To confirm the existence of poppies and to
verify the aerial photographs, he frequently flew over suspected fields

before the maps were handed over to Mexican officials, who then directed the defoliation flights that would desiccate the plants.[1]

Although it was first proposed during the Nixon years, the herbicide program in Mexico came to fruition under President Gerald Ford in early 1976.[2] Ford's successor, President Jimmy Carter likewise strongly favored aerial defoliation of poppies in Mexico, as did Peter G. Bourne, the head of the White House Office of Drug Abuse Policy—today Bourne would be known as a "drug czar." In May 1977, after a two-day trip to Mexico, Bourne recommended that Carter make a public announcement about the success of the herbicide campaign in curtailing the availability of Mexican heroin in the United States. Bourne reported to Carter that "everyone I spoke to both in the Mexican government and in the U.S. mission felt the opium eradication program had been almost 100% successful during this growing season; the most persuasive evidence being the extreme, visible economic distress that has developed in Sinaloa, Durango, and Chihuahua (the prime opium growing areas) among farmers and merchants since the eradication program went into full effect."[3]

But it was not the Carter administration's support for spraying herbicides on poppies that drew scrutiny. Rather, the defoliation of marijuana in Mexico with the herbicide paraquat created controversy as the Department of Health, Education, and Welfare (HEW), in March 1978, released a report suggesting that smoking paraquat-laced marijuana might lead to lung cancer.[4] The paraquat controversy—which lasted through 1979—and the herbicide program overall offers scholars many avenues of inquiry regarding the links between drug history, U.S. foreign relations history, and environmental history.[5] One pressing concern an environmental reading of the herbicide program prompts is how U.S. officials in the mid-1970s negotiated a seemingly inhospitable atmosphere regarding the role of defoliation programs in U.S. foreign policy.

In January 1975, Ford signed the 1925 Geneva Protocol on biological and chemical weapons, which restricted the first use of such weapons. Though the Nixon administration intended—in its support of the protocol—that the defoliation program in Vietnam (Operation Ranch Hand) would be exempt from the strictures of the international agreement, the opposite occurred. Indeed, during congressional debates and hearings on the protocol, from 1970 to 1974, Operation Ranch Hand (which ended in early 1971) became a leading issue for the United States's ratification of the Geneva Protocol.[6] Coupled with the Geneva Protocol was a new federal regulatory apparatus on environmental issues, foremost among them the 1969 National Environmental Protection Act (NEPA). Beyond these federal measures was the presence and influence of a strong environmental movement that had gained force during the 1960s, expanded during the 1970s, and led to a host of new local, state, and federal environmental legislation.

Even as environmentalism in the United States during the 1970s presented challenges to the continuing role of chemical defoliation programs in U.S. foreign policy, drug control officials were able to successfully negotiate this context of environmentalism and ensure that defoliation in the name of drug control was not thwarted. In fact, at the same time that controversy over Operation Ranch Hand ensued in the halls of Congress, U.S. officials, in cooperation with the governments of Jamaica and Mexico, initiated testing of drug crop defoliation (poppies and marijuana) in those two countries. U.S. policy makers—and their Jamaican and Mexican counterparts—were well aware that developing defoliation programs in foreign nations would certainly draw criticisms and comparisons to Operation Ranch Hand, but they employed a set of rationales to preserve chemical defoliation as a weapon in the war on drugs. Two rationales were most used. First was the appeal to "the discourse of agriculture," meaning that policy makers asserted that the herbicides proposed for eradicating drug crops were already used for domestic agriculture in the United States, Mexico, and Jamaica, and hence the chemicals' environmental safety was ensured. Second was the rationale that foreign governments invited U.S. assistance and that defoliation programs were *foreign nations' programs*, not U.S. programs.

When aerial defoliation became a fixture of U.S. drug control during the 1970s, the testing of drug crop defoliation in Jamaica and Mexico, and the implementation of a sustained program in Mexico, served as the "proving grounds" for the rehabilitation of aerial herbicides in U.S. foreign policy. While the proving grounds discussed in other chapters in this volume point to a direct connection between U.S. military bases and their effects on the environment, the link between the U.S. military, the drug war, and their environmental consequences is more circuitous. U.S.-supported aerial defoliation programs have occurred in numerous Central and South American nations, but Colombia (from the 1980s through today) is the nation where defoliation of drug crops with herbicides has occurred on the largest and most sustained level. Indeed, the spraying of coca crops in Colombia during the 2000s under Plan Colombia constituted the largest drug defoliation program in history.

Washington, D.C.-backed defoliation programs in the Americas are directed by the State Department, not the U.S. military. The U.S.-supported fumigation program in Colombia, however, is directly tied to the militarization of drug policy in the Western Hemisphere since the 1980s. The drug war's militarization by the United States and its drug control partners in the Americas resulted in a greater presence of the U.S. military in Latin America and the Caribbean. In the specific case of Colombia, the spraying of herbicides on drug crops was facilitated by two interlocking factors. One, the deep connection between insurgent groups and drug trafficking in Colombia led to a militarized drug control policy in that nation as the United States aided Bogotá in defeating narcoguerrillas.[7] Two, the massive fumigation program facilitated by the U.S. State Department was not only deemed central to defeating narcoguerrillas but was only possible because of U.S. military assistance to the Colombian army tasked with securing coca-growing areas under insurgent control. Such U.S. aid emanated from a series of U.S. military installations in Central and South America and the Caribbean (for example, the bases in Manta, Ecuador, and Aruba)—themselves markers of drug policy militarization. Inside Colombia, official U.S. civilian and military personnel and private contractors operated alongside Colombian police and military units at the Larandia and Tres Esquinas military bases, for instance. In the end, a militarized drug war in Colombia resulted in a range of environmental effects within that nation and rehabilitated aerial herbicides in the post–Vietnam War era.

From the 1970s on, public and private discussions among officials about defoliation of drug crops has focused on the discourse of agriculture. Not surprisingly, U.S. officials during the Kennedy and Johnson administrations claimed that the herbicides applied in Vietnam were also commonly used in the United States.[8] The revelation of the toxicity (from dioxins) of herbicides like Agent Orange is what led to their disuse and demonization within the environmental movement. But when U.S. officials in the mid-1970s employed the discourse of agriculture to defend herbicides in the service of international drug control, their statements came with the assurance that the chemical defoliants—namely 2, 4-D and paraquat—and their application met the standards of the regulatory apparatus then in place in the United States.

Unlike the defoliants sprayed in Vietnam, the herbicides tested and used were "nonpersistent," meaning that the chemical agents that destroyed plant cells did not build up in soil and water; instead, they broke down in a manner of weeks or months. Similarly, U.S. officials regularly pointed to EPA approval of particular herbicides when properly applied. The case studies of Jamaica and Mexico bear out how policy makers in the United States sought to avoid and defend against criticisms that drug crop defoliation was similar to Operation Ranch Hand, even as they had to contend with such uncomfortable facts as 2, 4-D being a component of Agent Orange.[9] The herbicide programs in Mexico and Jamaica reveal how American officials used the legislation and regulations that resulted from the U.S. environmental movement to thwart critics who argued that drug crop defoliation posed a danger to the environment and public health.[10]

In the spring of 1974, U.S. and Jamaican officials began discussions on how to halt marijuana cultivation and trafficking in Jamaica. In May 1974, Eli Matalon, Jamaica's minister of national security and justice, sent a letter to the U.S. State Department, "making an official request for the assistance of three technical experts to train Jamaican personnel in the destruction of marijuana by means of herbicides and in crop substitution programs." The State Department, whose office of international narcotics matters oversaw the bulk of U.S. drug control programs, made it clear that all spraying of Jamaican marijuana be "done by Jamaican personnel using Jamaican equipment or by privately owned equipment under contract to the Jamaican government." In contrast to Operation Ranch Hand, no U.S. personnel or equipment would be directly involved in the spraying operations, and the Jamaican government would "assume full responsibility and cost for [the] herbicide campaign."[11]

During the development and testing phase of the proposed herbicide program in Jamaica, U.S. officials repeatedly argued that herbicides were key weapons for severely limiting marijuana cultivation and trafficking in Jamaica. The application of herbicides from helicopters was deemed vastly superior to manually eradicating fields, which required a large commitment of manpower.[12] Aerial herbicides deleted the protective effect of Jamaica's "antagonistic terrain" that restricted easy access to marijuana fields. The U.S. ambassador to Jamaica, Sumner Gerard, summarized his and the U.S. government's enthusiasm for herbicides when he argued that the "GOJ decision to employ selective herbicides, which kill marihuana when sprayed on the plant, has brought accomplishment of the essential element of destroying the growing fields within grasp." For Gerard and his fellow herbicide supporters in the State Department and the DEA, herbicides would likewise undermine the morale of Jamaican cultivators because tending a field of marijuana "represents a considerable investment in time and effort to the farmer, [and] the psychological impact of seeing his labor go up in smoke, must be profound."[13]

At the center of the proposition that chemical defoliation of marijuana in Jamaica was environmentally safe was USDA plant scientist Dr. Walter A. Gentner. In conjunction with agents from the Jamaican Department of Agriculture, Gentner conducted field tests of various herbicides on marijuana. Herbicides such as paraquat, glyphosate, 2, 4-D, and lynusol were tested, but Gentner and his Jamaican counterparts determined that paraquat proved most effective in destroying marijuana when sprayed from helicopters.[14] Employing the discourse of agriculture and its implicit assurance of environmental safety, the U.S. embassy in Kingston highlighted the legitimacy and safety of the herbicide program by noting that "due in great measure to [Gentner's] wealth of experience and technical acumen, the tests were conducted in a truly legitimate fashion."[15]

However, the proposed defoliation program was bound to generate criticism because of the climate of environmentalism in the United States and the ongoing publicity and controversy over Operation Ranch Hand. In late August 1974 columnists Jack Anderson and Les Whitten wrote an article about U.S. drug control operations in Jamaica. The article revealed that "so intense is the fight against the traffickers that the United States has obtained permission to spray Jamaican fields with Vietnam-style defoliants." In response, Minister Matalon issued a rejoinder to the journalists' claims—one that framed the proposed herbicide program in a post–environmental movement discourse of agriculture. In addition to emphasizing that Jamaica had requested U.S. assistance and that the program was under Jamaican, not U.S. control, Matalon defended the use of herbicides by reminding critics that the herbicides selected were "commonly used for agricultural purposes," that the herbicides were not those used in Vietnam, and that the Jamaican government would not engage in any program that would be "detrimental to legitimate agricultural production or could result in the contamination of our water supplies."[16]

Regardless of Matalon's justifications, though, the proposed defoliation operations never materialized. In the aftermath of the news report, Matalon first postponed the program's implementation and then indefinitely delayed it in late September 1974. For Matalon, the program's political risks proved too high and the perception that the United States, not the Jamaican government, was leading the push for aerial defoliation was one that Matalon could not overcome. The setback in Jamaica came from Matalon, not from U.S. environmental regulations. The United States remained committed to assisting Jamaica if it ever decided to initiate aerial defoliation, and the U.S. embassy in Kingston concluded that "if [the] GOJ makes full commitment to spraying, publicity to make clear eradication and interdiction programs are theirs and not ours might be useful."[17]

Ultimately the herbicide program in Jamaica was not implemented, but a larger-scale program developed in Mexico—the nation considered of greatest importance in the U.S. drug war in the 1970s because it supplied the bulk of heroin to the American market.[18] The same rationales used to defend herbicide use in Jamaica were employed by U.S. and Mexican officials to support defoliation in Mexico. On November 8, 1975, Pedro Ojeda Paullada, Mexico's attorney general, agreed that Mexico would begin aerial spraying in January 1976. According to policy makers, this agreement came only after many months of U.S. and Mexican officials ensuring the environmental safety of the proposed defoliants and debating the merits of using chemicals on Mexican soil. Two types of herbicides were initially under consideration for use—paraquat and glyphosate (sold as Roundup in the United States). The EPA had validated the safety and efficacy of both herbicides in March 1975.[19] By the last weeks in December 1975, the decision to begin widespread use of herbicides had been made, and any concerns over environmental safety had supposedly been addressed. As the Mexican public would be told, paraquat was already in use in Mexican agriculture, and experimental spraying had yielded no new health concerns. The Mexican government ultimately determined, as had Jamaica, that paraquat was best used on marijuana fields and that 2, 4-D, another herbicide tested, "was superior for killing poppies."[20]

Before the 1976 eradication campaign, to start in January 1976, the State Department and the DEA, well aware of the sensitive atmosphere that Operation Ranch Hand had created, reminded its personnel in Mex-

ico that the herbicides (2, 4-D and paraquat) were "field tested by personnel of the [Mexican] Attorney General's office and had been given the
stamp of approval by the Mexican Agriculture department." The State
Department and the DEA also reminded its staff in Mexico to expect
criticisms—in particular, that if defoliation proved effective in Mexico,
cultivators and traffickers would produce "propaganda concerning the
alleged deadly use of herbicides" including "the alleged death of children
and animal stock."[21] The 1976 and 1977 herbicide campaigns seemed to
prove effective in reducing poppy cultivation and heroin trafficking in
Mexico. The Carter administration lauded the herbicide program, but
in 1977 and 1978 the controversy over Mexico's use of paraquat to spray
marijuana fields threatened to derail it.

Nearly a year before the March 1978 HEW report on paraquat-tainted
marijuana, Bourne had commissioned the investigation into paraquat's
health risks in mid-1977 after meeting with an aide to Senator Charles
Percy of Illinois and Keith Stroup, the executive director of the National
Organization for Reform of Marijuana Laws (NORML). Stroup and Percy's aide were worried about the defoliant's health effects on marijuana
users. In 1978, Percy conducted investigations on paraquat, introducing
in September an amendment to the International Security Assistance
Act that called for an end to U.S. support of herbicide use "for any program" in foreign nations. The Percy Amendment for a time threatened to
undermine the entire program. By the fall of 1979, however, the White
House, aided by Congressman Lester L. Wolff of New York, succeeded
in altering the amendment so that only U.S. support for defoliation of
marijuana with paraquat was prohibited. Washington's backing of poppy
eradication with 2, 4-D remained intact.[22]

Washington's ability to fund and assist defoliation programs with
paraquat was halted, but the interruption was short-lived. In 1981
the U.S. Congress—spurred by a conservative backlash against rising
domestic drug use in the 1970s—repealed the Percy Amendment, free-
ing Washington from restrictions on supporting paraquat spraying
programs in drug-producing nations.[23] Hence the legal basis of aerial
defoliation backed by the United States was solidified by the early 1980s,
through the 1990s, and into the 2000s. The U.S. government's support
for defoliation programs in the Americas expanded. Concurrent with
the expansion, which would increasingly focus on coca cultivation in the
Andean region of South America, was the "militarization" of drug con-

DANIEL WEIMER

trol policy in the Americas as the U.S. military, along with the armed forces of South American nations, came to play larger roles in antinarcotics efforts. The drug war's militarization, integrated with fumigation operations, occurred in a host of South American nations, most notably Bolivia, Colombia, and Peru.[24] The intertwined polices of militarized drug control and aerial defoliation are best exemplified by events in Colombia, where the most extensive and sustained fumigation programs in history were implemented by the Colombian and U.S. governments. In Colombia the presence of U.S. officials, members of the U.S. armed forces, and private defense contractors at Colombian military bases (such as Larandia), coupled with supporting U.S. military locations in places like Ecuador and El Salvador, created a host of environmental concerns resulting from militarized drug control policies.

By the second half of the 1970s, a thriving marijuana industry had developed in Colombia's Guajira Peninsula and the Sierra Nevada de Santa Maria. Before the 1970s marijuana was cultivated in Colombia, but on a small scale and for domestic consumption. The mid-1970s crackdown on Jamaican marijuana production and trafficking together with the defoliation program in Mexico, which temporarily reduced cultivation there—coupled with U.S. marijuana consumers' fears of paraquat-tainted pot from south of the border—spurred a marijuana boom in northern Colombia on the Caribbean coast. There, the blessings of geography, an impoverished agricultural sector, enterprising traffickers, and a regional history of smuggling created a marijuana bonanza that soon attracted the attention of the Carter administration and the Julio César Turbay (1978–82) government in Bogotá.[25]

Given the apparent success of the defoliation program in Mexico, the Carter administration in 1978 inquired if Turbay might enact a similar approach in Colombia, which now stood as the world's foremost marijuana producer. For the moment, though, Turbay demurred on spraying paraquat because of the ongoing controversy in the United States and questions about environmental effects. In late 1978 he authorized the use of the Colombian military to manually uproot and burn illicit marijuana. The eradication campaign—Operation Fulminante—was part of the joint U.S.-Colombian "Two Peninsulas" campaign that targeted growers and traffickers in Colombia's Guajira Peninsula and smugglers along the Florida coast. In 1979, Washington continued to query Turbay about the efficacy of defoliation, but a large-scale program did not develop during his presidency.

At the time, the 1979 revision of the Percy Amendment precluded Washington's support of paraquat spraying, which meant that Colombia would have to finance a defoliation program itself. In June 1979 the attorney general of Colombia traveled to Mexico to observe its marijuana eradication program with paraquat, but a government commission tasked with studying a possible paraquat program did not recommend defoliation for environmental and health reasons. Paraquat spraying, which was conducted on an experimental basis in the Sierra Nevada de Santa Marta, was also studied by another government commission made up of members of numerous official agencies dealing with health and law enforcement. That group likewise opposed a large-scale, ongoing defoliation program.[26]

Although a chemical fumigation program failed to materialize under Turbay, his successor, Belisario Betancur (1982–86), instituted aerial defoliation of marijuana in 1984. Betancur initially opposed fumigation for the same reasons as his predecessor, but by the 1980s Colombian traffickers who had amassed wealth and power—particularly from cocaine trafficking, not just marijuana smuggling—were a destabilizing and violent force within the country. The infamous Cali and Medellín cartels that pioneered the trafficking of mass quantities of cocaine in the late 1970s used violence against competitors and the government to ensure a quiescent state and society.[27] When the Betancur administration—fully supported by the United States—began to confront traffickers by targeting cocaine laboratories, the traffickers responded with attacks against the government. The 1984 assassination of the minister of justice, Rodrigo Lara Bonilla, by the Medellín cartel served as a watershed moment in Colombia's drug wars. Betancur responded by authorizing extradition of traffickers—a fate most hated by the provincial narcotraffickers who sought societal and political status within Colombia's stratified class system—and the institution of chemical fumigation.[28] The same government council that had opposed paraquat spraying in 1979 approved the chemical in May 1984. The Betancur government decided that glyphosate (Roundup) rather than paraquat would be best because the herbicide did not carry the controversy that surrounded paraquat and was determined to be less dangerous to human and environmental health. Between 1984 and 1987 about twenty-seven thousand hectares of marijuana fields were forcibly eradicated, with defoliation accounting for much of the destruction.[29]

Another distinguishing factor of the herbicide eradication operations under Betancur was the inclusion of spraying coca as well as marijuana plants.[30] By the 1980s Colombia was home to successful cocaine traffickers and ever-expanding coca cultivation. Colombian traffickers moved from importing coca paste from Bolivia and Peru to growing their own coca—an innovation that altered the dynamics of Colombia's drug economy by adding another source of illegal revenue within the nation's borders. As with marijuana production in the nation's northern Caribbean region, the areas of Colombia where coca cultivation took root harbored natural and social "competitive advantages" that allowed coca production to expand from 3.7 percent of the world's cultivation in 1981 to Colombia leading global production by 1998.[31] Southeastern Colombia's humid and hilly tropical regions along the Amazon basin are amenable to the hardy and adaptive coca bush. Traditional coca cultivation in the Andes (particularly in Bolivia and Peru) centered on the genus *Erythroxylum coca* and *Erythroxylum novogranatense*, but in Colombia traffickers introduced a hybrid variety bred for greater adaptability and production.[32]

Reflecting the situation of many illicit drug producers across the globe, poor small holders in Colombia—many of them recent settlers to the frontier areas of Putumayo, Caquetá, and Guaviare where coca farming flourished during the 1980s and 1990s—viewed coca as an economically viable crop that required little to no expensive inputs (such fertilizers). The crop did not rot after harvesting and drying, was lightweight and thus not dependent on extensive infrastructure to transport to market, and the leaf commanded a stable price. Coca's environmental and economic advantages were complimented by the coca-growing regions' remoteness and thin state presence, which facilitated illicit production and trafficking.[33] The weak state presence and geographical remoteness points to many of the reasons why the largest drug crop defoliation campaign in history developed in Colombia. By the early 1980s, Colombia's long-running insurgent movements had become intertwined with the nation's narcotrafficking. Three leftist groups—the rural-based guerrilla movement the Revolutionary Armed Forces of Colombia (FARC), the National Liberation Army (ELN), and the urban Movimiento 19 de Abril (M-19)—challenged the Colombian state from the 1950s to the present.

Of the three, the FARC took the largest and most sustained role in the drug-trafficking industry, financing organization and operations.[34]

When the guerrillas first came into contact with traffickers and illicit cultivation in the late 1970s, the FARC initially spurned involvement with the drug economy for ideological reasons. But by the early 1980s, the FARC—operating in Colombia's southern regions where coca cultivation took hold—realized the utility of the drug trade in terms of garnering support among cultivators (by ensuring, for example, traffickers paid coca producers fair wages) and generating revenue. Over that decade the FARC levied a tax on cultivators then expanded taxation to the importing of the precursor chemicals used to formulate cocaine from coca leaves. The group also began charging traffickers for protecting laboratories and landing strips in FARC territory. But relations with traffickers frayed over the 1980s and into the 1990s, when the FARC began to oversee coca cultivation themselves as well as demanding ever-increasing amounts of protection money from traffickers. By this time, half of the FARC's income came from drug trafficking, which also included marijuana and poppy cultivation and attendant heroin processing and trafficking. With the drug-trafficking revenue, complemented by funds generated by kidnapping and extortion, the FARC expanded numerically, materially, and geographically. From thirty-six hundred soldiers in 1986 to seven thousand in 1995 to between fifteen and twenty thousand by the decade's end, the FARC had evolved into a well-armed and equipped force that operated in dozens of "fronts" across southern Colombia.[35]

While the FARC fed off of the drug trade during these years, the U.S. and Colombian governments were focused on dismantling the Cali and Medellín cartels. For the United States, in the midst of the crack cocaine scare, the cartels were the main source of cocaine for U.S. users.[36] For Bogotá, the cartels were a fearsome antistate force, particularly because of their violent opposition to extradition and their ability to corrupt government officials. As a result of U.S. and Colombian cooperation, Pablo Escobar, head of the Medellín cartel, was killed in 1993 by the Colombian police. His organization along with the Cali cartel was effectively dismantled by 1995. The effective end of the two cartels in no way spelled the end of the illegal drug trade in Colombia, however. Rather, the trade fractured into smaller organizations with transnational reach, often specializing in facilitating trafficking along particular links in the cocaine commodity chain.[37] Coca cultivation continued apace throughout the 1990s with the Colombian government estimating that cultivation expanded from forty-three thousand hectares in 1994 to nearly eighty thousand in 1997. In 1994, Colombia's "head of the counternarcotics police described the south-central province of Guaviare as a 'sea of coca.'" This remark proved applicable on a larger scale when in 1998 Colombia became the world's largest producer of coca.[38]

This statistic brings us back to the interlocking issues of aerial defoliation of drug crops, drug war militarization by the U.S. and Colombian governments, and the environmental effects of drug trafficking and drug control in Colombia. With U.S. encouragement of the Turbay government to enact paraquat defoliation, Washington's willingness to provide defoliation assistance (equipment, training, funding, and chemicals) has been a continuous theme in U.S. relations with Colombia since the late 1970s. Spraying of illicit crops—coca, marijuana, and opium poppies—occurred with varying intensity throughout the 1980s to the mid-1990s.[39] In 1994 the Clinton administration was able to secure an agreement with the new Ernesto Samper (1994–98) government to initiate a larger-scale and more consistent aerial fumigation program. The renewed effort came about in part because of charges that the Medellín cartel had funded Samper's presidential campaign. An official Colombian investigation cleared the new president of any formal crimes, but to help counter allegations of ties to traffickers, Samper ramped up the spraying of drug crops. In 1995 the Colombian president pledged to eradicate illegal coca, marijuana, and poppies within two years. As part of these efforts, in addition to spraying glyphosate, the Colombian government broadcast the granulated herbicide imazapyr from aircraft over coca fields. Though Samper's claims of decisive eradication proved to be tired drug war hyperbole, over the course of his administration the Colombian government—with much U.S. assistance ranging from aircraft to training and spare parts for equipment—managed to fumigate more than 140,000 hectares of coca and thousands of hectares of marijuana and poppies.[40]

U.S. military and police assistance to Colombia in the 1980s and 1990s was generally couched in terms of drug control. This discursive strategy was a legacy of the Vietnam War and Washington's support of counterrevolution in Central America in the 1980s, which made direct counterinsurgency aid to Colombia controversial.[41] Yet, in practice, neatly separating drug control from counterinsurgency was difficult to maintain. A December 1991 Defense Intelligence Agency (DIA) report on FARC cultivation of poppies illustrates this reality. The report indicated that the Colombian army's use of U.S. military aid to attack drug trafficking was difficult to gauge "given the close relationship between subversion and narco trafficking." As the report noted, "it is not possible to differentiate exactly which [i.e., guerrillas or traffickers] the [Colombian] army units are attacking." The DIA went on to characterize the FARC as an "independent cartel" and concluded that the "Colombian military forces [sic] argument supporting the levels of USG military assistance has been that the narco guerrilla relationship makes it impossible to combat narcos without fighting the guerrillas at the same time."[42] Hence drug control and counterinsurgency remained inevitably entwined.

The DIA's reference to U.S. military assistance to the Colombia armed forces also speaks to the drug war's militarization since the 1980s. The Pentagon assumed a new role in hemispheric drug control, with a focus on interdiction in the air and at sea. With the ending of the Cold War, the U.S. Southern Command (Southcom) found a new role in counternarcotics operations. In 1988, Congress added to Title 10 of the United States Code that directs the armed forces. The addition, Section 124, "made the Pentagon the 'single lead agency' for detecting and monitoring illegal drugs transiting to the United States by air or sea."[43] Contemporaneous with this change was President George Bush's 1989 National Security Directive 18, "International Counternarcotics Strategy," and the "Andean Initiative" that enlisted South American militaries into drug control. President Ronald Reagan in 1986 had declared illegal drugs as a national security threat, and Washington had supplied Bolivia with Blackhawk helicopters to assist in the destruction of cocaine laboratories—Bush's actions continued his predecessors' militarization.[44] In effect, the Andean Initiative and Section 124 provided the broad contours of hemispheric drug control and U.S. policy in Latin America by charging Andean nations' militaries—supported by the United States—with "source control" in the form of crop eradication and destruction of processing laboratories while the U.S. military would use its technical and material capabilities in interdicting sea and air shipments of drugs.[45] Under this policy, for instance, the Colombian military received in 1989 and 1990 $73.1 million and $93.2 million, respectively, in counterdrug aid from the Pentagon.[46]

In contrast to the Bush administration, the Clinton White House focused its drug control assistance on Colombian police units rather than the Colombian military. This decision was based on human rights abuses connected to the Colombian armed forces, government-linked paramilitary forces, and the legacy of U.S. counterinsurgency support in Central America. As a result, the State Department's Bureau of International Narcotics Control and Law Enforcement (INL) and its International Narcotics Control (INC) program grew in size and importance during the Clinton administration in supplying counterdrug aid to Latin American nations. The program surpassed the Pentagon in the 1990s as the main entity through which drug control aid flowed. Through the INC, nations received police training, weapons transfers, helicopters, airplanes, ground vehicles, and a whole range of aid, such as surveillance devices and herbicide spraying equipment.[47] Likewise, with the breakup of the Cali and Medellín cartels by the mid-1990s, the focus of U.S. aid shifted to a reemphasis on crop destruction through fumigation.

Defoliation operations are only possible because of Southcom's role in Colombia and the system of U.S. military installations throughout the Americas and the Caribbean that support aerial defoliation in Colombia. During the 1990s, as Southcom's drug war mission solidified, U.S. bases in Panama and Puerto Rico provided the logistic and material support for interdiction programs. In 1999, when control of the Panama Canal Zone was transferred to Panama, the U.S. military installation there closed. A system of forward operating locations (FOLs) or cooperative security locations (CSLs) in Manta, Ecuador, Comalapa, El Salvador, and Hato and Reina Beatrix airports in Aruba and Curacao filled the gap. These facilities host and are run by the U.S. Air Force, Navy, Coast Guard, and U.S. Customs Service.[48] The U.S. State Department's INL is run from Patrick Air Force Base in Florida. All told, the militarization of the drug war resulted in an expanded role for and presence of the U.S. armed forces in Latin America and Caribbean, with 92 percent ($2.7 billion) of all U.S. military and police assistance to the regions emanating from Washington's drug control programs from 1997 through 2002.[49]

In 1998, Colombia's new president, Andrés Pastrana, inherited a situation in which the FARC had grown in power and presence—operating in or controlling some 50 percent of the country. Pastrana initiated peace talks with the FARC and—aiming to reduce violence—ceded control of much of two provinces to the insurgents. Pastrana hoped to reduce the drug trade (and its role in fueling conflict) while assisting many small holders who cultivated coca by proposing a large-scale, internationally funded development program that would provide coca growers with economic alternatives. Pastrana dubbed these peace and development proposals as Plan Colombia. But in the United States, and within the Colombian military, allowing the FARC free reign in coca-producing regions was not viewed as a path toward drug control or lasting peace in Colombia. Adhering to past reasoning that harming the insurgents promoted drug control and vice versa, General Barry McCaffrey, former Southcom commander (1994–96) and President Clinton's drug czar, recommended increased aid to the Colombian military to dampen the FARC's drug trafficking and insurgency. As in the past, drug control offered justification for military aid, particularly since the logic of the "narcoguerrilla" concept had taken root over the past decade. Within a year of its initial proposal from Pastrana, Plan Colombia had morphed into a $1.2 billion security-focused aid package in which the Colombian military would benefit from U.S. largess.[50]

Because U.S. aid was predicated on fostering drug control in Colombia, defoliation was judged the most effective and efficient means to eradicate illicit drug crops—a logic that had supported defoliation since the 1970s. Since much of the coca cultivation took place in FARC-controlled areas, spraying operations would be subject to insurgent attacks. The revised Plan Colombia used this fact to funnel aid to the Colombian military by asserting that the Colombian army would first—in the counterinsurgency euphemism—"clear" coca-producing regions of insurgents so that defoliation flights could take place. By the end of 1999 a small group of U.S. Special Operations Forces working in Colombian military bases had trained and equipped a new Colombian army counternarcotics battalion tasked with confronting and ridding the coca fields of Putumayo and Caquetá of insurgents.[51] Targeting the two regions, home to prodigious coca cultivation, was part of the U.S.-Colombian "push into southern Colombia" to "break the links" between insurgents and illegal drug profits.[52]

By 2000 two more counternarcotics battalions were created, three in all that constituted the "counternarcotics brigade" of the Colombian army: a twenty-three-hundred-man force augmented by forty-five helicopters (Huey and Blackhawk) with which to penetrate remote regions and "secure" the areas for fumigation. Highlighting the drug war's militarization and the role of the U.S. State Department and Pentagon in

Colombia's overlapping drug and civil wars, the journalist Adam Isacson observed that "units like Colombia's Antinarcotics . . . use U.S.-funded weapons and ammunition, fly U.S.-funded helicopters or sail U.S.-funded boats, and in some cases even wear U.S.-funded uniforms, eat U.S.-funded rations, and sleep in barracks on bases built in part with U.S. funds."[53]

The events of September 11, 2001, and the ensuing "war on terror" by the George W. Bush administration transformed Plan Colombia (renamed the Andean Counterdrug Initiative in 2001) into a six-billion-dollar aid package over the course of Bush's two terms in office.[54] In short, the administration's war on terror, the breakdown of peace talks the under Pastrana, and the election of Alvaro Uribe as president of Colombia in 2002 widened the scope and intensity of U.S. counternarcotics and counterinsurgency programs in Colombia, including fumigation. The failed peace negotiations and the continuation of violence paved the way for Uribe's hardline approach to insurgents. This development, coupled with Washington's war on terrorism (the FARC had been deemed a terrorist organization by the State Department in the late 1990s), allowed for the United States to eschew any restrictions on aid to Colombia being limited to counterdrug operations.[55]

Spraying of drug crops in Colombia thus reached new levels in the 2000s. The State Department's INL and U.S. embassy-based Narcotics Affairs Section supplied "technical and scientific advice, herbicide [glyphosate, aka Roundup], fuel, spray aircraft, and a limited number of escort helicopters." U.S.-supplied fixed-wing aircraft included "10 OV-10 Broncos, 6 T-6 Turbo Thrushes, 8 AT-802 Air Tractors."[56] The INL used the private defense firm DynCorp Aerospace Technologies to provide pilots for spraying operations. This privatization of defoliation operations reflects a feature of drug war militarization as well as a trend in twenty-first-century U.S. military operations. DynCorp employed "U.S. citizens, Colombians, and third-country nationals" to operate the aircraft and "provide maintenance, training, and logistical support."[57] The State Department had been using private contractors, particularly DynCorp, since the mid-1990s, when the Clinton administration secured a revived fumigation program with the Samper government.[58]

The INL did not route fumigation aid (such as helicopters or herbicide) through U.S. military locations in Latin America but rather provided the aid directly to Colombia. In-country Colombian military bases, such as those in Larandia and Tres Esquinas in Caquetá, served as the nerve centers of the fumigation program. These bases housed DynCorp and INL personnel, aircraft, and equipment and acted as staging grounds for the Counternarcotics Battalions' assaults on FARC-held coca fields. Similarly, in Villagarzón in Putumayo the Colombian Anti-narcotics Police maintained a base, which also housed a counterguerrilla battalion and served as a center for fumigation operations.[59] In effect, these bases were the outer ridges of the U.S. military's presence in the Americas. They exemplified the logic of drug war militarization and the persistent and integral role of aerial defoliation; the full force of U.S. material and technical commitment to drug-crop eradication became manifest at these sites. From 47,000 hectares in 2000, the amount of land sprayed increased significantly, particularly after 2002 with the Uribe presidency and the post-9/11 grafting of the war on terror to the drug war. More than 120,000 hectares were fumigated in 2002 and 2003; "the number of hectares sprayed increased each year until 2006, when it peaked at 171,613 hectares; thereafter it declined to 153,133 hectares in 2007 and 133,496 hectares in 2008."[60] The FARC-heavy areas of Putumayo and Caquetá experienced the bulk of the fumigation operations.

Because of the intensified spraying during the Plan Colombia years (circa 2000–8), debates and protests about the environmental and health risks of fumigation came from officials and citizens in both Colombia and the United States. Neither protests (official or civilian) nor official legislation concerning the environment prevented the aerial defoliation program. In September 2001 a group of two thousand Ecuadorian peasants and farmers filed a lawsuit against DynCorp in U.S. federal court charging the contractor with damaging their land, livestock, and health. The plaintiffs accused DynCorp of spraying nontarget land along the Colombian-Ecuador border and that "drift" from fumigation operations resulted in economic, human, and environmental harm. Citing the Alien Tort Claims Act that "permits foreign citizens to sue U.S. companies in U.S. courts over actions committed abroad," the Ecuadorians sought billions of dollars in damages as well as a halt to the spraying operations.

In February and March 2013 the Washington, D.C., federal court issued two rulings that denied the Ecuadorians' claims. U.S. district judge Richard Roberts determined that their main scientific witness, Dr. Michael Wolfson, an occupational and environmental health expert, had failed to adequately and scientifically demonstrate the link between glyphosate exposure and the land, livestock, and fisheries damage claimed, as well as the personal injury claims of "acute illness—skin irritation, vomiting, and respiratory problems . . . [and] an increased risk of cancer."[61] Dyn-Corp's lead counsel, Eric Lasker, asserted that "the company's position from the beginning has been that the spraying operations were completely safe, and that view was confirmed by the United States Department of State, the EPA, and the U.S. Department of Agriculture, and an independent expert panel appointed by the Organization of American States."[62] Indeed, Lasker's comments encapsulated how the U.S. government used environmental legislation and agencies to justify fumigation under Plan Colombia. During these years U.S. officials presented a continuity of rationales with their predecessors in the 1970s and early 1980s to preserve aerial defoliation as a weapon in the drug war.[63]

In the immediate aftermath of the first round of spraying in Putumayo in late 2000, a number of U.S. congresspeople expressed concerns about fumigation's potential risks. Among them was Senator Paul Wellstone of Minnesota, who visited Putumayo in December 2000 to observe a spraying operation. To his surprise, a Turbo Thrush passing overhead released the spray directly on the senator and his cohort, which included the U.S. ambassador to Colombia. Medical examination found no harm to Wellstone, and a Colombian policeman told journalist Robin Kirk that the senator had been doused to emphasize the herbicide's safety.[64] Nonetheless, the U.S. Congress added a provision to U.S. aid to Colombia that required the State Department to consult with the EPA to assess glyphosate's environmental and health risks. The State Department, starting in fiscal year 2002, had to provide a satisfactory report each year to Congress in order for fumigation aid to be released. Each subsequent report upheld glyphosate's overall safety while acknowledging—as Roundup's labeling indicates—that the herbicide can cause eye, skin, and mucous membrane irritation.

Employing the discourse of agriculture and echoing past State Department reports on herbicides used for drug crop eradication, the department's 2002 fact sheet on aerial eradication declared that glyphosate is "the most widely used agricultural chemical in the world. It is commercially available under many different brands in Colombia and worldwide. The aerial eradication program uses less than 13% of the total amount of glyphosate used in Colombia each year. The majority of the glyphosate used in Colombia is used by local farmers' weed control in crop fields."[65]

Similarly, the USDA's secretary of agriculture noted that "glyphosate is the most widely used herbicide in the world, available through both commercial and retail distributors. Glyphosate poses minimal health risks to humans and animals, is environmentally benign, and degrades rapidly in soil and water. It is USDA's determination that the risks involved with using glyphosate with commercially available adjuvants for narcotics eradication are minimal."[66]

Despite official assurances of environmental and health safety, critics pointed out flaws in the annual reports—namely, that the EPA was unable to conduct tests on the ground in Colombia and that overall EPA and USDA assessments of glyphosate had been conducted in a vacuum devoid of the specific environmental conditions in Colombia. The EPA in 2002 stated that glyphosate may cause acute eye irritation but was unable to determine this conclusively, given the lack of sufficient data and testing.[67] In 2005 an independent panel of agricultural and toxicology experts commissioned by the Organization of American States released a final report on glyphosate's environmental and health risks associated with coca and poppy eradication. Based upon the existing scientific literature and the five-person team's own observations and testing in Colombia, the report upheld U.S. and Colombian officials' claims about glyphosate's safety.

Placing the fumigation campaign within the context of glyphosate's wide use in agriculture in Colombia and worldwide, the team noted that the herbicide "is not highly mobile in the environment and is rapidly and tightly bound on contact with soil and aquatic sediments. Glyphosate has a very short biological activity in soils and water, does not biomagnify or move through the food chain, and does not leach into groundwater from soil."[68] The report concluded that "glyphosate itself has low toxicity to non-target organisms other than green plants. It is judged to have low acute and chronic toxicity, carcinogenic, mutagenic, or a reproductive toxicant. With respect to humans, is not considered hazardous, except for the possibility of eye and possibly skin irritation (from which recovery occurs)."[69] Combined with the surfactant Cosmo-flux, the mixtures' toxicity to humans, mammals, and aquatic life was deemed low and short-lived. Frequent overspraying of "surface waters" and possible damage to aquatic organisms was the area of greatest potential damage, according to the study, but the authors stated that further testing was needed.[70]

DANIEL WEIMER

Just as the discourse of agriculture allowed officials to use environmental legislation and government agencies (e.g., the EPA) to proclaim fumigation's safety, policy makers invoked environmentalism to level charges at traffickers and cultivators, whom they claimed were responsible for "ecological degradations." In 2003 the State Department's fact sheet "Environmental Consequences of the Illicit Coca Trade" listed a host of environmentally damaging practices associated with cocaine production and trafficking. These included deforestation (totaling 5.9 million acres over twenty years) due to slash-and-burn (swidden) agricultural practices that destroy "rain forest"; erosion and soil depletion that results from unsustainable swidden farming; the loss of biodiversity that comes with deforestation; the massive use of fertilizers, pesticides, and herbicides (ironically paraquat is mentioned) to grow illicit crops; and the soil and water pollution that comes from the many chemicals used in processing coca leaves into coca paste and refined cocaine (e.g., "millions of liters of kerosene, ethyl ether, sulfuric acid, potassium permanganate, acetone, and thousands of tons of lime and carbide"). The State Department noted that the loss of tropical rain forest resulted in species depletion—including species that may lead to medical advances—as well as releasing "large quantities of greenhouse gases, [which contribute] to global warming."[71]

These charges are certainly accurate on one level. However, official justifications of fumigation predicated on environmentalism ignore a critical flaw in policy makers' thinking. Rather than discourage illegal production, aerial eradication often encourages more cultivation and thus amplifies the environmental damage that comes with coca, poppy, and marijuana farming. From the 1970s through the 2000s, eradication displaced cultivators and cultivation, pushing them to new forest that was then cut down for drug crop agriculture. Eradication of these areas in turn generates another cycle of dislocation and deforestation, along with the other harms of drug production and processing.[72] Eradication temporarily diminished cultivation while growers and traffickers adapt to forced eradication through displacement into additional and often more remote terrain and the tending of smaller, harder-to-detect plots.

While the drug control gains are fleeting, the prices paid to growers and traffickers remain constant, thus highlighting the oft-reiterated fact that the source control (supply reduction) logic at the heart of fumigation proponents is fatally flawed. In Colombia, for instance, coca growing was more extensive in 2007 than in 2000, when Plan Colombia began. There was a drop in cultivation in 2002 and 2003 due to eradication, but again this slowdown was momentary as the growers and traffickers adapted by moving cultivation. Since a peak of 167,000 hectares in 2007, production in Colombia has declined and leveled off to between 60,000 to 70,000 hectares between 2008 and 2011.[73] Although this drop from 2007's peak may seem to confirm the logic of eradication, current levels of cultivation in Colombia (where coca farming has continued to spread into new regions, such as the Pacific Coast) are more than adequate to supply the global demand for cocaine.[74] The price and availability of cocaine throughout the globe has remained steady, hence nullifying the assertion that reduced supply equates to higher prices and diminished consumption.[75] Lastly, and critically, the fumigation program in Colombia (and in other nations) illustrates that aerial defoliation—by itself or within the context of militarized drug control and counterinsurgency operations—does not solve the long-term socioeconomic factors promoting drug crop cultivation and drug trafficking.

In September 2010, then U.S. secretary of state Hillary Clinton, speaking about rampant drug-related violence in Mexico, where aerial defoliation first appeared, remarked that Plan Colombia had succeeded in reducing bloodshed in Colombia. At the time of her comments (and since), the United States has continued to provide counterdrug and counterinsurgency aid to Colombia beyond the approximately six billion dollars afforded under Plan Colombia between 2000 and 2008.[76] Fumigation had continued, with one hundred thousand hectares sprayed in 2012.[77] Moreover, in 2013 the Colombian government began substantive peace talks with insurgents, with the FARC in 2014 requiring that cessation of defoliation operations be a main tenet of any peace program.[78] As these developments indicate, the story of drug trafficking and insurgency is an ongoing saga in Colombia.

When taken as a whole, events in Colombia over the past four decades reveal that the militarization of drug control, fostered by the United States, provided the context in which aerial fumigation persisted and escalated within U.S. foreign policy. Aerial eradication of drug crops performed an integral function within the militarization of drug policy in the Americas by acting as a *means* by which to attack so-called narcoguerrillas. This, in turn, served as the *rationale* for why the United States needed to assist the Colombian military tasked with providing security for fumigation operations. The U.S. military sites with drug control mandates in Latin American and the Caribbean, along with Colombian bases (particularly those at Tres Esquinas, Larandia, and Villagarzón), provided the logistical, material, and training architecture undergirding fumigation-cum-counterinsurgency operations. Ultimately, drug crop defoliation went hand in hand with the heightened and multivalent military and militarized U.S. presence in Latin America. In this sense, the drug war and the lens of environmental history affords fresh insights into U.S. military and foreign relations history, illuminates another chapter in the *longue durée* of herbicides in U.S. foreign policy, and helps detail distinct ways in which the global U.S. military presence has altered the environment. In 1976, when Thomas Mace flew reconnaissance flights over Mexican poppy fields, he may not have foreseen the long-term corollaries of his work, but his actions were part of the first episode in what grew into a decades-long war on plants.

NOTES

1   Author e-mail correspondence with Thomas H. Mace, May 10 and 11, 2012; June 20 and 21, 2012; and December 2 and 3, 2012.

2   Kate Doyle, "Operation Intercept: The Perils of Unilateralism," Document 2: June 18, 1969 [Task Force Report], White House, memorandum, National Security Archive, Nixon Presidential materials, White House Central Files: Subject Files, FG 221, Box 5, available at www.gwu.edu/~nsarchiv/NSAEBB/NSAEBB86?index2 .htm.

3   Memorandum, Peter Bourne to the President, "Mexican Narcotic Program," May 19, 1977, Folder "WHCF, SF Countries," Box CO 44, CO 104 7/1/77–12/31/77. See also Telegram, American Embassy Mexico to the Secretary of State, "Narcotics: Visit of Bourne and Falco," May 19, 1977, Folder Mexico, 5/10/77–6/7/78 [CF, O/A 155], Box 40, Special Assistant to the President—Peter Bourne, Jimmy Carter Library, which illustrates U.S. and Mexican officials' high hopes of defoliation's efficacy.

4   David F. Musto and Pamela Korsmeyer, *The Quest for Drug Control: Politics and Federal Policy in a Period of Increasing Substance Abuse, 1963–1981* (New Haven, CT: Yale University Press, 2002), 214.

5   For overviews of the cross-fertilization of diplomatic and environmental history, see Kurk Dorsey, "Dealing with the Dinosaur (and Its Swamp): Putting the Environment in Diplomatic History," *Diplomatic History* 29 (September 2005): 573–87; (entire issue) "Special Forum with Environmental History," *Diplomatic History* 32 (September 2008): 515–651; and J. R. McNeill and Corinna R. Unger,

eds., *Environmental Histories of the Cold War* (Cambridge: Cambridge University Press, 2010). See also Richard P. Tucker, *Insatiable Appetite: The United States and the Ecological Degradation of the Tropical World* (Berkeley: University of California Press, 2000); David Biggs, *Quagmire: Nation-Building and Nature in the Mekong Delta* (Seattle: University of Washington Press, 2011); and Edmund Russell, *War and Nature: Fighting Humans and Insects with Chemicals from World War I to Silent Spring* (Cambridge: Cambridge University Press, 2001).

In pointing out the corresponding interests of environmental and diplomatic history, Dorsey, in his essay "Dealing with the Dinosaur," notes that "nature transcends borders in a way that nothing else does" (page 576). Drugs and drug crops similarly dissolve borders (to the great frustration of drug control officials). Drugs, like the environment, are a transnational issue ripe for analysis from foreign relations and environmental scholars. For the applicability of drugs and drug control to transnational history, see Paul Gootenberg, "Talking about the Flow: Drugs, Borders, and the Discourse of Drug Control," *Cultural Critique* 71 (Winter 2009): 13–25.

6   David Zierler, "Against Protocol: Ecocide, Détente, and the Question of Chemical Warfare in Vietnam, 1969–1975," in McNeill and Unger, *Environmental Histories of the Cold War*, 227–56.

7   The term "narcoguerrilla," attributed to the U.S. ambassador to Colombia, Lewis Tambs, appeared in 1984 after the destruction of a cocaine laboratory in insurgent-held territory. Francisco E. Thoumi , *Illegal Drugs, Economy, and Society in the Andes* (Baltimore, MD: Woodrow Wilson Center and the Johns Hopkins University Press, 2003), 101–3.

8   Evelyn Krache Morris, "Into the Wind: The Kennedy Administration and the Use of Herbicides in South Vietnam" (PhD dissertation, Georgetown University, 2012), chapter 4; and Edwin A. Martini, *Agent Orange: History, Science, and the Politics of Uncertainty* (Amherst: University of Massachusetts Press, 2012), 56–57, 61.

9   Agent Orange is composed of 50 percent 2,4-D and 50 percent 2,4,5-T.

10 In this respect, the legality of the herbicide programs in Jamaica and Mexico during the 1970s relates to recent studies of Agent Orange and DDT by Edwin Martini and David Kinkela, respectively, which examine how U.S. foreign policy officials had to contend with new environmental regulations that affected the conduct of American foreign relations. See Martini, *Agent Orange*, 97–145; and Kinkela, *DDT and the American Century: Global Health, Environmental Politics, and the Pesticide That Changed the World* (Chapel Hill: University of North Carolina Press, 2011), 136–81.

11 Telegram, U.S. Embassy Kingston to D.C., "Narcotics: Operation Buccaneer," May 10, 1974; Telegram, U.S. Embassy Kingston to D.C., "Operation Buccaneer," June 21, 1974, Central Foreign Policy Files, 1973–1975, RG 59 [retrieved from Access to Archival Databases (hereafter AAD)].

12 In the development and execution of Operation Ranch Hand, American officials made similar arguments—that herbicides were a replacement for manpower. See

David Zeiler, *The Invention of Ecocide: Agent Orange, Vietnam, and the Scientists Who Changes the Way We Think about the Environment* (Athens: University of Georgia Press, 2011), 81–82; and Krache Morris, "Into the Wind," chapter 6.

13 Ambassador Gerard to D.C., "Operation Buccaneer," June 21, 1974, Central Foreign Policy Files, 1973–1975, RG 59, AAD.

14 Telegram, American Embassy Kingston to DEA, D.C., "Operation Buccaneer Sitrep 2," July 9, 1974; Telegram, American Embassy Kingston to DEA, D.C., "Operation Buccaneer Sitrep 3," July 17, 1974; and Telegram, American Embassy Kingston to DEA, D.C., "Dr. Walter Gentner, US Department of Agriculture Operation Buccaneer," July 26, 1974, Central Foreign Policy Files, 1973–1975, RG 59, AAD.

15 Telegram, American Embassy Kingston to DEA, D.C., "Dr. Walter Gentner, US Department of Agriculture Operation Buccaneer," July 26, 1974, Central Foreign Policy Files, 1973–1975, RG 59, AAD.

16 Telegram, American Embassy Kingston, D.C., "Operation Buccaneer: Matalon Statement," September 6, 1974, Central Foreign Policy Files, 1973–1975, RG 59, AAD.

17 Telegram, American Embassy Kingston, D.C., "Codel Murphy," September 25, 1974, Central Foreign Policy Files, 1973–1975, RG 59, AAD. The DEA publication *Drug Enforcement* ran an extensive article on Operation Buccaneer (the name for the joint U.S.–Jamaican drug control program in 1974), but the article made no mention of herbicide use—either the proposed program or possible future programs. Walter E. Sears, "Operation Buccaneer," *Drug Enforcement* (Winter 1975): 6–15.

18 Domestic Council Drug Abuse Task Force, *White Paper on Drug Abuse* (Washington, D.C.: Government Printing Office, 1975), 97–98; Memorandum for Jim Cannon, "Drug Review Task Force," August 29, 1975, White House Central Files, Subject File, Box 7, HE 5–1: 8/22/75–10/11/75, Gerald R. Ford Library (hereafter GRFL); Memorandum for Secretary of State, *White Paper on Drug Abuse*, October 16, 1975; U.S. Department of State Response to the *White Paper on Drug Abuse*, December 12, 1975, RG 59, Box 32, 150/72/7/1, Thailand 1975, NA; Memorandum for Brent Scowcroft, December 18, 1975, White House Central Files, Subject File, Box 7, HE 5–1: 12/11/75–12/20/75, GRFL.

19 Telegram, Secretary of State, Washington to American Embassy, Mexico, "Herbicides for Poppy Eradication," March 21, 1975, Central Foreign Policy Files, 1973–1975, RG 59, AAD.

20 For a detailed look at the development of the herbicide program in Mexico, see Daniel Weimer, *Seeing Drugs: Modernization, Counterinsurgency, and U.S. Narcotics Control in the Third World, 1969–1976* (Kent, OH: Kent State University Press, 2011), 172–89.

21 Telegram, DEA/Mexico City to DEA, D.C., "Herbicides," September 24, 1975, RG 59, Box 20, "Mexico Program Development," International Narcotics Matters Country Files, NA.

22 The preceding paragraphs on the paraquat controversy are drawn from Musto and Korsmeyer, *Quest for Drug Control*, 212–15, 226–30; "U.S. Gives Ways to Avoid Mar-

ijuana-Paraquat Danger," *New York Times*, May 13, 1979; Senate Committee on the Judiciary, *The Mexican Connection: Hearings Before the Subcommittee to Investigate Juvenile Delinquency of the Committee on the Judiciary*, February 10 and April 19, 1978, 95th Cong., 2nd sess. (Washington, D.C.: Government Printing Office, 1978), 142–43; and Telegram, Lee Dogoloff to Congressman Lester Wolff, "Percy Amendment," August 7, 1979, NLC-16–122–5–23–9; Memorandum, From Stu Eizenstat and Lee Dogoloff to Griffin Bell, Attorney General, "Mexican Marihuana Spraying Program," August 9, 1979, Folder DPS, Eizenstat, Box 189, Drug Policy [CF, O/A 727] [1]; and Memorandum, Warren Christopher to the President, September 127, 979, NLC-128–14–11–17–4, Jimmy Carter Library.

In mid-1978, NORML filed a lawsuit against the State Department requesting an injunction of U.S. support for the herbicide program. NORML claimed that U.S. aid violated NEPA because the State Department did not complete an Environmental Impact Statement (EIS) required under NEPA. The U.S. District Court ruled that while the State Department needed to complete an EIS, it did not grant an injunction, and thus U.S. environmental law did not prohibit Washington's backing of defoliation in Mexico. *National Organization for the Reform of Marijuana Laws (NORML) v. U.S. Department of State*, 452 F. Supp. 1226 (1978)-U.S. District Court-District of Colombia Memorandum Opinion at http://scholar.google.com/scholar_case?case=4020276725637732144&q=National+Organization+for+the+Reform+of+Marijuana+Laws+%28NORML%29+v.+U.S.+Department+of+State,+452+F.+Supp.+1226+&hl=en&as_sdt=2,49; and U.S. Department of State, Bureau for International Narcotics Matters, *Narcotics Control in Mexico: Environmental Analysis of Effects in Mexico* (Washington, D.C.: Government Printing Office, 1979).

23   House Committee on the Judiciary, *Eradication of Marihuana with Paraquat: Hearings Before the Subcommittee on Crime, October 5 and November 17, 1983*, 98th Cong., 1st sess., 128–29. On the backlash against drug abuse in the late 1970s and early 1980s, see David F. Musto, *The American Disease: Origins of Narcotics Control*, 3rd ed. (New York: Oxford University Press, 1999), 259–67.

24   Bolivia, which conducted fumigation operations between 1982 and 1986, ceased chemical eradication because of cultivator protests and environmental concerns, as did Peru for the same reasons, where in 2000 the government banned aerial defoliation programs that occurred intermittently during the 1990s. On Peru, see David Scott Palmer, "Peru, Drugs, and Shining Path," in *Drug Trafficking in the Americas*, ed. Bruce M. Bagley and William O. Walker III (Miami, FL: University of Miami North-South Press, 1996), 181–82; and Isaías Rojas, "Peru: Drug Control Policy, Human Rights, and Democracy," in *Drugs and Democracy in Latin America*, ed. Coletta A. Youngers and Eileen Rosin (Boulder, CO: Lynne Rienner Publishers, 2005), 211–13. For Bolivia, see Rensselaer W. Lee III, *The White Labyrinth: Cocaine and Political Power* (Brunswick, NJ: Transaction Publishers, 1989), 206–7.

25   Lina Britto, "A Trafficker's Paradise: The 'War on Drugs' and the New Cold War in Colombia," *Contemporanea: Historia y problemas del siglo XX* 1, no. 1 (2010): 159–66, available at www.geipar.udelar.edu.uy/wp-content/uploads/2012/05/10_Dossiero8.pdf.

26   Juan Gabriel Tokatlian, "The United States and Illegal Crops in Colombia: The Tragic Mistake of Futile Fumigation," UC Berkley Center for Latin American Studies, Working Paper No. 3, June 2003, pages 3–6, available at http://clas.berkeley .edu/sites/default/files/shared/docs/papers/Tokatlianwithcover.pdf; Britto, "Trafficker's Paradise," 167; and Ricardo Vargas, "The Anti-Drug Policy, Aerial Spraying of Illicit Crop and Their Social, Environmental, and Political Impacts in Colombia," *Journal of Drug Issues* 32 (Winter 2002): 11–60, 12.

27   For a critique of inaccuracies inherent in the term "cartel," see Michael Kenney, *From Pablo to Osama: Trafficking and Terrorist Networks, Government Bureaucracies, and Competitive Adaptation* (University Park: Pennsylvania State University Press, 2007).

28   Álvaro Camacho Guizado and Andreés López Restrepo, "From Smugglers to Drug Lords to *Traquetos*: Changes in the Colombian Illicit Drug Organizations," in *Peace, Democracy, and Human Rights in Colombia*, ed. Christopher Welna and Gustavo Gallán (South Bend, IN: University of Notre Dame Press, 2007), 73–79; Tokatlian, "United States and Illegal Crops in Colombia," 6–7; and María Clemencia Ramírez Lemus, Kimberly Stanton, and John Walsh, "Colombia: A Vicious Circle of Drugs and War," in *Drugs and Democracy in Latin America: The Impact of U.S. Policy*, ed. Coletta A. Younger and Eileen Rosin (Boulder, CO: Lynne Reinner Publishers, 2005), 103–4.

29   Vargas, "Anti-Drug Policy," 16–17; and Tokatlian, "United States and Illegal Crops in Colombia," 8.

30   Tokatlian, "United States and Illegal Crops in Colombia," 7.

31   Thoumi, *Illegal Drugs, Economy, and Society*, 84–85; and Thoumi, "Why the Illegal Psychoactive Drugs Industry Grew in Colombia," in *Drug Trafficking in the Americas*, ed. Bruce Bagley and William O. Walker III (Miami, FL: University of Miami North-South Press, 1996), 77–96.

32   Kenneth R. Young, "Environmental and Social Consequences of Coca/Cocaine in Peru: Policy Alternatives and a Research Agenda," in *Dangerous Harvest: Drug Plants and the Transformation of Indigenous Landscapes*, ed. Michael K. Steinberg, Joseph J. Hobbs, and Kent Mathewson (New York: Oxford University Press, 2004), 250; and Paul Gootenberg, *Andean Cocaine: The Making of a Global Drug* (Chapel Hill: University of North Carolina Press, 2008), 315.

33   Vanda Felbab-Brown, *Shooting Up: Counterinsurgency and the War on Drugs* (Washington, D.C.: Brookings Institution Press, 2010), 72; and Thoumi, "Why the Illegal Psychoactive Drugs Industry Grew in Colombia," 79–84.

34   For the drug-trafficking activities of M-19 and the ELN, see Felbab-Brown, *Shooting Up*, 89–94.

35   Ibid., 79–81; and Ramírez Lemus, Stanton, and Walsh, "Colombia," 106.

36   The best starting point for exploring the myths and dynamics of the crack scare in the United States is Craig Reinarman and Harry G. Divine, eds., *Crack in America: Demon Drug and Social Justice* (Berkeley: University of California Press, 1997).

37   Kenney, *From Pablo to Osama*, 88–90; and Ramírez Lemus, Stanton, and Walsh, "Colombia," 104–5.

38 Ramírez Lemus, Stanton, and Walsh, "Colombia," 105.

39 See Tokatlian, "United States and Illegal Crops," 8–14, for a more detailed look at the ebb and flow of fumigation during these years.

40 Ramírez Lemus, Stanton, and Walsh, "Colombia," 104–5; and Tokatlian, "United States and Illegal Crops," 20–23.

41 On U.S. counterinsurgency aid and policy in Central America, see Odd Arne Westad, *The Global Cold War* (New York: Cambridge University Press, 2007), 331–48; and Stephen G. Rabe, *The Killing Zone: The United States Wages Cold War in Latin America* (New York: Oxford University Press, 2012), 144–74.

42 Document 21, Defense Intelligence Agency, Intelligence Agency Report, "Drug Cultivation and Guerrilla Support," December 11, 1991, in National Security Archive Briefing Book No. 69, *War in Colombia: Guerrillas, Drugs, and Human Rights in U.S.-Colombia Policy, 1988–2002,* vol. 2, *Counterdrug Operation: The Most Dangerous Flying in the So-Called Drug War,* available at www.gwu.edu/~nsarchiv/NSAEBB/NSAEBB69/part2.html.

43 Adam Isacson, "The U.S. Military in the War on Drugs," in *Drugs and Democracy,* ed. Youngers and Rosin, 28. Regarding drug policy militarization within the United States, see Timothy J. Dunn, *The Militarization of the U.S.-Mexico Border, 1978–1992: Low-Intensity Conflict Doctrine Comes Home* (Austin: Center for Mexican American Studies, University of Texas at Austin, 1996), 103–45.

44 National Security Archive Briefing Book, *War in Colombia: Guerrillas, Drugs, and Human Rights in U.S.-Colombia Policy, 1988–2002,* vol. 1, *The Andean Strategy: "Attacking Drugs by Hitting the Insurgency,"* available at www.gwu.edu/~nsarchiv/NSAEBB/NSAEBB69/part1.html.

45 The formalization of charging foreign militaries with source control within U.S. drug policy did not mean that the policy was wholly novel. For instance, during the 1970s the United States provided aircraft and surveillance equipment to the Burmese military for counternarcotics/counterinsurgency operations against leftist rebels tied to heroin production and trafficking. Given this, the "narcoguerrilla" concept popularized in the 1980s was already established in theory and practice. Weimer, *Seeing Drugs,* 144–71, 189–92.

46 Juan Gabriel Tokatlian, "Drug Summitry: A Colombian Perspective," in *Drug Trafficking in the Americas,* ed. Bagley and Walker, 138.

47 Isacson, "U.S. Military in the War on Drugs," 18–19, 26.

48 Ibid., 29–30, 32; Adam Isacson, Joy Olson, and Lisa Haugaard, "Below the Radar: U.S. Military Programs with Latin America, 1997–2007," Latin American Working Group, March 2007, 19–21.

49 Isacson, "U.S. Military in the War on Drugs," 34.

50 Ramírez Lemus, Stanton, and Walsh, "Colombia," 105–7.

51 Juan Forero, "U.S. Training Readies New Colombian Antidrug Warriors," *New York Times,* December 10, 2000.

52 Ramírez Lemus, Stanton, and Walsh, "Colombia," 107–8; and Lesley Gill, *The School of the Americas: Military Training and Political Violence in the Americas* (Durham, NC: Duke University Press, 2004), 181–82.

53   Isacson, "U.S. Military in the War on Drugs," 40–41

54   Felbab-Brown, *Shooting Up*, 101.

55   Because of human rights abuses by the Colombian military and paramilitary groups, the Clinton administration had halted aid to Colombian military and police units with verified human rights violations. However, the events of 9/11 changed the thinking in Washington, D.C. In 2002, Congress lifted the restriction on U.S. aid to be used only on counterdrug operations—the United States could now directly support the Colombian military's operations against insurgents. Adam Isacson, "Washington's 'New War' in Colombia: The War on Drugs Meets the War on Terror," *NACLA Report on the Americas*, March–April 2003; Ramírez Lemus, Stanton, and Walsh, "Colombia," 109–10; and Felbab-Brown, *Shooting Up*, 101–2. A good account of the complicated logic behind Washington's counterdrug-cum-counterinsurgency aid to Colombia and the issue of human rights and paramilitaries is Robin Kirk's *More Terrible Than Death: Massacres, Drugs, and America's War in Colombia* (New York: Public Affairs, 2003).

56   Connie Veillette and Jose E. Arvelo-Velez, "Colombia and Aerial Eradication of Drug Crops: U.S. Policy and Issues," Congressional Research Service Report, RL32052, August 28, 2003, 1–2, available at www.hsdl.org/?view&did=451623.

57   Ramírez Lemus, Stanton, and Walsh, "Colombia," 112.

58   Document 42, U.S. Embassy Colombia cable, "Request for Training Plan and Phaseout Timeline for DynCorp Operations in Colombia," April 22, 1998, in National Security Archive Briefing Book No. 69, *War in Colombia: Guerrillas, Drugs, and Human Rights in U.S.-Colombia Policy, 1988–2002*, vol. 2, *Counterdrug Operation: The Most Dangerous Flying in the So-Called Drug War*, available at www.gwu.edu/~nsarchiv/NSAEBB/NSAEBB69/part2.html.

59   Isacson, Olson, and Haugaard, "Below the Radar," 21; e-mail correspondence with Adam Isacson, September 9, 2013; and Asociacion Minga, "The Armed Conflict in Lower Putumayo," November 20, 2008, with the Support of the Center for International Policy and Witness for Peace, pages 3–4.

60   Felbab-Brown, *Shooting Up*, 102.

61   "Plaintiffs to Appeal Dismissal of 'Plan Colombia' Lawsuit against DynCorp," *BLT: The Blog of the Legal Times*, March 11, 2013, available at http://legaltimes.typepad.com/blt/2013/03/plaintiffs-to-appeal-dismissal-of-plan-colombia-lawsuit-against-dyncorp-1.html.

62   Ibid.

63   On public and private protest against defoliation within Colombia protests during the 1990s and 2000s, see Tokatlian, "United States and Illegal Crops in Colombia," 22–23; Ramírez Lemus, Stanton, and Walsh, "Colombia," 120–21; and Kirk, *More Terrible Than Death*, 243.

64   Kirk, *More Terrible Than Death*, 263–64.

65   "State Department Q & A on Aerial Eradication Program in Colombia," March 24, 2003, *IIP Digital*, available at http://iipdigital.usembassy.gov/st/english/article/2003/03/20030325113253neergeo.3604242.html#axzz2YwnmXG0s.

66   U.S. Department of State, "Response for Secretary of Agriculture to Secretary of

State," August 14, 2002, available at www.state.gov/j/inl/rls/rpt/aeicc/13246.htm.

67 Ramírez Lemus, Stanton, and Walsh, "Colombia," 119–20.

68 OAS, "Environmental and Human Health Assessment of the Aerial Spray Program for Coca and Poppy Control in Colombia," a report prepared for the Inter-American Drug Abuse Control Commission (CICAD) section of the OAS, Washington, D.C., March 31, 2005, 10.

69 Ibid.

70 Ibid., 11.

71 U.S. Department of State, "Environmental Consequences of the Illicit Coca Trade," March 17, 2003, available at http://2001–2009.state.gov/p/inl/rls/fs/3807.htm.

72 Vargas, "Anti-Drug Policy," 15–19, 28; and Martin Jelsma, *Vicious Circle: The Chemical and Biological "War on Drugs"* (Amsterdam: Transnational Institute, March 2001), 4–8, also available at www.tni.org/sites/www.tni.org/files/download/viciouscircle-e.pdf; and Stephanie Joyce, "Environmental Casualties of the War on Drugs," *Environmental Health Perspectives* 107 (February 1999): 74–77, 75.

73 Felbab-Brown, *Shooting Up*, 102; and United Nations Office of Drug Control (UNDOC), *Colombia: Monitoreo de Cultivos de Coca 2011*, June 2012, page 11, available at www.unodc.org/documents/crop-monitoring/Colombia/Censo_cultivos_coca_2011.pdf.

74 UNDOC, *Colombia: Monitoreo de Cultivos de Coca 2011*, June 2012, page 21, available at www.unodc.org/documents/crop-monitoring/Colombia/Censo_cultivos_coca_2011.pdf. For an intriguing anthropological and theoretical account of coca cultivation's and trafficking's inroads into the Pacific coastal regions, see Michael Taussig, *My Cocaine Museum* (Chicago: University of Chicago Press, 2004), 139–47.

75 See, for instance, the statistics on global cocaine prices in UNODC, *World Drug Report 2012*, 35–42, chapter 1, available at www.unodc.org/documents/data-and-analysis/WDR2012/WDR_2012_Chapter1.pdf.

76 Kevin Young, "Two, Three, Many Colombias," *Foreign Policy in Focus*, December 29, 2010, available at http://fpif.org/two_three_many_colombias/. In 2009 the United States and Colombia signed a defense cooperation agreement that would have allowed the U.S. military to operate in seven Colombian military bases and installations for a ten-year period, during which time U.S. military commanders would not be required to receive authorization from Colombia for each deployment of U.S. personnel. In August 2010 the Colombian Constitutional Court invalidated the agreement. As of April 2013, no new deal has been reached between the United States and Colombia, but U.S. personnel and private defense contractors still regularly operate in Colombia with Bogotá's approval as they have for the past two decades. See "U.S.-Colombia Defense Cooperation Agreement," available at www.securityassistance.org/latin-america-and-caribbean/blog/2009/11/04/us-colombia-defense-cooperation-agreement; and "Colombian Court Strikes Down U.S. Defense Agreement," available at www.securityassistance.org/latin-america-and-caribbean/blog/2010/08/18/colombian-court-strikes-down-us-defense-agreement.

77   INL, U.S. State Department, "2013 International Narcotics Control Strategy
     Report," March 1, 2013, available at www.state.gov/j/inl/rls/nrcrpt/2013/
     vol1/204048.htm#Colombia.
78   "The Twilight of Fumigation in Colombia," available at www.securityassistance.
     org/latin-america-and-caribbean/blog/2014/04/03/twilight-struggle-over
     -fumigation-colombia.

CHAPTER 6

ADDRESSING ENVIRONMENTAL RISKS AND MOBILIZING DEMOCRACY?

Policy on Public Participation in U.S. Military Superfund Sites

JENNIFER LISS OHAYON

A LTHOUGH they are no longer commissioned for battle, former military lands around the United States have become sites of struggles over environmental remediation. Since 1988, hundreds of major military installations have been closed under the direction of the federal government.[1] A legacy of toxic contamination is often left behind, with many of these installations being listed among the nation's most hazardous waste sites. This chapter reviews the federal policy on public participation in the environmental remediation of former U.S. military sites, investigating actual practices of public participation and stakeholder inclusion at remediation sites. While many sites expanded participation to include citizen advisory boards, which are important venues for debate as compared to traditional public participation methods such as comment periods, deliberation is not necessarily democratic.

There are few mechanisms built into these efforts to ensure agencies are responsive to public input, which can be particularly problematic in sites where long-standing socioeconomic and environmental inequalities have strained military-community relations and led to a lack of trust for governmental agencies. Through a case study approach looking at disbanded deliberative bodies, I argue that for citizen advisory boards to be meaningful vehicles for public participation in contentious environments, the boards need to have rigorous evaluations of governmental accountability. Rather than aiming at securing public trust in, or even acceptance of, cleanup plans, these programs must pay attention to the historical and political variables that structure institutional relationships and reactions to environmental risks.

MILITARY CONTAMINATION

The amount of lands damaged by military activities grew substantially in the twentieth century, both domestically and abroad, as a result of two world wars, the Vietnam War, and the Cold War. The closure and realignment of more than a hundred major U.S. military bases and hundreds of smaller military installations increased public awareness of military pollution.[2] Before the 1980s millions of acres of soil and water were contaminated in and near Department of Defense (DOD) sites in the United States and its territories, although a widespread lack of record keeping has made it difficult to comprehensively calculate the extent and nature of that contamination. In the mid-1990s it was projected that there were approximately 20,000 potentially contaminated sites at 1,722 active installations and about 8,000 potential sites at 1,632 former bases.[3] Contamination from "industrial" uses includes petroleum products, heavy metals, polychlorinated biphenyls, and volatile organic compounds. It can also include more "exotic" military compounds used in training exercises and experimentation, such as explosives (e.g., trinitrotoluene, dinitrotoluene), unexploded ordnances, radioactive materials, and nerve agents. Contamination is complex in the majority of sites, including groundwater, soil, and surface water.[4] In some cases, contamination spreads far beyond the points of origin in military sites, through transport by wind currents, leaching in groundwater, or bioaccumulation in wildlife species.

Environmental Regulation of Military Lands

Decommissioned military bases are currently subject to federal, state, and local government oversight, and they have attracted various forms of public and scientific scrutiny. Until the late 1970s, few laws regulated the disposal of hazardous wastes by private industry, and none applied to the military. The passage in 1980 of the Comprehensive Environmental Response, Compensation, and Liability Act (CERCLA), also known as the Superfund Act, gave the EPA authority and limited funding to identify and compel responsible parties to remediate land with hazardous substances that may endanger public health and ecosystems. Within the Superfund program, the EPA developed a National Priorities List (NPL) of the most contaminated and hazardous sites. CERCLA did not initially cover federal properties, and the military was at first exempt from environmental regulation. Congress passed the Superfund Amendments and Reauthorization Act (SARA) in 1986, which requires the Department of Defense to comply with the regulations. To date, the EPA lists 130 of the 1,320 Superfund sites, in which the responsible party can be a "private" or federal entity, such as military sites. Military sites thus comprise about 10 percent of the total most hazardous designated sites in the United States.[5] Over 80 percent of the Superfund sites in which the responsible party is a federal agency are DOD sites. The Department of Energy is responsible for many of the remaining federal facilities on the Superfund list, in large part because of its nuclear weapons programs. Furthermore, military sites tend to be of greater size than contaminated sites in which the responsible party is a private entity. Thus military-related activities are responsible for the majority of the contaminated federal lands in the United States.[6]

DOD sites encompass some of the country's most difficult, largest, and expensive cleanup sites. Under the Superfund program, the DOD is the lead agency during cleanup, meaning the military determines the resources it is willing to spend on cleanup and can select its own cleanup strategies and postremedial monitoring approach. CERCLA, however, gives the EPA oversight of investigations, cleanup, and plans for long-term operation and maintenance for sites on the National Priorities List. CERCLA does not establish regulatory standards for substances but requires compliance with the standards established by the EPA or other regulatory agencies, when they are present.[7] Other governmental agencies, such as the state-level EPA and the Department of Toxic Substances Control, can be members of base cleanup teams and influence remedial activities. Although local governmental entities have a limited role under the Superfund program, remediated land is often transferred to cities or counties, and the military will enter into negotiations with these actors over acceptable cleanup standards.

Policy Surrounding Public Participation in Military Superfund Sites

In order to increase accountability and incorporate the priorities of the public into scientific policy decisions, academic scholars, activists, and practitioners called for extending public participation programs. The call for participatory methods appealed to the democratic ideal of the public having a fundamental right to participate in decisions that affect them. In addition to expanding participatory processes on democratic grounds, academics and the public outlined substantive rationales. According to these arguments, "lay" judgments are important because of the chronic uncertainty of risk calculations and to influence federal and state authorities to incorporate societal values into decision-making processes.[8] Incorporating public participation can bring about more precautionary sampling and monitoring, evaluate the credibility of experts based on potential conflicts of interest, and critique the issues receiving priority policy attention.

As the disastrous environmental consequences of militarism and certain technological developments became increasingly apparent to the public, it stood to reason that new hazardous waste legislation, such as the Superfund Act, passed in part as a response to public advocacy, would have provisions to incorporate public participation into decisions on environmental remediation.[9] The National Contingency Plan (NCP), the primary regulation of the Superfund program, mandates public notices and formal public comment periods during key stages of the cleanup, including when the Proposed Plan (a document that outlines a preferred cleanup remedy) is released. The NCP establishes nine criteria for selection of a cleanup program, with community acceptance being one criterion.[10]

The traditional mechanisms for public participation required by the NCP, such as public notices and comment periods, have been critiqued as focusing primarily on agency-to-public communication and soliciting a limited set of public views.[11] As a result, public participation efforts have been criticized as attempts to defuse public challenges and ensure agencies have credibility rather than allow community engagement efforts to shape political decisions.[12] Later initiatives for public participation

JENNIFER LISS OHAYON

thus aimed to guarantee that community involvement would be more meaningful and effective. In addition to meeting its public participation requirements as per the NCP, the DOD established citizen advisory boards as the primary way for the public to have a two-way dialogue with the military and regulatory agencies over cleanup.[13] Restoration advisory boards (RABs), a type of citizen advisory board, were established in 1994 through a DOD/EPA partnership at most major closing bases; the program was later expanded to cover more than three hundred active, former and closing facilities.[14] The RABs are intended to be the primary forum for partnership among local residents, community and environmental groups, the installation, the EPA, and local and state agencies; they provide a mechanism for public input on remedial programs, including cleanup strategies, standards, and technologies.[15]

A committee made up of state and federal officials, environmental activists, labor unions, and representatives of Native peoples, on whose lands many hazardous wastes sites are located, originally advised the DOD and the EPA on the structure of citizen advisory boards. The committee produced the Consensus Recommendation of the Federal Facilities Environmental Restoration Dialogue Committee (FFERD), also known as the Keystone Report.[16] A year later, the DOD/EPA partnership promulgated its own joint guidelines on the RAB, which drew from and modified the Keystone Report. The report called for RABs to be independent of officials and envisioned the ability for community members to produce inclusive agendas including such topics as land use and social, cultural, and aesthetic issues. In contrast, according to the DOD/EPA guidelines, RABs cannot address future land use of the site and must have a base official as a strong cochair.[17]

Despite the widespread implementation of these boards and the resources dedicated to them, there has been little formal study of their effectiveness in practice. Although there has been academic interest in public participation programs, there is no consistent measure to evaluate the success of participatory methods, with the criteria for successful participation changing across settings, participatory forms, and the expectations of stakeholders.[18] Measures for evaluating the success of participatory mechanisms include informing the public of specific issues or a general increase in public awareness, incorporating residents' values and preferences in policy decisions, as well as increasing the legitimacy of decision making and institutions.[19] Social scientists have critiqued more instrumental approaches to public participation, which aim, for example, to increase the trust in government institutions or assist in policy compliance.[20] According to the RAB guidelines, the boards are meant to offer communities an opportunity to provide input into the remedial process and ensure that cleanups are "responsive to community needs."[21] The programmatic objectives convey that they are meant to have substantive outcomes for how the public engages the issues at stake in environmental remediation.

This chapter examines two case studies of RAB implementation in which there was active participation by the public and the environmental risks of site pollution were perceived to be high. Despite the enthusiasm around citizen advisory boards in the participatory era, the actualization of this policy was contentious in the military context, with struggles over the authority of these boards, the accountability of agencies, and the social responsibilities of the military beyond technical environmental remediation.

CASE STUDIES AND METHODS

This chapter explores two case studies from California—sites at Hunters Point Naval Shipyard and the former Fort Ord—to assess how DOD/EPA public participation programs have functioned in practice. I designed and conducted a case study approach to examine the implications of policy and program design for public participation. I investigate the gap between policy promise and outcomes and analyze why certain RABs were disbanded. In both case studies the military disbanded the RAB; in Fort Ord it was disbanded in 1999 (five years after formation), and in the Shipyard in 2009 (sixteen years after formation) because of competing visions concerning their purpose and significant conflict among actors. Both sites currently rely on public outreach programs that focus on newsletters and fact sheets, meetings and workshops, site tours, and technical assistance grants. Why did the citizen advisory boards fail to function as intended? Deliberation is an essential part of public participation, but more attention is needed as to how deliberation is structured. How in particular can deliberative spaces function when military-public relations are strained as a result of historical and institutional variables and there are disagreements over board authority and agency accountability?

Approximately 10 percent of military Superfund bases are found in

California, home to Hunters Point Naval Shipyard and Fort Ord. In 2012 and 2013, I conducted eighteen semistructured interviews and numerous informal discussions involving key players and institutions, including former RAB members, community technical advisers, community involvement coordinators and remedial project managers from the EPA, and project managers from the California Department of Toxic Substances Control (DTSC; the primary state oversight agency) as well as military personnel. In the interviews I ask about the purposes and goals of community involvement activities, the scope of issues that should be considered, and the development of agendas, decision-making processes, and meeting facilitation. Ethics approval was obtained for this research, and interview participants are kept confidential throughout this chapter, with reference only to community status or agency affiliation. I recorded the interviews, and quotations from interviews are verbatim. I also relied on participant observation of twenty-four workshops, meetings, and tours in both sites from 2011 to 2014. Meetings were not recorded, and quotations from meetings are taken from field notes and thus may be paraphrased. These methods are complemented by additional available documents, including community involvement plans, policy guidelines, and minutes from RAB meetings.

Both Fort Ord and the Shipyard have complex contamination and wide-ranging cleanup programs. Each site had active involvement from community members and groups exposed to disparate environmental hazards, causing tensions among public participants and agency representatives. Although RABs have typical problems with implementation across sites, particularly related to issues with time commitment and access to information, some RABs have been less acrimonious. In both case studies community members invested significant time in public participation processes and a high level of public awareness existed, as a result of local media coverage, legal disputes, and issues arising during cleanup. Surveys across different sites have found that a majority of respondents are often not aware that there is a Superfund site near their home.[22] An absence of public challenges on a cleanup program is not necessarily indicative of community acceptance; instead, it can be a result of lack of public awareness or acquiescence.[23] Examining public participation in areas with high interest and debate over cleanup programs gives insights into the opportunities and barriers for these programs to incorporate public input, particularly when issues of social rights are at stake.

Hunters Point Naval Shipyard

The San Francisco Bay Area became deeply entwined with militarism in the twenty century. Located in southeastern San Francisco, adjacent to the San Francisco Bay, Hunters Point Naval Shipyard consists of 866 acres, 420 acres on land and 446 acres under water. Between 1941 and 1991 the Shipyard was subjected to a number of naval and industrial activities that left its land, groundwater, and bay sediments polluted with heavy metals, polychlorinated biphenyls, volatile organic compounds, pesticides, petroleum compounds, and radionuclides.

The Shipyard's main activities during World War II were building, repairing, and maintaining naval ships and submarines. The Shipyard was the site for radiological decontamination efforts and disposal of ships involved in Operation Crossroads, the two underwater nuclear blasts at Bikini Atoll in 1946, as well as ships involved in other atomic weapons tests. The Shipyard's Naval Radiological Defense Laboratory (NRDL), operational from 1946 until 1969, did research and experiments on the effects of radiation. The NRDL decontaminated these irradiated warships of residual plutonium from bombs and fission products through sandblasting ship bodies and burning fuel in the Shipyard's boilers. From the time of its commission to throughout the 1950s, the NDLR did experiments on tens of thousands of live animals to investigate the biological effects of radiation exposure. It also conducted research on nuclear by-products sent from other laboratories. Although much of the waste was removed in barrels to be sunk near the Farallon Islands, thirty miles offshore, radionuclides were discharged into the sewer and storm drain lines from buildings used for radiological research and maintenance, littered the lab and storage rooms, and also went into an on-site landfill.[24] These areas are currently being investigated and remediated under CERCLA. From 1976 to 1986 the site was leased to a private ship repair company and, in response to violations of safeguards for toxic substances and massive illegal toxic dumping, the facility was eventually raided by the U.S. Federal Bureau of Investigation and the San Francisco District Attorney's Office.

The surrounding community in Bayview–Hunters Point is composed predominantly of low-income people of color, including African-American and Asian-identified populations.[25] At its peak employment level during the close of World War II, the Shipyard employed over seventeen thousand civilians, many of them African-American migrants from the Southern states, escaping Jim Crow laws and in search of more steady employment. They arrived in San Francisco to be faced with different segregation laws and customs in the form of a restrictive job market and discriminatory housing polices for many of the city's neighborhoods. As a result, many African Americans settled in the Bayview–Hunters Point neighborhood, around their main source of employment, the Shipyard. When naval operations ceased at the Shipyard in 1974, thousands of people lost their jobs. In 2011, the Hunters Point Shipyard community had approximately 54 percent unemployment.[26] This reality contributed to great interest regarding the possibility for jobs in environmental cleanup as well as concern over the gentrifying potential of base redevelopment. The Shipyard is the most expensive redevelopment project of a former naval base in the United States and will house business and commercial centers and private residences.

In 1989, the EPA placed the Shipyard on its National Priorities List, making it the only federal Superfund site in San Francisco. The Department of Public Health, federal and state agencies, community organizations, and the media disagree about the nature and extent of environmental risks from the Shipyard. Studies by the Department of Public Health indicate the surrounding communities have the highest levels of cancer and respiratory disease in San Francisco, although there is etiological uncertainty regarding the relationship between the health issues and specific environmental effluents originating from the Shipyard as the area is heavily industrialized. Other issues that strained community relations in the Shipyard include a landfill fire in 2000, for which the navy was fined by the EPA for its failure to notify the agency or the community, and problems with air monitoring during redevelopment activities. Significant conflict has occurred between the navy and community groups on various remedial strategies, including containment measures that create a physical barrier between contaminated soil and the surrounding environment. In 1994 the navy was sued by a coalition of environmentalists, anglers, and public interest groups, including original RAB members, for nineteen thousand violations of the Clean Water Act. The lawsuit, based on the navy's own self-monitoring reports, alleged that toxic discharges, including metals, vinyl chlorides, and polychlorinated biphenyls, from the Shipyard's deteriorating sewer and storm system were entering San Francisco Bay.[27]

Fort Ord

The almost twenty-eight-thousand-acre Fort Ord, located in Monterey County, California, was established in 1917 as a basic army training base and closed in 1994. The site was added to the National Priorities List in 1990. At closure at least twelve thousand acres were contaminated by munitions used in training exercises, including land mines, hand grenades and bombs; groundwater plumes remain an issue. Before closure, the base employed more than fifteen thousand active military personnel and around five thousand civilians. Many individuals migrated to the areas for employment and became unemployed or underemployed after operations were shut down.[28] Environmental justice concerns have not been as prominent at Fort Ord as at the Hunters Point Shipyard, although an environmental justice organization has been a long-term member of public participation efforts. Several nearby towns have large Latino, African-American, and Asian-American populations. Much of the land at Ford Ord has been repurposed: designated as a nature reserve and a state university or transferred to local cities to be developed for commercial and residential purposes.

Cleanup activities have been controversial in the past, drawing several lawsuits from community members. Heavy metals—particularly lead, originating from munitions and explosives—are found across Fort Ord in levels higher than the recommended standards of the state and federal EPA. Members of the restoration advisory board brought a lawsuit against the army for burial of lead-contaminated soil in an on-site landfill, charging that the plan to bury was not appropriately reviewed under environmental legislation. As part of the cleanup program, there have been prescribed burns to clear vegetation so that munitions can be removed. This has raised concerns about health impacts from particulate matter exposure. In 1998 some RAB members spearheaded a lawsuit that maintained the army's unexploded munitions cleanup program had violated CERCLA requirements to thoroughly evaluate alternative detection and remediation technologies for unexploded munitions and solicit public oversight. Shortly after a judge issued a tentative ruling in the plaintiffs' favor, the army voluntarily conceded to clean up unexploded munitions at closing bases in accordance with CERCLA directives. Following this conflict, the army implemented an extensive notification and relocation program during prescribed burns. The same year that RAB

JENNIFER LISS OHAYON

members and the army entered a settlement on the unexploded munitions case, the restoration advisory board was disbanded. RAB members
then brought another suit against the army, claiming that the RAB was
disbanded in retaliation for their prior lawsuit and that shutting down
the board had not been done "in consultation with the community as a
whole."[29] This lawsuit was ultimately unsuccessful.

REPRESENTATION IN NONDELIBERATIVE FORUMS

After the failure of the RABs at both Hunters Point Shipyard and Fort
Ord, the military emphasized its dedication to the participatory process
by instituting a variety of public participation activities. These activities, however, reverted back to an older concept of public participation
as based on the transmission of information from agencies to the public
rather than providing similar opportunities as the RAB for debate about
environmental risks and challenges to cleanup programs. In effect, none
of these forums solicit deliberation, generally defined as a process of
debate and discussion, meant to give opportunities for political challenge and orient the political and policy processes around incorporating
the positions and concerns of interested and affected groups.[30]

Current community involvement initiatives—including surveys,
newsletters and fact sheets, meetings and workshops, public comment
periods, site tours, a website, and mailing lists—are outlined in community involvement plans (CIP). These documents are formally required
by the Superfund's National Contingency Plan (NCP). The CIP for the
Hunters Point Shipyard is modeled after the plan produced for Fort Ord.
The activities, delineated in the current CIPs for both sites, go beyond
the basic criteria for public participation required by the Superfund's
NCP. Interviewees from the military and regulatory agencies repeatedly emphasized that current activities to engage the public are not only
more diverse and inclusive than many other private and federal Superfund sites, but they are more diverse and inclusive than the RABs they
replaced. As one military representative put it for Fort Ord: "We see a
lot more diverse crowds, not just the same people coming to the same
meetings, but different people, which is wonderful. This was not the way
things were when the RAB was active. That was a very static group of
people that came."[31] An EPA representative at the Shipyard discussed a
similar phenomenon at her site: "What is good about the new system is

we do see new interests from a broader sense of the community that we didn't see in the past. It seemed like the RAB was locked down with a specific group of people."[32] These interviewees presented the restoration advisory boards as the standard approach, an inversion of the original policy intention for these boards to be more innovative and meaningful approaches to public participation.

Although some current variants of public participation, such as site tours, may include more individuals than the RABs, whose membership typically range from ten to twenty-five individuals, these activities are more oriented toward outreach, education, and disseminating information rather than on sustained and in-depth discussion and debate on remedial activities. One community group commented in the 2011 CIP for the Hunters Point Shipyard that their fundamental concern with the community involvement activities is that "all of the action and activities are geared toward one-way communication from the navy to community."[33] The navy responded by asserting that two-way communication occurs in activities such as community meetings with a question-and-answer period, presentations at established group meetings, and a dedicated call-in line.

In the new activities, however, participants do not have the time to readily assimilate the information presented, weigh the evidence on issues, and discuss and debate potential alternatives, nor do these forums provide the technical resources for the general public to critically engage in the analysis. Unlike the RABs, where community members would become informed and debate on issues over typically multiyear tenures, workshops consist mainly of presentations by the military and occasionally regulators and contractors. At the community information workshops that I attended from 2011 to 2014, the majority of time was spent transitioning through slides outlining cleanup remedies and describing schedules for completion of work. Some workshops also have breakout groups for community members to ask specific questions of agency representatives. One community interviewee stated that an issue with the community involvement workshops is that public participants cannot ask questions about issues for which they have limited knowledge. While remedial approaches were prone to deconstruction in more politically oriented and adversarial settings, such as the restoration advisory boards, within workshops public participation is more restricted to a question-and-answer format. Although some workshops and meetings

JENNIFER LISS OHAYON

have received high turnout, for both Fort Ord and the Shipyard, community members have complained that the attendance is skewed toward military, regulators, and paid contractors; this has been substantiated by agency attendance records.[34]

At both sites, the military and regulators have emphasized the success of site tours, including bus and walking tours, for attracting a large and diverse group of public participants who have not previously been involved. The tours give participants a chance to see the areas of the sites that are typically closed off to the public; they also allow military representatives to explain the different cleanup remedies employed. Although participants have the opportunity to ask specific questions (as in workshops and meetings), tours focus on unidirectional transfer of information (i.e., from agencies to the general public), and there is less opportunity for participants to challenge cleanup activities. At Fort Ord, at the beginning of every bus tour, the organizer emphasizes that there "will be no three Ps on this tour: that is politics, protests, and petitions."[35] When I asked a community organizer from an environmental justice group in Fort Ord what she thought of the bus tours and community involvement meetings, she replied, "You know, the problem is that there always seems to be a contest for the governmental agencies about how good everything is. They want everything to be accomplishment, accomplishment, accomplishment. But how can you have accomplishments all the time with no failures?"[36] In response to military-led bus tours, her group had organized an alternative Fort Ord Tour that had discussion points including potential risks from leachate at the landfill and stops at the low-income housing on Fort Ord where there is lead and asbestos contamination.

Participatory programs should not be seen as engaging an already fully developed and intransigent public perspective; instead, they are simultaneously creating, transforming, and eliciting different public "faces" based on their design. Current methods of public participation in these sites often mobilize a more passive participant than deliberative forums that assemble a different understanding, acceptance, and interest in environmental cleanup. The military uses surveys to assess the effectiveness of public participation approaches. Surveys, however, are limited in their ability to communicate and stimulate in-depth views about complex issues and have elicited less controversial responses than some of the interactions that occurred during the restoration advisory boards. A 2009 public survey conducted by the army, for example, constructed a general public that is more trusting of the army's cleanup program at Fort Ord and satisfied with the public participation response.[37] This is in contrast to the reactions to the cleanup by community members who have become involved in ongoing discussions. The RABs facilitated a participatory process that allowed community members to be effectively integrated into the process, familiarized with the site, conversant in the issues, and able to formulate recommendations on the cleanup program. Particularly in the environmental risk arena, where knowledge is not settled, these debates are especially important.

ISSUES WITH THE IMPLEMENTATION OF RABs

The legitimacy of a political response is predicated not only on the amount of participation but also on the quality of that participation. Although RABs mobilize small segments of the population, they solicit ongoing discussions and debate. Despite the resources devoted to the restoration advisory boards, however, the deliberative process failed in the cases of Fort Ord and the Hunters Point Shipyard. Regulators and community members, with experience collaborating with RABs in multiple sites, have highlighted numerous issues with the implementation of the RAB model across the country. Many cited in interviews that the technical complexity of cleanup decisions has been a barrier to public participation. RAB members do not necessarily have the time or the technical expertise to review the immense amounts of technical reports produced, nor do citizen advisory boards have the funds to hire independent technical consultants. Although there is available limited EPA funding for technical assistance grants, grants are typically awarded to just one community group. Others have argued that the RABs should have ongoing, independent technical support or a better balance between public interest representatives and those with technical expertise from nonmilitary academic and environmental sources. Several scholars have likewise documented that public participation activities can have a lack of participants because of the time commitments of evaluating the large number of documents produced, attending meetings and events, and keeping track of rapid changes in problem definitions.[38]

The RABs in the Hunters Point Shipyard and Fort Ord were particularly adversarial. Both sites experienced similar issues, including fighting

JENNIFER LISS OHAYON

among community members, regulators, and the military, and infighting within the community. Both RABs were said to be exclusionary in practice. Long-term board members became highly familiarized with issues and this, in addition to hostile interactions within the boards, sometimes created an intimidating environment for new board members at the beginning stages of understanding the cleanup program. The Fort Ord RAB members included federal, state, and local agencies, former civilian base employees, environmentalists concerned with conservation and technical aspects of cleanup, environmental justice advocates, a lawyer involved in the litigation against the army, and (according to skeptical members) politicians and business representatives with designs on local office positions and particular reuse plans. For the Shipyard, a mix of individuals and organizations sat on the restoration advisory board, including government agencies, those with interests in human rights and environmental justice, and a local environmental organization with technical expertise. Both RABs, however, were not representative of the racial, cultural, and economic diversity of the surrounding communities (for example, Latino and Asian populations were underrepresented within the boards).

The RABs were disbanded in both sites by the military, in consultation with regulators, who noted the "hostile tone" of the meetings and the focus on issues outside of RAB purview, such as employment and site reuse.[39] In both cases the participating community members were held responsible for the problems in the restoration advisory boards, as evidenced in officials' statements during interviews and by government documentation submitted to disband the RABs.[40] The participatory trend in science comes rooted with expectations. While the RABs turned out to be contentious settings, underlying much of this conflict were questions about the authority and accountability of these boards. Also in play was the type of redress these boards provided for historical and present-day social and environmental health inequities.

THE STRUCTURE AND FUNCTION OF CITIZEN ADVISORY BOARDS

Participants had different expectations of the boards for the interrelated issues of accountability and authority. What do different social actors believe should be the authority of these boards? How is accountability connected to these efforts, and in what ways is it measured? Accountability to whom and for what types of issues?

Conflict ensued as public participants witnessed a gap between discussion and agency action and came to see citizen advisory boards as lacking significant authority, undermining the democratic rationale for public participation. The original DOD/EPA policy clearly states that the RAB is not intended to be a body that directly makes cleanup decisions; instead, it serves as a way for the communities to become informed and deliver advice to agencies, as the word *advisory* indicates. RAB participants, though, had differing views of the purpose of these boards. As one community interviewee stated: "It was the only process that they seemed to come up with that we are supposed to have some sort of voice, and hopefully some sort of equality in the decisions that are being made."[41] The guidelines of the DOD/EPA policy stress, in contrast to this participant's understanding of the process, that the RAB "is *not* a decision-making body."[42]

In the case of Fort Ord, in particular, conflicts about the lack of authority were often reflected in arguments over procedural matters. Facilitators at Fort Ord stated that "the underlying cause of the Fort Ord RAB's procedural difficulties is a widespread apparent misunderstanding of the RAB's role in the cleanup decision-making process. . . . RAB procedures at Fort Ord and the attitude of many of the participants, seem to treat the body as if it were a city council or other local decision-making body."[43] Although RAB meeting minutes reveal that many topics related to the remedial program were addressed in these bodies, the military, regulators, and community members in Fort Ord unanimously agreed that a disproportionate amount of time was spent arguing over procedural matters and distracted from the RAB's ability to focus its efforts on the cleanup programs. Actors differed, however, in the weight of importance that they gave to the procedural aspects of the advisory boards. For community members, procedural matters could be controversial as they reflected differences in opinion over the board's authority, the resources and support dedicated to the board, and what constituted a procedurally fair and legitimate public participation process. There was significant disagreement over such procedural matters as the facilitation of meetings, whether meeting minutes were reflective of dissenting opinions (or intentionally edited key conflicts out of the public record), and the military's role in selecting the original membership of the RAB boards.

For Fort Ord, there was conflict over a lack of transparency in the original RAB selection process, which the army reasoned was for privacy issues. The first RAB cochair, a retired army colonel and businessman, sat on the original selection committee for the twelve RAB community members. Some saw this as symbolic of the infiltration of army and business interests on the community side of the RAB.[44] A former RAB member asserted that "[the RAB] became procedural because the army was ignoring what the community wanted to do in so far as self-governance and the army kept inserting these people into the RAB that had conflicts of interest, like those affiliated with the army and commerce. They were exploiting the criteria for community members. Community members were very loosely defined."[45] As such, the member demanded more openness and community input into the early formations of the boards.

In both cases public concerns that participation was not factored as an important input into policy making came up repeatedly during RAB meetings and interviews. Community members complained that remedial decisions were made in closed meetings of the base cleanup team, which consists of the military as well as federal and state regulators. Because of constraints in public authority over decision making, the process would frequently become displaced. Community members participated in the RABs to acquire information and skills yet would frequently appeal to the media and courts to compel agency action in the face of an absence of power sharing. As one EPA representative from Fort Ord stated with respect to the munitions lawsuit: "They needed to go through the lawsuit to impact munitions cleanup because the army wasn't listening. They were blowing up munitions in place and no one was being notified. No one was really part of that process."[46] An activist from Fort Ord stated he was happy when an environmental lawyer joined the RAB because "I always knew that we'd have to sue. That was just a given, because the powers that be were not going to listen until you put teeth in your argument."[47] As the army's decision to disband the RAB came shortly after the settlement of the successful munitions suit, community members argued that it was a retaliatory response to members' legal activism. While official documents point to the antagonistic interactions that occurred during RAB meetings as the rationale for disbanding the citizen advisory committees, a military representative indicated that the lawsuits further strained relationships. "Members of the RAB were suing the Army," she stated, "which made things particularly difficult, because we were in a lawsuit situation. It just doesn't make for easy conversation."[48]

Conflict over prescribed rules and proceedings became the locus of political struggle, particularly for Fort Ord, as they reflected disagreements over the function of the boards and the political power afforded to them. How much control the military, as lead agency, had over the cleanup and public participation programs was contentious, compounded by its power, albeit with regulatory approval, to disband these bodies. A Fort Ord former RAB community member asserted, "They'll point the finger and say I ended the RAB, I will point the finger and say they did it. But they had all the money, they had all the means, and they had an obligation to follow the guidelines. I was arguing for a legitimate participation process and they say we ended up in process hell."[49] Deliberative dialogues have typically been evaluated within a narrow theoretical frame (e.g., Is there mutual respect among actors?).[50] Scholars have challenged the exclusion of an analysis of the role of power within political institutions and status inequalities when evaluating deliberative dialogues, as communities react to risks based on a lack of control to influence and consent to the source of risks rather than on technical evidence alone.[51]

RAB Accountability

A lack of authority for these boards became particularly contentious without a stringent and open process of accountability to ensure public input was considered. Participatory bodies such as citizen advisory boards are not directly elected, or otherwise authorized, by their communities; it is therefore difficult for the larger public to hold them accountable. Some democratic theorists thus argue that these bodies limit themselves to a consultative capacity rather than making legally binding decisions.[52] Representatives from the military, the EPA, and other main decision makers are typically appointed rather than directly authorized by the public, while community members involved in RABs might bear more resemblance to their publics. As those who bear the burdens of environmental and health problems, community members may push for more precautionary cleanup programs and be more responsive to public concerns.

The RABs revealed fault lines among different actors in appropriate standards for evaluating evidence and meriting action, including

JENNIFER LISS OHAYON

the investigation of hazards. In many instances, community members pushed for positions that admitted more uncertainties and embraced precautionary measures. However, there are no mechanisms to ensure the military is responsive to public concerns, particularly if they view the concerns as being unduly cautious. In Fort Ord community members contended that base officials should expand sampling efforts outside of site perimeters, to investigate how elevated levels of contaminants might have spread downstream into surrounding communities. These concerns were initially dismissed by the military, but contaminated groundwater plumes were later discovered to extend outside of the base boundaries. As one EPA representative put it: "Military bases take pride in that they can contain the plume on the base and so when it goes off base, they go crazy, and that's exactly what happened. . . . If there's any way for the military to say to the community that 'we can sample that,' just to say that 'we understand your concerns,' it would help."[53] While community members may need help from experts and may be characterized as overly cautious in their input, sociologist Steve Fuller has called for a type of responsive public deliberation that is protected by "the right to be wrong."[54]

Agencies have been responsive to some community requests during multiyear tenures of public participation. For the Shipyard the military and regulators have increased air monitoring, adjusted work hours, and varied truck routes in response to public input.[55] At Fort Ord the army has modified prescribed burn programs and investigated at least one area previously designated a "no action site."[56] Most struggles applied knowledge acquired from the RAB to advocacy across multiple communications, policy, and legislative venues. The outcomes of the process were not always knowable and transparent to participants, however, and community members expressed concern that much of their input failed to gain resonance with federal and state bodies. In this context disenchanted participants came to see deliberative forums as "just talk"—a process that does not substantively shape agency goals.[57] "The military just wanted to have a box checked off that said they talked to community," one community member stated, indicating a perception that the restoration advisory board was merely incorporated as a result of regulatory specification.[58]

Deliberative democrats have envisioned accountability in democracy as "giving an account" for the reasons for political decisions. While this is not equivalent to a framework that assures all public preferences and concerns influence decision making, "giving an account" could require implementing a stringent and transparent process that weighs reasons for incorporating or not incorporating the input of interested and affected groups. An evaluation process for the RABs could indicate whether public feedback systematically fails to influence decision-making processes. This includes considering at what point in decision making public input is solicited (e.g., Are there still opportunities to make fundamental changes to cleanup programs?) and what types of public input have influence. Some recommendations from public participants, such as changes to website design or additions to an information repository, are easier to implement than more substantive changes, such as modifications to land use, monitoring, or the selection of experts.

The selection process for the citizen advisory boards became a question of both who has the authority to influence member selection and to whom should the boards be accountable? Defining a community is an act that necessarily draws boundaries around which concerns matter. For example, the Keystone Report—produced by a committee largely made up of environmental activists, labor unions, and indigenous groups—originally advised the DOD/EPA to "seek out and solicit the full diversity of public stakeholders in communities, particularly communities of color, indigenous peoples, low-income communities, and local governments."[59] Furthermore, the document recommends the inclusion of "representatives of citizen, environmental, and public interest groups whose members live in the communities or regions affected by the environmental contamination and related cleanup efforts at the facility."[60] In interviews with government officials as well as in DOD/EPA promulgated guidelines, stakeholders were also emphasized to be the business community, installation officials, and homeowner associations.[61] Thus Keystone laid out a more restricted vision of who was significantly impacted by contamination and cleanup activities. Some saw agency demands to incorporate more diverse views on the boards not as directed toward addressing racial and ethnic exclusion, but rather as a ruse for packing the boards with individuals from business communities who were supportive of preferred reuse plans and not as critical of environmental restoration projects.

Conflict can negatively impact accountability processes, with interviewees alleging military authorities discounted their advice because of "bad blood" or in retaliation for their activism. An interviewee from the Shipyard drew parallels to another closed California military base, McClellan Air Force Base, where he assisted with litigation against the air force after the RAB was disbanded due to extended disagreements between community members and base officials. "The Air Force complained 'the community is nasty to us,'" the interviewee stated, "but they were nasty because they were scared that their surrounding neighborhoods were contaminated. Many of these people worked on McClellan Air Force Base as military employees and buried the waste. . . . But [the air force] didn't like the RAB members and to look into their concerns would have been to encourage these people."[62] Soon after the RAB dissolution, the air force discovered barrels of buried radioactive waste.[63] Evaluations of deliberative processes could account for whether institutions are less responsive to concerns when publics are perceived as adversarial.

ADDRESSING A FEDERAL MANDATE FOR PUBLIC PARTICIPATION: REDRESSING LOCAL ISSUES?

The design of the RABs does not address full democratic participation, nor do they have stringent and transparent mechanisms to ensure accountability for public participants. This in part contributed to a failure of policy implementation as intended, as participants felt frustrated over a lack of decision-making influence. At both Fort Ord and the Hunters Point Shipyard, military and regulatory agencies cited that community members pressed issues outside of the purview of RAB—namely, employment and base reuse. As a result, presentations and discussions about environmental cleanup were not always completed. According to policy, RAB discussions are meant to be restricted to the technical aspects of base cleanup, but for some public members environmental remediation could not be separated from concerns relating to economic well-being, social inclusion, and health. It is not in the design of RAB or CERCLA policy, nor is it within the jurisdiction of the military, to address these more inclusive agendas. An emphasis on technical progress forward, without necessarily addressing the residual impacts of long-term military land tenure, affected agency-community relations, particularly in the neighborhoods surrounding the Shipyard where many disenfranchised groups reside.

Community RAB members critiqued the technical aspects of remedial strategies, as evidenced in struggles surrounding remedial alternatives (e.g., prescribed burns and on-site capping of contaminants) and the thoroughness of investigations, monitoring, and risk assessments. Beyond particular technical comments, however, publics have challenged the bifurcation of politics and science in the framing of environmental remediation. While environmental remediation is framed primarily as a technical endeavor in documents and current public forums, cleanup decisions are made in a climate of conflicting accounts of environmental, ecological, and social risks, mutable environmental standards, competing political priorities, budgets, and resources, and varying degrees of private and public investments into land reuse and redevelopment projects. For example, publics insisted that who carries out environmental remediation, and under which legislative process, matters. The Defense Authorization Act of 1997 contained a provision that allows for the DOD to "defer" the CERCLA covenant that all necessary remedial actions have been taken before transfer of contaminated property.[64]

Community RAB members worried that the transfer of still contaminated parcels could encourage faster regulatory approval of insufficient cleanups if the benefits of reuse were high and that public input would be more restricted than under traditional CERCLA oversight. In Fort Ord, when questioned whether RAB members would review property scheduled for early release to local reuse committees, the army cochair emphasized that the RAB addresses the technical aspects of the cleanup not site reuse.[65] While community RAB members tackled technical issues and critiqued the representation of science and politics into neatly partitioned spheres, the boards were also strategically used by participants at the Hunters Point Shipyard and Fort Ord to advance a broader political agenda on employment and reuse. The forums thus turned out to be more discursively undisciplined and disorderly than a well-intentioned federal policy had originally envisioned.

The Shipyard, once the economic driver for that part of San Francisco, is currently bordered by one of the most economically depressed areas of the city. A technical adviser to the community commented that for a community with long-term socioeconomic and environmental inequalities, environmental remedial activity would be seen as an important source of employment and economic renewal. He further critiqued the navy of failing to take advantage of a city-based citizens' advisory subcommittee on contracting and other employment concerns that was cre-

JENNIFER LISS OHAYON

ated in part to take pressure off the RAB by instituting an alternative forum for these discussions. Had "the Navy partnered with the Subcommittee as was proposed," he alleged, "the RAB might not have been burdened by these questions over the past sixteen years." The reply was that "the Navy disagrees with the idea that if it had invested more time in the [citizens advisory committee] subcommittee that the RAB would have been more effective."[66]

Similarly, in Fort Ord the discussions would veer toward local contracting and employment as RAB members included workers who had lost their jobs with base closure. Not all RAB community participants agreed with what they considered to be a disproportionate focus on employment and other livelihood issues. A former Fort Ord community RAB member stated that "[one environmental justice activist] would come to a RAB member where the whole agenda was to address cleanup issues, but she would argue about jobs and housing."[67] A community member in the Shipyard emphasized: "We warned the group that kept bringing it up that the navy would use employment arguments as a justification to get rid of the RAB. And that's exactly what happened."[68]

The topic of land reuse is also considered by DOD/EPA policy to be outside of the scope of the RABs. Despite this, the issue would continually surface during meetings. The shipyard at Hunters Point is the largest swath of land left in the city for redevelopment. Surrounding low-income residents expressed fears that they would be displaced through a process of gentrification, and thus those who for years endured the environmental hazards would not benefit from its subsequent cleanup and reintegration into a profitable urban real estate market. As such, a project of environmental remediation could not be understood apart from one that could potentially deepen existing inequalities as the marking of the area as one that is economically and socially desirable.[69] Likewise, a former RAB community member from Fort Ord particularly interested in the site's reuse stated: "[The agencies] say 'we are cleaning up this land, this parcel, and we are cleaning it up for a purpose, so that we can have redevelopment here.' But, what redevelopment is going here, who will benefit, how will the community benefit?"[70]

Just as RABs were not designed to tackle employment or reuse issues, they did not satisfactorily address residents' concerns about elevated rates of acute and chronic health problems in their communities. Public health assessments and epidemiological studies are not encompassed in the jurisdiction of base cleanup teams. As a Department of Toxic Substances Control representative said, "We aren't epidemiologists, we can't study people. And it's because of the regulatory structure that we are limited to overseeing remediation of the properties."[71] Cleanup remedies are intended to be protective of present and future human health and, although uncommon, external health consultations can be solicited for an issue with significant public concern, such as the EPA requested with an industrial landfill fire in the Shipyard. The military representatives and regulators in charge of identifying and addressing pollution are not epistemologically or legislatively equipped to address public health concerns. When I asked a former Fort Ord RAB member if she trusts how the cleanup team characterizes environmental risks, she responded, "They are not doctors, that's self-evident. They have no business interpreting anything that has to do with health. They can't be experts on everything."[72]

Furthermore, CERCLA is oriented toward reducing human and ecological risk through current remedial activities rather than redressing past health exposures, for much of which the data is lacking and inconclusive. As one EPA regulator said, "Superfund is more forward thinking than backward thinking, even though the liability goes way backwards, as you know [i.e., early land managers can be held potentially responsible for contamination]. But as far as what we are trying to do in terms of protecting human health and the environment, it's present and future risk. Our whole motto is protecting future generations, and the health effects of what may or may not have happened is not in CERCLA at all."[73] Another EPA regulator reiterated this during a RAB meeting in response to a community inquiry about the possible associations between high asthma rates in Bayview–Hunters Point and remedial activities at the Shipyard. "This cannot be determined," he stated, "as the EPA is dealing with the substances at present and not with past levels or activities."[74]

Community members were often referred to other committees, such as reuse authorities, when they tried to bring up issues relating to land use, redevelopment, and employment. It sometimes proved difficult to attend additional meetings for those involved in a volunteer capacity. While community involvement workshops are spent transitioning through slides on remedial achievements, hence portraying the military's role as environmental restorer, RABs, in contrast, troubled themselves with the persisting health, social, and economic impacts of a history of militarism.[75] Cleanup programs encompass vast projects of digging and hauling away tons of known contaminated soils, engineering durable covers to keep other contaminants in place, designing and installing groundwater treatment technologies, and removing subsurface volatile organic compound gases with vapor extraction systems. From the Shipyard alone, over twenty-four thousand dump trucks of chemical and radiological contaminated soil has been removed as of mid-2012, and several groundwater plumes have achieved required cleanup levels through in situ chemical degradation of contaminants into nontoxic components.[76] These activities are impressive technological feats meant to degrade, remove, or contain well over half a century of military and industrial waste production. Just as some contaminants cannot be physically broken down—only contained in place or displaced, as is the fate for both sites' industrial landfills—some harm is not easily redressed.

The technical task of environmental remediation thus moved into social and political domains of justice that institutions and regulatory frameworks, such as CERCLA policy, are ill-equipped to address. Public participation programs today seek to have less adversarial climates or, as a military representative evoked, settings that are free from "politics, protests, and petitions." The technical imaginary is that these problems can be remediated, posing a dilemma for how to re(member) science in these contexts—that is, both to re-member the scientific decision-making process with those affected while recalling the variables that structure public reactions to institutions and cleanup programs.

DISTRUST AND CONTESTATION

For the Hunters Point Shipyard and Fort Ord, hostility was cited as a reason to disband the RABs. As one EPA representative from the Shipyard stated: "Towards the end of the Navy's RAB, it just got too political and too personal, too attack-driven."[77] Although during interviews the conflict was often reduced to an interpersonal problem with agency representatives, debates over authority and accountability, and the overarching institutional, political, and historical contexts structured these relationships and contributed to community distrust. Some of these issues were stronger contributing factors to conflict in different sites and at different times (i.e., procedural issues plagued the Fort Ord RAB whereas discussions at the Shipyard could become mired by issues of employment). Nonetheless, these issues reflected and intensified feelings of distrust surrounding the responsiveness of military authorities and regulators. This underpins a need for a shift in analysis from the distrusting community member, and the interpersonal conflicts that manifest as a result, to an evaluation of the trustworthiness of institutions.[78]

Public participation has transitioned from contentious RABs to community events that aim to solicit good relations and mutual trust. As a Fort Ord army representative stated, "On the bus tour, people can argue and ask questions, but in the end we all sang a song together and that's a reminder of trust."[79] This representative also emphasized that a hotline during the prescribed burn programs in Fort Ord is there to offer "reassurance" to people nervous about smoke impacts. Agency representatives in the Shipyard, in contrast, have not put the same overt emphasis on trust. When a technical adviser commented that it was unrealistic for the navy to believe that RAB members would "immediately give over their trust to an entity whose actions in 1974 helped drive the community into poverty," the agency response was that "the Navy has never stated that a goal of the RAB is for community members to 'give over their trust' to the Navy."[80] Current events at the Shipyard have, however, minimized conflict among social actors, focusing more on information transfer than animated debate.

Policy documents and agency representatives often emphasize that a key goal of public involvement initiatives is to develop trust, respect for different perspectives, and a spirit of collaboration among stakeholders, and scholars cite distrust as a barrier to public participation.[81] Distrust, however, can be a productive response to past state violations and current environmental and political conditions. According to this view, rather than a barrier to overcome, distrust is treated as a rational response to living within a stratified society.[82] Military culture could itself be a source of public mistrust. Institutional issues associated with transitioning to a more open process were complicated by a military culture that traditionally viewed disclosure and broad participation as breaches of security.[83] Early regulation under the Superfund program was plagued by difficulties as the military adjusted to the new environmental regulations, requirements for cleanup and documentation of remedial activities, and mandates for public openness after decades of secrecy surrounding base operations and little experience in cooperating with the public. Moreover, RAB formation is typically a community-led initiative, a process that requires fifty people petition for its implementation. In this case a federal mandate from above is spearheaded from below, with local base officials in the middle responsible for board formation despite not requesting the boards themselves or having previous experience working with the public. While some members identified with or trusted military authorities more, the military careers of staff, either as civilian or uniformed, caused some participants to feel intimidated and heightened their distrust of officials' commitment to the restoration advisory boards.

According to a San Francisco civil grand jury report, the high level of community distrust of the agencies responsible for managing the Hunters Point Shipyard's cleanup and reuse was exacerbated by unexplained fires, a lack of complete data and documentation of the extent of contamination, missed deadlines for cleanup and reuse, and failures to study and account for cluster illnesses among nearby residents.[84] This report was published two summers after a 2000 landfill fire containing industrial wastes exacerbated military-community relations. The U.S. EPA fined the navy for its failure to notify the regulatory agency during the first three weeks of the fire and directed the navy to install air monitors and establish a community outreach program. Sentiments that the navy initiated neither the notification of community members nor the collection of air data continually appear during meetings and in the popular press. Less than a year after the fire, a published investigative report drew on historical research of declassified documents and accused the navy of conducting nuclear research and mishandling radioactive waste on a scale greater than previous revealed. When accused of insufficiently investigating and informing regulators and the public of the site's nuclear history, the Shipyard's base environmental coordinator replied that the navy was not purposely obfuscating this information, but until 2002 no one with the technical and scientific expertise to do so had constructed a formal radiological assessment.[85] Nonetheless, the narrative of nuclear fallout particles captured the imagination of residents and contributed to an ongoing social fallout between less trusting community members and the navy.

Key struggles in Fort Ord centered on the boundaries of contaminated groundwater plumes, the munitions remedial approach, and lead concentrations in the beach dunes. These conflicts escalated when participants did not feel that institutions were accountable to their concerns. For example, an environmental testing firm for the Shipyard and Fort Ord was suspended by the EPA for failing to follow proper testing procedures and falsifying results at another base.[86] A Fort Ord community RAB member felt his inquiries as to the implications of this for Fort Ord's data from the lab were dismissed. "When it came up this lab was fraudulent," he stated, "it all went back to the issues we were raising at the RAB. When we raised issues, they told us not to worry about it. I didn't have confidence in their ability to do what they say they are doing and therefore I told them that we need a very strong RAB."[87] In addition to providing a venue for input on public values, this assertion forwards citizen advisory boards as public oversight committees, a position that entails scrutiny. With respect to ensuring cleanup programs are adequate, it could be productive for deliberative forums like the RABs to invite public expressions of skepticism and make space for conflicting interests.[88] This conflict would be different than one rooted in intimidation or interpersonal attacks, as characterized much of the fighting in these sites.

At the Hunters Point Shipyard and Fort Ord, public trust eroded in the military and the oversight capabilities of regulatory agencies. Conversely, agencies did not have faith in the intentions of community members for joining these boards. Disparate social groups perceive and experience institutions and environmental risks differently, and the removal of the military, regulators, and the politicians from their representative communities was a recurring theme. When a community member in the Shipyard asked an EPA regulator during a public meeting if he would ever live in Bayview–Hunters Point, his response was, "If I had an opportunity to move to the Shipyard after the cleanup, I would absolutely do that. I'm close to the data. I watch the samples be taken to the lab and that gives me confidence in the data."[89] An agency representative emphasized the veracity of scientific data, while residents emphasized the gulf between agencies and the public, governmental failures in containing hazardous waste, disagreements among experts, inadequate past notification systems, and the experiences of being sick.

Debates about toxins dissolved to questions about authority and accountability, the social responsibilities of agencies, and the motivations and trustworthiness of institutions. Public reactions to environmental hazards and regulations are not solely responses to perceived physical risks but also take into account the equity of risk distribution; the social identifiability, competence, and trustworthiness of institutions and their actors; and the public's power to influence and consent to the source of the risk.[90] As such, public participation programs need to recognize that public participants in the citizen advisory boards often have a different suite of evaluative criteria as compared with state authorities for what constitutes an adequate investigation and monitoring of site conditions. While community members were often officially blamed for the failure of the RABs, the unraveling of these experiments in participation and democracy brought other questions to the fore. How much influence should community input have over remedial programs? Who should the programs be accountable to and for what types of issues?

Both the Shipyard and Fort Ord have participatory processes that are more expansive and diverse than many other federal sites and the majority of "private" sites regulated under the Superfund program. In both case studies, current public participation activities are defined largely in terms of making technical information accessible and allowing the public to submit recommendations. There is no participatory process, however, that encourages ongoing discursive challenges to the ways in which state actors represent and respond to risks. While deliberative bodies only mobilize a small segment of the population, they complement broader public participation activities by facilitating cultivation of the skills and knowledge required to evaluate technically and politically complex cleanup issues.

While citizen advisory boards incorporate the important democratic principles and procedures of deliberation and representation, the boards are not panaceas for democracy and guaranteeing that cleanup programs are receptive to social concerns and values. In practice, RABs allowed for a more managed form of public participation than that envisioned by scholars, activists, and social movements that have called for a direct influence and substantial contribution to decision making.[91] Many participants were unsatisfied with the lack of formal mechanisms within the citizen advisory boards to ensure that the military and regulators would investigate public concerns and make substantive changes to cleanup programs and agency practices. Rigorous evaluations that assess whether community input is systematically excluded from decision-making processes could be particularly important when relationships

among stakeholders are strained as a result of a lack of trust in the institutions that manage risk and current and past threats to civil liberties
and health.

NOTES

1   The author wishes to thank Edwin A. Martini for all his work and dedication
in bringing together this edited volume. The author also thanks Greg Gilbert,
Zdravka Tzankova, David Winickoff and his lab as well as Josephine Liss Ohayon
and two anonymous reviewers for their comments on an earlier version of this
chapter. Thanks for funding and inspiration on (re)membering science go to
Jenny Reardon and the Science and Justice Research Center. Additional funding
was provided by the EPA STAR Fellowship and the UCSC Environmental Studies
Department.

2   In particular, since 1988, the Department of Defense (DOD) has streamlined its
domestic base infrastructure in five rounds of base realignments and closures,
governed by the Base Realignment and Closure Commission (BRAC). Early BRAC
rounds focused on reducing infrastructure as the Cold War drew to a close,
whereas the last BRAC round, in 2005, focused on realigning military capabilities
due to operations in Afghanistan and Iraq as well as counterterrorism activities.

3   U.S. DOD, *Annual Report for Fiscal Year 1993* (Washington, D.C.: Defense Technical
Information Center, 1994), 45.

4   See CERCLIS Public Access Database for profiles for individual Superfund sites,
U.S. Environmental Protection Agency, available at http://cfpub.epa.gov/super
cpad/cursites/srchsites.cfm; accessed November 16, 2013.

5   The number of sites on the National Priorities List (NPL) of Superfund sites is a
small percentage of the overall number of contaminated sites under the military's
jurisdiction. Other sites might be unlisted because of political pressure or subject
to other environmental regulations, such as the Resource Conservation and
Recovery Act.

6   Statistics compiled by the author from data on individual sites from the EPA's
NPL database, available at www.epa.gov/superfund/sites/query/queryhtm/nplfin
.htm; accessed November 16, 2013.

7   Sometimes regulatory standards do not exist, such is the case with arsenic, and
the military can establish its own safety levels for cleanup. Other times, regulatory standards are controversial and unsettled. For example, the DOD challenged
the EPA's efforts to set new pollution limits on two common military contaminants: perchlorate, a munitions ingredient, and trichloroethylene, a solvent.

8   For example, there is uncertainty due to assumptions being made in the selection
of samples, sample and size, models for exposure to contaminants, and from the
inherent complexity of biological and technological systems. Mark Brown, *Science
in Democracy: Expertise, Institutions, and Representation* (Cambridge: Massachusetts Institute of Technology Press, 2009); Brian Wynne, "Public Participation in

Science and Technology: Performing and Obscuring a Political-Conceptual Category Mistake," *East Asian Science, Technology, and Society* 1, no. 1 (2007): 99–110; Brian Wynne, "May the Sheep Safely Graze? A Reflexive View of the Expert-Lay Knowledge Divide," *Risk, Environment, and Modernity: Towards a New Ecology* (1996): 44–83; Harry Collins and Robert Evans, *Rethinking Expertise* (Chicago: University of Chicago Press, 2007); Jason Corburn, "Environmental Justice, Local Knowledge, and Risk: The Discourse of a Community-Based Cumulative Exposure Assessment," *Environmental Management* 29, no. 4 (2002): 451–66; Alan Irwin, *Citizen Science: A Study of People, Expertise, and Sustainable Development* (New York: Routledge, 1995); Silvio Funtowicz and Jerome Ravetz, "Science for the Post-Normal Age," *Futures* 25, no. 7 (1993): 739–55; and Kristin Shrader-Frechette, *Risk and Rationality: Philosophical Foundations for Populist Reforms* (Berkeley: University of California Press, 1991).

9   The Superfund Act itself was passed in response to the environmental activism of residents seeking relocation and compensation after becoming aware that their homes were located above an abandoned toxic waste dump in Love Canal, New York. Before that, the EPA did not have the authority to respond to environmental emergencies such as that at Love Canal.

10   There are nine criteria for the acceptance of a cleanup alternative. "Community acceptance" is a modifying criteria, meaning that it is not mandatory but rather is a factor that shapes the adoption of a cleanup alternative.

11   Brian Adams, "Public Meetings and the Democratic Process," *Public Administration Review* 64, no. 1 (2004): 43–54; Margaret A. Moote, Mitchel P. McClaran, and Donna K. Chickering, "Theory in Practice: Applying Participatory Democracy Theory to Public Land Planning," *Environmental Management* 21, no. 6 (1997): 877–89; and Lawrence E. Susskind, "The Siting Puzzle: Balancing Economic and Environmental Gains and Losses," *Environmental Impact Assessment Review* 5, no. 2 (1985): 157–63, 159.

12   Irwin, "Citizen Science"; and Andrew Szasz and Michael Meuser, "Public Participation in the Cleanup of Contaminated Military Facilities: Democratization or Anticipatory Cooptation?" *International Journal of Contemporary Sociology* 34, no. 2 (1997): 211–33.

13   Citizen advisory boards are used increasingly by government agencies. The Department of Energy and the EPA have also established a variant of these boards.

14   Lucie Laurian, "Deliberative Planning through Citizen Advisory Boards," *Journal of Planning Education and Research* 26, no. 4 (2007): 415–34, 420.

15   U.S. DOD and U.S. EPA, *Restoration Advisory Board Workshop Guidebook* (San Francisco, CA: Joint DOD/EPA Restoration Advisory Board Workshop, August 1994).

16   Federal Facilities Environmental Restoration Dialogue Committee (FFERDC), *Final Report of the Federal Facilities Environmental Restoration Dialogue Committee: Consensus Principles and Recommendations for Improving Federal Facilities Cleanup* (Keystone, CO: Keystone Center, April 1996).

17   Szasz and Meuser, "Public Participation," 221.

18   Julia Abelson, Pierre-Gerlier Forest, John Eyles, Patricia Smith, Elisabeth
      Martin, and Francois-Pierre Gauvin, "Deliberations about Deliberative Methods:
      Issues in the Design and Evaluation of Public Participation Processes," *Social Sci-
      ence and Medicine* 57, no. 2 (2003): 239–51; and Thomas Beierle and Jerry Cayford,
      Democracy in Practice: Public Participation in Environmental Decisions (New York:
      Routledge, 2002).

19   Laurian, "Deliberative Planning," 416. Roger Kasperson, Dominic Golding, and
      Seth Tuler, "Social Distrust as a Factor in Siting Hazardous Facilities and Com-
      municating Risks," *Journal of Social Issues* 48, no. 4 (1992): 161–87. U.S. National
      Research Council (NRC), Committee on Risk Characterization, *Understanding
      Risk: Informing Decisions in a Democratic Society* (Washington, D.C.: National Acad-
      emy Press, 1996).

20   Brown, *Science in Democracy*; Szasz and Meuser, "Public Participation"; Irwin,
      Citizen Science; and Sherry Arnstein, "Ladder of Citizen Participation," *Journal of
      the American Institute of Planners* 35, no. 4 (1969): 216–24.

21   U.S. DOD/U.S. EPA, *Restoration Advisory Board Workshop Guidebook*.

22   Laurian, "Deliberative Planning," 425; and Lucie Laurian, "A Prerequisite for
      Participation Environmental Knowledge and What Residents Know about Local
      Toxic Sites," *Journal of Planning Education and Research* 22, no. 3 (2003): 257–69,
      263.

23   Brian Wynne, *Risk Management and Hazardous Waste: Implementation and the
      Dialectics of Credibility* (Berlin: Springer-Verlag, 1987).

24   U.S. Government Accountability Office (GAO), *Military Bases: Opportunities Exist
      To Improve Future Base Realignment and Closure Rounds* (Washington, D.C.: GAO,
      2013); and Base Realignment and Closure Program Management Office West,
      *Final Radiological Addendum to the Revised Feasibility Study for Parcel D, Hunters
      Point Shipyard, San Francisco, California* (San Diego, CA: BRAC Program Manage-
      ment Office West, 2008).

25   Self-identified Blacks/African Americans constitute 19.7 percent and self-iden-
      tified Asian populations constitute 34.6 percent of the Hunters Point Shipyard
      community, as defined by three zip codes. In the area's poorest zip code, Blacks/
      African Americans constitute 38.0 percent and Asians 29.2 percent of the popula-
      tions (according to a 2010 survey conducted by the Neilsen Company).

26   U.S. Department of the Navy, BRAC Program Management Office West, *Final
      Community Involvement Plan (CIP): Hunters Point Shipyard, San Francisco, California*
      (San Francisco, CA: BRAC Program Management Office West, 2011), Appendix
      D-7.

27   Jennifer Bjorhus, "Group To Sue Navy over Pollution of the Bay," *San Francisco
      Chronicle*, July 20, 1994.

28   U.S. Department of the Army, Fort Ord Base Realignment and Closure Office,
      Final Community Relations Plan (CRP) (Fort Ord, CA: U.S. Army, 2006), 1–70, 17.

29   Scott Allen, "Notice of Intent To Sue," Fort Ord, California, August 7, 2000 (in
      author's possession).

30   Simone Chambers, "Deliberative Democratic Theory," *Annual Review of Political*

Science 6 (2003): 307–26, 309; Brown, Science in Democracy; Sheila Jasanoff, Designs on Nature: Science and Democracy in Europe and the United States (Princeton, NJ: Princeton University Press, 2005); Abelson et al., "Deliberations about Deliberative Methods"; and John Dewey, The Public and Its Problems (Athens, OH: Swallow Press, 1954).

31 Interview with the author, Fort Ord, August 26, 2011.

32 Interview with the author, Hunters Point Shipyard, August 6, 2013.

33 U.S. Navy, Final Community Involvement Plan (CIP), Appendix J-10.

34 For example, in 2009 and 2010 there were four community involvement workshops held each year in Fort Ord. An average of thirty-four people attended these meetings, of which an average of eight people were community members (U.S. Army, Community Survey).

35 Community bus tour in Fort Ord, Monterey, August 23, 2011.

36 Interview with the author, Fort Ord, Monterey, February 12, 2012.

37 U.S. Army, Community Survey.

38 Laurian, "Deliberative Planning"; Abelson et al., "Deliberations about Deliberative Methods"; and Daniel Fiorino, "Citizen Participation and Environmental Risk: A Survey of Institutional Mechanisms," Science, Technology, and Human Values 15, no. 2 (1990): 226–43.

39 Letters distributed by the navy to community participants, now in author's possession: U.S. Navy, Notice to Dissolve the HPS RAB, 1–2; and U.S. Army, Letter to Disband the Fort Ord RAB, 1–2.

40 Ibid.

41 Interview with author, Fort Ord, Monterey, February 10, 2012.

42 U.S. DOD/U.S. EPA, Restoration Advisory Board Workshop Guidebook, 4, emphasis in the original.

43 Aimée Hougton and Lenny Siegel, Fort Ord Restoration Advisory Board Interim Report and Recommendations (San Francisco, CA: SFSU Career/Pro, July 1997), 1.

44 Fort Ord RAB Meeting Minutes (February 1994), page 56 (in author's possession).

45 Interview with the author, Fort Ord, April 17, 2013.

46 Interview with the author, Fort Ord, September 29, 2011.

47 Interview with the author, Fort Ord, February 9, 2012.

48 Interview with the author, Fort Ord, August 26, 2011.

49 Interview with the author, Fort Ord, February 9, 2012.

50 Abelson et al., "Deliberations and Deliberative Methods."

51 M. N. Peterson, M. J. Peterson, and T. R. Peterson, "Conservation and the Myth of Consensus," Conservation Biology 19, no. 3 (June 2005): 762–67; Barry Hindess, Discourses of Power: From Hobbes to Foucault (Oxford: Blackwell, 1996); and Maarten Hajer, The Politics of Environmental Discourse: Ecological Modernization and the Policy Process (Oxford: Clarendon Press, 1995), 6.

52 Brown, Science in Democracy.

53 Interview with the author, Fort Ord, September 29, 2011.

54 Steve Fuller, The Governance of Science (Buckingham: Open University Press, 2000).

55   U.S. Department of the Navy, BRAC Program Management Office West, *Final Community Involvement Plan (CIP)*, (San Francisco, CA: U.S. Navy, 2011), 1–56, 54.

56   Kris Wernstedt and Robert Hersh, *Land Use and Remedy Selection: Experience from the Field: The Fort Ord Site* (Washington, D.C.: Resources for the Future, 1997), 40.

57   Michael X. Delli Carpini, Fay Lomax Cook, and Lawrence R. Jacobs, "Public Deliberation, Discursive Participation, and Citizen Engagement: A Review of the Empirical Literature," *Annual Review of Political Science* 7 (2004): 315–44.

58   Interview with the author, Fort Ord, May 5, 2012. Brown, *Science in Democracy*; and Chambers, "Deliberative Democratic Theory."

59   FFERDC, *Final Report of the Federal Facilities Environmental Restoration Dialogue Committee*, xiii.

60   Ibid., 57

61   U.S. DOD/U.S. EPA, *Restoration Advisory Board Workshop Guidebook*.

62   Interview with the author, Hunters Point Shipyard, May 22, 2013.

63   Sam Stanton, "Toxic Radioactive Waste at Air Force Dump," *Sacramento Bee*, July 25, 2002.

64   "National Defense Authorization Act for Fiscal Year 1997," Public Law 104–201, September 23, 1996 (110 U.S. Statutes at Large, 2421–2870).

65   Fort Ord, RAB Meeting Minutes, February 1994, page 41.

66   U.S. Navy, *Final Community Involvement Plan (CIP)*, Appendix J-25.

67   Interview with the author, Fort Ord, April 17, 2013.

68   Interview with the author, Hunters Point Shipyard, June 11, 2013.

69   Lindsey Dillon, "Race, Waste, and Space: Brownfield Redevelopment and Environmental Justice at the Hunters Point Shipyard," *Antipode* (2013): 1–17.

70   Interview with the author, Fort Ord, February 10, 2012.

71   Interview with the author, Hunters Point Shipyard, August 13, 2013.

72   Interview with the author, Fort Ord, February 10, 2012.

73   Interview with the author, Hunters Point Shipyard, August 6, 2013.

74   Hunters Point Shipyard, RAB Meeting Minutes, August 25, 1999.

75   David Havlick, "Logics of Change for Military-to-Wildlife Conversions in the United States," *GeoJournal* 69, no. 3 (2007): 151–64.

76   Environmental Protection Agency, "Hunters Point Naval Shipyard," online at http://yosemite.epa.gov/r9/sfund/r9sfdocw.nsf/vwsoalphabetic/Hunters+Point+Naval+Shipyard?OpenDocument; accessed March 15, 2014.

77   Interview with the author, Hunters Point Shipyard, August 6, 2013.

78   Benjamin Ruha, *People's Science: Bodies and Rights on the Stem Cell Frontier* (Palo Alto: Stanford University Press, 2013), 153.

79   Interview with the author, Fort Ord, August 26, 2011.

80   U.S. Navy, *Final Community Involvement Plan (CIP)*, J-24.

81   Paul Slovic, "Perceived Risk, Trust, and Democracy," *Risk Analysis* 13, no. 6 (1993): 675–82.

82   Ruha, *People's Science*, 146.

83   Laurian, "Deliberative Planning"; Diane Rahm, "Controversial Cleanup: Superfund and the Implementation of U.S. Hazardous Waste Policy," *Policy Studies*

Journal 26 (2005): 719–34; and Szasz and Meuser, "Public Participation."

84 County of San Francisco Civil Grand Jury, "Hunters Point Naval Shipyard," Superior Court of California, June 6, 2002.

85 Sarah Phelan, "Nuclear Fallout," *San Francisco Bay Guardian*, July 16, 2008.

86 Erik Ingram, "EPA Ends Suspension of Santa Rosa Testing Lab," *Chronicle North Bay Bureau*, August 1, 1996.

87 Interview with the author, Fort Ord, April 17, 2013.

88 Chantal Mouffe, *The Democratic Paradox* (New York: Verso Books, 2000).

89 Community Involvement Meeting, Hunters Point Shipyard, April 12, 2012.

90 Sheila Jasanoff, "Bridging the Two Cultures of Risk Analysis," *Risk Analysis* 13, no. 2 (April 1993): 123–29; Kristin Shrader-Frechette, *Burying Uncertainty: Risk and the Case against Geological Disposal of Nuclear Waste* (Berkeley: University of California Press, 1993); Wynne, *Risk Management and Hazardous Waste*; and Peter Sandman, "Getting to Maybe: Some Communications Aspects of Siting Hazardous Waste Facilities," *Seton Hall Legislative Journal* 9 (1985): 437.

91 Jonathan London, Julie Sze, and Raoul S. Lievanos, "Problems, Promise, Progress, and Perils: Critical Reflections on Environmental Justice Policy Implementation in California," *UCLA Journal of Environmental Law and Policy* 26 (2008): 255–90, 255; Ryan Holifield, "Neoliberalism and Environmental Justice in the United States Environmental Protection Agency: Translating Policy into Managerial Practice in Hazardous Waste Remediation," *Geoforum* 35, no. 3 (2004): 285–97; and Arnstein, "Ladder of Citizen Participation."

CHAPTER 7

REALITY REVEALED

U.S. Military Bases, Environmental Impact, and Civil Society in South Korea

HEEJIN HAN AND YOOIL BAE

THE Korean War (1950–53) and the subsequent division of the Korean Peninsula by an armistice resulted in an extended stay of the U.S. military in the Republic of Korea (ROK, or South Korea). This direct physical presence of the U.S. military during the Cold War period and beyond has provided deterrence against a potential threat from North Korea, facilitating South Korea's rapid economic growth and political liberalization through security and stability. As South Korea transitioned to democracy in the late 1980s, however, activists and civil society organizations began to question the validity of the traditional United States–South Korean alliance. In particular, they started to see the status-of-forces agreement (SOFA), signed in July 1966 under Article IV of the Mutual Defense Treaty between the two countries, as an unequal and unfair agreement.[1] While the SOFA has granted the U.S. Forces in Korea (USFK) legal rights and privileges, it has systemically prevented the South Korean government from exercising sovereign authority and jurisdiction over crimes and wrongdoings committed by USFK personnel on Korean soil.

Despite their crimes, many of the U.S. military personnel have avoided trials in Korean courts as this principle of extraterritoriality under the

SOFA has provided them immunity. Accordingly, such criminal acts as murder and rape of Korean civilians have not been punished in South Korean courts. About one hundred thousand crimes committed by GIs were recorded from 1945 to 2001.[2] Since the signing of the SOFA, as of 1987, only 0.7 percent of crimes committed by Americans (39,453) were brought under jurisdiction of the Korean government, and this figure is surprisingly low compared with 32 percent in NATO countries and 21.2 percent in the Philippines.[3] As a result, the SOFA has become a source of public resentment toward U.S. military and a symbol of South Korea's compromised sovereignty.[4] As the Korean public and civil society have become increasingly aware of the near immunity provided to U.S. military personnel under the SOFA, progressive democratic activists and people from all social strata have begun to harbor some levels of anti-Americanism.[5]

For the past few decades, the focus of South Koreans' concern on the presence of U.S. military forces has gradually shifted from individual cases of criminal acts on the part of U.S. soldiers to the broader social influence of U.S. forces in Korea on South Korean society as a whole. South Korea's nongovernmental organizations (NGOs) and civic activists have recently begun to pay attention to environmental pollution such as water and soil contamination at U.S. military bases. This rising concern about the negative environmental impact of the U.S. military presence became particularly acute during the transfer of the base back to the Republic of Korea from the early 2000s on. In reaction to civil society's demand for incorporation of environment-related provisions and for proper remedial actions, several supplementary agreements on environmental issues have been added to the SOFA. However, the USFK has not faithfully implemented these new agreements, and the burden of environmental restoration remains with the South Korean government and taxpayers.

This chapter provides a historical overview of the U.S. military's environmental footprint in South Korea and discusses how the SOFA has changed in response to growing demand for environmentally friendly actions from South Korean civil society and the general public. The USFK and the SOFA have become sources of growing anti-Americanism in South Korea, particularly during the country's economic and political transition. Environmental protection and remediation at U.S. military bases has become an increasingly important policy issue that has escalated tension between the two countries. Several environmental provisions in supplementary documents added to the SOFA are interpreted differently by the two governments. This calls into question responsibility for restoration of the damaged environment at the returned and soon-to-be-returned bases. Two case studies—allegations of dioxin contamination at Camp Carroll and an oil spill at Camp Kim—illustrate how the existing environmental agreements under the current SOFA have failed to resolve the tension between the United States and South Korea.

THE U.S. MILITARY PRESENCE AND THE RISE OF ANTI-AMERICANISM

The presence of U.S. military forces on the Korean Peninsula as well as in other Asian countries such as Japan and the Philippines has been crucial in preventing a potential North Korean invasion and strengthening the U.S.–South Korean alliance since 1953. The U.S. military presence has also played an important role in improving South Korea's defense system and military power by allowing the transfer of material resources, weapons, and technology within a short span of time. Partly because of the continual military presence and assistance (figure 7.1), the South Korean government has been able to focus solely on economic development for decades; a tremendous amount of money has been saved because of low defense spending.[6]

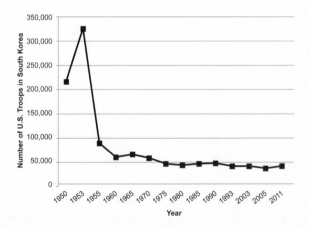

7.1 Number of Troops in Korea since 1953. Data compiled by the author based on *The Hankyoreh,* March 21, 2013; C. Murphy and G. Evans, "U.S. Military Personnel Strength by Country of Location since World War II, 1948–1973," in *Report on Korea,* ed. U.S. Embassy (Seoul: U.S. Embassy, 1976); and Sejong Institute, *U.S. Forces Korea and ROK-U.S. Security Alliance* (Seoul: Sejong Institute, 1996), 86.

Changing International and Domestic Environments

Geopolitical shifts in the region and domestic political-economic change has gradually begun to affect South Koreans' perspectives on the U.S. military presence.[7] First, the collapse of the Cold War system raised questions about the necessity of continued U.S. presence in Asia. North Korea's isolation from strong military allies such as the Soviet Union and China, coupled with the South's policy of Nordpolitik, in the 1990s diluted expectations of war in the region substantially.[8] This circumstance gave rise to the election of civilian presidents from progressive opposition parties from 1998 through 2007 to pursue a reconciliatory approach (i.e., the Sunshine policy) toward the North.

The public sentiment toward the United States and the U.S. forces in Korea has also changed over time, as South Korea has gone through rapid economic growth and democratization.[9] The enhancement of national pride among the South Korean people has led them to reflect upon the U.S.-ROK alliance and the U.S. role during Korea's struggle for democracy. As more progressive students and leaders have begun to see the United States as a behind-the-scene supporter of military dictatorship, believing that South Korea's democratization and reunification with the North could be deterred by the American presence, the antigovernment movement in the 1980s shifted its emphasis from a struggle against the authoritarian dictatorship to a struggle against the United States.[10] For the first time since the mid-1980s, dissidents and activists in Korea have started to criticize the United States, crying, "Yankee, go home."[11]

The most recent incident that triggered a bout of nationwide anti-Americanism involved the tragic deaths of two middle-school girls in 2002. On June 13, 2000, a sixty-ton U.S. Army armored vehicle hit two teenagers who were heading to a friend's birthday party. The USFK initially saw the case merely as an accident and did not have a plan to prosecute the two American soldiers involved. This decision provoked large-scale mass protests demanding the United States hand over the army sergeants to the South Korean Ministry of Justice for further investigation.[12] The subsequent refusal by the United States to surrender primary jurisdiction to the Republic of Korea following a trial before the U.S. military tribunal enraged even more people.[13] Continuous demonstrations eventually led to an official apology for the accident by the U.S. president George W. Bush and other senior officials. This event became a major issue during Korea's presidential election, held in December 2000. Roh Moo-hyun, the opposition candidate who later became president, promised, "If elected, I will deal with the Bush administration with national assertiveness. I will not kowtow to Washington. The US-ROK alliance should be transformed into horizontal relations—'equal partnership.'"[14]

The accident served as a focus for the subsequent negotiation for revamping the SOFA.[15] The rise of anti-Americanism, illustrated by this incident, has been an inevitable by-product of democratization; the transition has created political space for people to demand more equality in their nation's relations with the United States.[16] Various studies have argued that democratization became associated with the rise and spread of a strong brand of anti-Americanism.[17] These studies argue that increased national confidence—born of economic development, democratization, and heightened nationalism—led some South Koreans to discount the importance of the U.S.-ROK alliance and the U.S. forces in Korea.

Growth of Civil Society and Public Awareness

In addition to these broad economic and political changes, the growth of Korean civil society since the late 1990s has also generated new political avenues through which people can vent their grievances against the USFK. The historical roots of the civil society movement in Korea can be traced back to the intense movement for democratization during the authoritarian regimes. Since South Korea's democratization in 1987, civil society groups have transformed themselves from pro-democracy to policy-oriented advocacy groups and have started to discuss such social issues as labor, human rights, and the environment. Civil society activism in these arenas has played a crucial role in the country's democratic consolidation.[18] In the postdemocratization era, various civic organizations with different political ideologies and agendas have sought to participate in policy processes through collective action.[19] For example, sizable civic organizations such as Citizens' Coalition for Economic Justice (CCEJ) and People's Solidarity for Participatory Democracy (PSPD) to professional groups like Korea Federation for Environmental Movement (KFEM) and Green United Korea (GKU) have become important players in Korean politics.

The anti-American movement in the late 1990s and early 2000s served as a platform that united different civic groups around common goals.[20] These groups began to question the fairness of the SOFA and the legal rights and privileges the U.S. forces in Korea enjoy under the agreement.[21] As these groups mobilized to express their anti-American stance and a freer media started to report wrongdoings of GIs from the mid-1980s on, anti-Americanism became more pronounced.[22] The legislative politics and increasing political outlets for advocacy under the democratic system have enabled civil society organizations to criticize the United States for violating South Korea's domestic regulations (e.g., raping women and assaulting citizens) and international norms (e.g., human rights).[23]

Various changes in the geopolitics surrounding the Korean Peninsula and in the domestic political landscape have led many South Koreans—particularly democracy activists, civil society organizations, and younger generations—to cast doubts on Korea's traditional relationship with the United States. Many Koreans have witnessed the ambiguous attitude of the U.S. government toward Korea's military authoritarian governments. More recently, U.S. foreign policy toward North Korea—in particular, the Bush administration's policy in 2000s—created a political cleavage of sorts among Koreans over the future of the bilateral relationship between the United States and South Korea. These factors led the South Korean public to become more assertive, independent, and nationalistic in their relationship with the United States, prompting them to call for a new, equal partnership.[24]

ENVIRONMENTALISM AND THE NEW PHASE OF ANTI-AMERICANISM

Three kinds of anti-Americanism have been observed in Korea: the ideological variety, which is represented by radical student organizations, leftist scholars, and journalists; the pragmatic variety, represented by moderate NGOs concerned with specific issues such as the SOFA, environmental damage and operational control, rather than denying the United States; and the popular variety, which is episodic and emotionally responsive to certain incidents.[25] The vast majority of recent anti-American sentiment expressed by Korean civil society and the general public is the issue-oriented type. It is generally targeted at such issues as crimes against South Koreans perpetrated by the USFK or the terms and condi-

HEEJIN HAN AND YOOIL BAE

tions on which military facilities are being returned to South Korea.[26] This type of anti-Americanism is arising from Korea's pragmatic and policy-oriented concerns. This variant of anti-American sentiment has recently gained increasing scholarly attention. The environmental footprint of U.S. military bases in Korea and the damage created, the focus of this chapter, is an example of this issue-oriented anti-Americanism.

The environmental impact of the U.S. military bases was first exposed by media reports in the 1990s, but U.S.-ROK relations were not greatly affected until the early 2000s. Most of the environmental pollution cases have been reported annually by internal USFK whistleblowers or Korean residents living within the vicinity of U.S. bases.[27] A number of South Korean civil society organizations have also investigated the environmental impact of the U.S. bases. Their field reports have brought the seriousness of the environmental damage to the fore since the mid-1990s.[28] In 1996, Green Korea United and the "National Countermeasure Commission for the Return of Our Land from U.S. Bases" conducted a joint research project on the environment surrounding U.S. military bases.[29] This joint research committee found at least twenty-three known instances of environmental pollution over ten years (from 1990) at the time of their investigation.[30] It reported that the pollution level of soil, underground water, and noise in areas near the bases already significantly exceeded South Korean environmental standards. The committee started to inform this "inconvenient truth" to the public.

This problem solving–oriented civil society has continued to put pressure on the USFK to revise the SOFA; they have raised public awareness about the cost and negative impact of pollution and contamination caused by USFK operations.[31] But the issue was not viewed as alarming in the 1990s, largely because environmental consciousness among ROK officials and the general public was at a relatively low level. Environmental protection remained secondary to other interests, such as economic growth and national security. As more environmental pollution cases were reported in the 2000s, however, Koreans began to realize the severity of the damage caused by U.S. forces in Korea. Oil spills and leaks from dilapidated underground storage tanks at some U.S. military bases have continued to pollute water and soil.[32] Moreover, the noise from aircraft landings and takeoffs, gunfire, artillery fire, and the sounds of helicopters and vehicles has continued to disrupt local residents' daily lives and impact their properties.[33] Illegal disposal of construction materials and toxic chemical waste have caused pollution of water and soil. These problems have often gone beyond the immediate vicinity of the military bases, negatively affecting surrounding areas.

In 2000, an environmental organization disclosed that the USFK had illegally disposed of 470 bottles of highly toxic formaldehyde from the Yongsan base mortuary into the Han River without proper treatment.[34] The Han River is a major source of drinking water for more than ten million people in Seoul metropolitan area. The USFK refused to prosecute the wrongdoer and continued to engage in actions that cause negative environmental externalities.[35] According to Green United Korea, since the 2000 formaldehyde dumping incident, an average of 8.8 cases of pollution-related incidents have occurred per year, which was more than twice that occurred throughout the 1990s.[36] These kinds of incidents began to alert South Koreans of the severity of the environmental damage caused by U.S. military bases.[37]

Environmental Provisions Incorporated into the SOFA

The United States responded to the growing public concern about environmental conditions at U.S. military bases and vicinities by adding various environmental provisions to the SOFA.[38] For the first time since the SOFA was signed in 1966, the two governments acknowledged the need to incorporate an environmental protection policy. In 2001 they signed the "Memorandum of Special Understanding on Environmental Protection," which says that the United States would adopt and comply with environmental governing standards, updated every two years to reflect the advancement in each country's domestic environmental standards. The United States would also establish a procedure regarding information exchange between the two parties and provide Korean officials access to U.S. bases for environmental surveys, monitoring, and evaluation. Moreover, the United States agreed to undertake remedial action in cases of contamination that present "known, imminent, and substantial endangerment" (KISE) to human health.[39] This document was not binding but was a meaningful step toward mutual commitment to environmentally friendly actions by introducing procedural rules for environmental surveys and responses.

Following this agreement, the "Joint Environmental Information Exchange and Access Procedures" (the so-called TAB A) was announced in

2002. According to this document, the USFK bases are subject to Korean experts' investigation for any possible pollution and contamination incidents, and if any damage to the soil or water is identified, the sites should be restored to their original condition based on negotiations between the two countries. TAB A also states that remedial process should be jointly monitored before the bases are returned to Korea.[40] Under this agreement the joint investigation for a pollution case proceeds in three steps. First, the USFK provides information regarding base facilities and environmental conditions of bases to the Korean government (within thirty days). The second step involves field access, research, investigation, and analyses (within sixty days). The third step entails exchange of investigation reports and information between the two governments (within fifteen days). If any environmental damage is detected, the USFK should pay for proper remedial measures for the polluted bases before their return to the Republic of Korea. In 2003, the two governments signed another supplementary document, titled "Procedures for Environmental Survey and Consultation on Remediation for Facilities and Areas Designated to Be Granted or Returned." This document stated that the United States will plan and execute at its own expense remedial measures in accordance with the SOFA and any relevant agreements by the United States before its bases and facilities are returned to the Republic of Korea.[41] The two governments also agreed to release information to the media and the general public regarding these procedures, with the exception of some specific categories of information that may be subject to approval by the cochairs of the SOFA Environmental Subcommittee.[42]

Redeployment of the USFK and the Struggle over Cleanup

The U.S. decision to redeploy its troops in the early 2000s presented an opportunity for South Korea to test the USFK's commitment to these newly incorporated environmental provisions. Various factors—including the end of the Cold War, reduced threat from communist countries, and the development of military technology—led to changes in U.S. strategic plans in the early 2000s. The United States recognized that a large number of soldiers and heavily armed forces were no longer necessary in the region.[43] In South Korea it decided to relocate the forward-deployed USFK south of the Han River, based on the Pentagon's "Global Defense Posture Review," revised after the attacks of September 11, 2001.[44] U.S.

secretary of defense Donald Rumsfeld strongly argued that the U.S. military should adapt to new challenges coming from terrorist groups that might use weapons of mass destruction to launch attacks at unexpected times and places.[45] In the eyes of the Pentagon's transformation planners, the large contingents of U.S. ground forces on the Korean Peninsula equipped with heavily armored vehicles appeared outdated and less adaptable to the requirements of new missions of the twenty-first century.[46] The United States also planned to expand USFK missions outside South Korea under the broad scheme of realigning its overseas forces.[47] In July 2004 the United States and the Republic of Korea laid down a blueprint for realigning the USFK through a consultative body called the "Future of the ROK-U.S. Alliance Policy Initiative"; the two governments agreed to reduce U.S. ground forces by 12,500 by the end of 2008.[48]

Another reason for the redeployment was that the Korean government suffered a shortage of land available for its growing economy and population. This pressure for more space led the two countries to sign the Land Partnership Plan in 2002 and in 2004 and to agree on relocation of the USFK from the city center to local areas. According to this plan, the USFK agreed to return more than thirty bases and sixty training sites to Korea (approximately 170 million square meters of land), and South Korea agreed to grant 2,973 acres of new land for relocation of facilities.[49] The redeployment decision also partially reflected the anti-American sentiment among South Koreans.[50] Defense Secretary Rumsfeld said, "We do need to rearrange our footprint there. We are irritating the South Korean people. What we need to do is have a smaller footprint, fewer people and have them arranged not so much in populated areas."[51] Although the USFK spokesman stated that the relocation plan had nothing to do with the public sentiment, it would be fair to say that anti-Americanism and public concerns about environmental conditions at and near base areas partially prompted the decision to relocate U.S. bases.[52]

After signing redeployment agreements, the two countries embarked on an environmental survey in 2005 at U.S. military bases planned for return to South Korea. From June through September of that year, SOFA's Environmental Subcommittee convened to review the survey results and negotiate the remedial measures and terms. The meetings were stalled, however, as Korea's Ministry of Environment demanded compensation for damage at USFK bases be offered in accordance with Korea's domestic laws, including the Soil Environment Preservation Act. The USFK insisted that it did not bear any responsibility for cleanup, arguing that the pollutants found in its bases did not pose "known, imminent, and substantial endangerment" threats to human beings, so-called KISE threats—the required criteria for U.S. remedial action.[53]

As the two sides could not resolve their differences, the issue of cleanup at the returned bases was taken to the Security Policy Initiative, a body led by defense ministers and attended by high-ranking policy makers from both governments. This heightening of the returned base issue to a security talk level meant that the environmental issue was discussed only at the margin, together with other highly sensitive and politicized security issues, such as the transfer of wartime operation control (OPCON). As a result, the issue of the USFK's environmental responsibility for cleanup was eclipsed by other politically charged agendas influenced by the power politics between the two countries. The Republic of Korea, which had insisted on the "polluter pays principle," eventually yielded to the U.S. decision and accepted the earlier-than-scheduled return of the bases; it refused to release any information to the Korean public and media regarding contamination at the bases.

Actions of the two governments infuriated South Korea's general public and civil society, forcing the National Assembly (parliament) to hold hearings on June 25 and 26. The assembly's Committee for Environment and Labor requested the results of environmental investigations at a total of twenty-nine bases along with the contents of the United States–Korean deal. The submitted investigation report revealed that at least twenty-six of twenty-nine bases in such cities as Chunchon, Gunsan, and Inchon were severely polluted (ten soil pollution and sixteen water pollution cases), and some of the pollution levels exceeded the South Korean domestic limit by more than 150 times.[54] Despite this revelation, parliamentary hearings could not demand accountability from those responsible for the contamination and reached rather ambiguous conclusions: (1) There were no agreed-upon standards about the pollution caused by the USFK and its cleanup; (2) the problem of environmental damage at returned bases was secondary only to the maintenance of amicable relationships between the two countries; and (3) revision of the SOFA was necessary for implementation of the newly established environmental policy.[55]

The inaction of the two governments regarding the severity of the environmental damages and the lukewarm pressure by the National Assembly triggered much stronger protests in South Korea by civil society organizations. They continued to pressure both governments to conduct more comprehensive investigations at every base to be returned. Secretary General Kyungsu Park-Jung of the National Campaign for the Eradication of Crimes by U.S Troops in Korea—an NGO established in late 1993 to protect victims of crimes committed by the USFK and to call for amendment of the SOFA—said that "an all-out investigation not just at returned bases but at all U.S. army bases is necessary. We also need to revise SOFA's environmental contents."[56] The environmental pollution at the returned bases and the USFK's lack of action thus resulted in a fresh wave of anti-Americanism and a new round of environmental activism calling for a drastic revision of the SOFA.

The USFK did not faithfully comply with the newly added environmental provisions under the SOFA regime. It failed to inform the Korean Ministry of Environment and the concerned local governments of the degrees of pollution and contamination at USFK facilities. Despite the U.S. claim that inspections were conducted according to its environmental governing standards, Korean government authorities or experts were not allowed to confirm their findings.[57] Nor did the USFK grant the public access to information regarding the investigation. The two governments could not reach a deal through SOFA's Environmental Subcommittee as a mechanism for communication and conflict resolution. The final decisions made at the Security Policy Initiative thus simply reflected the asymmetrical balance of power between the United States and South Korea.

WHERE EACH PARTY STANDS

The United States has developed one of the most rigorous environmental legal and regulatory systems in the world. In the post–Cold War era, it began to take measures to hold the military accountable to its environmental and natural resources (ENR) laws.[58] The administrations of George H. W. Bush and Bill Clinton wanted the military to incorporate ENR protection into day-to-day operations and go beyond compliance to take a more proactive role in avoiding ENR violations.[59] As environmental concerns were incorporated as part of security in the 1990s, the United States created a new deputy secretary of defense position focusing on environmental security and increased its budget for restoration of military facilities suffering from environmental degradation.[60]

The United States urged its military to become much greener in its overseas operations and management of bases.[61] For instance, since the disclosures of serious environmental damage at other U.S. bases (for example, in the Philippines), the U.S. government set forth minimum standards on the disposal of hazardous and toxic materials and wastes.[62] However, compared to the well-developed and clearly structured domestic environmental standards, the U.S. environmental policies applied to overseas bases and military operations are much more obscure and flexible, allowing great discretion to policy makers. As a result, the U.S. policies frequently depend on negotiations with individual countries, and outcomes of the bilateral negotiations often reflect the balance of power between the United States and its counterparts.[63] Despite the Department of Defense's policy of nondiscrimination, it has applied different environmental guidelines and liability schemes in different countries with which it has defense agreements.[64]

The USFK adheres to three sets of laws in Korea: the SOFA, its own internal environmental regulations (environmental remediation for Department of Defense activities overseas and environmental governing standards), and South Korea's environmental laws. The USFK established the internal environmental governing standards in 1997 and amended them in 2004. However, this internal regulation, composed of nineteen chapters, does not have any effective enforcement mechanism.[65] In South Korea's case, the SOFA has remained most important set of laws because it has allowed the U.S. forces in Korea to shirk their responsibility in cleaning up the pollution and contamination by referring to Article IV, which states that the United States bears "no duty of restoring to the original state."[66] Based on this, the USFK has argued that it does not bear any responsibility to restore the returned bases, and South Korea does not need to pay the USFK for the value of facilities it leaves behind. The United States has maintained that the increase in value of returned bases and the U.S. facilities during the period of its usage will offset the expense for cleanup. Given that the United States would not demand compensation from the Republic of Korea for the increased value of the returned bases, Koreans should not expect the United States to pay for cleanup.

To make matters worse, the newly added environmental provisions have proven too ambiguous to ensure any remedial action by the USFK for the pollution it has caused so far. For instance, the "Procedures for Environmental Survey and Consultation on Remediation for Facilities and Areas Designated to be Granted or Returned" only "recommends" necessary remedial works to the USFK without binding power and does not provide any specific requirement about condition, cost sharing, and duration of the works.[67] Even if "known, imminent, and substantial endangerment" human health can be established, the USFK is not legally obliged to remedy the pollution. Although it was only a matter of "respecting," not enforcing, South Korean environmental laws, the USFK has continued to deny the possibility of imminent and substantial damage to the environment stemming from the daily operations of its bases.

The stance that the South Korean government (particularly the Ministry of Environment) and civil society activists have taken can be summarized as follows: First, the USFK should abide by the Soil Environment Preservation Act and the Groundwater Act of Korea.[68] The government has argued that the threats posed by contamination and pollution were already imminent and substantial, exceeding the criteria specified in relevant Korean laws. Second, the most critical issue is the cost of cleanup. The South Korean government and the general public believe that the U.S. forces in Korea should follow the "polluter pays principle"—a widely accepted international environmental norm. The expense of the cleanup of the returned bases and soon-to-be-returned bases amounts to 300 billion won (US$290 million), which has been put forth by Korean taxpayers so far, and the cost of USFK's reluctance to fulfill its environmental commitment has been rising.[69] In the case of twenty-three bases returned in 2007, the initial committee report estimated cleanup costs at 119.7 billion won (US$84.6 million). However, a Defense Ministry project estimate in August 2008 put it at 190.7 billion won, and an in-depth study conducted in November of the same year estimated an even higher figure: 320 billion won.[70] In a recent survey, about 79 percent of South Koreans said they believe the United States should clean up pollution within U.S. military bases, while only 4 percent said South Korea is responsible for cleanup.[71] Critics have also argued that Korean taxpayers should no longer bear any extra burden of cleanup when it already provides bases for free to the USFK and pays approximately 40 percent of the USFK's annual costs.[72]

Third, South Korean environmental NGOs and activists have argued that the SOFA should be revamped. From their perspectives, it is not fair when compared to SOFAs between the United States and NATO or between the United States and Germany, for instance.[73] In the case of the latter, strict regulations and rules under German environmental laws apply to all U.S. military activities.[74] A secretary-general of GKU argued that the United States has applied double standards in its environmental policy at its overseas military bases by applying much more stringent policies in advanced countries than in less powerful countries like Korea and the Philippines.[75] Many civil society organizations thus believe that the SOFA itself should be revamped to include more detailed provisions and provide clear standards for environmental remedy and monitoring procedures.[76] This idea is shared by the broader South Korean society. When Green United Korea asked Korean people about the possible solutions to pollution at U.S. military bases, about 59.6 percent chose amendment of the U.S.–South Korea SOFA, while 25 percent said the United States should take greater responsibility.[77]

CASE STUDIES: AGENT ORANGE AND OIL SPILLS

The Camp Carroll Controversy

The controversy since 2011 over Camp Carroll, located in Chilgok County, Kyungsang-buk-do (North Kyungsang, a province southeast of the peninsula), illustrates the ongoing tension between the two countries over environmental contamination at U.S. military bases. Although this case is merely one of scores of similar cases, it demonstrates how different the two governments' approaches and perspectives toward environmental investigation and remediation policy are. The existing SOFA regime continues to pose obstacles to fast discovery and treatment of damage of hazardous substances by the U.S. military.

The controversy started when a former U.S. staff who worked at Camp Carroll told a radio show in Arizona that he remembered at least 250 barrels (each 55 gallons) of defoliants (mostly Agent Orange) having been disposed underground at the base in the late 1970s.[78] Shortly thereafter, Chilgok County cautiously raised the question of whether the high incidence of cancer observed among residents of a village close to Camp Carroll could possibly be explained by the underground disposal by the United States of highly toxic chemical materials such as Agent Orange, pesticides, and solvents. The village people had drunk water directly from their wells until just a few years ago, when a modern water and sewage system was finally installed. This alleged connection between toxic waste disposal at Camp Carroll and local residents' health conditions ignited the debate on locating and remediating of a large amount of Agent Orange that was supposedly brought to the camp in the late 1960s. Some argued that the remaining quantities of Agent Orange might have been stored at Camp Carroll after its usage at the Demilitarized Zone (DMZ) area in the late 1960s, contaminating soil and water and affecting the health of local residents.

In May 2011 environmental NGOs and civil society organizations agreed to form an alliance called Agent Orange Risk, launching campaigns calling for a response from the USFK. On June 1, South Korea and the USFK convened a meeting of the SOFA Environmental Subcommittee and agreed to apply sophisticated methods to conduct investigation inside the camp. Both sides established their respective investigation teams. The Korean team included not only governmental entities but also local governments and civic organizations, reflecting a more democratic composition. Both parties agreed that once the ground-penetrating radar investigation had located the areas where the barrels had been buried, soil and water samples from the area would be taken for separate research by both governments. Then the two parties would invite experts and host discussion sessions before reaching a final conclusion.[79] Based on this agreement, the joint investigation began on June 2. The USFK maintained the position that it would conduct water and radar investigations first before it conducted soil investigation; the ROK's Ministry of Environment repeatedly demanded that both water and soil investigation be carried out simultaneously.

On May 27 the joint investigation team took ten samples of underground water from the south of Camp Carroll. The mayor of Chilgok County asked the USFK to establish clear criteria for the investigation, study the impact on local people, and discuss environmental and remedial measures (in case contamination is confirmed). In mid-June, an alliance of about eighty South Korean civil society organizations hosted a conference under the theme of "Agent Orange Contamination at Camp Carroll and the Problems with the Government's Response," maintaining that Camp Carroll was already contaminated by dioxin. They argued that the USFK should conduct soil investigations, and any data on storage, usage, transfer, and disposal of Agent Orange collected through the monitoring process should be disclosed.[80] The alliance urged the USFK to allow the Korean investigation team composed of governmental and civil society actors to enter the camp to conduct in-depth environmental impact assessment.

The joint investigation team concluded on August 5 that it could not find any defoliant disposed at the camp and that neither soil nor water samples contained any significant amount of dioxin.[81] The U.S. Eighth Army Commander repeated the same position: although there was some evidence that Agent Orange left over from the Vietnam War was sent to areas including Utah, quantities sent to Korea had been completely used up in the DMZ area in 1968.[82] This announcement did not address public concerns about the health impact of the disposed chemicals. Cognizant of this and to alleviate fears, the Republic of Korea in September 2011 ordered the Ministry of Environment to investigate the health situation of local residents. The investigation was conducted over a period of a year, covering five thousand residents. It found neither dioxin in residents' blood samples nor direct health impact from drinking water in the vicinity of Camp Carroll.[83] This investigation also did not provide any proper explanation for the higher-than-national-average incidence of cancer, high blood pressure, and asthma among local residents, particularly among those who lived longer, failing to mitigate the public distrust of the investigation procedures and outcomes.[84] Local residents and NGOs continued to question the validity and credibility of the investigation and its outcomes. At an USFK-organized meeting in June 2011, one local resident shouted: "The USFK disposed defoliants, which is an outright criminal act. Who in the world lets the accused do the investigation?"[85]

Oil Spills at Yongsan Garrison and Camp Kim

Oil-contaminated water at Yongsan District, in central Seoul, was first found in 2001 around Noksapyeong Station near Yongsan Garrison. Contaminated water was found again in 2008 at Namyeong Station, near Camp Kim. The soil contamination near Noksapyeong Station is believed to have been caused by a cracked old tank underneath the garrison. The USFK announced that it had finished the cleanup in 2006, but the Seoul city government has continued to detect polluted groundwater near the station.[86]

Yongsan Garrison and Camp Kim were identified as the sources of this oil spill; the leaked oil contained substances such as Jet Propellant 8, a type of jet fuel used by the USFK, not by Koreans for any civilian purposes. The Seoul Metropolitan City presumes that at least 12,225 square meters of land (11,766 square meters around Noksapyeong Station and 459 square meters around Camp Kim) and more than seven million liters of underground water have been polluted thus far.[87] The water and land from these two sites contain various harmful chemicals (benzene, toluene, and xylene), and the degree of contamination is quite severe. According to Representative Jang Ha-na of the main opposition Democratic Party, more than 1,430 milligrams of total petroleum hydrocarbons (TPH) per liter, an amount 958 times acceptable levels, was detected in underground water in the neighborhood of Camp Kim in 2011.[88]

As of this writing, the USFK has not responded to the government's request to collaborate in an investigation of this case. The U.S. force's unwillingness to cooperate has led the Seoul city government to take remedial measures itself. It has removed about 2,000 tons of oil-contaminated underground water around U.S. Army bases in Seoul since the early 2000s.[89] It has extracted at least 568 liters of floating oil and 1,970 tons of polluted underground water released from Yongsan Garrison and Camp Kim.[90] According to a report from the Korea Rural Community Corporation, more than 5 billion won has been spent on cleaning up the area near Noksapyeong Station, and nearly 800 million won has been spent since 2003 on purification of the polluted area near Camp Kim.[91]

As the cost of remedy rose, the Seoul Metropolitan City filed an administrative suit against the Korean central government for compensation. In 2009, Seoul city won a lawsuit that demanded the central government pay the sum of 2.2 billion won (US$2 million) the city had spent for the cleanup around Noksapyeong Station between 2001 and 2008. Seoul city lodged another suit, demanding 650 million won in compensation for similar operations in 2009 and 2010.[92] In 2011, the city urged the central government to pay 263.9 million won (US$229,115) that it had spent in 2010 to purify polluted groundwater around Noksapyeong Station.[93] These lawsuits have taken place because under the current SOFA the South Korean government, not the USFK, had to bear the burden of compensating third parties who suffer damage caused by the USFK.[94] Based on this policy, the Seoul Central District Court ruled in favor of the Seoul Metropolitan Government and ordered the Korean central government to compensate the city for environmental damage caused by oil spills. So far, the city has received 2.91 billion won in compensation against expenses it has incurred on investigation and purification from 2001 to 2010.[95]

The fact that the Seoul city government has had to spend considerable financial resources on cleanup since the early 2000s indicates that the USFK has failed to repair cracked and rundown oil tanks and their pipes. All remedial measures for this environmental damage have been paid for by South Korean taxpayers, who ironically are potential victims directly affected by contamination of water and soil, in the absence of remedial measures. Knowing that ROK authorities can conduct investigations only at points of pollution sources (i.e., Yongsan Garrison and Camp Kim) with permission from the USFK under the SOFA rules, both the central government and the Seoul city government have been asking the USFK to cooperate. But the USFK has not answered these calls and has denied the Korean government access to these locations.

As the criticism from the city government under its mayor Park Wonsoon and NGOs intensified, the USFK finally agreed in May 2013 to discuss the matter in the SOFA Environmental Subcommittee. In June 2013, Korea's Ministries of Environment, Foreign Affairs, and Defense as well as Seoul Metropolitan City Government and the USFK representatives and environmental experts met, mutually recognizing the severity of the pollution issue, to discuss a joint investigation and agreed to organize an Environmental Joint Working Group[96] However, it remains to be seen whether the USFK will conduct joint investigations at these locations and take proper remedial measures. The USFK announced that it is too early to say whether there will be any investigation inside the camps.[97] Both the central government and the Seoul city government want the pollution issue to be addressed by 2016, when the garrison and camp will be returned to South Korea. They expect the contamination and pollution to be much more serious inside these facilities and believe that further damage to water and land and public health can be prevented by taking prompt actions.

CHARTING THE FUTURE OF THE ALLIANCE

Since the mid-1990s, and particularly after the early 2000s, when the United States decided to return its military bases under the new strategic plan to redeploy its troops, environmental pollution and contamination at U.S. bases and their impact on local environment and local residents' health have become a fresh source of anti-American sentiment in Korea. South Korea's growing civil society and public opinion, informed by liberal investigative journalism, have put pressure on both the USFK and the South Korean government to address the environmental externalities produced by U.S. military bases and their operations from environmental sovereignty and social justice perspectives. In response to this pressure and criticism, the USFK and the ROK have added several covenants to the SOFA that contain provisions regarding environmental standards, exchange of information, access to bases, results of environmental performance, and environmental remedies.

These supplementary documents have not resolved environmental pollution and contamination problems at U.S. military bases, however, as the SOFA does not hold the USFK legally accountable to South Korean domestic laws. Moreover, the SOFA's supplementary agreements do not specify any clear standards for pollution or remediation, nor do they have any enforcement mechanisms. Therefore, the controversy over who is responsible for environmental damage and cleanup continues today, as the case studies illustrate. As long as environmental clauses remain proclamatory rather than legally binding, and as long as the USFK possesses exclusive jurisdiction over all facilities and land within U.S. military bases, environmental protection and remedies will remain only a secondary concern to the USFK, compared with other priorities such as strategic interests or budgetary concerns.[98] The environmental impact of U.S. military bases and other relevant issues (such as local people's rights to environmental safety and rights to know) have been neglected in favor of security concerns.[99]

The revision of the SOFA in the direction of incorporating more stringent environmental clauses does not seem so easy. Given the security role that the USFK has played for several decades under the broader framework of the United States–ROK alliance, the Korean government feels reluctant to demand any drastic reform on environmental issues.[100] In light of continuous threats posed by the nuclear brinkmanship of North Korea and the continuous importance of South Korea to the economic and political interests of the United States and vice versa, the need to maintain a healthy U.S.–South Korea alliance remains the primary political and strategic need for both parties. Based on this shared acknowledgment, the two governments should consider adopting a broader definition of security that incorporates such nontraditional dimensions as environmental challenges and people's health and well-being.[101]

Both governments have sacrificed environmental security in favor of the traditional notion of security. However, the USFK's unwillingness to reduce its negative environmental footprint can feed into growing anti-American sentiment among Korean people, posing a threat to the U.S.-ROK alliance itself. Despite a decrease in military presence and influence exerted by the United States, a significant number of USFK personnel will continue to interact with Koreans for years to come; this interaction has been an important component of the healthy alliance between the two countries.[102] Continued conflicts and dissonance between the USFK and local citizens over such issues as environmental protection might hurt the U.S. force's morale, which was one of the reasons that prompted the USFK to decide to realign its bases in the early 2000s.[103] The U.S. force's failure to address the anti-American sentiment exacerbated by its neglect of environmental externalities from its military presence in a more transparent and responsible manner might morph into a broad nationalistic opposition to the United States–ROK alliance. Such negligence might undermine the international trust, prestige, and soft power of the U.S. government in the long run.[104] For a healthy future of the alliance, the two governments should design ways to respond to South Koreans' growing concerns about the environmental impact of U.S. military bases.

NOTES

1   The official name of the SOFA is the Agreement under Article IV of the Mutual Defense Treaty between the Republic of Korea and the United States, Regarding Facilities and Areas and the Status of United States Armed Forces in the Republic of Korea. It was revised in 1991 and 2001. For the amended agreement, see www.state.gov/documents/organization/129549.pdf.

2   Elisabeth Schober, "Encounters: The US Armed Forces in Korea and Entertainment Districts in and near Seoul," in *Korea: Politics, Economy, and Society*, ed. Rüdiger Frank, James E. Hoare, Patrick Köllner, and Susan Pares (Boston: Brill, 2011), 207–31.

3   Jinwung Kim, "Recent Anti-Americanism in South Korea: The Causes," *Asian Survey* 29 (1989): 749–63, 758.

4   James Feinerman, "The U.S.-Korean Status of Forces Agreements as a Source

of Continuing Korean Anti-American Attitudes," in *Korean Attitudes toward the United States' Changing Dynamics*, ed. David I. Steinberg (Armonk, NY: M. E. Sharpe, 2005), 196–212.

5   Thomas Kern, "Anti-Americanism in South Korea: From Structural Cleavages to Protest," *Korea Journal* 45 (2005): 257–88, available at http://iis-db.stanford .edu/pubs/22961/Kim-Hakjoon_FINAL_May_2010.pdf; and Chang Hun Oh and Celeste Arrington, "Democratization and Changing Anti-American Sentiments in South Korea," *Asian Survey* 47, no. 2 (2007): 327–50.

6   Japan followed the same course, although much earlier than South Korea. The U.S.-Japan security alliance since 1951 has played a crucial role in promoting the Japanese postwar economic miracle. See, for example, Aaron Forsberg, *America and the Japanese Miracle: The Cold War Context of Japan's Postwar Economic Revival, 1950–60* (Chapel Hill: University of North Carolina Press, 2000); and Richard J. Samuels, *Rich Nation, Strong Army: National Security and the Technological Transformation of Japan* (Ithaca, NY: Cornell University Press, 1994).

7   Gi-Wook Shin, "South Korean Anti-Americanism: A Comparative Perspective," *Asian Survey* 36, no. 8 (1996): 787–803.

8   "Nordpolitik" (northern policy), the centerpiece of the Roh Taw-woo administration's foreign policy, refers to Korea's open-door policies toward Communist countries and North Korea.

9   Kim, "Recent Anti-Americanism in South Korea."

10   Ibid.; and Gi-Wook Shin and Hilary Ian Izatt, "Anti-American and Anti-Alliance Sentiments in South Korea," *Asian Survey* 51 (2011): 1113–33.

11   Kim, "Recent Anti-Americanism in South Korea," 761.

12   Don Kirk, "Koreans Protest US Military's Handling of a Fatal Accident," *New York Times*, August 4, 2002, available at www.nytimes.com/2002/08/04/world/ koreans-protest-us-military-s-handling-of-a-fatal-accident.html; and Ji-Ho Kim, "U.S. Military Refuses to Relinquish Jurisdiction over American Soldiers," *Korea Herald*, August 8, 2002, available at http://news.naver.com/main/read.nhn?mode =LSD&mid=sec&sid1=108&oid=044&aid=0000032139.

13   Yoon-Ho Alex Lee, "Criminal Jurisdiction under the US–South Korea Status of Forces Agreement: Problems to Proposals," *Journal of Transnational Law and Policy* 13 (2003): 213–49.

14   Hakjoon Kim, "A Brief History of the US-ROK Alliance and Anti-Americanism in South Korea," *Walter H. Shorenstein Asia-Pacific Research Center Report* 31, no. 1 (2010): 1–45.

15   BBC News, "US Soldiers Charged for Korean Deaths" July 5, 2002, available at http://news.bbc.co.uk/2/hi/asia-pacific/2097137.stm.

16   Kathrine H. S. Moon, "Korean Nationalism, Anti-Americanism, and Democratic Consolidation," in *Korea's Democratization*, ed. Samuel S. Kim (New York: Cambridge University Press, 2003), 135–57.

17   Shin and Izatt, "Anti-American and Anti-Alliance." Kim, "Brief History of the US-ROK Alliance."

18   Sunhyuk Kim, *The Politics of Democratization in Korea: The Role of Civil Society*

(Pittsburgh: Pittsburgh University Press, 2000).

19   Yooil Bae, Dong-Ae Shin, and Yong Wook Lee, "Making and Unmaking of Trans-national Environmental Cooperation: The Case of Reclamation Projects in Japan and Korea," *Pacific Review* 24 (2011): 201–23.

20   Moon, "Korean Nationalism," 145.

21   Mark Ruppert, "Criminal Jurisdiction over Environmental Offenses Committed Overseas: How to Maximize and When To Say 'NO,'" *Air Force Law Review* 40 (1996): 1–48, available at www.afjag.af.mil/shared/media/document/AFD-081204–039.pdf.

22   Oh and Arrington, "Democratization and Changing Anti-American Sentiments," 335.

23   Ibid., 140.

24   Kim, "Recent Anti-Americanism in South Korea," 758.

25   Sung-han Kim, "Anti-American Sentiment and the ROK-U.S. Alliance," *Korean Journal of Defensive Analysis* 15 (2003): 105–30.

26   Bruce Cumings, "The Structural Basis of 'Anti-Americanism' in the Republic of Korea," in *Korean Attitudes toward the United States: Changing Dynamics*, ed. David I. Steinberg (Armonk, NY: M. E. Sharpe, 2005), 91–115.

27   "Juhan migun hwankyung ohyum sangseupjuk . . . deuruhnangutman yishib-nyungan 47gun" [Habitual environmental pollution by the U.S. military . . . 47 'exposed' cases in twenty years]," *Hankyoreh*, May 22, 2011, available at www.hani.co.kr/arti/society/environment/479193.html.

28   Moon, "Korean Nationalism," 147.

29   Working Group for Environmental Research on Damage Caused by the U.S. Military, "Report on Environmental Damage Caused by U.S. Military Bases in South Korea," available at www.usacrime.or.kr/frame-data.htm.

30   Donga-A Ilbo, "U.S. Military Bases' Oil Spill . . . Why Is It Continued?" September 18, 2002, available at http://news.donga.com/List/Series_70030000000040/3/70030000000040/20020509/7817536/1.

31   Working Group, "Report on Environmental Damage," 2; and Moon, "Korean Nationalism," 147.

32   Oil spills have been the most common forms of environmental harms caused by the U.S. forces in Korea, with 77 percent of soil and water pollution attributed to them. See Manjong Lee, "Banhwan migun gijiyui hwankyung ohyum munje e daehan bubjuk gochal: Hanmi SOFA hwankyung gyujungyui munjejumgwa gaesunbangahn jungsim" [Study on environmental pollution in returned American military bases regarding its legal aspects—centered on finding and settling the problems of SOFA environmental provision established between Korea and America], *Hwankyungbub yungu* [Environmental law studies] 30 (2008): 139–62.

33   Chang-Hee Nam, "Relocating the U.S. Forces in South Korea: Strained Alliance, Emerging Partnership in the Changing Defense Posture," *Asian Survey* 46 (2006): 613–31.

34   National Archives of Korea, "US Military's Discharge of Toxic Chemicals into the Han River," available at http://archives.go.kr/next/search/listSubjectDescription.do?id=006947&pageFlag=.

35   Green Korea United, "The Eighth US Army Division Discharged Toxic Fluid (Formaldehyde) into the Han-River," available at http://green-korea.tistory .com/74, accessed May 30, 2013.

36   Green Korea United, "Environmental Problem Related to Military Activities," available at http://green-korea.tistory.com/44, accessed June 19, 2013.

37   Working Group, "Report on Environmental Damage," 5.

38   Lee, "Banhwan migun gijiyui," 143.

39   Young Geun Chae, "Environmental Contamination at U.S. Military Bases in South Korea and the Responsibility to Clean Up," *Environmental Law Reporter* 40 (2010): 10078–97.

40   Lee, "Banhwan migun gijiyui," 149.

41   "Banhwan migun giji ohyum miguni chaekimjinda" [U.S. takes charge of the pollution at returned bases], *Hankyoreh*, May 30, 2003, available at http://legacy .www.hani.co.kr/section-003100000/2003/05/003100000200305301856744.html.

42   Chae, "Environmental Contamination," 10,086.

43   Foreign Press Centers, U.S. Department of State Archives, "U.S. Global Force Posture Review," July 29, 2013, http://2002–2009-fpc.state.gov/35246.htm, accessed July 30, 2013.

44   Nam, "Relocating the U.S. Forces."

45   Ibid., 620.

46   Ibid.

47   Sung-Ki Jung, "USFK Seeks To Expand Role Outside Peninsula," *Korea Times*, February 24, 2010, available at www.koreatimes.co.kr/www/news/nation/2010/02/ 205_61388.html.

48   Nam, "Relocating the U.S. Forces," 615.

49   "Korea's Military Allowance to the U.S," *Hankyoreh*, February 2, 2007, available at www.hani.co.kr/arti/politics/defense/188045.html.

50   Nam, "Relocating the U.S. Forces," 618.

51   Rumsfeld as quoted in Schober, "Encounters," 228.

52   Nam, "Relocating the U.S. Forces."

53   Young Geun Chae, "Problems with the 2007 US-ROK Base Return Agreement and Future Agenda," paper presented at the Workshop in Commemoration of the Publication of the Report on Environmental Damage of U.S. Military Bases, Seoul, South Korea, August 7, 2008.

54   "Severe Pollution Levels Detected at 13 U.S. Bases Scheduled for Return to S. Korea," *Hankyoreh*, March 18, 2009, available at http://english.hani.co.kr/arti/ english_edition/%20e_national/344760.html.

55   Working Group, "Report on Environmental Damage," 1.

56   Jiekyu Goh and Eunji Kim, "Chunchon Camp Page migun giji oyumjung choiak" [Chunchon Camp Page, the worst pollution among U.S. military bases], *Shisa-In* [Inside current events], June 2, 2011, available at http://media.daum.net/society/ others/view.html?cateid=3000&newsid=20110602101254915&p=sisain.

57   Working Group, "Report on Environmental Damage," 12.

58   Robert F. Durant, *The Greening of the U.S. Military: Environmental Policy, National*

Security, and Organization Change (Washington, D.C.: Georgetown University Press, 2007); and Robert F. Durant, "National Defense, Environmental Regulation, and Overhead Democracy: A View from 'Greening' of the U.S. Military," *Public Organization Review* 10 (2010): 223–44.

59 Durant, "National Defense," 224.

60 Lee, "Banhwan migun gijiyui," 148.

61 Ibid., 144–45.

62 For further discussion of environmental damage at U.S. bases overseas, see Kiminori Hayashi, Oshima Ken'ichi, and Yokemoto Masafum, "Overcoming American Military Base Pollution in Asia: Japan, Okinawa, Philippines," *Asia-Pacific Journal: Japan Focus* 28 (2009), available at www.japanfocus.org/-Oshima-Ken_ichi/3185.

63 Yusun Woo, "Environmental Problems on the US Military Bases in the Republic of Korea: Who Is Responsible for the Cleanup Expenses and Whose Environmental Standards Will Apply?" *Southeastern Environmental Law Journal* 15 (2007): 577–612.

64 Kim David Chanbonpin, "Holding the United States Accountable for Environmental Damages Caused by the U.S. Military in the Philippines, A Plan for the Future," *Asian-Pacific Law and Policy Journal* 4 (2003): 320–81, available at http://blog.hawaii.edu/aplpj/volume-4-issue-2/.

65 Chae, "Environmental Contamination," 10,092.

66 Lee, "Banhwan migun gijiyui," 150–53.

67 Ibid., 149.

68 Ibid., 151–52.

69 "Banhwan migun giji junghwae 3000uk soyo" [300 billion won necessary for environmental remedy of the returned bases], *Money Today*, May 27, 2011, available at www.mt.co.kr/view/mtview.php?type=1&no=2011052717592861069&outlink=1.

70 "Severe Pollution Levels Detected," *Hankyoreh*.

71 Green Korean United, "79.1% of Koreans Believe That the U.S. Should Clean Up Pollution within US Military Bases," available at http://green-korea.tistory.com/49, accessed May 20, 2013.

72 Taeho Kang and Wonje Sohn, "Korea's Military Allowance to the U.S.," *Hankyoreh*, February 2, 2007, available at www.hani.co.kr/arti/politics/defense/188045.html.

73 Jimmy H. Koo, "The Uncomfortable SOFA: Anti-American Sentiments in South Korea and the U.S.-South Korea Status of Forces Agreement," *National Security Law Brief* 1, no. 1 (2011), available at http://digitalcommons.wcl.american.edu/nslb/vol1/iss1/5.

74 Chanbonpin, "Holding the United States Accountable," 354.

75 Authors' personal communication, June 27, 2013.

76 Chae, "Environmental Contamination," 10092; Chae, "Problems with the 2007 US-ROK Base Return Agreement," 26; and Woo, "Environmental Problems on the U.S. Military Bases," 611.

77 Green Korea United, "Polluted Land and Water of Seoul: Investigation Needed at the Yongsan Camp," available at www.greenkorea.org/?p=32679.

78 Bongsuk Son, "Juhan miguni kyungbuk chilgoke goyubjie daeryang maeyib, mi

bangsong pockro" [U.S. broadcast a large quantity of defoliants disposed by the USFK at Kyungbuk Chilgok], *The Kyunghyang Shinmun*, May 19, 2011, available at http://news.khan.co.kr/kh_news/khan_art_view.html?artid=201105191205571& code=910302.

79 Jeongsu Sun, "'Camp carroll radar': Tamsa hu shichu habyi . . . mi palgunsar-youngguan hankuken nameun goyupjie upda doipuri" [Camp Carroll agreement to drill after radar investigation . . . U.S. the Eighth Army commander repeats the position that there is no Agent Orange left in Korea], *Kuki News*, June 1, 2011, available at http://news.kukinews.com/article/view.asp?page=1&gCode=all&arcid=0005017202&code=11131100.

80 "Goyubjie daecheak huiyi, camp carol giji yimi ohyum" [Agent Orange risk reveals Camp Carroll already polluted by dioxin], *Herald News*, June 13, 2011, available at http://news.heraldcorp.com/view.php?ud=20110613000909&md=20120422133319_AS.

81 "Chilgok migunbudae goyubjie ubda, dioxine miliang gumchil" [No defoliants found at Chilgok U.S. military base, only a small quantity of dioxin found], *Newsis*, August 5, 2011, available at http://news.naver.com/main/read.nhn?mode=LSD&mid=sec&sid1=100&oid=003&aid=0004006981.

82 Sun, "Camp Carroll Radar."

83 Seungim Jung, "Camp Carroll goyunjie muhae" [Defoliants at Camp Carroll, no harms]," *Hankook Ilbo*, September 21, 2012, available at http://news.hankooki.com/lpage/society/201209/h2012092102373221950.htm.

84 Jonguk Lee, "Chilgok Goyubjie guanlyun jisokjuk yungu jiegi" [Further study needed about Chilgok defoliant case], *Kyungbuk Ilbo*, October 22, 2012, available at www.kyongbuk.co.kr/main/news/news_content.php?id=600541&news_area=110&news_divide=&news_local=24&effect=4.

85 Maeil Daily, "Bulshingamman duh hwakinhan migun-Chilgok jumin goyunjie gandamhui" [Distrust intensified at USFK-Chilgok residents meeting], June 10, 2011, available at www.imaeil.com/sub_news/sub_news_view.php?news_id=29899&yy=2011.

86 Rahn Kim, "Underground Water Pollution Serious Near U.S. Bases in Seoul," *Korea Times*, June 7, 2013, available at http://koreatimes.co.kr/www/news/nation/2011/06/113_88489.html.

87 "Yongsan giji gireum yuchulro hwakindeun ohyummyunjeokman samcheon chilbaekpyeong" [12,231 square meters of land found polluted by oil spills from Yongsan U.S. military base], *Yonhap News*, May 27, 2013, available at http://news.naver.com/main/read.nhn?mode=LSD&mid=sec&sid1=100&oid=001&aid=0006280110.

88 "USFK Ignores Requests for Pollution Inspection," *Korea Times*, May 27, 2013, available at http://koreatimes.co.kr/www/news/nation/2013/05/113_136445.html.

89 Kim, "Underground Water Pollution."

90 Ibid.

91 "Yongsan giji," *Yonhap News*.

92   Kim, "Underground Water Pollution."

93   "S. Korean Gov't Ordered to Pay for Cleanup of Pollution around U.S. Base,"
Yonhap News, June 25, 2013, available at www.globalpost.com/dispatch/news/
yonhap-news-agency/130625/s-korean-govt-ordered-pay-cleanup-pollution
-around-us-base.

94   Ibid.

95   "S. Korean Gov't Ordered," *Yonhap News*.

96   Seung-hun Kang, "Yongsan migun giji gireum yuchul hanmi shilmuyui
gusung habyi" [US-ROK agree to form a joint working group to investigate
the oil leak], *Aju News*, June 18, 2013, available at www.ajunews.com/kor/view
.jsp?newsId=20130618000340.

97   Jae-won Kim, "Gov't, USFK Agree to Discuss Land Pollution," *Korea
Times*, June 18, 2013, available at http://koreatimes.co.kr/www/news/
nation/2013/06/113_137690.html.

98   Jahng-hee Lee, "Commentary: The SOFA's Environmental Clause Must be
Amended," *Kyunghyang Daily News*, June 2, 2011, available at http://english.khan
.co.kr/khan_art_view.html?artid=201106021644247&code=710100.

99   Giju Park, "Mugun gijiyui hwankyung munje gaesun banghyange gwanhan
gochal" [Study on U.S. bases in Korea in the direction of environmental improve-
ment], *Hwankyungbub yungu* [Environmental law studies] 31 (2009): 87–108.

100   Ibid., 88.

101   Lina Gong, "Traditional Security as a Source of Nontraditional Insecurities—The
Case of Okinawa," NTS Alert, September 2012, RSIS Center for Nontraditional
Security (NTS) Studies for NTS Asia, Singapore.

102   Mark E. Manyin, "South Korean Politics and Rising 'Anti-Americanism': Implications for U.S. Policy toward North Korea," *Congressional Research Service Report*
(November 2003), available at http://fpc.state.gov/documents/organization
/27530.pdf.

103   Nam, "Relocating the U.S. Forces," 619.

104   Durant, "National Defense," 224.

CHAPTER 8

A WILDLIFE INSURGENCY

The Endangered Species Act, Citizen-Initiated Lawsuits, and the Department of Defense at the End of the Cold War

KATHERINE M. KEIRNS

THE red-cockaded woodpecker is a small, black-and-white-striped "undistinguished" bird, one of the more than two hundred wood-pecker species in the world, which nests in southern longleaf pine trees sought after by the logging industry.[1] At one point the species ranged all over the southeastern United States; today the largest concentrations are on the coastal plains of Georgia and the Carolinas and in particu-lar on military reservations in those states.[2] Although it had been listed under the Endangered Species Act since the late 1960s, in the late 1990s the red-cockaded woodpecker became the poster species for the Defense Department's environmental protection and conservation efforts. Doz-ens of articles in the country's leading newspapers have trumpeted the military's cooperation with environmental groups such as the Nature Conservancy and environmental regulators such as the Department of the Interior's Fish and Wildlife Service to help bring this species back from the brink of extinction.[3] In 2010, Fort Bragg, home of the largest concentration of red-cockaded woodpeckers, won the secretary of the army's Environmental Award for Natural Resources Conservation for the efforts that culminated in the Fish and Wildlife Service declaring the bird population in full recovery on the base the year before, lifting restrictions on more than three thousand acres that had been closed to training for almost two decades.[4] But this feel-good environmental story about soldiers and conservationists teaming up to save an endangered species has a much more complicated past.

Only a few years before the soldiers and the birds became friends in the press, commanders at Fort Benning, Georgia, and Fort Bragg, North Carolina, had stumbled into a war with not only the birds but also with the Fish and Wildlife Service and a well-funded environmental group, Defenders of Wildlife. In 1989 commanders at Fort Benning had little understanding of what was required of them under the Endangered Species Act. Largely out of ignorance, they had delegated responsibility for managing environmental questions to the army civilians in charge of timber sales from the base. Those same forestry managers would face criminal indictments under the Endangered Species Act in 1992 after it was found that they had deliberately concealed the presence of wood-peckers to avoid delays in logging.[5] But the situation was much worse at Fort Bragg, where the contempt in which the senior base commanders held conservation requirements trickled down so that troops would not speak to wildlife managers and pictures of woodpeckers were seen taped on top of firing range targets.[6]

Engineering officers who did have experience dealing with the legal requirements of the Endangered Species Act had little influence with the leadership and could not negotiate in good faith with wildlife regulators. Relations between the garrison commanders and the Fish and Wildlife Service had completely broken down in the face of outright hostility in a conflict that threatened to send senior base officials to prison for con-tempt of court.[7] Officials from the Pentagon were forced to intervene and order base officials to cooperate fully with Fish and Wildlife in complying with federal environmental law. The result of the war between the wood-peckers and a few rogue colonels resulted in the army's complete sur-render to the forces of environmental preservation. To some people this may seem a surprising result, but it came after a decade of encounters between the military and endangered species represented by citizens' groups in court—encounters in which the law systematically favored the wildlife.

During the 1990s the Pentagon came to understand their conserva-tion responsibilities as important to their war-fighting mission, in part

KATHERINE M. KEIRNS

because of their experience with endangered species citizen-initiated lawsuits. The Endangered Species Act of 1973 is one of the cornerstones of American environmental law, and by the early 1990s it was understood to be the most stringent such law in the world because of its lack of exceptions or qualifications.[8] In the mid-1990s there were 220 endangered species listed on the Department of Defense's twenty-five million acres of land.[9] Roughly half the land and species could be found on army installations.[10] By 2008, when formal surveys were done by the Nature Conservancy, it was found that, despite the fact that the Department of Defense managed just 3 percent of federal land, they hosted more endangered species than any other group including the National Forest Service and the National Park Service.[11] Like these other federal land management entities, it took the armed forces more than a decade of bitter experience with citizen-initiated lawsuits to understand the power that the Endangered Species Act held over their activities.

A series of court cases throughout the 1980s, and the attendant publicity received, taught the armed services that failure to account for endangered species could have drastic effects on military operations. At the same time, the end of the Cold War caused a dramatic change in both the power of the military and the willingness of the American public to accept environmental degradation in the name of national security.[12] The legal realities of the Endangered Species Act, as well as the changes in public opinion, caused a shift in Pentagon policy. Fighting the conservationists was a losing battle, and joining them had the potential of not only putting the armed forces on the right side of public opinion—it could protect the military from further disruption to their operations.

These lessons were not easily learned, and the process took defense officials nearly a decade of legal contests that pitted nuclear missiles against desert fish, navy gunners against goats, and paratroopers against woodpeckers. The Endangered Species Act attracted little notice when it was first passed in the early 1970s, but a Supreme Court case at the end of the decade signaled that this law with its clear language and lack of exceptions had changed the landscape of environmental law. Massive government projects thought to have unstoppable institutional inertia were suddenly vulnerable if only an activist group could find their own endangered species champion. Throughout the 1980s the Department of Defense learned through bitter, and sometimes surreal experience, that simply complying with the law did not save them from a legal morass.

As the military lost authority and credibility at the end of the Cold War, they needed to partner with outside environmental groups to prove good faith to not only the courts but also the outside groups that had learned how to use the Endangered Species Act to force compliance.

The relationship between the U.S. military and the environment is a complex one, with a long history of military involvement in conservation as well as troubling legacies of environmental pollution.[13] Most recent efforts by the U.S. military to conserve and clean up previous environmental damage can be justified under strictly practical lines: water contamination threatens troops' health, inefficient use of fuel in Afghanistan risks the lives of soldiers transporting that fuel over mountain roads, and climate change may cause political instability leading to future wars.[14] Yet of all the environmental issues for the Pentagon to align itself with in the last decade of the twentieth century, it was the cause of endangered wildlife that had the largest public profile and shows the clearest changes in attitudes and actions by the armed services. The Endangered Species Act is the most prominent environmental law for which there is no direct link between the goals of the law and the health or well-being of the military and its people. Compliance with the National Environmental Policy Act of 1969 or the Clean Water Act of 1972 could easily be justified by a military officer as important for the protection of his own soldiers, sailors, airmen, or their families.[15] There is no direct public health consequence to violating or complying with the Endangered Species Act. Yet this is the environmental law that the Defense Department has gone out of its way to associate with itself, because military leaders have learned that it is the single environmental law they cannot avoid.[16]

The history of the Endangered Species Act of 1973 has been well documented; the legislation is the culmination of some of the earliest environmental protection efforts.[17] The initial federal effort to protect endangered species was the Lacey Act of 1900, signed by Theodore Roosevelt, which prohibited the commerce in the products of illegal hunting of fish or wildlife, but the practical reach of this law was limited.[18] The original effort to create a list of federally protected endangered species came under the Endangered Species Act of 1966, which directed federal agencies to protect the listed species "insofar as is practicable and consistent with the[ir] primary purposes."[19] This relatively weak mandate on federal actions was accompanied by the fact that the Endangered Spe-

KATHERINE M. KEIRNS

cies Act of 1966 had little or no enforcement mechanisms. The powers of the secretary of the interior to list species not native to the United States and to limit commerce in the products that harmed these species was expanded in the Endangered Species Conservation Act of 1969. With each strengthening of the law, Congress was responding to lobbying by scientists and environmental activists who were more and more concerned about diminishing biological diversity.

Continued fears over rapid extinction of species caused Congress to revisit the issue in 1973, when the scope and power of the act was increased yet again. However, nearly all the bills introduced that year retained the exception language from the 1966 law, language opposed by conservation groups, fearful that an agency's primary purpose would always overrule the welfare of an endangered species.[20] The conservationists' pressure was successful, and the qualifying language was completely absent from the version that eventually passed the House, and largely absent from the version that passed the Senate. The Supreme Court has relied heavily on the removal of that language from the final bills in its interpretation of federal agencies' responsibilities under Section 7 of the Endangered Species Act.[21] The act was passed by overwhelming margins in both the House and the Senate, and signed into law by President Richard Nixon.[22] In later years, when the act became controversial among conservatives and business owners, several members of Congress claimed that they thought it would protect eagles, condors, and bears, collectively known by ecologists as "charismatic mega fauna."[23]

The Endangered Species Act, written in clear, plain language, states that it is "declared to be the policy of Congress that all Federal departments and agencies shall seek to conserve endangered species and threatened species and shall utilize their authorities in furtherance of the purposes of this Act."[24] Conflicts between the agency's primary mission and the act must be resolved in favor of protecting the endangered species, and there are effectively no exceptions built into the law.[25] Under the Endangered Species Act of 1973, primary responsibility for management of threatened and endangered species is assigned to the secretary of the interior, the U.S. Fish and Wildlife Service (FWS), and the National Oceanic and Atmospheric Administration (NOAA).[26] These agencies investigate criminal violations of the act and work in consultation with state and federal agencies to ensure their compliance with Section 7 of the ESA. A Fish and Wildlife "biological opinion" must be issued should any government activity affect a listed threatened or endangered species. If a finding of jeopardy is reached by Fish and Wildlife, recommendations will be made to mitigate harm to the species while still allowing the activity to move forward. If the activity cannot be altered so as not to harm the endangered species, it cannot go forward. This new law was unlike any of the previous federal conservation measures in its power and reach.

Despite the broad political support under which it was passed and the sweeping scope of the legislation, the ESA drew very little notice from either the public or the defense establishment for its first six years. In the mid-1970s, Cold War military priorities were assumed to trump any environmental policy. This can be seen in the air force's handling of a controversy involving the Channel Islands in California and the proposed launching of space shuttles from Vandenberg Air Force Base. In the early planning stages of the shuttle program, it was thought that civilian missions would launch from the Kennedy Space Center in Florida, while military and classified flights would take place at Vandenberg.[27] Shuttle launches would fly over the Channel Islands, home to the endangered brown pelican, creating sonic booms roughly fifteen times more powerful than typical supersonic military flights. Environmental groups and ecologists from the University of California at Irvine were concerned that the sonic booms would crack eggs and frighten adult birds away from their nests, thus decimating the population.[28]

The air force's proposed solutions to the problem ranged from the serious—changing the velocity and inclination of the launches to take the booms away from the islands—to the utterly bizarre. These included "conditioning" the birds to the sonic booms by flying many high speed planes over the islands, drugging the birds during launches to avoid frightening them, or the flying of massive plastic sheets from helicopters to block the islands from the sonic booms.[29] The air force may not have taken these solutions seriously—and the ecologists at UC–Irvine were "speechless" after reading them.[30] It seems likely that these options were included almost as a kind of legalistic boilerplate to say that the air force was studying the problem. That kind of unfeasible mitigation plan would not have been included in any biological mitigation plan acceptable to the courts ten years later. The legal and environmental landscape in which the military operated was about to drastically change. After a 1979 Supreme Court ruling, the Channel

Island pelicans were seen as a significant threat to the entire Vandenberg shuttle launch project.[31]

The first major court challenge to the Endangered Species Act was not a Department of Defense project, but a massive dam project of the Tennessee Valley Authority (TVA). The Tellico dam was a TVA development project on the Little Tennessee River, which would impound water over 16,500 acres and create a reservoir roughly thirty miles long. The dam project was controversial with both local farmers and environmentalists from the start, as it would destroy large amounts of productive farm land and drown the last free-flowing segment of the Tennessee River.[32] Shortly before the passage of the ESA, a University of Tennessee biology professor discovered a small three-inch grey fish, the endangered snail darter, in the portion of the Little Tennessee that would be impounded at the completion of the Tellico dam. Negotiations between Fish and Wildlife and the TVA on means to protect the fish were fruitless; the TVA insisted that the dam would be built and that the only way to protect the fish was to relocate the population.[33] Environmental groups brought suit under the ESA against the Tennessee Valley Authority to prevent the completion of the dam that would kill the entire known population of the snail darter. The TVA encouraged congressional appropriations committee members to believe the lawsuit was a simple nuisance case, and in no way a threat to the project.

The case, *Tennessee Valley Authority v. Hiram G. Hill*, did not initially go well for the environmentalists. Though the district court did find that the TVA was in violation of the Endangered Species Act, it did not order the injunction sought. The court believed that doing so would lead to the "absurd result of requiring a court to halt impoundment of water behind a fully completed dam if an endangered species was discovered in the river the day before such impoundment was scheduled to take place." The lower court could not conceive that Congress would intend such a result. However, the ruling was overturned on appeal and the Supreme Court affirmed the appeals court's decision. Writing for the majority, Chief Justice Warren E. Burger said that it was difficult to find a statute whose terms were more clear than the Endangered Species Act and that any attempt by the courts to impose an economic balance of the cost of a federal project against the value of an endangered species would require that the courts ignore the "ordinary meaning of plain language" in the act.[34] As the Tellico dam could not be operated without killing the entire known population of the snail darter, the Supreme Court's interpretation of the law was that the dam project had to be abandoned.[35]

The idea that a multimillion-dollar project could be halted by a tiny fish no one had heard of struck many people as a massive waste of taxpayers' money. There were calls to repeal the Endangered Species Act, or to amend it to impose the same kind of exceptions that had existed under previous endangered species legislation; there were also those who saw defending the act as important to protecting the future.[36] In the summer of 1979 some Republican lawmakers (and staff) claimed that massive projects in just about every state would be blocked by spiders or slugs.[37] From this moment, for many conservatives the Endangered Species Act became the prime example of the madness of government regulation. When the Supreme Court ruled that a fish was more important than a dam, or by extension that any small plant or animal on private land could prevent a property owner from doing as he wished, the world was turned upside down. Newspapers described these late 1970s cases with headlines reading, "The U.S. vs. the Snail Darter et al." or, in the case of the Channel Islands, the "Pelican vs. the Space Ship."[38] This rhetoric of a small obscure animal against a large and important project dominates the way the press described endangered species conflict for the first few years after *TVA v. Hill*, but it also carried the connotation of David versus Goliath. Many groups began looking for their own endangered species champion in any fight with the federal government.

Nine months after the Supreme Court ruling in *TVA v. Hill*, Catholic Action of Hawaii and the Peace Education Project, primarily anti–nuclear weapons activists with no apparent environmental expertise or previous interest in biological diversity, filed suit to block the expansion of a munitions holding facility at the West Loch Branch of the Pearl Harbor Naval Base in Honolulu, Hawaii. The navy had been storing munitions at a number of facilities across the island and wished to consolidate and expand them so that they would be capable of holding nuclear weapons. The navy, under national security regulations promulgated by the Atomic Energy Act, would not confirm the location or number of nuclear weapons but had publicly announced that the proposed facility could house them.

Catholic Action argued that the environmental impact assessment (EIA) filed by the navy was inadequate because it failed to take into account the possibility of accidents involving the nuclear weapons or the effect on the habitat of the Hawaiian stilt—a listed endangered species that nested near the facility. They wanted the court to require a much more costly and time-consuming environmental impact statement (EIS). An EIA is a more superficial document than an EIS. If a federal agency believes that an action does not present any significant environmental impact under the National Environmental Policy Act of 1969, they may write a short EIA. If there will be any significant impact—or because of the threat of lawsuits, any impact at all—the agency must write a full EIS. The EIS does not need to present a plan to mitigate damage done, but it must represent a "hard look" and include significant input from such scientists as ecologists and biologists either from the EPA or contracted from outside of the government.[39] Many environmental lawsuits against federal agencies dispute either the use of the EIA over an EIS or the rigor of the EIS. As preparing a complete environmental impact statement costs a great deal of time and money, the process can be used to indefinitely delay a project or make it cost prohibitive.

The antinuclear groups did not attempt to argue any specific harm to the stilt; simply that the presence of nuclear weapons near the birds would be a violation of the Endangered Species Act.[40] The case was dismissed at the district court level because the plaintiffs failed to make a specific claim regarding the Endangered Species Act, but the Ninth Circuit ordered the navy to write an expanded EIS on the grounds that it must account for the possible presence of nuclear weapons if that potential presence is publically acknowledged.[41] The inclusion of an Endangered Species Act claim by the plaintiffs in *Catholic Action v. Brown* can most charitably be read as an afterthought, or less so as disingenuous, but it sent an important signal. The citizen-initiated lawsuit provision, which allows private parties to sue a federal government agency to require enforcement of the ESA, gave any group standing to sue the military over environmental threats.[42] If the antinuclear activists had presented any evidence that the building of the West Loch facility would have had an effect on the Hawaiian stilt, the case could have come out differently. As it was, the case opened the Pentagon up to a vast array of environmental legal claims.

The power of the Endangered Species Act as a weapon to attack unpopular military projects can better be seen in a series of early 1980s court cases filed in an ongoing and long-term quasi colonial war between the Commonwealth of Puerto Rico and the U.S. Navy over the narrow island of Vieques, six miles off the coast of the main island of Puerto Rico.[43] Large tracts of the island that had historically been home to sugar plantations were bought by the navy in the 1940s, amounting to twenty-six thousand of the island's thirty-three thousand acres. The naval reservation on the island is in two sections, with the island's civilian population of more than seven thousand living between them on a small strip of land. The western section was largely used for ammunition storage and non-live-fire training, while the eastern portion was used for amphibious assaults, naval gunnery bombardment, and aerial target practice. The entire Vieques military reservation comprises the inner range of the navy's Atlantic Fleet Weapons Training Range, operated out of Roosevelt Roads Naval Station on the main island of Puerto Rico. Highly unpopular with the island's civilian population, the range operated between 6 a.m. and 11 p.m. The population considered the noise, perceived danger, and environmental impact extremely disruptive to the island's fishing and tourist industries and lobbied the territorial government to help end the activity.[44]

The governor of Puerto Rico, as well as a number of Vieques residents, filed suit in U.S. District Court against the Department of Defense and the navy, alleging a wide variety of violations of environmental and nuisance laws, including the Federal Water Pollution Control Act, the Rivers and Harbors Act, the Clean Air Act, the Noise Control Act, the Coastal Zone Management Act, the Manatee and the Marine Mammal Protection Act as well as the Endangered Species Act. Many of the plaintiffs' claims were novel at best, including arguing that the firing of ammunition out of guns or the dropping of bombs from aircraft constituted illegal dumping. Although the court did find some violations of the various acts listed, it did not issue the injunction the governor wanted; instead, the court ordered the navy to fix the violations with deliberate speed.[45] With the exception of the Endangered Species Act claims, the entire raft of complaints was dismissed by the Court of Appeals.[46]

In a case that involved a raft of complicated environmental claims, the only one that turned out to carry the power to actually stop activity on the firing range was the Endangered Species Act. The ESA claim was initially dismissed but revived on appeal. The island, at the time the lawsuits were initiated, was home to six species designated as threatened or endangered: the brown pelican, the manatee, the leatherback turtle, the hawksbill turtle, the loggerhead turtle, and the green turtle.[47]

The district court argued the presence of the endangered species on navy land (and not on the civilian portions of Vieques) was itself evidence that the navy was not doing harm to the animals.[48] The appeals court found that the lower court judge inappropriately substituted his own judgment about the "refuge effect" on the birds and turtles, ruling that the courts could not substitute its own judgment for that of a formal biological opinion by the Fish and Wildlife Service.[49] The court did express some doubt about how the navy could argue that practicing tracked amphibious landings over turtles' nests could not cause harm to the animals.[50] When the case was taken up by the Supreme Court the following year, the court affirmed that portion of the ruling.[51]

As it turned out, the navy had sought a biological opinion from the Fish and Wildlife Service for their Vieques training exercises but not until well into the case. In the written opinion the First Circuit Court chided the navy, pointing out that much of the litigation would have been avoided had they acted in consultation with Fish and Wildlife earlier. In the Supreme Court ruling, Justice Byron White went so far as to use the Endangered Species Act as a model to show how water pollution laws do not carry the same requirements to cease actions found to be harmful to the environment as the ESA does for actions that threaten endangered species.[52] The biological findings of Fish and Wildlife, along with the publicity achieved through the lawsuits, caused the navy to reach a memorandum of understanding with the governor of Puerto Rico in 1983. It required conservation efforts beyond that of those required under the Fish and Wildlife's biological opinion as well as investments by the navy into the island's economy.[53] Although the Endangered Species Act represented the most powerful weapon in Puerto Ricans' arsenal against the navy, it was not a magic bullet; this was a temporary victory in a longer political war.

Cooperation with the Fish and Wildlife Service was a defense in court, but it was not an absolute protection against public embarrassment for the military. Endangered Species Act cases could take on a surreal life of their own. Around the same time of the navy's conflict with the Commonwealth of Puerto Rico, it was in a no-win situation with a massive herd of goats off the coast of California. San Clemente Island, about seventy-five miles northwest of San Diego, was owned entirely by the navy, and aside from a limited number of scientific researchers, the island was closed to the public and used by the navy for gunnery practice.[54] In 1977 the Fish and Wildlife Service had issued a biological opinion, in support of the San Clemente loggerhead shrike, an endangered songbird, requiring the navy to remove a herd of anywhere between ten thousand and twenty-seven thousand feral goats from the island.[55] The goats had been introduced to the island sometime in the late nineteenth century in hopes of establishing a source of fresh meat for passing ships. By the 1970s the goats had destroyed much of the island's native vegetation, obliterating the nests of many songbirds and shorebirds.[56]

Beginning in 1979, the navy proposed removing the goats through aerial eradication, "which involved using Navy marksmen to shoot the goats from helicopters" with automatic shotguns.[57] This began a cycle of alternating firestorms in the Los Angeles press, attempts by animal rights groups to capture the goats, and court filings.[58] Each time the navy would announce its plan to kill the goats, California animal rights organizations would denounce the navy as cold-blooded and cruel, suggesting that the eradication effort was some kind of recreational effort by the military: "The Navy seems to come up with something like this every Christmas. It seems to be their idea of the Nativity."[59] The navy halted its efforts to quiet the publicity and various animal rights NGOs attempted to organize a capture program, netting only a couple of hundred animals. Often the number of animals captured would be smaller than the birth rate in the goat population.[60] Following the failed goat capture attempts, the navy again announced plans to shoot the goats.

Each time the matter was brought to federal court, the navy prevailed. When the first group, the Fund for Animals, lost two early court cases, they bowed out of the fight only to be replaced by another group, the Animal Lovers Volunteer Association. The animal rights groups' complaints were repeatedly dismissed for lack of standing. In its ruling, the Ninth Circuit pointed out that if the groups had been suing on behalf of the endangered birds, or if the goats themselves had been endangered, they would have had standing.[61] The law did not protect every animal from harm—specifically listed species only. Simply protecting an animal was not a valid reason to sue the navy. The navy's actions, far from being recreational, were an attempt to protect endangered wildlife. But winning in court did not stop allegations in the press that the navy's training activities were the primary cause of danger to the animals. When the goats were finally removed completely from the island in 1992, the navy faced criticism from conservation groups that it allowed the situation to go on for so long "through neglect."[62] Even a good-faith effort to follow the best scientific advice offered does not always shield the military from suspicion by environmental groups, and it certainly did not keep them out of court, but it did ensure that those cases were dismissed quickly. The lesson from the San Clemente goats was that the Pentagon needed to partner with environmental groups in order to avoid drawn-out legal proceedings and public embarrassment.

In contrast to the relatively small geographic reach of the battle over the goats of San Clemente Island, the largest 1980s military project with major environmental opposition centered on the consequences to endangered species was the LGM-118A Peacekeeper Intercontinental Ballistic Missile (ICBM). Better known as the MX, it was to be the air force's next generation nuclear deterrent. During the Cold War, American nuclear weapons doctrine relied on a triad of nuclear delivery mechanisms, manned bombers, land-based ICBMs, and submarine launched ICBMs. Critics charged that land-based missiles were vulnerable to attack and would be destroyed in the first wave of a nuclear war. The MX was controversial on many grounds, including cost, delivery, survivability, and accuracy, but most of all some questioned the relevance of land-based missiles in the age of submarine-based missiles.[63] The original proposal was that roughly one hundred missiles would be placed in silos and bunkers in the Nevada and Utah desert; the rest would be placed on roving trains that would be sent out to travel the U.S. rail network at times of heightened tension—an idea that carried its own set of concerns about security and accidents.[64]

The Nevada scheme had powerful political enemies and ran afoul of two paradoxical problems: there was too little water and too many fish. Many community leaders in Nevada were concerned about the amount of water that would be needed for the large installations in the desert, fearing that the water demands of the silos would harm development in the already dry state.[65] In particular, the project was opposed by powerful Nevada senator and former governor Paul Laxalt.[66] Strangely enough given the climate, Nevada was host to more endangered fish species than any other state in the early 1980s, and those fish complicated a number of building projects.[67] Most of the fish species were prehistoric remnants from the vast oceans that once covered the western United States; they now existed in discrete water holes in the desert fed by groundwater. Ecologists from the University of Nevada and environmentalists with the Nevada Desert Fish Council allied themselves with local political and community leaders and property developers to help stop the missile placement through denial of appropriations money.[68]

The next plan was to put the missiles in existing Minuteman III silos in Colorado, Nebraska, and Wyoming as proof of the country's "national will" to update the nuclear force.[69] Unfortunately for the air force, this assessment of the national will was not that of their neighbors in these three western states. Opposition around the MX missile in the West is significant for several reasons. By the late 1980s people who had been willing to accept the loss of parts of their property—not to mention the risk of living next to a standoff nuclear weapon—were less willing to do so. Many ranchers had leased small portions of their land to host nuclear missile silos in the 1960s with the understanding that it was a sacrifice for national defense. The air force had allowed inhabited structures as close as 1,200 feet from a Minuteman silo but were demanding a safety buffer of 1,750 for the MX. In some cases this would condemn the homes of ranchers who had hosted missiles for twenty-five years.[70] One rancher, Rodney Kirkbride of Wyoming, remarked, "I've gotten used to the Minuteman, I guess, but they want more land, more water, more everything for the MX."[71]

These ranchers made political alliances with environmental groups who challenged the air force's environmental impact statements, which treated the project like any other public works road extension. When more extensive environmental impact statements were released, they indicated potential harm to a number of endangered species in Nebraska and Wyoming.[72] Without explanation, the air force chose to limit its environmental impact statements to those two states, without ever looking at the sites in Colorado where they planned to place the missiles.[73] Public hearings on the environmental impact statements were held in Nebraska and Wyoming but not in Colorado. When the air force was challenged on this point, it attempted to claim that its existing environmental impact statements were sufficient for all the silos. As a result, the governor of Colorado, as well as a large number of municipalities, filed suit, pointing out that among other things, Colorado had a different set of endangered species. The courts ruled in favor of Colorado, ruling that environmental impact statements must be site-specific in part because of the requirements of the Endangered Species Act.[74]

The underlying question in many of the MX missile debates was a doubt by many Americans that a new nuclear weapons system was needed at all when the country already had thousands of missiles dotting the West and dozens of nuclear ballistic missile submarines at sea.[75] Ranchers and western politicians, many of them Republican supporters of the Reagan administration, were becoming unwilling to trade property rights and environmental damage for Cold War policy; they were willing to ally themselves with conservation and environmental groups to fight defense projects.[76] "National security" was no longer a trump card to gain land concessions in the West. A similar dynamic could be seen over a proposed army project at the Dugway Proving Ground in Utah. A Washington D.C.–based environmental group, the Foundation for Economic Trends, sued the Department of Defense with the support of local Utah community leaders over plans to build a biological weapons lab.[77] By the early 1990s it had become nearly impossible for the military to take control of even public lands without unified opposition from previously antagonistic western interest groups.[78]

The majority of citizen-initiated lawsuits under the provisions of the Endangered Species Act during the 1980s were directed at navy and air force projects. Isolated cases of the closure of firing ranges on army posts were the furthest reach of the act into army operations until 1988, when conflicts over training operations at Fort Bragg came to a head over the red-cockaded woodpecker. The woodpeckers live in cooperative groups, taking years to hollow out nests in living but diseased pine trees.[79] The standard federal management habitat around this time was determined to "a central 4-ha [hectare] nesting area, which contains the cluster of relict cavity trees where a social group of 1–5 birds roosts and nests, plus foraging habitat."[80] Once ranging all over the American Southeast, the woodpeckers had experienced loss of much of their habitat by the late 1980s development and logging of the native longleaf pine forests. In the 1970s Fort Bragg officials had rejected a management plan for the red-cockaded woodpecker because it conflicted with the base's timber management operations.[81] It was within the culture of the base to assume that timber sales—not part of the primary military mission—were more important than environmental concerns. In 1986 the Department of Defense, in concert with the Fish and Wildlife Service, had begun instituting army-wide protocols for the protection of the red-cockaded woodpecker on military installations across the South. Wildlife officials told investigators working for the Rand Corporation that Fort Bragg officials had been repeatedly informed that they were in violation of not only army policy but of the Endangered Species Act.[82]

In May 1988 the Fish and Wildlife Service informed Fort Bragg that the military activity on the base might be endangering the woodpecker; the base responded with a simple denial that it was not. When forced by higher authority to conduct a review, the officials at Fort Bragg wrote a report that although admitting that military activity may affect the woodpecker, it "could not be allowed to affect the military mission" and demanded the flexibility to train "without environmental consideration." This was contrary to army policy, and there was some suggestion by investigators later that this was a deliberate attempt by Fort Bragg officials to pick a fight with Fish and Wildlife, with little understanding of the power of the FWS when it came to enforcing the Endangered Species Act.[83] Once again ordered to cooperate with wildlife investigators, the garrison commanders delegated the consultation to personnel with little authority; combat training officers acted as if the entire process was unimportant, refusing to prevent incidental habitat destruction. In an act that appeared to Fish and Wildlife to be an attempt to intentionally provoke the conservation officials, Fort Bragg held a massive artillery training exercise including seventeen artillery battalions, which caused tremendous damage to habitat and the killing of woodpeckers.[84]

Given the antagonism directed at the Fish and Wildlife Service, the base personnel's contempt for the wildlife, and apparently their complete ignorance of the requirements of the law, Fish and Wildlife issued a strongly worded biological opinion stating that base activity jeopardized the birds and recommended massive restrictions on activity all over the base. The opinion included restricting all activity around woodpecker nesting and forage sites to transitory foot and vehicle traffic on existing roads for a fifteen-hundred-foot radius, along with further restrictions to protect endangered plant habitat, amounting to nearly a third of the facility's land.[85] Fort Bragg was also ordered to begin a three-year controlled burn cycle meant to restore the pine barren ecosystem, which would further disrupt military activity.[86] The same day that the Fish and Wildlife jeopardy opinion was issued, the Environmental Defense Fund gave notice to the army of its intent to file a lawsuit charging violation of the Endangered Species Act Sections 7 and 9, alleging criminal misconduct.[87] At that point the Pentagon took power away from Fort Bragg officials, and the army accepted all the Fish and Wildlife recommendations

KATHERINE M. KEIRNS

for protecting the woodpecker on the base, placing dramatic restrictions on one of the United States's most famous military bases.

In the immediate aftermath of the debacle at Fort Bragg, which threatened to send the commander of the army's most active military installation to trial for criminal violations of the Endangered Species Act, the army and the Defense Department attempted to understand how the situation had gotten that bad. Studies of the incident were published by the U.S. Army War College, the Judge Advocate General's Corps, and the Rand Corporation.[88] Defense Department officials, including then secretary of defense Dick Cheney, directed that the armed forces were to become the "federal leader" in compliance with the Endangered Species Act: "Defense and the environment is not an either/or proposition. To choose between them is impossible in this real world of serious defense threats and genuine environmental concerns."[89] The conclusion reached by all of these studies was that the only way to prevent severe disruption to military activity was to "provide more effective endangered species management and reduce the conflict with mission requirements."[90] Both Rand and the Army War College study emphasized education of army leaders about their responsibilities under the act, and a survey taken at the War College of army senior officers suggested that a drastic change in attitude had already taken place: 78 percent of respondents believed that environmental issues were extremely important, and more than 56 percent considered environmental neglect a threat to national security.[91]

The experience of the Department of Defense with citizen-initiated lawsuits under the Endangered Species Act in the 1980s had taught the military that if they placed themselves or their missions in conflict with endangered species, they were almost certainly going to lose in court. At the same time, they faced a rapidly changing world at the end of the Cold War, in which American citizens were no longer willing to accept that environmental destruction was an acceptable cost for national security.[92] But it was not until senior army officials at two of the premier installations in the service, Fort Benning and Fort Bragg, blundered their way toward potential jail time that a wholesale attitude shift in the armed forces took place. That shift gave the Pentagon an attractive environmental cause with which to align itself as it came under attack for the environmental destruction that is inevitable in many operations.

It is worth questioning if the positive press the military received in the late 1990s and 2000s for their endangered species conservation efforts is an effort at greenwashing a largely negative environmental record. There are thousands of toxic waste cleanups due to military pollution going on around the country, and bases handed over to conservationists often come deeply contaminated. But that does not change the fact that military operations have been accommodated to protect endangered species at great cost and inconvenience. Officials know that the military will never be seen as a benign force in the environment, but they come from a profession that operates closer to the environment than many of their fellow citizens, and they often see environmental degradation firsthand. The armed services has adapted to environmental challenges.

The power of the Endangered Species Act lies in the fact that is the one environmental law effectively with no exceptions, the one in which any citizen can force any government agency to comply though the federal courts. It requires no science training to understand that there are different species at risk in different places, so the assessment and management plans have to be highly place-specific rather than boilerplate used from site to site. This is, of course, also true of pollution of land, air, and water, but it takes expert testimony from geologists, hydrologists, and meteorologists to explain why to judges. The process under which the U.S. military shifted from bad environmental actor to complicated conservationist is important in understanding how environmentalism has penetrated American culture far beyond its traditional left/right polarization.

NOTES

1   Cornell Lab of Ornithology, "Red-Cockaded Woodpecker, Life History," available at www.allaboutbirds.org/guide/Red-cockaded_Woodpecker/lifehistory.

2   David N. Diner, "The Army and the Endangered Species Act: Who's Endangering Whom?," *Military Law Review* 143 (1994): 200–201. This article was originally published as a staff study in 1992 for the Army Judge Advocate General's Office. Only minor changes exist between the original staff study and the law journal article.

3   There are dozens of newspaper articles about the red-cockaded woodpecker on military bases from major newspapers around the country; this small sampling includes the first appearance of the subject in the *New York Times*. Every few years journalists seem to discover the subject anew and write as if they are the first to discover the partnership between the military and the wildlife. William K. Stevens, "Wildlife Finds Odd Sanctuary on Military Bases," *New York Times*, January 2, 1996. Christopher Joyce, "Fort Bragg's Woodpeckers: Soldiers, Wildlife Find Common Ground in North Carolina," NPR, available at www.npr.org/templates/

story/story.php?storyId=1143060. Martin L. Calhoun, "Cleaning up the Military's Toxic Legacy," *USA Today*, September 1995.

4   Cathy Kropp, "Fort Bragg's Award Is for the Birds," U.S. Army, available at www.army.mil/article/37653/fort-braggs-award-is-for-the-birds/; and Daniel Cusick, "FWS, Army Declare Red-Cockaded Woodpeckers 'Recovered' at Fort Bragg," *E&ENews*, available at www.eenews.net/public/eenewspm/2006/06/07/9.

5   Diner, "Army and the Endangered Species Act," 204–5.

6   Jerry Aroesty, David Rubenson, and Charles Thompsen, *Two Shades of Green: Environmental Protection and Combat Training* (Santa Monica, CA: Rand Corporation, 1992), 36.

7   Diner, "Army and the Endangered Species Act," 206–8.

8   Oreb Ashland, "Species Act Called Most Stringent in the World," *Christian Science Monitor,* May 18, 1992.

9   Numbers are difficult to pin down during this period in part because of the annual discovery of new species, because of the drastic reduction in land under DOD management directly after the Cold War, and because of classified land-holdings. The numbers cited come from L. Peter Boice, "Managing Endangered Species on Miltiary Land," U.S. Department of Defense, available at www.umich.edu/~esupdate/library/96.07–08/boice.html. Boice was director of conservation for the Department of Defense at the time of the writing (in 1996), and these figures are cited by most sources. For a longer discussion of why DOD land numbers in general are hard to pin down, look to Trevor Paglen, *Blank Spots on the Map: The Dark Geography of the Pentagon's Secret World* (New York: Dutton, 2009).

10   Robert P. Barrens and Michael McKee, "Balancing Army and Endangered Species Concerns: Green vs. Green," *Environmental Management* 27, no. 1 (2001): 123–33.

11   Bruce A. Stein, Cameron Scott, and Nancy Benton, "Federal Lands and Endangered Species: The Role of Military and Other Federal Lands in Sustaining Biodiversity," *BioScience* 58, no. 4 (2008): 339–47.

12   An example of this can be seen in the opposition surrounding the extension of a bombing range in Idaho in the late 1980s and 1990s. See Rick Atkinson, "Range War in Idaho: Air Force's Vast Expansion Plan Is Resisted," *Washington Post*, May 9, 1990.

13   David Zierler, *The Invention of Ecocide: Agent Orange, Vietnam, and the Scientists Who Changed the Way We Think about the Environment* (Athens: University of Georgia Press, 2011); Karl Jacoby, *Crimes against Nature: Squatters, Poachers, Thieves, and the Hidden History of American Conservation* (Berkeley: University of California Press, 2001); Richard P. Tucker and Edmund Russell, eds., *Natural Enemy, Natural Ally: Toward an Environmental History of Warfare,* 1st ed. (Corvallis: Oregon State University Press, 2004); and Edmund Russell, *War and Nature: Fighting Humans and Insects with Chemicals from World War I to Silent Spring*, Studies in Environment and History (Cambridge: Cambridge University Press, 2001). Also see Lisa M. Brady, *War upon the Land: Military Strategy and the Transformation of Southern Landscapes during the American Civil War, Environmental History and the American South* (Athens: University of Georgia Press, 2012).

14 J. R. McNeill and Corinna R. Unger, *Environmental Histories of the Cold War* (Cambridge: Cambridge University Press, 2010); Robert F. Durant, *The Greening of the U.S. Military: Environmental Policy, National Security, and Organizational Change* (Washington, D.C.: Georgetown University Press, 2007); "Casualty Costs of Fuel and Water Resupply Convoys in Afghanistan and Iraq," *Army-Technology.com*, available at www.army-technology.com/features/feature77200/; and John M. Broder, "Climate Change Seen as Threat to U.S. Security," *New York Times*, August 8, 2009.

15 In the military this is described as "force readiness" and amounts to generalized concern for the well-being of the troops. "Force readiness" includes adequate training for troops, good quality food, protection from predatory-lending practices, and high-quality schools for their children. As such, the health and wellness of families living on post and subject to environmental contamination can be—and often is—characterized as a "force readiness" issue.

16 I have chosen to exclude from this analysis Endangered Species Act lawsuits against the U.S. Army Corps of Engineers that dealt exclusively with civil projects. The USACE is charged with the enforcement of environmental regulations in wetlands and navigable waters and, as such, is the defendant in many ESA suits. However, these are nearly always about USACE's role as a regulator, not as a military service. I have also excluded one case filed in the mid-1990s against the U.S. Coast Guard that dealt primarily with the Coast Guard as a regulator of civilian boat traffic and not as a quasi-armed service. The Coast Guard case is *Richard Max Strahan v. Rear Admiral John L. Linnon*, 967 F.Supp. 581 (1997).

17 Douglas Brinkley, *The Wilderness Warrior: Theodore Roosevelt and the Crusade for America*, 1st ed. (New York: HarperCollins, 2009); and Zygmunt J. B. Plater, *The Snail Darter and the Dam: How Pork-Barrel Politics Endangered a Little Fish and Killed a River* (New Haven, CT: Yale University Press, 2013).

18 *Tennessee Valley Authority v. Hill*, 437 U.S. 153, 98 S.Ct 2279 (1978). See footnote 20 of Chief Justice Burger's opinion in *Tennessee Valley Authority v. Hill*, which focuses on the trouble enforcing the Lacey Act.

19 Section 1(b) of the Endangered Species Act of 1966 as quoted in *Tennessee Valley Authority v. Hill*, 17.

20 Ibid., 20. Specifically the Sierra Club worried that the language "could be construed to be a declaration of congressional policy that other agency purposes are necessarily more important than the protection of endangered species."

21 Section 7 of the ESA sets out the requirements of federal agencies in protecting endangered species, while Section 9 deals with criminal violations of the law by private citizens. Broadly speaking, the ESA requires that private citizens only avoid "taking" a plant or animal. The act defines the term "take" to mean to "harass, harm, hunt, shoot, wound, kill, trap, capture, or collect, or to attempt to engage in any such conduct." The key term on the list is "harm," which has been interpreted by both the Interior Department and the courts to include the destruction of critical habitat. This is the basis under which private land owners have opposed the ESA because they believe it denies them use of their private

property. Section 7 takes this further for federal agencies in that it requires all federal agencies, regardless of their primary missions, to actively protect endangered species.

22   For more background on the Nixon administration's understanding of the environmental laws passed during this period, see Bruce J. Schulman, *The Seventies: The Great Shift in American Culture, Society, and Politics* (New York: Free Press, 2001); and Rick Perlstein, *Nixonland: The Rise of a President and the Fracturing of America* (New York: Scribner, 2008).

23   Just two of many examples: Seth S. King, "Snail Darter and Whooping Crane Win the First Test of Species Act," *New York Times*, January 24, 1979; and Peter Steinhart, "Those Endangered Species: What Good Are They?," *Los Angeles Times*, July 2, 1978.

24   Endangered Species Act of 1973, Section 2(c)(1).

25   *Tennessee Valley Authority v. Hill*. There is an exception for national security concerns within the law, but it has never been used. It is understood by the Pentagon and the Army Judge Advocate General's Office that this exception, which would have to be made by the secretary of defense, is strictly a wartime exception. Interview with Major Craig Teller, U.S. Army Environmental Law Division, Office of the Judge Advocate General, as quoted in Diner, "Army and the Endangered Species Act," 196. Following the court's ruling in *Tennessee Valley Authority v. Hill*, the act was amended to create an appeals mechanism for federal agencies, but the requirements were strict and it was used only a couple of times during the act's first three decades.

26   Endangered Species Act of 1973, Section 8. This has the effect of giving Fish and Wildlife authority over endangered species on land, birds, and freshwater fish, while NOAA is given authority in protection of oceangoing fish and marine mammals in conjunction with the Marine Mammal Protection Act of 1973. Most of the cases discussed in this chapter deal with Fish and Wildlife.

27   At the time it was also believed that the shuttle would launch every few weeks, so having two launch sites was a requirement of the schedule.

28   Robert A. Jones, "Air Force Will Probe Sonic Boom Threat to Channel Islands," *Los Angeles Times*, October 14, 1977.

29   Ibid.

30   Ibid.

31   "Environmental Conflict: Pelican vs. Space Ship," *Washington Post*, January 15, 1979.

32   *Tennessee Valley Authority v. Hill*; and *Environmental Defense Fund V. TVA*, 339 F.Supp. 806 ED Tenn. (1972).

33   *Tennessee Valley Authority v. Hill*. The TVA continued to insist to the congressional appropriations committee that their efforts to transplant the snail darter were promising, but the court found that these statements were at best misleading.

34   *Tennessee Valley Authority v. Hill*, 15–16.

35   The Tellico dam, along with another dam, were the first cases brought before the Endangered Species Committee after it was created in amendments to the

ESA following the Supreme Court decision, where the Tellico dam project did not receive the exception that its supporters assumed it would. Congress then passed a single-case exception to the law and the dam was finally opened. They attempted to eliminate the Endangered Species Committee, but that bill never passed the Senate. This series of events, where a review system is created and fails to rule in the way that its creators desired, led to attempts to undermine that review system and create another. Brian Balogh describes this process in his institutional history of the Atomic Energy Commission; see Brian Balogh, *Chain Reaction: Expert Debate and Public Participation in American Commercial Nuclear Power, 1945–1975* (Cambridge: Cambridge University Press, 1991).

36   "Senate Bill Threatens Rare Wildlife," *Christian Science Monitor*, May 26, 1978; "The U.S. vs. Snail Darter et al.," *Chicago Tribune*, June 5, 1978; King, "Snail Darter and Whooping Crane"; Steinhart, "Those Endangered Species"; and "Protecting Endangered Species," *Irish Times,* June 17, 1978.

37   Steinhart, "Those Endangered Species."

38   "Environmental Conflict: Pelican vs. Space Ship," *Washington Post*, January 15, 1979; "The U.S. vs. Snail Darter et al."; and "Fish vs. Military-Battle Plans Ready," *The Sun*, March 8, 1980.

39   National Environmental Policy Act of 1969, Title I, Section 102.

40   *Catholic Action of Hawaii/Peace Education Project v. Harold Brown, Secretary of Defense*, 468 F.Supp. 190 (1979).

41   *Catholic Action of Hawaii/Peace Education Project v. Harold Brown, Secretary of Defense*, 643 F.2d 469 (1980).

42   Endangered Species Act of 1973, Section 11(g).

43   *Carlos Romero-Barcelo v. Harold Brown*, 478 F.Supp. 646 (1979); *Carlos Romero-Barcelo v. Harold Brown*, 643 F.2d 835 (1981); and *Caspar W. Weinberger, Secertary of Defense v. Carlos Romero-Barcelo*, 456 U.S. 305, 102 S.Ct. 1798 (1982). Carlos Romero-Barcelo was the governor of Puerto Rico, while Brown and Weinberger were the secretaries of defense under Carter and Reagan, respectively.

44   *Carlos Romero-Barcelo v. Harold Brown* (1979), 11–13.

45   Ibid.

46   *Carlos Romero-Barcelo v. Harold Brown* (1981)

47   *Carlos Romero-Barcelo v. Harold Brown* (1979), 9–10.

48   Ibid., 48–50.

49   The "refuge effect" is the idea that areas of wilderness cut off from human activity because of military or human health concerns can become thriving areas for wildlife. The classic areas for this are the Korean Demilitarized Zone between North and South Korea and the Chernobyl Exclusion Zone. For an extended discussion of the refuge effect, see Mary Mycio, *Wormwood Forest: A Natural History of Chernobyl* (Washington, D.C.: Joseph Henry Press, 2005).

50   *Carlos Romero-Barcelo v. Harold Brown* (1981), 25–28.

51   *Caspar W. Weinberger, Secertary of Defense v. Carlos Romero-Barcelo.*

52   Ibid.

53   Mireya Navarro, "Uproar against Navy War Games Unites Puerto Ricans," *New*

York Times, July 10, 1999. The memorandum of understanding did little to end the controversy over the navy's use of the island, however. In April 1999 a security guard on the range was killed when a bomb went off course and destroyed his gate. Dozens of protesters have been arrested trespassing on the range in the two decades since the court battle.

54   *Animal Lovers Volunteer Association, Inc v. Caspar Weinberger,* 765 F.2d 937 (1985); and Les Line, "Navy Moves to Aid Strike Imperiled by Its Gunnery Practice," *New York Times,* January 7, 1997.

55   Exactly how many goats lived on San Clemente at any one time during this period is impossible to determine, with court filings on behalf of animal rights groups and newspaper reports relying on their information giving low figures, while counterfilings and other news reports relying on the navy or Fish and Wildlife numbers put the number of goats much higher. Line, "Navy Moves to Aid Strike"; and *Animal Lovers Volunteer Association, Inc v. Caspar Weinberger.*

56   Feral goats have a particularly storied legal history under the Endangered Species Act. One of the most prominent early case involves a population of goats and sheep living in the critical habitat of an endangered native Hawaiian bird. The state of Hawaii managed the population through the issuance of hunting permits. The courts ruled that the population as a whole was a risk to the endangered species and ruled that state (and federal) agencies may be required to remove non-native species that threaten the habitat of listed species. The Palila cases came down at the beginning of the navy's saga with the goats of San Clemente. See *Palila v. Hawaii Department of Land and Natural Resources,* 471 F.Supp. 985 (1979); and *Palila v. Hawaii Department of Land and Natural Resources,* 639 F.2d 495 (1981).

57   *Animal Lovers Volunteer Association, Inc v. Caspar Weinberger.*

58   Ibid.; Gordon Grant, "Navy Defends Its Plan to Kill 1,200 Wild Goats," *Los Angeles Times,* December 21, 1984; Gordon Grant, "Navy Kills 461 Goats on San Clemente Island," *Los Angeles Times,* July 12, 1986; and Lyle V. Harris, "Adopt-a-Goat Program Seeks Homes for a Herd: Group Seeks Homes for Herd of Rescued Goats," *Washington Post,* September 25, 1986.

59   Fund for Animals president Cleveland Amory, as quoted in Grant, "Navy Defends Its Plan to Kill 1,200 Wild Goats."

60   *Animal Lovers Volunteer Association, Inc v. Caspar Weinberger.*

61   Ibid.; *Animal Lovers Volunteer Association v. Richard Cheney,* 795 F.Supp. 991 (1992); and *Animal Lovers Volunteer Association v. Richard Cheney,* 795 F.Supp. 994 (1992).

62   Line, "Navy Moves to Aid Strike."

63   Donald A. Mackenzie, *Inventing Accuracy: An Historical Sociology of Nuclear Missile Guidance, Inside Technology* (Cambridge: Massachusetts Institute of Technology Press, 1990).

64   Anthony Ramirez, "The Secret Bomber Bugging Northrop," *Fortune,* March 14, 1988.

65   Marc Reisner, *Cadillac Desert: The American West and Its Disappearing Water* (New York: Viking, 1986).

66   Mackenzie, *Inventing Accuracy,* 229.

67 "Fish vs. Military-Battle Plans Ready"; and "Rare Fish Block Nevada Projects," *Los Angeles Times*, June 4, 1980.

68 "Endangered Fish Pose Problem in Developing Nevada's Deserts," *New York Times*, March 2, 1980; and "Rare Fish Block Nevada Projects."

69 Ramirez, "Secret Bomber Bugging Northrop."

70 Brad Knickerbocker, "MX Missile Runs into Opposition from Its Prospective Neighbors," *Christina Science Monitor*, October 14, 1983. This is one of several news articles about rancher unrest over the program. In the case of one rancher, Glenda Parson, her home, barns, and shop would be condemned by the air force.

71 Ibid.

72 "MX Placement Held Risky to Rare Species," *Washington Post*, October 9, 1983.

73 Available public statements do not give any reason for the exclusion of Colorado from the Peacemaker EIS. It could have been that Colorado was added to the plan at a late date while the complicated EIS was well under way, or that the air force believed that there would be more opposition to the project in Colorado. Further study of internal air force documents would be needed to understand the reasoning, as no justification was offered in the court filings other than that they should be able to use the EIS from the other states.

74 *Roy R. Romer v. Frank C. Carlucci*, 847 F.2d 445 (1988). Romer was the governor of Colorado; Carlucci the secretary of defense under Reagan.

75 Mackenzie, *Inventing Accuracy*.

76 Richard White, *"It's Your Misfortune and None of My Own": A New History of the American West*, 1st ed. (Norman: University of Oklahoma Press, 1991), 566.

77 *Foundation on Economic Trends v. Caspar W. Weinberger*, 610 F.Supp. 829 (1985); and "Army Says Germ Warfare Lab Would Be Safe," *New York Times*, February 7, 1988.

78 Colman McCarthy, "The Pentagon's Land Sighting," *Washington Post*, January 21, 1990; Rick Atkinson, "Range War in Idaho: Air Force's Vast Expansion Plan Is Resisted," *Washington Post*, May 9, 1990; Steven Lee Myers, "Cold War Over, Air Force Must Compete for Space," *New York Times*, July 16, 1998; and Paglen, *Blank Spots on the Map*.

79 Cornell Lab of Ornithology, "Red-Cockaded Woodpecker, Life History."

80 Frances C. James et al., "Ecosystem Magement and the Niche Gestalt of the Red-Cockaded Woodpecker in Longleaf Pine Forests," *Ecological Applications* 11, no. 3 (2001): 855–70.

81 Diner, "Army and the Endangered Species Act," 205.

82 Aroesty, Rubenson, and Thompsen, *Two Shades of Green*, 33–34.

83 Diner, "Army and the Endangered Species Act," 207.

84 Aroesty, Rubenson, and Thompsen, *Two Shades of Green*, 36. Diner, "Army and the Endangered Species Act," 207.

85 Aroesty, Rubenson, and Thompsen, *Two Shades of Green*, 37–41.

86 Ibid., 45.

87 Aroesty, Rubenson, and Thompsen, *Two Shades of Green*.

88 Mark D. Ahner, "Can the United States Army Adjust to the Endangered Species Act of 1973?" Staff Study, U.S. Army War College, 1992; Diner, "Army and the

Endangered Species Act; and Aroesty, Rubenson, and Thompsen, *Two Shades of Green*.

89   Ahner, "Can the United States Army Adjust," 2 and 22. It is not unreasonable to question if Dick Cheney really believed this in 1991. Given the hierarchical nature of the military, it almost doesn't matter what was in Cheney's heart; the command structure would adapt to what it was ordered to do. It is worth debating how Cheney's position changed in the post-2001 world, but that is not within the scope of this chapter.

90   Diner, "Army and the Endangered Species Act," 199.

91   Ahner, "Can the United States Army Adjust." The survey was relatively small, but given that the respondents were all army field grade officers (above the rank of major) attending the Army War College, the numbers remain significant.

92   McNeill, *Environmental Histories of the Cold War*.

CHAPTER 9

RESTORATION AND MEANING ON FORMER MILITARY LANDS IN THE UNITED STATES

DAVID G. HAVLICK

A MID-AUTUMN visit to the Big Oaks National Wildlife Refuge in southern Indiana is easy to recommend. The hardwood forests tint red, orange, and yellow as leaves flag their final colors before dropping for winter, the streams that course through the refuge run clear and cool, and the seasonal influx of deer and turkey hunters has yet to break the calm of this fifty-thousand-acre tract of forest, wetlands, and grasslands that rests anomalous amid the region's agricultural landscape. The Big Oaks refuge is renowned for its bird life. Designated a Globally Important Bird Area of the United States, the refuge is home, at least seasonally, to more than two hundred species of birds, including Henslow's sparrows, cerulean warblers, wood ducks, orchard orioles, Acadian flycatchers, and wood thrush.[1] Mammals abound, too: river otter ply the refuge waters, and federally endangered Indiana bats live here, as do coyotes, bobcats, beaver, white-tailed deer, and the occasional black bear. In the grasslands, adult crawfish frogs dig their burrows, while mossy enclaves shelter the tiny four-toed salamander.[2]

Yet there is also this: to enter the Big Oaks refuge, visitors must watch a thirty-minute safety video that details the hazards of unexploded military ordnance (UXO), then sign a hold-harmless agreement that acknowledges they understand and accept the risks of entering this site, which still holds 1.5 million rounds of UXO, 7 million projectiles with live fuses or small explosive charges, and 165,000 pounds of depleted uranium shells. Only about 10 percent of the refuge is open to the public, and at the center of the off-limits portion the Indiana Air National Guard operates a laser-guided air-to-ground firing range. All of this, habitat and hazards alike, at some level can be traced back to the refuge's earlier incarnation as the U.S. Army's Jefferson Proving Ground (JPG). For much of the time from 1940 to 1994, the JPG functioned as one of the army's principal munitions testing sites and firing ranges, a place where howitzers, antiaircraft guns, antipersonnel mines, air-to-ground artillery, and antitank munitions were tested. Fires set both incidentally and intentionally kept portions of the site from reforesting. These areas transitioned to grasslands, while outside the core impact zones, the farmlands condemned by the army were abandoned and steadily thickened with trees. Among these dangerous lands are a variety of rare and endangered (and also relatively well-protected) habitat types and species. The result is a landscape that is unique in scale and composition for this part of the United States.

The mix of conditions at Big Oaks provides a set of paradoxes and contrasts that highlight the social and ecological complexity of transitioning militarized landscapes. The site is in many respects severely degraded, most dramatically in terms of the prohibitive explosive hazards that prevent human occupancy, but Big Oaks is also ecologically privileged. Beyond its physical characteristics, Big Oaks harbors multiple cultural layers: traces of indigenous Americans mingle with stories of nineteenth-century slaves passing north to freedom along the Underground Railroad. Members of twentieth-century farm families who worked the land, then found themselves evicted on less than one month's notice to make way for army munitions, still make their way on occasion to visit their shattered homesteads.

The Big Oaks refuge, and similar sites of military-to-wildlife conversion, can productively be considered socioecological or hybrid landscapes where human and nonhuman elements become difficult to separate, where historical agency blurs, and where landscape conditions are, in important respects, integrated cultural and ecological productions.[3] This chapter highlights examples from recent military-to-wildlife refuge conversions to illustrate the disparate meanings we may draw from such places. These meanings, in turn, influence traditional assumptions about ecological restoration and how we interpret the relationship between militarism and the environment more broadly. My analysis emerges from particular places and data from specific sites of military transition, pointing more widely to important conceptual claims about military-environment compatibility. The research is based on more than five dozen interviews with refuge personnel and other key constituencies involved in recent military-to-wildlife conversions, visitor surveys conducted at three such refuges, document analysis, and fieldwork at dozens of sites of recent military-to-wildlife conversion in the United States and central Europe.

MILITARY-TO-WILDLIFE CONVERSIONS

Since 1988, more than four hundred U.S. military installations have been closed or repurposed. Most of these recent transitions are the result of five rounds of streamlining and updating military assets guided by a congressionally designated Base Closure and Realignment Commission (BRAC). Spurred by geopolitical changes following the end of the Cold War, as well as other efforts to modernize the U.S. military, BRAC closures have affected numerous small sites and some 125 "major" installations consisting of more than ten acres, or $1.5 billion in assets.[4] Nearly two dozen of these major military installations have subsequently been redesignated to become national wildlife refuges.[5]

At first glance, transitioning military bases to new purposes of wildlife conservation may seem an odd fit. Many of these sites have seen heavy impacts and upon closure include an array of military remnants ranging from infrastructure such as roads, landing strips, telecommunication facilities, and office complexes to more exclusive military features such as concrete ammunition bunkers (or "igloos"), high-security fencing, chemical contamination, and unexploded ordnance. Curiously, this legacy of military activity and production often works in *favor* of wildlife-oriented conversions. At sites where military hazards, contamination, or substantial infrastructures remain, conversion to civilian purposes can be difficult and prohibitively expensive. Quite a few military sites characterized by severe contamination also now contain, ironically, valuable ecological characteristics. The particular land use patterns at many military installations, where core areas receive devastating impacts or intensive development but the periphery remains relatively unused as buffer zones, over time provided inadvertent protection to wildlife, plants, and habitat. The genuine ecological features of these former military installations, along with the fact that cleanup standards are minimal to maintain these places for wildlife conservation, helps explain why more than 15 percent of all major U.S. military installations closed since 1988 have become national wildlife refuges.

To understand and interpret more fully the role of militarization on these lands and their changing orientation from military use to conservation, it is helpful to identify some of the meanings these places hold. As dynamic ecological and cultural sites, military-to-wildlife refuges can challenge us to consider in a different light how environmental processes—what we might more loosely call "nature"—and human actions interact. Ecological restoration efforts, often initiated as part of base cleanup or conversion, bring a number of these nature-society relationships into focus as traditional assumptions about reference conditions or human agency no longer easily fit. Military-to-wildlife conversions bring into focus additional questions. How do these sites create new political spaces? That is, whose interests are protected, mobilized, enhanced, or threatened by this particular kind of land use change? What values and assumptions are expressed by the formulation that such refuges represent "win-win-win" scenarios where the military benefits by streamlining obsolete assets, the environment gains protections for wildlife and habitat, and local human communities see the liabilities of off-limits, hazardous military bases become new tourist or open space amenities?

Other questions are potentially broader in scope: How can military-to-wildlife conversions and ecological restoration at these sites inform our understanding of militarism as it relates to a clean or healthy environment? When expanded, this question presses us to consider whether military practices and productions contribute in genuine ways to environmental protection. Can there be, in other words, a more *ecological* militarization that goes beyond rhetoric or greenwashing and instead represents a deeper position of institutional responsibility for the military? And finally, how might ecological restoration practice and theory influence militarism?

DISPARATE MEANINGS OF MILITARY-TO-WILDLIFE REFUGES

As is evident in the Big Oaks National Wildlife Refuge, the diverse qualities of a military-to-wildlife refuge can make it difficult to categorize.

DAVID G. HAVLICK

The challenge becomes greater still when we consider the complexity of meaning not just within a single site but across different conversion lands. Since 1988, military-to-wildlife conversions have occurred in habitats ranging from boreal forest in northern Maine to subtropical dry forest in the Caribbean, from wetlands along the Chesapeake Bay to shortgrass prairie in Colorado to Pacific atolls. The physical environments of these sites are naturally very different, but so too are the human impacts and cultural contexts. Looking simply at the array of military legacies that remain across sites we find some—including Big Oaks, Vieques (Puerto Rico), and Nomans Land Island (Massachusetts)—burdened with unexploded ordnance. The Rocky Mountain Arsenal, just north of Denver, Colorado, was infamously contaminated by chemical weapons and pesticide production at the site for four decades beginning in 1942. A number of sites are dotted with massive concrete igloos used for ammunition or missile storage, others have obsolete communication towers, snarls of military-grade wiring, airstrips that once accommodated fighter jets, groundwater fouled by solvents and jet fuel, and streams laced with polychlorinated biphenyls (PCBs). There will of course never be one recipe, one cleanup plan, or a single template for restoration that fits all of these sites, but ecological restoration efforts can shine a more focused light to help us grapple with the meaning of these places and what we make of them.

According to the Society for Ecological Restoration International (SER), ecological restoration is "the process of assisting the recovery of an ecosystem that has been degraded, damaged, or destroyed."[6] The historical uses of an ecosystem are implicitly invoked here—something occurred to degrade, damage, or destroy the site. Elsewhere SER is more direct about the relationship between restoration and history: "Restoration attempts to return an ecosystem to its historic trajectory. Historic conditions are therefore the ideal starting point for restoration design."[7] The problem that quickly emerges for restoration at military-to-wildlife refuges, and other sites with complex or layered histories, is to identify *which historical conditions* will be used as the ideal starting point. The traditional approach used by many restoration projects has been to strive for a presettlement historical condition (often considered "natural") that resets the ecological clock to a time before the impacts of industrial society.

Although this approach has a certain romantic and/or ecological appeal, it has also been the source of criticism. In one influential broadside, the environmental philosopher Robert Elliot has argued that restoration is a case of "faking nature" that disingenuously substitutes a replica for the original.[8] In a related critique, the philosopher Eric Katz has labeled restoration a "big lie" that obscures the impacts humans have wrought.[9] More recently, global changes in climate, chemical deposition, and radioactive fallout have spurred recognition that pristine or preindustrial conditions no longer even exist on Earth, leading some scholars to embrace a shift to future-oriented restoration or to develop theories describing the qualities of entirely new, or *novel*, ecosystems.[10] Each of these approaches can fit military-to-wildlife refuges in certain ways, but a more immediate concern at such sites with important cultural histories may be that way ecological restoration can serve as an agent of historical erasure.[11] This is where the meaning of such sites comes into focus as a principal concern. If we are unable to agree upon the significance of a given site, how can we effectively set goals for how we would like to restore certain conditions present there?

The need to set goals for ecological restoration targets thus focuses our attention on the qualities of a given site that we wish to restore. To some, military-to-wildlife refuges provide examples of the resiliency of nature. In this view, ecological processes, particular organisms, or entire plant and animal communities (again, often cast as "nature") will eventually rebound or return, even to areas that have suffered heavy impacts and degradation. This redemptive storyline emerges in an upbeat Fish and Wildlife Service publication about the Rocky Mountain Arsenal, which proclaims: "In a way, it was the eagles that made it happen."[12] As the story goes, only after bald eagles returned to nest at the site did biologists, army officials, and elected officials start to think seriously about the Rocky Mountain Arsenal as a prospective wildlife refuge. With this framing, nature ("the eagles") asserts its own agency, which in turn catalyzes changes in human perceptions and policy measures relating to the contaminated site.

In turn, this affirmative account of thriving nature at military-to-wildlife sites can lend support more generally to a view promoting the success and dedication of the military's environmental stewardship.[13] Positive environmental qualities found today at former (and many current) military installations are well documented and receive considerable attention.[14] In fact, a number of military activities do create disturbances that can lead to rare habitat conditions—for example, planned

DAVID G. HAVLICK

or incidental fires on artillery ranges can create and maintain grasslands or savannas in areas where forest encroachment is the norm. The land use patterns often found on military sites, with intensive impacts at the core of an installation but perimeter areas kept mostly undisturbed, also have left tens of thousands of acres on U.S. Department of Defense (DOD) lands as de facto protected areas where plants and wildlife often proliferate. Although the primary goal in the case of these DOD sites is to restrict land use to accomplish military training, testing, or security objectives, the result is an array of protected areas that can surpass national parks, designated wilderness, or national wildlife refuges in the limits placed on public access and most human activities. In the absence of other industrial, commercial, or recreational impacts, off-limits military sites may steadily develop extraordinary qualities as unintentional nature reserves.

This phenomenon is not limited to the United States. Running north-south the length of central Europe, for instance, is a sixty-eight-hundred-kilometer Iron Curtain Trail that was designated by the European Union in 2005. The trail designation recognizes the growing appeal of the formerly heavily militarized borderlands that are in many places now characterized as a greenbelt of national and regional parks, natural areas, and biosphere reserves.[15] Similarly, though clearly at a different stage of its militarization, the DMZ of the Korean Peninsula is also gaining a reputation for its role as a de facto wildlife refuge.[16]

Conditions of DOD-managed lands are actually more varied than a simple "weapons to wildlife" framing suggests. On the whole, they are the most biologically diverse and the most contaminated of any category of federal land in the United States.[17] This, and the underlying actions that created these disparate qualities, is what has moved anthropologist Joseph Masco to cast a more critical eye on military-to-wildlife transitions.[18] For Masco, it is essential that we consider the broader temporal and geographic context that "involves a massive state-sponsored territorial sacrifice during the Cold War that has been wildly productive in specific areas."[19] With this, he emphasizes the "dual structure" of such spaces "as both wildlife refuge *and* sacrifice zone."[20] The geographer Rachel Woodward has similarly argued that we need to examine the "suite of moral, political, and economic commitments" that produce the conditions now found on these lands, rather than focus on the more superficial presentation of them as ecological havens.[21] It is not enough, in other words, to understand the ecological flourishing of militarized sites simply in terms of what is now *visible*.

To consider the question of how to find meaning in landscapes with layered or complex histories, we might look to the environmental philosopher Martin Drenthen. Recognizing that older layers may be obscured by contemporary activities or meanings, Drenthen provides the analogy of a palimpsest landscape where prior histories can be made legible as is sometimes possible with reused medieval parchments: "If we conceive of ecological restoration as the uncovering of ancient layers and the cultivation of the lessons learned from reading the older text, then the palimpsest landscape could be a landscape ideal worth striving for: a multi-layered legible landscape that reflects human history and 'grounds' our sense of place in an understanding of the earlier and deeper layers."[22] This approach offers a means by which it may be possible to recognize and appreciate current landscape forms, such as biologically diverse and protected military sites, while also "reading" the important but less visible or superficial layers that exist both physically in the form of contaminated groundwater or soils and less tangibly as political, economic, or other social processes. The geographer Sarah Whatmore has encouraged a similar understanding of complex landscapes with her treatment of *hybrid geographies*, where the social and the natural are seen as co-constituted and integrated so fully that it is no longer appropriate even to think of these as isolatable ontologically distinct categories.[23] These socially and ecologically integrated approaches to try to find meaning in military-to-wildlife landscapes surely present challenges of their own, but they effectively point to the need to consider such places more deeply, to view seemingly natural spaces also in cultural terms, and to think about how efforts to restore or conserve nature can relate to the militarization of societies in significant ways.

MILITARY-TO-WILDLIFE REFUGES AS POLITICAL SPACES

It is sometimes tempting to view military-to-wildlife conversions from the position of a triumphant and resilient nature. In this view, despite decades of neglect or abuse at the hands of the military, nature bounces back and in the end prevails. This rather reassuring perspective encourages us to imagine that no matter the insult, humans are mere bit players in the long arc of changing physical landscapes. But the subtle

DAVID G. HAVLICK

shift in agency that often accompanies this interpretation can serve to depoliticize transitioning military spaces in ways that carry very real consequences. As Woodward pointedly wrote, "The study of military geographies involves a moral decision. If we study the ways in which military activities inscribe themselves onto space, place, environment and landscape, should we ignore or accept unquestioned the politics of that process?"[24] When we cast nature or natural processes as taking hold in transformative ways—eagles reclaiming a chemical weapons plant, for example, or bats adopting obsolete ammunition bunkers or missile silos as hibernacula—we may render our own actions inconsequential. Decades of military activities, environmental contamination, dramatic physical impacts, or the displacement of human communities in this way can be written off as mere bumps in the course of natural succession.

Masco, Woodward, Drenthen, and other scholars contend that we ought to retain at least the memory of these activities, impacts, and displacements as significant, for these are not only ecological or natural places but also social or cultural ones. A closer look at military-to-wildlife conversions reveals a complex picture, with underlying motives, intentions, actions, and historical layers that need to be considered to evaluate the military's—and other actors'—true position more accurately. Among the more obvious changes that take place with these conversions are the shifts in nomenclature and institutional responsibility. In this, we find the U.S. Army's Jefferson Proving Ground recast as the U.S. Fish and Wildlife Service's Big Oaks National Wildlife Refuge, the army's Fort McClellan becomes Fish and Wildlife Service's Mountain Longleaf National Wildlife Refuge, and the Pease Air Force Base turns into Great Bay National Wildlife Refuge. One question I pursued in my document analyses and interviews with wildlife refuge officials was whether these name changes came from an intentional effort to obscure the past military histories or more simply as an affirmative means by which to recognize the new wildlife conservation mission and managers. Wildlife refuge officials on the whole expressed surprise that the change in names was even a source of questioning, and though the latter, more innocent intention clearly prevailed, the more suspect effect of obscuring prior histories may still result.

The Rocky Mountain Arsenal National Wildlife Refuge is one of the exceptions to this renaming, although an early refuge proposal from Colorado congressman Wayne Allard (later a U.S. Senator) sought to drop "arsenal" from the converted base's name. In 1991 he introduced a bill to Congress calling for "legislation which will establish the Colorado Metropolitan National Wildlife Refuge."[25] This version of the name was also used in the bill introduced in the U.S. Senate by Colorado's Hank Brown (and cosponsored by senator Tim Wirth), but Colorado congresswoman Patricia Schroeder consistently labeled the site "Rocky Mountain Arsenal" in a parallel bill she introduced and ultimately pushed through Congress.[26] Even at the Rocky Mountain Arsenal, however, the site's new orientation as a wildlife refuge seems to have become quickly normalized in the perception of the visiting public. In our surveys conducted here in 2010, visitors conveyed a set of expectations that characterized the place predominantly in terms of "natural" features such as native plants and wildlife.[27] When we asked visitors to list three words to describe the refuge, the responses overwhelmingly identified the site as "natural," "beautiful," and "peaceful." Despite the arsenal's four decades as a chemical weapons and pesticides manufacturing facility, infamous regionally for contaminating local groundwater and soils, very few visitors included words relating to this past.

At the Rocky Mountain Arsenal refuge, the most dramatic changes at the site are physical rather than rhetorical or institutional. The name changed little, and the army still holds title to more than 10 percent of the refuge area, as the most severe sites of contamination and subsequent remediation areas will remain their obligation in perpetuity. To the average visitor, however, the arsenal appears as a site transformed. As part of a remediation costing more than two billion dollars, all infrastructure relating directly to chemical production has been demolished, contaminated soils and structures were removed and contained in on-site landfills, and an extensive shortgrass prairie restoration has occurred, including the introduction of a thriving herd of bison. This transformed physical landscape is doubtless responsible, at least to some degree, for the dramatic shift in public perception of the site from a place of severe contamination and hazard to one of natural beauty and tranquility.

Interestingly enough, despite different historical and contemporary settings, when in similar surveys of visitors at Assabet River National Wildlife Refuge in 2011 and 2012, my research found nearly identical results to this same open-ended question. Assabet River refuge was known from 1942 to 2000 as the U.S. Army's Sudbury Annex Ammunition Depot. The depot contained a few areas of chemical con-

9.1 Concrete ammunition storage igloo, Assabet River National Wildlife Refuge, Massachusetts. Image courtesy of David G. Havlick.

tamination—primarily from pesticides sprayed along railroad beds and coolants used in a telecommunications facility at the site—but after these were cleaned up, the most dramatic features remaining from the military's use are fifty massive concrete ammunition igloos scattered throughout the woods of the refuge's twenty-one hundred acres (figure 9.1). Since it opened to public use in 2005, the Assabet River refuge has grown increasingly popular as a recreational destination for local people in the Boston area. The Fish and Wildlife Service built a new visitors center in 2010, including exhibits featuring the site's wildlife and habitat as well as displays describing the military, agricultural, colonial, and Native American uses that predate its refuge designation. Not all visitors stop in at the visitors center, but even those who come to the refuge only to run, hike, or bicycle could scarcely miss finding ammunition igloos (commonly called "bunkers") during their visit. Several times each year local historians and refuge volunteers offer popular bunker tours for busloads of paying visitors. Unlike the situation at Rocky Mountain Arsenal refuge, visitors to Assabet River National Wildlife Refuge find a physical landscape that clearly still includes military relicts, even as the site's discursive presentation (i.e., its name and institutional presence) is more wholly associated with its new national wildlife refuge status.

There are other more subtle political spaces to be considered with these military-to-wildlife sites, including how elected officials, federal agencies, and local boosters often present such conversions as win-win-win opportunities that streamline obsolete military assets and turn restricted military sites (or brownfields) into open space amenities that will benefit local economies and the natural environment.[28] Even from very different physical qualities found at these sites and varying discursive changes that accompany the transitions, each military-to-wildlife conversion can generate a substantially different set of public perceptions that, in turn, have important political implications.

The emergence of former military installations as fresh sites of ecological production carries important political meaning not simply to these specific places and the people who interact with them, but also more broadly to the institutions responsible for their management. The sites' current custodian, the U.S. Fish and Wildlife Service, is the least well funded of any major federal land management agency and finds itself with an expanding land base that includes military installations in dire need of cleanup and remediation. For a number of such conversions, congressional action has effectively foisted military sites upon the Fish and Wildlife Service, which in several cases received these "gifts" despite having little interest in the wildlife or habitat features they contain. At other sites, such as Big Oaks National Wildlife Refuge, the Fish and Wildlife Service has pursued military-to-wildlife transfers due to unique habitat or conservation characteristics but has failed to convince the DOD to clear the military hazards or buildings that remain. Such cases highlight the asymmetrical institutional relationship between the world's most potent and heavily funded military and a wildlife agency forced to make do with an annual budget that falls far short of staffing its facilities or meeting its backlog of maintenance projects, even without adding liabilities to its refuge system.

The Department of Defense, meanwhile, has ample incentive to encourage all the military-to-wildlife transfers it can. Cleanup of these lands, when it occurs, need only meet a safety standard for a refuge worker exposed on site forty hours a week, not a more stringent level that would apply for a residential or commercial development. Obsolete or contaminated military holdings can therefore be relatively cheap to off-load as wildlife refuges, and the military gains the substantial benefit of pointing to its fine record of environmental stewardship that has allowed former bases to adopt opportunistic purposes of wildlife conservation.[29] The apparent greening of military sites can be scaled up to provide evidence for a broader position of environmental responsibility to which the DOD increasingly seems eager to lay claim.

ECOLOGICAL MILITARIZATION AND ECOLOGICAL RESTORATION

In recent years the U.S. Department of Defense has increasingly sought to highlight its dedication to a "triple bottom line" of mission, environment, and community.[30] The DOD typically is careful to maintain its "mission first" policy and quietly emphasizes that the environmental and community portions of this triple bottom line do not rest on par with the military mission. Within those parameters, however, the military goes to some lengths to establish its environmental bona fides. Dating back to 1960, with the passage of the Sikes Act, every DOD installation has been required to create a plan for the conservation of fish and wildlife, their habitats, and, where necessary, rehabilitation measures.[31] In many ways foreshadowing public lands legislation and executive orders that would come in the following decades, the Sikes Act stipulated that threatened and endangered wildlife and plants be afforded protections and that activities such as off-road vehicle use should be strictly controlled.[32]

More broadly, a suite of U.S. environmental laws that passed in the latter half of the twentieth century subjected DOD lands to regulations that simply did not exist before the 1960s. Among these, the National Environmental Policy Act (NEPA) required that significant federal actions include environmental analyses or impact statements, opening subsequent decisions to a process of public participation. In order to fend off extinctions, the Endangered Species Act (ESA) prohibited "takings"—meaning direct mortality or, less directly, habitat destruction—of species that are severely imperiled. The Resource Conservation and Recovery Act (RCRA) prescribed management protocols for hazardous materials and solid waste cleanups; the Comprehensive Environmental Response, Compensation, and Liability Act (CERCLA) clarified the chain of financial liability for hazardously polluted sites and created the

Superfund program to pay for remediation costs at dozens of the nation's most contaminated locations. These and other laws apply today in most instances on military and other federal lands (the ESA also applies on private lands).

Going beyond these legal requirements, however, the DOD has recently worked to position itself as a leader in the environmental management of its lands and facilities. DOD publications routinely tout the agency's accomplishments in sustainability, and its installation-level programs include ambitious efforts to achieve net-zero status in solid waste production, energy, and water consumption.[33] Such facilities as the army's Fort Carson and the U.S. Air Force Academy are implementing sustainability programs for renewable energy and carbon neutrality that easily surpass those of most municipalities or universities in the United States.

Recent decades have also found top DOD officials making clear statements about their agency's commitment to the environment. In 1990 secretary of defense Dick Cheney announced to a gathering of military leaders and other federal officials that "defense and the environment is not an either/or proposition. To choose between them is impossible in this real world of serious defense threats and genuine environmental concerns."[34] The secretary of the army routinely issues an Earth Day memo with a similar message of military environmentalism. In 2008, for example, army secretary Pete Geren sounded this environmental call to arms: "For all the advances mankind made in the twentieth century, it has become increasingly clear that we borrowed heavily against our environmental future. Environmental threats, such as climate change, are impacting areas of the world least capable of absorbing these shocks."[35] Geren memorably concluded by pronouncing, "To be Army Green is to be Army Strong!"

Much like military lands with their contrasting qualities of contamination and protection, the discursive positioning and environmental programs of the DOD also come with their share of disjuncture. The military's mission that ostensibly partners with environment and community for a "triple bottom line," for example, is predicated upon its ability to assert dominant, deadly force across any region of the planet. According to its own publications, the air force is based upon "one common foundation—persistent, lethal, overwhelming air, space and cyberspace power massed and able to be brought to bear anywhere at any time."[36]

Similarly, the U.S. Army's mission to "provide the capability—by threat, force, or occupation—to promptly gain, sustain, and exploit comprehensive control over land, resources, and people" seems to leave little room for the lighter bootprint advocated in military sustainability directives.[37]

That said, not every aspect of the military mission mobilizes against the DOD's pro-environment posture. In combat operations in Iraq and Afghanistan, U.S. supply lines and convoys have routinely been some of the costliest and most dangerous aspects of the war-fighting mission. During peak operations to support the war in Iraq, the United States moved approximately 2.4 million gallons of fuel *daily* across dangerous territory. Even discounting entirely the thousands of lives lost attempting to safeguard these supply lines—and the tens of thousands of shattered limbs—the DOD estimated the "fully burdened" cost of this fuel at $15 to $150 per gallon.[38] In Afghanistan the cost commonly exceeds $400 per gallon—with some estimates ranging upwards to $1,000 per gallon—to deliver and protect fuel to reach combat locations.[39] This of course completely ignores the human cost of lives lost or torn apart en route. An estimated 80 percent of U.S. military casualties in Afghanistan have been a result of improvised explosive devices (IEDs), and the majority of these are placed along roads and supply routes.[40] According to a 2009 Government Accountability Office report, more than forty trucks and approximately 220,000 gallons of fuel were lost due to attacks or other events while delivering fuel to a single airfield in Afghanistan in a single month in 2008.[41] It should come as no surprise that military planners, facing such conditions, increasingly recognize the need to reduce or eliminate extended convoys as a matter of tactical advantage and security. The fact that doing so would contribute handily to cost savings and military sustainability efforts only burnishes this resolve.

With this firmly in mind, the military actively funds research and development for an array of "green" technologies. In 2009, for example, the Office of Naval Research supplied U.S. Marines with a three-hundred-watt photovoltaic battery system (the Ground Renewable Expeditionary Energy System, or GREENS) designed to provide continuous power for communication and electronic devices in advanced field positions.[42] The ability to use computers, telecommunications, and targeting systems without being burdened with petroleum-powered generators or supply lines would add considerably to the mobility and security of forward parties of Marines and U.S. soldiers. In light of contrasting visions for how the military relates to the environment, the prospect of a more *ecological militarization* that renders the military mission as compatible with environmental protection is quite problematic. The military can legitimately point to its sustainability programs, the condition of military-to-wildlife lands, and its research and development funding for environmentally (and militarily) beneficial technologies, but these remain housed within the broader tent of the world's most powerfully destructive institution.

THE ROLE OF ECOLOGICAL RESTORATION

Considering the broader contexts of the military-environment relationship highlighted in this chapter, ecological restoration on former military lands may seem to play only a minor role. In terms of finances dedicated and institutional purposes, this is much the case, but restoration at military-to-wildlife sites remains important to consider for several reasons. The process of ecological restoration often brings the public into conversation with militarized landscapes in new and intimate ways. Restoration and remediation efforts are typically prerequisite to opening contaminated former military lands. Restoration work opens these sites physically as well as discursively. Perhaps most significant, ecological restoration on military lands presses us to think carefully about the condition of these lands, how they ought to be deliberately modified, and how the changes we make will in turn influence the meanings these landscapes convey.

One of the most fundamental aspects of active military lands is their restricted access. Military training and testing operations occur almost entirely out of view of the domestic public, and the bases themselves are mostly known by the populace only from the outside. At Big Oaks National Wildlife Refuge, one former army employee who remains actively engaged with the site described his interest in documenting and commemorating what happened there throughout its sixty-three-year history as an army proving ground. In one of our interviews he explained that people want to know "what happened here throughout the whole history of it. You know, what is behind that rusty fence? Why is that fence there?" Since the army did not conduct any comprehensive remediation of UXO (unexploded military ordnance) before transferring the refuge to the Fish and Wildlife Service, Big Oaks persists in a somewhat liminal state as a public national wildlife refuge that is open to the visiting pub-

DAVID G. HAVLICK

lic in only a very restricted capacity. A more dedicated effort to clean the site would broaden the scope of public engagement to be sure, but even in its current limited form—just about 10 percent of refuge lands are open and only on Mondays, Fridays, and the second and fourth Saturdays of each month from mid-April through November from 7:00 a.m. to 4:30 p.m.—the refuge still has an active public interface. An annual winter bird count attracts birders from across the region, hunters come each fall for popular deer and turkey seasons, academic researchers collaborate with refuge staff to conduct ecological research, and the refuge's growing reputation as a haven for rare wildlife and an abundance of birds make it a destination for dedicated naturalists. Prescribed burning, vegetation management, and other restoration work conducted by refuge staff contribute to these publicly valued features.

The public interface that exists at Big Oaks and other military-to-wildlife refuges helps focus visitors' attention on what these places are in all their complexity. Visitor surveys conducted at selected refuges seem to indicate a rapid naturalization of these sites simply *as wildlife refuges*, but allowing people to visit at least provides some opportunity for interpretation and education in visitors centers (where these exist), kiosks, trail signs, tours, and other forms of outreach. For casual visitors or tourists simply passing through, these brief engagements provide fairly limited exposure to the multiple cultural layers of these conversion sites, but for refuge volunteers and regular visitors, surveys and interviews have found considerably more attention to interpreting cultural elements and commemorating a full complement of histories from these places. For example, at Big Oaks a local group of citizens and former employees at the site founded a Jefferson Proving Ground Heritage Partnership "to help ensure the full story is told about the creation, support and history of Jefferson Proving Ground and that present and future generations are reminded of the sacrifice and contributions rendered by ordinary people in support of our nation."[43]

Restoration efforts at Big Oaks and other military-to-wildlife conversion sites face many questions and challenges, including the fact that the multiple histories, layers of use, and mix of impacts can provide little clear guidance in terms of restoration objectives. Choosing between different reference conditions as a target for ecological restoration, for example, will orient toward different goals, landscape characteristics, and historical periods. Facing a landscape that is dramatically the product of both human impacts *and* ecological processes, we are pressed to navigate the complexity of these mixed features to adequately account for cultural as well as ecological values. Finally, if restoration is at some level predicated upon acts of *erasure*—in the sense of removing degraded conditions and replacing them with more desirable forms and functions—the layered geographies at sites such as Big Oaks prompt us to be more attentive to the potential losses that can accompany this erasure as well as the gains we achieve. Recognizing and appreciating the complexity of these landscapes ought to move us toward a more deliberative restoration that accounts for ecological and cultural values, including the evolving relationship between environmental protection and militarization.

Military-to-wildlife conversions since 1988 have affected a significant number of sites across a diverse set of conditions. Of course, these particular transitions during this bracketed period of time represent a minority of the lands that currently exist as former military sites. How, then, can focusing upon conversions and ecological restoration at these sites inform our understanding of militarism as it relates to the larger concern of protecting or restoring a clean and healthy environment? Most immediately, these conversions provide a set of case studies by which we can evaluate whether military practices and productions contribute in genuine ways to environmental protection. This is an essential condition if the military is, in fact, going to go beyond rhetorical posturing or greenwashing to achieve a more ecological form of militarization.

What we find from these cases remains open to interpretation, but three significant observations emerge from studying military-to-wildlife transitions. First, military environmentalism remains subordinate to the dominant mission of the military. DOD environmental stewardship is in many respects genuine, promulgated by dedicated officers, enlisted personnel, and civilian employees, and produces measurable outcomes that in a number of instances benefit the environment. However, many of these instances of consilience are also either accidental byproducts of military activities or are accommodated principally because of related tactical or strategic military benefits. The fires that for decades cleared forests and maintained grasslands at Jefferson Proving Ground, for example, were started not with any ecological objectives in mind but rather were simply a side effect of military ordnance tests. The fact that refuge managers today at the Big Oaks National Wildlife Refuge value these openings and set fires each year to preserve them reflects primarily a happy coincidence of military and ecological outcomes, not a deeper commitment by decades of army managers to bring these two spheres into agreement.

Second, the discourse of ecological militarization can serve to obscure deeper and more far-reaching impacts of militarization, both domestically and abroad. Reflecting back to Secretary of Defense Cheney's 1990 statement to consider the complementarity of national defense and environmental protection, it is worth recalling the next line in the speech: "The real choice is whether we are going to build a new environmental ethic into the daily business of defense."[44] It is possible to find a variety of means by which to judge the DOD's current environmental ethic, but in terms of carbon emissions, biological destruction, geophysical impacts on the environment, human dislocations, or financial allocations to weapons versus wildlife, it would seem difficult to feel sanguine about the verdict. There are, of course, a number of significant environmental accomplishments for which the DOD can legitimately take credit, but despite the increase in military sustainability publications, proclamations, and programs, many of the most widespread and damaging impacts of militarization remain very much connected to the institution's core mission.

Third, ecological restoration conducted at former military sites can serve to influence public perceptions as well as the physical conditions of militarized sites. Restoration practices often engage local communities and can foster new connections between people and place. To some restoration scholars, this propensity of restoration to bring people into closer communion with the environment represents perhaps its greatest value.[45] Of course, the goal of most restoration efforts is primarily focused on making changes to the land itself, to improve ecological function, and, in some cases, reestablishing landscape forms that existed prior to human disturbance. In both these domains—the affective and the physical—restoration has an important role to play. Depending upon the choices we make about restoration goals, privileging ecological or cultural histories, and revealing or obscuring the many layers of impact and meaning found at military-to-wildlife conversions and similar sites, ecological restoration may serve to shape not just the past and present of militarized landscapes but also how we relate to these places in the future.

NOTES

1   Globally Important Bird Areas of the United States, American Bird Conservancy, available at www.abcbirds.org/abcprograms/domestic/iba/index.html, accessed August 22, 2013; and "Big Oaks National Wildlife Refuge Bird Checklist brochure," February 2012, U.S. Fish and Wildlife Service, Big Oaks National Wildlife Refuge, Madison, IN.

2   Big Oaks National Wildlife Refuge, available at www.fws.gov/refuge/big_oaks, accessed July 22, 2013.

3   Bruno Latour, *We Have Never Been Modern* (Cambridge, MA: Harvard University Press, 1993); Jonathan Murdoch, "Towards a Geography of Heterogeneous Associations," *Progress in Human Geography* 21, no. 3 (1997): 321–37; and Sarah Whatmore, *Hybrid Geographies: Natures, Cultures, Spaces* (London: Sage, 2002).

4   BRAC Executive Summary, 2003, available at www.brac.gov/docs/final/ExecutiveSummary.pdf, accessed October 3, 2013; and U.S. Department of Defense (DOD), *Base Structure Report Fiscal Year 2003 Baseline* (Washington, D.C.: DOD, 2002).

5   David G. Havlick, "Logics of Change for Military-to-Wildlife Conversions in the United States," *GeoJournal* 69 (2007): 151–64; and David G. Havlick, "Disarming Nature: Converting Military Lands to Wildlife Conservation," *Geographical Review* 101, no. 2 (2011): 183–200.

6   "SER International Primer on Ecological Restoration," version 2, Society for Restoration International, Washington, D.C., 2004, available at www.ser.org/resources/resources-detail-view/ser-international-primer-on-ecological-restoration, accessed October 4, 2013.

7   Ibid.

8   Robert Elliot, "Faking Nature," *Inquiry* 25 (1982): 1–93.

9   Eric Katz, "The Big Lie: Human Restoration of Nature," in Katz's *Nature as Subject: Human Obligation and Natural Community* (New York: Rowman and Littlefield, 1997).

10   Bill McKibben, *Eaarth: Making a Life on a Tough New Planet* (New York: Henry Holt and Co., 2010); and Bill McKibben, *The End of Nature* (New York: Random House, 1989). Young D. Choi, "Restoration Ecology to the Future: A Call for a New Paradigm," *Restoration Ecology* 15, no. 2 (2007): 351–53. Richard J. Hobbs, Eric Higgs, and James A. Harris, "Novel Ecosystems: Implications for Conservation and Restoration," *Trends in Ecology and Evolution* 24, no. 11 (2009): 599–605.

11   See Marion Hourdequin and David G. Havlick, "Restoration and Authenticity Revisited," *Environmental Ethics* 35, no. 1 (2013): 79–93; and Marion Hourdequin and David G. Havlick, "Ecological Restoration in Context: Ethics and the Naturalization of Former Military Lands," *Ethics, Policy, and Environment* 14, no. 1 (2011): 69–89.

12   U.S. Department of the Interior, Fish and Wildlife Service, *Rocky Mountain Arsenal National Wildlife Refuge: A Place Like No Other* (Commerce City, CO: U.S. Fish and Wildlife Service, Department of the Interior, 1999), 5.

13 E.g., Linda D. Kozaryn, "Environmental Protection Key to Readiness," American Forces Press Service, U.S. Department of Defense, November 26, 1996, available at www.defense.gov/News/NewsArticle.aspx?ID=40641, accessed October 11, 201; and U.S. DOD, DOD Sustainability, available at www.defense.gov/home/features/2010/1010_energy/, accessed October 11, 2013.

14 E.g., Michele Leslie, Gary K. Meffe, and Jeffrey L. Hardesty, *Conserving Biodiversity on Military Lands: A Handbook for Natural Resource Managers* (Washington, D.C.: U.S. DOD Biodiversity Initiative, U.S. DOD, and the Nature Conservancy, 1996); and Peter Coates, Tim Cole, Marianna Dudley, and Chris Pearson, "Defending Nation, Defending Nature? Militarized Landscapes and Military Environmentalism in Britain, France, and the United States," *Environmental History* 16, no. 3 (2011): 456–91.

15 See Michael Cramer, *Iron Curtain Trail, Part 3* (Rodingersdorf, Austria: Verlag Esterbauer, 2010); Michael Cramer, *Iron Curtain Trail, Part 2* (Rodingersdorf, Austria: Verlag Esterbauer, 2012); "Iron Curtain Trail," available at www.ironcurtaintrail.eu/en/index.html, accessed June 23, 2013; and Christian Schwägerl, "Along Scar from Iron Curtain, a Green Belt Rises in Germany," *Yale Environment 360* (2011), available at http://e360.yale.edu/feature/along_scar_from_iron_curtain_a_green_belt_rises_in_germany/2390/, accessed April 4, 2011.

16 See Hiroyoshi Higuchi, Kiyoaki Ozaki, Go Fujita, Jason Minton, Mutsuyuki Ueta, Masaki Soma, and Nagahisa Mita, "Satellite Tracking of White-naped Crane Migration and the Importance of the Korean Demilitarized Zone," *Conservation Biology* 10, no. 3 (1996): 806–12; and Ke Chung Kim, "Preserving Biodiversity in Korea's Demilitarized Zone," *Science* 278, no. 5336 (October 1997): 242–43.

17 Seth Shulman, *The Threat at Home: Confronting the Toxic Legacy of the U.S. Military* (Boston: Beacon Press, 1992); Leslie, Meffe, and Hardesty, *Conserving Biodiversity on Military Lands*; and Robert L. Fischman, *The National Wildlife Refuges: Coordinating a Conservation System through Law* (Washington, D.C.: Island Press, 2003).

18 Joseph Masco, "Mutant Ecologies: Radioactive Life in Post–Cold War New Mexico," *Cultural Anthropology* 19, no. 4 (2004): 517–50.

19 Ibid., 533.

20 Ibid., 532, emphasis in the original.

21 Rachel Woodward, *Military Geographies* (Oxford, U.K.: Blackwell, 2004).

22 Martin Drenthen, "Ecological Restoration and Place Attachment: Emplacing Non-Places?" *Environmental Values* 18, no. 3 (2009): 285–312.

23 Whatmore, *Hybrid Geographies*.

24 Woodward, *Military Geographies*, 9.

25 "Introduction of Legislation Establishing Colorado Metropolitan Wildlife Refuge," U.S. House of Representatives, July 15, 1991, H5436.

26 On March 14, 1991, four months before Allard initially introduced his Colorado Metropolitan Refuge bill, Schroeder submitted legislation for a Rocky Mountain Arsenal National Urban Wildlife Refuge; see Congressional Record, Extension of Remarks, March 14, 1991, 102nd Congress, 1st Session, 137 Cong. Rec. E944.

27 David G. Havlick, Marion Hourdequin, and Matthew John, "Examining Restora-

tion Goals at a Former Military Site," *Nature and Culture* 9, no. 3 (2014, in press).

28   For more on this, see Havlick, "Logics of Change."

29   See David G. Havlick, "Opportunistic Conservation at Former Military Sites in the United States," *Progress in Physical Geography* 38 (2014): 271–85.

30   E.g., U.S. Army Strategy for the Environment, 2004, Washington, D.C., available at www.sustainability.army.mil/overview/ArmyEnvStrategy.pdf, accessed October 13, 2013.

31   U.S. Department of Defense, *Defense Environmental Quality Program Annual Report to Congress, FY 2001* (Washington, D.C.: U.S. General Printing Office, 2001); Robert F. Durant, *The Greening of the U.S. Military: Environmental Policy, National Security, and Organizational Change* (Washington, D.C.: Georgetown University Press, 2007); and Coates et al., "Defending Nation, Defending Nature?"

32   U.S. DOD, *Defense Environmental Quality Program, FY 2001.*

33   E.g., Department of Defense Energy Programs, "Army Net Zero Energy Initiative," available at www.nrel.gov/defense/projects_army_net_zero.html, accessed October 14, 2013; and U.S. DOD, DOD Sustainability.

34   Dianne Dumanoski, "Pentagon Takes First Steps toward Tackling Pollution," *Boston Globe*, September 9, 1990.

35   "2008 Army Earth Day Message," Secretary of the Army, Washington, D.C., available at www.asaie.army.mil/Public/IE/earthday08message.pdf, accessed October 31, 2013.

36   U.S. Air Force, *U.S. Air Force Energy, Environment, Safety, and Occupational Health: Managing for Operational Sustainability, 2007 Inaugural Report* (Washington, D.C.: Department of the Air Force), 1.

37   U.S. Army, "Chapter 2: The Strategic Environment and Army Organization," in *U.S. Army Field Manual (FM 1),* Washington, D.C., 2005, available at www.army.mil/fm1/chapter2.html#section6, accessed October 14, 2013.

38   Barry Sanders, *Green Zone: The Environmental Costs of Militarism* (Oakland, CA: AK Press, 2009); and Wharton Aerospace and Defense Report, "U.S. Military Hopes To Be Energized by Alternative Fuels," January 30, 2009, available at http://executiveeducation.wharton.upenn.edu/wharton-aerospace-defense-report/upload/Military-Hopes-Energized-by-Fuel.pdf, accessed March 22, 2010.

39   Roxana Tiron, "$400 per Gallon Gas to Drive Debate over Cost of War in Afghanistan," *The Hill*, October 15, 2009, available at http://thehill.com/homenews/administration/63407–400gallon-gas-another-cost-of-war-in-afghanistan-, accessed October 16, 2009.

40   Ibid.

41   Ibid., citing "Defense Management: Increased Attention on Fuel Demand Management at DOD's Forward-deployed Locations Could Reduce Operational Risks and Costs," Government Accountability Office GAO-09-388T, March 3, 2009.

42   Office of Naval Research, "Solar Energy Powers Marines on Battlefield," December 7, 2009, press release, available at www.onr.navy.mil/en/~/link.aspx?_id=685466B603734B9DB20FCFA8F3883E23&_z=z, accessed March 25, 2010.

43   Jefferson Proving Ground Installation Support Management Agency, Madison,

IN, 2005, available at www.jpgbrac.com/environmental/heritage-partnership
.htm, accessed October 14, 2013.

44 Cheney as quoted in Dumanoski, "Pentagon Takes First Steps."

45 Eric S. Higgs, *Nature by Design: People, Natural Process, and Ecological Restoration*
(Cambridge: Massachusetts Institute of Technology Press, 2003); Eric S. Higgs,
"Restoration Goes Wild: A Reply to Throop and Purdom," *Restoration Ecology* 14,
no. 4 (2006): 500–3; William R. Jordan III, *The Sunflower Forest: Ecological Restora-
tion and the New Communion with Nature* (Berkeley: University of California Press,
2003); and Andrew Light, "Ecological Restoration and the Culture of Nature: A
Pragmatic Perspective," in *Readings in the Philosophy of Technology,* ed. David M.
Kaplan (New York: Rowman and Littlefield, 2009), 452–67.

Selected Bibliography

Abelson, Julia, Pierre-Gerlier Forest, John Eyles, Patricia Smith, Elisabeth Martin, and Francois-Pierre Gauvin. "Deliberations about Deliberative Methods: Issues in the Design and Evaluation of Public Participation Processes." *Social Science and Medicine* 57, no. 2 (2003): 239–51.

Adams, Brian. "Public Meetings and the Democratic Process." *Public Administration Review* 64, no. 1 (2004): 43–54.

Agamben, Giorgio. *State of Exception.* Chicago: University of Chicago Press, 2005.

Arnstein, Sherry. "Ladder of Citizen Participation." *Journal of the American Institute of Planners* 35, no. 4 (1969): 216–24.

Aroesty, Jerry, David Rubenson, and Charles Thompsen. *Two Shades of Green: Environmental Protection and Combat Training.* Santa Monica, CA: Rand Corporation, 1992.

Bacevich, Andrew J., ed. *Long War: A New History of United States National Security Policy since World War II.* New York: Columbia University Press, 2007.

Bae, Yooil, Dong-Ae Shin, and Yong Wook Lee. "Making and Unmaking of Transnational Environmental Cooperation: The Case of Reclamation Projects in Japan and Korea." *Pacific Review* 24 (2011): 201–23.

Baker, Anni. *American Soldiers Overseas.* Westport, CT: Praeger, 2004.

Balogh, Brian. *Chain Reaction: Expert Debate and Public Participation in American Commercial Nuclear Power, 1945–1975.* Cambridge: Cambridge University Press, 1991.

Beck, John. *Dirty Wars: Landscape, Power, and Waste in Western American Literature.* Lincoln: University of Nebraska Press, 2009.

Beck, Ulrich. *Ecological Enlightenment: Essays on the Politics of the Risk Society.* New York: Humanity Books, 1995.

———. *Risk Society: Toward a New Modernity.* 1982. Reprint, Thousand Oaks, CA: Sage Publications, 1992.

Beierle, Thomas, and Jerry Cayford. *Democracy in Practice: Public Participation in Environmental Decisions.* New York: Routledge, 2002.

Bellia, Patricia. "Executive Powers in Youngstown's Shadows." *Constitutional Commentary* 19 (2002): 87–154.

Biggs, David. *Quagmire: Nation-Building and Nature in the Mekong Delta.* Seattle: University of Washington Press, 2011.

Brady, Lisa M. "Life in the DMZ: Turning a Diplomatic Failure into an Environmental Success." *Diplomatic History* 32, no. 4 (September 2008): 585–611.

———. *War upon the Land: Military Strategy and the Transformation of Southern Landscapes during the American Civil War, Environmental History and the American South.* Athens: University of Georgia Press, 2012.

Brenkman, John. *The Cultural Contradictions of Democracy: Political Thought since September 11.* Princeton, NJ: Princeton University Press, 2007.

Brinkley, Douglas. *The Wilderness Warrior: Theodore Roosevelt and the Crusade for America.* 1st edition. New York: HarperCollins, 2009.

Britto, Lino. "A Trafficker's Paradise: The 'War on Drugs' and the New Cold War in Colombia." *Contemporanea: Historia y problemas del siglo XX* 1, no. 1 (2010): 159–77.

Brown, Mark. *Science in Democracy: Expertise, Institutions, and Representation.* Cambridge: Massachusetts Institute of Technology Press, 2009.

Bruff, Harold H. "Executive Power and the Public Lands." *University of Colorado Law Review* 76 (2005): 503–20.

Calder, Kent. *Embattled Garrisons: Comparative Base Politics and American Globalism.* Princeton, NJ: Princeton University Press, 2007.

Camacho Guizado, Álvaro, and Andreés López Restrepo. "From Smugglers to Drug Lords to *Traquetos*: Changes in the Colombian Illicit Drug Organizations." In *Peace, Democracy, and Human Rights in Colombia*, edited by Christopher Welna and Gustavo Gallán, 60–89. South Bend, IN: University of Notre Dame Press, 2007.

Carpini, Michael X Delli, Fay Lomax Cook, and Lawrence R. Jacobs. "Public Deliberation, Discursive Participation, and Citizen Engagement: A Review of the Empirical Literature." *Annual Review of Political Science* 7 (2004): 315–44.

Cecil, Paul. *Herbicidal Warfare: The Ranch Hand Project in Vietnam.* New York: Praeger, 1986.

Chae, Young Geun. "Environmental Contamination at U.S. Military Bases in South Korea and the Responsibility to Clean Up." *Environmental Law Reporter* 40 (2010): 10078–97.

Chambers, Simone. "Deliberative Democratic Theory." *Annual Review of Political Science* 6 (2003): 307–26.

Choi, Young D. "Restoration Ecology to the Future: A Call for a New Paradigm." *Restoration Ecology* 15, no. 2 (2007): 351–53.

Closmann, Charles E., ed. *War and the Environment: Military Destruction in the Modern Age.* Lubbock: Texas A&M Press, 2009.

Coates, Peter, Tim Cole, Marianna Dudley, and Chris Pearson. "Defending Nation, Defending Nature? Militarized Landscapes and Military Environmentalism in Britain, France, and the United States." *Environmental History* 16, no. 3 (July 2011): 456–91.

Coggins, George C., Charles F. Wilkinson, and John D. Leshy. *Federal Public Land and Resource Law.* 5th edition. New York: Foundation Press, 2002.

Collins, Harry, and Robert Evans. *Rethinking Expertise.* Chicago: University of Chicago Press, 2007.

Commoner, Barry. "The Fallout Problem," *Science* 127, no. 3305 (May 1958): 1023–26.

Cooley, Alexander. *Base Politics: Democratic Change and the U.S. Military Overseas.* Ithaca, NY: Cornell University Press, 2008.

Corburn, Jason. "Environmental Justice, Local Knowledge, and Risk: The Discourse of a Community-Based Cumulative Exposure Assessment." *Environmental Management* 29, no. 4 (2002): 451–66.

Corwin, Edward S. *The President: Office and Powers, 1787–1984: History and Analysis of Practice and Opinion.* New York: New York University Press, 1984.

Cronon, William, ed. *Uncommon Ground: Rethinking the Human Place in Nature.* New York: W. W. Norton & Company, Inc., 1995.

Cumings, Bruce. "The Structural Basis of 'Anti-Americanism' in the Republic of Korea." In *Korean Attitudes toward the United States: Changing Dynamics,* edited by David I. Steinberg, 91–115. Armonk, NY: M. E. Sharpe, 2005.

Dewey, John. *The Public and Its Problems.* Athens, OH: Swallow Press, 1954.

Dillon, Lindsey. "Race, Waste, and Space: Brownfield Redevelopment and Environmental Justice at the Hunters Point Shipyard." *Antipode* (2013): 1–17.

Diner, David N. "The Army and the Endangered Species Act: Who's Endangering Whom?" *Military Law Review* 143 (1994): 200–201.

Divine, Robert A. "Eisenhower, Dulles, and the Nuclear Test Ban Issue: Memorandum of a White House Conference, 24 March 1958." *Diplomatic History* 2, no. 1 (October 1978): 321–30.

Dorsey, Kurk. "Dealing with the Dinosaur (and Its Swamp): Putting the Environment in Diplomatic History." *Diplomatic History* 29 (September 2005): 573–87.

Drenthen, Martin. "Ecological Restoration and Place Attachment: Emplacing Non-Places?" *Environmental Values* 18, no. 3 (2009): 285–312.

Dudziak, Mary L. "Law, Power, and 'Rumors of War': Robert Jackson Confronts Law and Security after Nuremberg." *Emory University School of Law Legal Studies Research Paper Series Research Paper,* no. 12–191 (2012): 366–85.

———. *War Time: An Idea, Its History, Its Consequences.* New York: Oxford University Press, 2012.

Dunn, Timothy J. *The Militarization of the U.S.-Mexico Border, 1978–1992: Low-Intensity Conflict Doctrine Comes Home.* Austin: Center for Mexican American Studies, University of Texas at Austin, 1996.

Durant, Robert F. *The Greening of the U.S. Military: Environmental Policy, National Security, and Organization Change.* Washington, D.C.: Georgetown University Press, 2007.

———. "National Defense, Environmental Regulation, and Overhead Democracy: A View from 'Greening' of the U.S. Military." *Public Organization Review* 10 (2010): 223–44.

Elliot, Robert. "Faking Nature." *Inquiry* 25 (1982): 1–93.

Enloe, Cynthia. *Bananas, Beaches, and Bases: Making Feminist Sense of International Politics.* Berkeley: University of California Press, 2000.

———. *The Morning After: Sexual Politics at the End of the Cold War.* Berkeley: University of California Press, 1993.

Evenden, Matthew. "Aluminum, Commodity Chains, and the Environmental History of the Second World War." *Environmental History* 16, no. 1 (January 2011): 69–93.

Fehner, Terrence R., and F. G. Gosling. *Atmospheric Nuclear Weapons Testing, 1951–1963.* Washington, D.C.: U.S. Department of Energy, 2006.

Feinerman, James. "The U.S.–Korean Status of Forces Agreements as a Source of Continuing Korean Anti-American Attitudes." In *Korean Attitudes toward the United States' Changing Dynamics*, edited by David I. Steinberg, 196–212. Armonk, NY: M. E. Sharpe, 2005.

Felbab-Brown, Vanda. *Shooting Up: Counterinsurgency and the War on Drugs.* Washington, D.C.: Brookings Institution Press, 2010.

Fernlund, Kevin J., ed. *The Cold War American West, 1949–1989.* Albuquerque: University of New Mexico, 1998.

Fiege, Mark. "The Atomic Scientists, the Sense of Wonder, and the Bomb." *Environmental History* 12, no. 3 (July 2007): 578–613.

Fiorino, Daniel J. "Citizen Participation and Environmental Risk: A Survey of Institutional Mechanisms." *Science, Technology, and Human Values* 15, no. 2 (1990): 226–43.

Fischman, Robert L. *The National Wildlife Refuges: Coordinating a Conservation System Through Law.* Washington, D.C.: Island Press, 2003.

Fisher, Louis, and Gordon Silverstein. *Presidential War Power.* Lawrence: University Press of Kansas, 1998.

Fleming, James Rodger. *Fixing the Sky: The Checkered History of Weather and Climate Control.* New York: Columbia University Press, 2010.

Forrestal, Dan J. *The Story of Monsanto: Faith, Hope, and $5000: The Trials and Triumphs of the First 75 Years.* New York: Simon and Schuster, 1977.

Forsberg, Aaron. *America and the Japanese Miracle: The Cold War Context of Japan's Postwar Economic Revival, 1950–60.* Chapel Hill: University of North Carolina Press, 2000.

Fradkin, Phillip L. *Fallout: An American Nuclear Tragedy.* Tucson: University of Arizona Press, 1989.

Franklin, Jane, ed. *The Politics of Risk Society.* Malden, MA: Blackwell Publishers, 1998.

Fuller, Steve. *The Governance of Science.* Buckingham: Open University Press, 2000.

Funtowicz, Silvio, and Jerome Ravetz. "Science for the Post-Normal Age." *Futures* 25, no. 7 (1993): 739–55.

Getches, David H. "Managing the Public Lands: The Authority of the Executive to Withdraw Lands." *National Resources Journal* 22 (1982): 279–335.

Gill, Lesley. *The School of the Americas: Military Training and Political Violence in the Americas.* Durham, NC: Duke University Press, 2004.

Gootenberg, Paul. *Andean Cocaine: The Making of a Global Drug.* Chapel Hill: University of North Carolina Press, 2008.

———. "Talking about the Flow: Drugs, Borders, and the Discourse of Drug Control." *Cultural Critique* 71 (Winter 2009): 13–25.

Gross, Oren, and Fionnuala Ní Aoláin. *Law in Times of Crisis: Emergency Powers in Theory and Practice.* New York: Cambridge University Press, 2006.

Hacker, Barton C. *Elements of Controversy: The Atomic Energy Commission and Radiation*

Safety in Nuclear Weapons Testing, 1947–1974. Berkeley: University of California Press, 1994.

Hajer, Maarten A. *The Politics of Environmental Discourse: Ecological Modernization and the Policy Process*. Oxford: Clarendon Press, 1995.

Hamblin, Jacob Darwin. *Arming Mother Nature: The Rise of Catastrophic Environmentalism*. New York: Oxford University Press, 2013.

Haraway, Donna. *Simians, Cyborgs, and Women: The Reinvention of Nature*. New York: Routledge, 1991.

Havlick, David G. "Disarming Nature: Converting Military Lands to Wildlife Conservation." *Geographical Review* 101, no. 2 (2011): 183–200.

———. "Logics of Change for Military-to-Wildlife Conversions in the United States." *GeoJournal* 69 (2007): 151–64.

Hersey, John. *Hiroshima*. 1946. Reprint, New York: Bantam Books, 1981.

Higgs, Eric S. *Nature by Design: People, Natural Process, and Ecological Restoration*. Cambridge: Massachusetts Institute of Technology Press, 2003.

———. "Restoration Goes Wild: A Reply to Throop and Purdom." *Restoration Ecology* 14, no. 4 (2006): 500–503.

Higuchi, Hiroyoshi, Kiyoaki Ozaki, Go Fujita, Jason Minton, Mutsuyuki Ueta, Masaki Soma, and Nagahisa Mita. "Satellite Tracking of White-naped Crane Migration and the Importance of the Korean Demilitarized Zone." *Conservation Biology* 10, no. 3 (1996): 806–12.

Hindess, Barry. *Discourses of Power: From Hobbes to Foucault*. Oxford: Blackwell, 1996.

Hise, Greg. *Magnetic Los Angeles: Planning the Twentieth-Century Metropolis*. Baltimore, MD: Johns Hopkins University Press, 1999.

Hobbs, Richard J., Eric Higgs, and James A. Harris. "Novel Ecosystems: Implications for Conservation and Restoration." *Trends in Ecology and Evolution* 24, no. 11 (2009): 599–605.

Höhn, Maria, and Seungsook Moon, eds. *Over There: Living with the U.S. Military Empire from World War Two to the Present*. Durham, NC: Duke University Press, 2010.

Holifield, Ryan. "Neoliberalism and Environmental Justice in the United States Environmental Protection Agency: Translating Policy into Managerial Practice in Hazardous Waste Remediation." *Geoforum* 35, no. 3 (2004): 285–97.

Hostetler, Darrin. "Wrong War, with the Wrong Enemy, at the Wrong Time: The Coming Battle over the Military Land Withdrawal Act and an Experiment in Privatizing the Regulation of Public Lands." *Environmental Law Review* 29 (1999): 303–38.

Hourdequin, Marion, and David G. Havlick. "Ecological Restoration in Context: Ethics and the Naturalization of Former Military Lands." *Ethics, Policy, and Environment* 14, no. 1 (2001): 69–89.

———. "Restoration and Authenticity Revisited." *Environmental Ethics* 35, no. 1 (2013): 79–93.

Hunner, John. *Inventing Los Alamos: The Growth of an Atomic Community*. Norman: University of Oklahoma Press, 2004.

Inoue, Masamichi. *Okinawa and the U.S. Military: Identity Making in the Age of Globalization*. New York: Columbia University Press, 2007.

Irwin, Alan. *Citizen Science: A Study of People, Expertise, and Sustainable Development.* New York: Routledge, 1995.

Isacson, Adam. "The U.S. Military in the War on Drugs." In *Drugs and Democracy in Latin America,* edited by Coletta A. Youngers and Eileen Rosin, 15–60. Boulder, CO: Lynne Rienner Publishers, 2005.

Jackson, Robert H. "Is Our Constitutional Government in Danger?" *Town Meeting* 4, no. 5 (1939): 3–28.

———. "Wartime Security and Liberty under Law." *Buffalo Law Review* 1 (1951): 3–17.

Jacoby, Karl. *Crimes against Nature: Squatters, Poachers, Thieves, and the Hidden History of American Conservation.* Berkeley: University of California Press, 2001.

James, Frances C., et al. "Ecosystem Magement and the Niche Gestalt of the Red-Cockaded Woodpecker in Longleaf Pine Forests." *Ecological Applications* 11, no. 3 (2001): 855–70.

Jasanoff, Sheila. "Bridging the Two Cultures of Risk Analysis." *Risk Analysis* 13, no. 2 (April 1993): 123–29.

———. *Designs on Nature: Science and Democracy in Europe and the United States.* Princeton, NJ: Princeton University Press, 2005.

Jelsma, Martin. *Vicious Circle: The Chemical and Biological "War on Drugs."* Amsterdam: Transnational Institute, 2001.

Johnson, Chalmers. *Blowback: The Costs and Consequences of American Empire.* New York: Metropolitan Books, 2000.

Jordan III, William R. *The Sunflower Forest: Ecological Restoration and the New Communion with Nature.* Berkeley: University of California Press, 2003.

Joyce, Stephanie. "Environmental Casualties of the War on Drugs." *Environmental Health Perspectives* 107 (February 1999): 74–77.

Kasperson, Roger, Dominic Golding, and Seth Tuler. "Social Distrust as a Factor in Siting Hazardous Facilities and Communicating Risks." *Journal of Social Issues* 48, no. 4 (1992): 161–87.

Katyal, Kumar Neal. "The Supreme Court, 2005 Term—Hamdan v. Rumsfeld: The Legal Academy Goes to Practice." *Harvard Law Review* 120 (2006): 65–123.

Katz, Eric. *Nature as Subject: Human Obligation and Natural Community.* New York: Rowman and Littlefield, 1997.

Kenney, Michael. *From Pablo to Osama: Trafficking and Terrorist Networks, Government Bureaucracies, and Competitive Adaptation.* University Park: Pennsylvania State University Press, 2007.

Kern, Thomas. "Anti-Americanism in South Korea: From Structural Cleavages to Protest." *Korea Journal* 45 (2005): 257–88.

Kim, Hakjoon. "A Brief History of the U.S.-ROK Alliance and Anti-Americanism in South Korea." *Walter H. Shorenstein Asia-Pacific Research Center Report* 31, no. 1 (2010): 1–45.

Kim, Jinwung. "Recent Anti-Americanism in South Korea: The Causes." *Asian Survey* 29 (1989): 749–63.

Kim, Ke Chung. "Preserving Biodiversity in Korea's Demilitarized Zone." *Science* 278, no. 5336 (October 1997): 242–43.

Kim, Sung-han. "Anti-American Sentiment and the ROK-U.S. Alliance." *Korean Journal of Defensive Analysis* 15 (2003): 105–30.

Kim, Sunhyuk. *The Politics of Democratization in Korea: The Role of Civil Society*. Pittsburgh: Pittsburgh University Press, 2000.

Kinkela, David. *DDT and the American Century: Global Health, Environmental Politics, and the Pesticide That Changed the World*. Chapel Hill: University of North Carolina Press, 2011.

Kroll-Smith, J. Stephen, and Worth Lancaster. "Bodies, Environments, and a New Style of Reasoning." *Annals of the American Academy of Political and Social Science* 584 (2002): 203–12.

Kroll-Smith, J. Stephen, Phil Brown, and Valerie Gunter, eds. *Illness and the Environment: A Reader in Contested Medicine*. New York: New York University Press, 2000.

Langston, Nancy. *Toxic Bodies: Hormone Disruptors and the Legacy of DES*. New Haven, CT: Yale University Press, 2009.

Latour, Bruno. *Pandora's Hope: Essays on the Reality of Science Studies*. Cambridge, MA: Harvard University Press, 1999.

———. *We Have Never Been Modern*. Cambridge, MA: Harvard University Press, 1993.

Laurian, Lucie. "Deliberative Planning through Citizen Advisory Boards." *Journal of Planning Education and Research* 26, no. 4 (2007): 415–34.

———. "A Prerequisite for Participation Environmental Knowledge and What Residents Know about Local Toxic Sites." *Journal of Planning Education and Research* 22, no. 3 (2003): 257–69.

Lee, Manjong. "Banhwan migun gijiyui hwankyung ohyum munjiee daehan bubjuk gochal: Hanmi SOFA hwanjkyung gyujungyui munjiejumgwa gaesunbangahn jungshim" [Study on environmental pollution in returned American military bases regarding its legal aspects—centered on finding and settling the problems of SOFA environmental provision established between Korea and America]. *Hwankyungbub yungu* [Environmental law studies] 30 (2008): 139–62.

Lee III, Rensselaer W. *The White Labyrinth: Cocaine and Political Power*. Brunswick, NJ: Transaction Publishers, 1989.

Lee, Yoon-Ho Alex. "Criminal Jurisdiction under the U.S.–South Korea Status of Forces Agreement: Problems to Proposals." *Journal of Transnational Law and Policy* 13 (2003): 213–49.

Leshy, John D. "Shaping the Modern West: The Role of the Executive Branch." *Colorado Law Review* 72, no. 2 (2001): 287–310.

Levinson, Sanford. "Why the Canon Should Be Expanded to Include the Insular Cases and the Saga of American Expansionism." *Constitutional Comment* 17, no. 2 (2000): 241–66.

Light, Andrew. "Ecological Restoration and the Culture of Nature: A Pragmatic Perspective." In *Readings in the Philosophy of Technology*, edited by David M. Kaplan, 452–67. New York: Rowman and Littlefield, 2009.

London, Jonathan, Julie Sze, and Raoul S. Lievanos. "Problems, Promise, Progress, and Perils: Critical Reflections on Environmental Justice Policy Implementation in California." *UCLA Journal of Environmental Law and Policy Review* 26 (2008): 255–90.

Loomis, David. *Combat Zoning: Military Land Use Planning in Nevada.* Reno: University of Nevada Press, 1993.

Lotchin, Roger W. *Fortress California, 1910–1961: From Welfare to Warfare.* New York: Oxford University Press, 1992.

———, ed. *The Martial Metropolis: U.S. Cities in War and Peace.* New York: Praeger, 1984.

Lutts, Ralph H. "Chemical Fallout: Rachel Carson's *Silent Spring*, Radioactive Fallout, and the Environmental Movement." *Environmental Review* 9, no. 3 (Autumn 1985): 210–25.

Lutz, Catherine, ed. *Bases of Empire: The Global Struggle against U.S. Military Outposts.* New York: New York University Press, 2009.

Lynch, Kevin. *The Image of the City.* Cambridge: Massachusetts Institute of Technology Press, 1960.

Lytle, Mark. "An Environmental Approach to American Diplomatic History." *Diplomatic History* 20, no. 2 (March 1996): 279–300.

Mackenzie, Donald A. *Inventing Accuracy: An Historical Sociology of Nuclear Missile Guidance, Inside Technology.* Cambridge: Massachusetts Institute of Technology Press, 1990.

Makhijani, Arjun, Howard Hu, and Katherine Yih, eds. *Nuclear Wastelands: A Global Guide to Nuclear Weapons Production and Its Health and Environmental Effects.* Cambridge: Massachusetts Institute of Technology Press, 1995.

Martini, Edwin A. *Agent Orange: History, Science, and the Politics of Uncertainty.* Amherst: University of Massachusetts Press, 2012.

———. "Incinerating Agent Orange: Operations Pacer HO, Pacer IVY, and the Global Legacies of the Chemical War." *Journal of Military History* 76 (July 2012): 809–36.

Masco, Joseph. "Mutant Ecologies: Radioactive Life in Post–Cold War New Mexico." *Cultural Anthropology* 19 no. 4 (2004): 517–50.

———. *Nuclear Borderlands: The Manhattan Projects in Post–Cold War New Mexico.* Princeton, NJ: Princeton University Press, 2006.

Mayer, Kenneth R. *With the Stroke of a Pen: Executive Orders and Presidential Power.* Princeton, NJ: Princeton University Press, 2002.

McCaffrey, Katherine. *Military Power and Popular Protest: The U.S. Navy in Vieques, Puerto Rico.* New Brunswick, NJ: Rutgers University Press, 2004.

McKibben, Bill. *Eaarth: Making a Life on a Tough New Planet.* New York: Henry Holt and Co., 2002.

———. *The End of Nature.* New York: Random House, 1989.

McNeill, J. R., and Corinna R. Unger, eds. *Environmental Histories of the Cold War.* Cambridge: Cambridge University Press, 2010.

Miller, Richard L. *Under the Cloud: The Decades of Nuclear Testing.* New York: Free Press, 1986.

Mittman, Greg, Michelle Murphy, and Christopher Sellers, eds. *Landscapes of Exposure: Knowledge and Illness in Modern Environments.* Chicago: University of Chicago Press, 2004.

Monaghan, Henry P. "The Protective Power of the Presidency." *Columbia Law Review* 93, no. 1 (January 1993): 1–74.

Montoya, Maria E. "Landscapes of the Cold War West." In *The Cold War American West,
1949–1989*, edited by Kevin J. Fernlund, 9–28. Albuquerque: University of New
Mexico, 1998.

Moon, Katharine H. S. "Korean Nationalism, Anti-Americanism, and Democratic Consolidation." In *Korea's Democratization*, edited by Samuel S. Kim, 135–57. New York:
Cambridge University Press, 2003.

Moote, Margaret A., Mitchel P. McClaran, and Donna K. Chickering. "Theory in Practice: Applying Participatory Democracy Theory to Public Land Planning." *Environmental Management* 21, no. 6 (1997): 877–89.

Morris, Evelyn Krache. "Into the Wind: The Kennedy Administration and the Use of
Herbicides in South Vietnam." PhD dissertation, Georgetown University, 2012.

Mouffe, Chantal. *The Democratic Paradox*. Brooklyn, NY: Verso Books, 2000.

Murdoch, Jonathan. "Towards a Geography of Heterogeneous Associations." *Progress in
Human Geography* 21, no. 3 (1997): 321–37.

Murphy, Michelle. *Sick Building Syndrome and the Problem of Uncertainty: Environmental
Politics, Technoscience, and Women Workers*. Durham, NC: Duke University Press,
2006.

Musto, David F. *The American Disease: Origins of Narcotics Control*, 3rd edition. New York:
Oxford University Press, 1999.

Musto, David F., and Pamela Korsemeyer. *The Quest for Drug Control: Politics and Federal
Policy in A Period of Increasing Substance Abuse, 1963–1981*. New Haven, CT: Yale
University Press, 2002.

Mycio, Mary. *Wormwood Forest: A Natural History of Chernobyl*. Washington, D.C.:
Joseph Henry Press, 2005.

Nam, Chang-Hee. "Relocating the U.S. Forces in South Korea: Strained Alliance, Emerging Partnership in the Changing Defense Posture." *Asian Survey* (2006): 613–31.

Nash, Gerald. *The American West Transformed: The Impact of the Second World War*. Bloomington: Indiana University Press, 1985.

———. *The Crucial Era: The Great Depression and World War II*. 2nd edition. New York: St.
Martin's Press, 1992.

Nash, Linda. *Inescapable Ecologies: A History of Environment, Disease, and Knowledge*.
Berkeley: University of California Press, 2007.

The Nevada Test Site: A Guide to America's Nuclear Proving Ground. Culver City, CA: Center
for Land Use Interpretation, 1996.

Oh, Chang Hun, and Celeste Arrington. "Democratization and Changing Anti-American Sentiments in South Korea." *Asian Survey* 47, no. 2 (2007): 327–50.

Paglen, Trevor. *Blank Spots on the Map: The Dark Geography of the Pentagon's Secret World*.
New York: Dutton, 2009.

Palmer, David Scott. "Peru, Drugs, and Shining Path." In *Drug Trafficking in the Americas*,
edited by Bruce M. Bagley and William O. Walker III, 179–97. Miami, FL: University
of Miami North-South Press, 1996.

Park, Giju. "Mugun gijiyui hwankyung munjie gaesun banghyange gwanhan gochal"
[Study on U.S. bases in Korea in the direction of environmental improvement].
Hwankyungbub yungu [Environmental law studies] 31 (2009): 87–108.

Paulsen, Michael Stokes. "Youngstown Goes to War." *Constitutional Commentary* 19, no. 87 (2002): 215–60.

Pearson, Chris, Peter Coates, and Tim Cole, eds. *Militarized Landscapes: From Gettysburg to Salisbury Plain.* New York: Continuum, 2010.

Perlstein, Rick. *Nixonland: The Rise of a President and the Fracturing of America.* New York: Scribner, 2008.

Peterson, M. N., M. J. Peterson, and T. R. Peterson. "Conservation and the Myth of Consensus." *Conservation Biology* 19, no. 3 (June 2005): 762–67.

Plater, Zygmunt J. B. *The Snail Darter and the Dam: How Pork-Barrel Politics Endangered a Little Fish and Killed a River.* New Haven, CT: Yale University Press, 2013.

Rabe, Stephen G. *The Killing Zone: The United States Wages Cold War in Latin America.* New York: Oxford University Press, 2012.

Rahm, Dianne. "Controversial Cleanup: Superfund and the Implementation of U.S. Hazardous Waste Policy." *Policy Studies Journal* 26 (2005): 719–34.

Ramírez Lemus, María Clemencia, Kimberly Stanton, and John Walsh. "Colombia: A Vicious Circle of Drugs and War." In *Drugs and Democracy in Latin America: The Impact of U.S. Policy,* edited by Coletta A. Younger and Eileen Rosin, 99–142. Boulder, CO: Lynne Rienner Publishers, 2005.

Reinarman, Craig, and Harry G. Divine, eds. *Crack in America: Demon Drug and Social Justice.* Berkeley: University of California Press, 1997.

Reisner, Marc. *Cadillac Desert: The American West and Its Disappearing Water.* New York: Viking, 1986.

Rojas, Isaías. "Peru: Drug Control Policy, Human Rights, and Democracy." In *Drugs and Democracy in Latin America: The Impact of U.S. Policy,* edited by Coletta A. Youngers and Eileen Rosin, 185–230. Boulder, CO: Lynne Rienner Publishers, 2005.

Roosevelt, Theodore. *Theodore Roosevelt, an Autobiography.* Cambridge, MA: Da Capo Press, 1985.

Rosenthal, Debra. *At the Heart of the Bomb: The Dangerous Allure of Weapons Work.* Reading, PA: Addison-Wesley Publishing, 1990.

Rossiter, Clinton L. *Constitutional Dictatorship: Crisis Government in the Modern Democracies.* Princeton, NJ: Princeton University Press, 1948.

Russell, Edmund. *War and Nature: Fighting Humans and Insects with Chemicals from World War I to Silent Spring.* Cambridge: Cambridge University Press, 2001.

Samuels, Richard J. *Rich Nation, Strong Army: National Security and the Technological Transformation of Japan.* Ithaca, NY: Cornell University Press, 1994.

Sanders, Barry. *Green Zone: The Environmental Costs of Militarism.* Oakland, CA: AK Press, 2009.

Sandman, Peter. "Getting to Maybe: Some Communications Aspects of Siting Hazardous Waste Facilities." *Seton Hall Legislative Journal* 9 (1985): 437–65.

Schober, Elisabeth. "Encounters: The U.S. Armed Forces in Korea and Entertainment Districts in and near Seoul." In *Korea: Politics, Economy, and Society,* edited by Rüdiger Frank, James E. Hoare, Patrick Köllner, and Susan Pares, 207–31. Boston: Brill, 2011.

Schulman, Bruce J. *The Seventies: The Great Shift in American Culture, Society, and Politics.* New York: Free Press, 2001.

Schulman, Seth. *The Threat at Home: Confronting the Toxic Legacy of the U.S. Military.* Boston: Beacon Press, 1992.

Sellers, Christopher. *Hazards of the Job: From Industrial Disease to Environmental Health Science.* Chapel Hill: University of North Carolina Press, 1997.

Shin, Gi-Wook. "South Korean Anti-Americanism: A Comparative Perspective." *Asian Survey* 36, no. 8 (1996): 787–803.

Shin, Gi-wook, and Hilary Ian Izatt. "Anti-American and Anti-Alliance Sentiments in South Korea." *Asian Survey* 51 (2011): 1113–33.

Shrader-Frechette, Kristin. *Burying Uncertainty: Risk and the Case against Geological Disposal of Nuclear Waste.* Berkeley: University of California Press, 1993.

———. *Risk and Rationality: Philosophical Foundations for Populist Reforms.* Berkeley: University of California Press, 1991.

Shulman. Seth. *The Threat at Home: Confronting the Toxic Legacy of the U.S. Military.* Boston: Beacon Press, 1992.

Slovic, Paul. "Perceived Risk, Trust, and Democracy." *Risk Analysis* 13, no. 6 (1993): 675–82.

Sorenson, David. *Shutting Down the Cold War: The Politics of Military Base Closure.* New York: Palgrave MacMillan, 1998.

Stein, Bruce A., Cameron Scott, and Nancy Benton. "Federal Lands and Endangered Species: The Role of Military and Other Federal Lands in Sustaining Biodiversity." *BioScience* 58 (2008): 339–47.

Stellman, Jeanne, Steven D. Stellman, Richard Christian, Tracy Weber, and Carrie Tomasallo. "The Extent and Patterns of Usage of Agent Orange and Other Herbicides in Vietnam." *Nature* 422 (April 2003): 681–87.

Susskind, Lawrence E. "The Siting Puzzle: Balancing Economic and Environmental Gains and Losses." *Environmental Impact Assessment Review* 5, no. 2 (1985): 157–63.

Swaine, Edward T. "Political Economy of Youngstown." *Southern California Law Review* 83, no. 2 (2010): 1–77.

Szasz, Andrew, and Micheal Meuser. "Public Participation in the Cleanup of Contaminated Military Facilities: Democratization or Anticipatory Cooptation?" *International Journal of Contemporary Sociology* 34, no. 2 (1997): 211–33.

Szasz, Ferenc M. *The Day the Sun Rose Twice: The Story of the Trinity Nuclear Explosion, July 16, 1945.* Albuquerque: University of New Mexico Press, 1985.

Taft, William H. *The Presidency.* New York: Charles Scribner's Sons, 1916.

———. *William Howard Taft: Essential Writings and Addresses.* Hackensack, NJ: Fairleigh Dickinson, 2009.

Taussig, Michael. *My Cocaine Museum.* Chicago: University of Chicago Press, 2004.

Thee, Marek. "The Pursuit of a Comprehensive Nuclear Test Ban." *Journal of Peace Research* 25, no. 1 (March 1988): 5–15.

Thornton, Joe. *Pandora's Poison: Chlorine, Health, and a New Environmental Strategy.* Cambridge: Massachusetts Institute of Technology Press, 2000.

Thoumi, Francisco E. *Illegal Drugs, Economy, and Society in the Andes.* Baltimore, MD: Woodrow Wilson Center and the Johns Hopkins University Press, 2003.

———. "Why the Illegal Psychoactive Drugs Industry Grew in Colombia." In *Drug Trafficking in the Americas,* edited by Bruce Bagley and William O. Walker III, 77–96. Miami, FL: University of Miami North-South Press, 1996.

Tokatlian, Juan Gabriel. "Drug Summitry: A Colombian Perspective." In *Drug Trafficking in the Americas*, editors Bruce M. Bagley and William O. Walker III, 131–47. Miami, FL: University of Miami North-South Press, 1996.

Tsutsui, William M. "Looking Straight at *Them!* Understanding the Big Bug Movies of the 1950s." *Environmental History* 12, no. 2 (April 2007): 237–53.

Tucker, Richard P. *Insatiable Appetite: The United States and the Ecological Degradation of the Tropical World.* Berkeley: University of California Press, 2000.

Tucker, Richard P., and Edmund Russell, eds. *Natural Enemy, Natural Ally: Toward an Environmental History of Warfare.* 1st edition. Corvallis: Oregon State University Press, 2004.

U.S. Department of Energy. *United States Nuclear Tests July 1945 through September 1992.* Las Vegas: Nevada Operations Office, 2000.

Utter, Jack, Stan Brickler, Brock Tunnicliff, and Margot Garcia. "Military Land Withdrawals: Some Legal History and a Case Study." *University of Arizona College of Agriculture Paper* no. 541 (1985): 1–74.

Vargas, Ricardo. "The Anti-Drug Policy, Aerial Spraying of Illicit Crop and Their Social, Environmental, and Political Impacts in Colombia." *Journal of Drug Issues* 32 (Winter 2002): 11–60.

Virilio, Paul, and Sylvere Lotringer. *Pure War: Twenty-Five Years Later.* Los Angeles: Semiotext, 1997.

Walker, J. Samuel. *Prompt and Utter Destruction: Truman and the Use of Atomic Bombs against Japan.* Chapel Hill: University of North Carolina Press, 2004.

Weimer, Daniel. *Seeing Drugs: Modernization, Counterinsurgency, and U.S. Narcotics Control in the Third World, 1969–1976.* Kent, OH: Kent State University Press, 2011.

Westad, Odd Arne. *The Global Cold War.* New York: Cambridge University Press, 2007.

Wheatley Jr., Charles F. "Withdrawals under the Federal Land Policy Management Act of 1976." *Arizona Law Review* 21 (1979): 311–27.

White, Richard. *"It's Your Misfortune and None of My Own": A New History of the American West.* 1st edition. Norman: University of Oklahoma Press, 1991.

Woo, Yusun. "Environmental Problems on the U.S. Military Bases in the Republic of Korea: Who Is Responsible for the Cleanup Expenses and Whose Environmental Standards Will Apply?" *Southeastern Environmental Law Journal* 15 (2007): 577–612.

Woodward, Rachel. "Khaki Conservation: An Examination of Military Environmentalist Discourses in the British Army." *Journal of Rural Studies* 17, no. 2 (2001): 201–17.

———. *Military Geographies.* Oxford, U.K.: Blackwell, 2004.

Wormuth, Francis Dunham. *To Chain the Dog of War: The War Power of Congress in History and Law.* Champaign: University of Illinois Press, 1989.

Wynne, Brian. "May the Sheep Safely Graze? A Reflexive View of the Expert-Lay Knowledge Divide." *Risk, Environment, and Modernity: Towards a New Ecology* (1996): 44–83.

———. "Public Participation in Science and Technology: Performing and Obscuring a Political-Conceptual Category Mistake." *East Asian Science, Technology, and Society* 1, no. 1 (2007): 99–110.

————. *Risk Management and Hazardous Waste: Implementation and the Dialectics of Credibility*. Berlin: Springer-Verlag, 1987.

Young, Alvin. *The History, Use, Disposition, and Environmental Fate of Agent Orange*. New York: Springer Books, 2009.

Young, Kenneth R. "Environmental and Social Consequences of Coca/Cocaine in Peru: Policy Alternatives and a Research Agenda." In *Dangerous Harvest: Drug Plants and the Transformation of Indigenous Landscapes*, edited by Michael K. Steinberg, Joseph J. Hobbs, and Kent Mathewson, 249–73. New York: Oxford University Press, 2004.

Zebrowski, Ernest, and Judith Howard. *Category Five: The Story of Camille, Lessons Learned from America's Most Violent Hurricane*. Ann Arbor: University of Michigan Press, 2005.

Zierler, David. *The Invention of Ecocide: Agent Orange, Vietnam, and the Scientists Who Changed the Way We Think about the Environment*. Athens: University of Georgia Press, 2011.

Contributors

YOOIL BAE is assistant professor of political science at the School of Social Sciences at Singapore Management University. His work has appeared in a variety of journals, including *Pacific Review, Democratization,* and the *International Journal of Urban and Regional Research.*

LEISL CARR CHILDERS is an assistant professor of history at the University of Northern Iowa and the coordinator of the Public History Program. She is the author of a forthcoming book about the history of multiple-use on public lands in the twentieth-century Great Basin.

BRANDON C. DAVIS is a PhD candidate in the Department of History at the University of British Columbia. His dissertation investigates the environmental history of two North American chemical and biological weapons proving grounds.

HEEJIN HAN is a lecturer in the Department of Political Science at National University of Singapore. She studies environmental politics with a regional focus on Northeast Asia and is particularly interested in politics and policy surrounding water governance issues in China and South Korea.

DAVID G. HAVLICK is an associate professor of geography and environmental studies at the University of Colorado–Colorado Springs. He is the author of *No Place Distant: Roads and Motorized Recreation on America's Public Lands* (2002) and a number of articles in publications including *Sci-*

ence, *Ecological Restoration, Geographical Review, Progress in Physical Geography, GeoJournal*, and *Ethics, Policy, and Environment*.

KATHERINE M. KEIRNS is completing a PhD in history at Princeton University. She brings previous experience in environmental history, geography, and the earth sciences to her work on American military officers' encounters with environmentalism, conservation, and the natural world.

EDWIN A. MARTINI is professor of history and associate dean of the College of Arts and Sciences at Western Michigan University. His publications include *Invisible Enemies: The American War on Vietnam, 1975–2000* (2007) and *Agent Orange: History, Science, and the Politics of Uncertainty* (2012).

NEIL OATSVALL is a historian of environment, war, technology, and agriculture. His current project is a book manuscript titled "Atomic Environments: Nuclear Technologies, the Natural World, and Policymaking, 1945–1960." His work has appeared in a variety of publications, including *Agricultural History* and *Environment and History*.

JENNIFER LISS OHAYON is a PhD candidate in the Environmental Studies Department at the University of California–Santa Cruz (UCSC) and a fellow at the Science and Justice Research Center at UCSC. She was a 2013–14 visiting academic at the University of California–Berkeley's Center for Science, Technology, Medicine, and Society.

DANIEL WEIMER is an associate professor of history at Wheeling Jesuit University. He is the author of *Seeing Drugs: Modernization, Counterinsurgency, and U.S. Narcotics Control in the Third World, 1969–1976* (2011).

Index

and endangered species, 239–41, 253–
55, 263n91; and military-to-wildlife
conversions, 266, 273–74, 278–80; and
nuclear testing/weapons, 81–82, 98;
and public lands, 31; and South Korea,
214, 222, 227–28; and Superfund sites,
184–85, 188–93, 196, 200; Third Infantry Division, 3, 16n2. *See also* military
bases; *names of army military bases*
Army Corps of Engineers (USACE), 88–89,
258n16
Army Judge Advocate General, 255, 256n2,
259n25
Army War College, U.S., 255, 263n91
Aruba, 146, 157
asbestos, 187
Asian American populations, 182–84, 189,
206n25
Assabet River National Wildlife Refuge
(Mass.), 274–76, 275*fig.*; visitors center
at, 275
asthma, 198, 227
Atlantic Fleet Weapons Training Range
(Vieques Island, P.R.), 247
atolls, 9, 52, 269. *See also* Bikini Atoll;
Eniwetok Atoll; Johnston Atoll
"Atom Damage Denied" (*NYT* article), 99
"Atomic Blast Six Miles Up to Test New
Air Defense" (AEC article), 62
Atomic Center, Inc. (New York), 92
Atomic Energy Act, 246
Atomic Energy Commission (AEC), 8,
46–47, 52–53, 56–65, 67, 67n7, 75,
259n35; and Bravo test, 60*fig.*, 61–63,
92–93; and cattle deaths, 9, 76, 78–79,
81, 84–85, 93, 97–105; Division of
Biology and Medicine (DBM), 70n18,
76, 78, 94, 97–98; Division of Military
Applications, 98; and hunger strikes,
65, 73n53; and international lawsuit,
65, 73n53; and mental maps, 9, 79,
81–85, 104–5; and Operation Teapot,
85–105, 88*fig.*; Santa Fe Operations
Office, 78, 89, 98, 100; and sheep

deaths, 85, 90, 94, 102, 104–5; Task
Force, 62; Test Division, 78, 87–88, 96
"Atomic Test Effects in the Nevada Test
Site Region" (AEC pamphlet), 86
atomic tests. *See* nuclear testing/weapons
Atomic Tests in Nevada (AEC film/informa-
tion booklet), 86, 91
Australia, 54

B

Bae, Yooil, 11–12, 14–15, **211–37**, 303
Bahamas, 119
Baker (nuclear test), 49–51, 50*fig.*; and
blast waves, 49–51
Baker, Anni, 5
Balogh, Brian, 259n35
*Bananas, Beaches, and Bases: Making
Feminist Sense of International Politics*
(Enloe), 5
Barstow (Calif.), 82
*Base Politics: Democratic Change and the
U.S. Military Overseas* (Cooley), 5
Base Realignment and Closure Commis-
sion (BRAC), 204n2, 267
*Bases of Empire: The Global Struggle against
U.S. Military Outposts* (Lutz), 6
bats, 265, 273; Indiana bats, 265
Bayview–Hunters Point community
(Calif.), 182–83, 198, 202, 206n25
beach dunes, 201
bears, 243; black bears, 265
Beatty (Nev.), 83
Beaty, Tim, 16n2
beaver, 265
Beck, John, 19
Beck, Ulrich, 142n56
benzene, 228
Betancur, Belisario, 152–53
Bhagavad Gita, 45*fig.*
Bien Hoa Air Base (S. Vietnam), 113–15,
135, 114*fig.*
Big Oaks National Wildlife Refuge (Ind.),
265–66, 268–69, 273, 276, 280–83; as
Globally Important Bird Area, 265

Cedar City (Utah), 94

Central America, 10, 119, 145–46, 150–51, 155, 157, 160, 170n41; counterrevolution in, 155. *See also names of Central American countries*

CERCLA (Comprehensive Environmental Response, Compensation, and Liability Act, 1980), 177–78, 182, 184, 195–96, 198–99, 205n9, 277–78

cerulean warblers, 265

Channel Islands (Calif.), 244–46

Chavez, Dennis, 98, 100–102

Chemical Corps, 120

chemicals, 9–10, 19, 64, 111–13, 116–17, 119–21, 123–27; chemical facilities, 117, 120–21; "chemical" spelled wrong, 133–34, 134*fig.*; chemical weapons, 123–26, 140n30, 144, 269, 273–75; and drug control, 144–49, 152, 154–55, 161, 163; on Johnston Atoll, 123–24, 133–34, 134*fig.*; and military-to-wildlife conversions, 267, 269–70, 273–75; "nonpersistent," 147; and risk society, 142n56; and South Korea, 225–28; and Superfund sites, 199. *See also* herbicides

Cheney, Dick, 255, 263n89, 278, 283

Chernobyl Exclusion Zone, 260n49

Chesapeake Bay, 269

Chicago (Ill.), 94

Chihuahua (Mex.), 144

Chihuahua Desert, 82

Childers, Leisl Carr, 8–9, 13, **75–110**, 303

children: and drug control, 150; and eye irritations, 76; in Mexico, 150; in South Korea, 214–15

Chilgok County (S. Korea), 225–26

China, 214

China Lake (Calif.), 82

chlorinolysis, 116

Chunchon (S. Korea), 221

CIPs (community involvement plans), 185–86

citizen advisory boards, 11, 175–76, 179–80, 188, 190–94, 202–3, 205n13; disbanded, 176, 180, 191; and local issues, 196–97; selection process for membership in, 190–91, 194; and trust/distrust, 202–3. *See also* RABs (restoration advisory boards)

Citizens' Coalition for Economic Justice (CCEJ, S. Korea), 215–16

civil defense, 85–87, 89, 91–92, 94–95, 97; Apple-2 civil defense test, 85, 87, 89, 95; and Bravo test, 92; and Operation Cue (Miscue), 85, 95

Civil Defense Administration, U.S., 95

civilization, 51

civil liberties, 20, 22, 204

Clean Air Act (1970), 124, 248

Clean Water Act (1972), 183, 242

climate change, 242, 270, 278

Clinton, Bill, 155–58, 171n55, 222

Clinton, Hillary, 164

Coastal Zone Management Act, 248

Coast Guard, U.S., 157, 258n16

Coates, Peter, 6

coca, 10, 145–46, 150, 152–55, 157–60, 162–64; coca paste, 153, 163; *Erythoxylum novogranatense*, 153; *Erythroxylum coca*, 153; hybrid variety of, 153

cocaine, 152–54, 156, 163–64; cocaine laboratories, 152, 154, 156, 166n7; crack cocaine, 154, 169n36

Code, U.S., 156; Section 124, 156; Title 10, 156

Cold War, 4–5, 9–10, 12–15; and drug control, 10, 14, 156; and endangered species, 13, 241–42, 244, 251, 253, 255, 257n9; and military-to-wildlife conversions, 12, 15, 267, 271; and movies, 68n10; and nuclear testing/weapons, 45–46, 60–61, 67n5, 68n10, 69n11, 81, 83, 105, 251, 253; and public lands, 7, 21; and South Korea, 211, 214, 219, 222; and Superfund sites, 10, 176, 204n2; and testing moratorium, 105. *See also* Soviet Union

Cole, Tim, 6

Colombia, 145–46, 151–65; and Agent Orange, 120; and Andean Counterdrug Initiative, 156, 159; and Anti-narcotics Police, 160; attorney general of, 152; civil war, 158–59; class system in, 152; Constitutional Court, 172n76; and corruption, 154–55; and "counternarcotics brigade," 158–60; and defense cooperation agreement with U.S., 172n76; drug trafficking in, 146, 151–60, 163–64; and human rights abuses, 157, 171n55; military of, 146, 156–60, 164–65, 171n55; Pacific Coast, 164; and paramilitary forces, 157, 171n55; and Plan Colombia, 146, 158–61, 164; protests in, 171n63; "Two Peninsulas" campaign, 151; violence in, 152, 154, 157, 159, 164

Colorado, 252, 262nn73–74, 269, 273–74, 285n26. *See also names of Colorado cities, towns, and military bases*

Colorado State College of Agriculture and Mechanic Arts, 100

Comalapa, 157

Committee to Observe the Atomic Bomb Tests, 51

Commoner, Barry, 47

community involvement plans. *See* CIPs (community involvement plans)

Comprehensive Environmental Response, Compensation, and Liability Act. *See* CERCLA

Conan, M., Mrs., 70n18

condors, 243

Congress, U.S.: acquiescence to withdrawal powers, 23–24, 26–27, 30, 34–35; and Agent Orange, 117–19, 127, 131–32; and drug control, 144–45, 150, 156, 161, 171n55; and endangered species, 242–45, 251, 259n35; and executive powers, 19, 22–30, 32–35, 37n13; and executive war powers, 25–28, 30; House Veterans' Affairs Committee, 132; and military-to-wildlife conver-

sions, 267, 273–74, 276, 285n26; and nuclear testing, 47, 57, 94, 100–102; and public lands, 19, 22–30, 32–35, 37n13, 38n31; Senate Committee of Public Lands, 26; silence of, 23–24, 26–27, 30, 34–35; and Superfund sites, 177

Consensus Recommendation of the Federal Facilities Environmental Restoration Dialogue Committee (FFERD, Keystone Report), 179, 194

conservation/conservationists: and endangered species, 239–44, 249–51, 253–56; and military-to-wildlife conversions, 267–68, 272–73, 276–77; and public lands, 22–23, 27, 33–34; and public participation programs, 189; and Superfund sites, 189. *See also* environmentalists/environmentalism

conservatives, 150, 243, 246, 253

conspiracy theorists, 105

Constitution, U.S.: accepted constitutional norms, 22; and emergency powers, 21–22, 29; and executive powers, 21–22, 24–25, 27–29; Property Clause, 37n13; return to constitutional normalcy, 21–22, 34–36, 37n13

contamination, 9–11, 15; and Agent Orange, 9, 113, 115–17, 119, 121, 125–28, 131–36; and Bravo test, 62, 92–93; and brownfields, 276; and drug control, 10, 148, 161, 163; and dumping in ocean waters, 125–26, 182; and endangered species, 242, 256, 258n15; of fish, 62, 92, 126–27, 135, 161, 183; of food, 91, 93–95, 97; and "force readiness," 258n15; and KISE ("known, imminent, and substantial endangerment"), 218, 221, 224; lack of record keeping on, 176; and military-to-wildlife conversions, 267, 269–78, 280; and nuclear testing, 50–51, 62, 64–65, 89–95, 124, 182; on-site capping of, 196; and South Korea, 11, 212, 217–30, 233n32; and

Denver (Colo.), 269

Denver Post, 70n18

Department of Agriculture (USDA): and Agent Orange, 111; Agricultural Research Service, 100; and cattle deaths, 97–102; and drug control, 10, 148, 161–62; and nuclear testing, 97–102

Department of Defense, U.S. (DOD): and Agent Orange, 111–13, 118, 128, 140n30; Defense Atomic Support Agency (DASA), 140n30; Defense Threat Reduction Agency (DTRA), 124, 140n30; and drug control, 156–59; and endangered species, 12, 239–42, 245, 247–48, 251, 253–55, 257n9, 259n25; and military-to-wildlife conversions, 15, 271, 276–80, 282–83; "mission first" policy of, 277, 282–83; and nuclear testing/weapons, 43–45, 91, 251, 253; as Pentagon, 111, 128, 156–59, 219–20, 240–42, 247, 251, 254–55, 259n25; and public lands, 19–20, 27, 31–35; and public participation programs, 179–80, 190, 194, 196–97; and South Korea, 219–20, 222–23; and Superfund sites, 176–77, 179–80, 190, 194, 196–97, 204n2, 204n7; and "triple bottom line," 277–80, 282–83; as War Department, 20, 27, 31, 43–45

Department of Energy, U.S., 177, 205n13

Department of Health, Education, and Welfare, U.S. (HEW): and Agent Orange, 111, 132; and drug control, 144, 150

Department of Interior, U.S.: and Agent Orange, 133; and endangered species, 239, 243, 258n21; and nuclear testing, 52, 54–56; and public lands, 22–23, 27, 30–32, 38n31. *See also* Fish and Wildlife Service, U.S. (FWS)

Department of State, U.S.: and Agent Orange, 112; Bureau of International Narcotics Control and Law Enforce-

ment (INL), 157, 159–60; and drug control, 10, 146–50, 157–61, 163–64, 167n22; International Narcotics Control (INC), 157; Narcotics Affairs Section, 159

Department of Toxic Substances Control, U.S., 177

deserts, 59, 75, 82–83, 90; and desert fish, 241, 251–52; and endangered species, 241, 251–52; and missile bunkers/silos, 251–52. *See also names of deserts*

dinitrotoluene, 176

dioxin: and Agent Orange, 111–12, 115–18, 120–22, 126–28, 132–36, 134*fig.*, 137n3, 146; and drug control, 146; and South Korea, 213, 226–27

diplomacy, 4, 15, 69n11

Diplomatic History, 7

dogs, 70n18, 95

Dorminey, Bruce, 16nn1–2

Doty, Dale E., 55

Dow Chemical, 120–21

Drenthen, Martin, 272–73

drones, 16, 57; drone warfare, 16

drug control, 10, 143–65; and Agent Orange, 146–47, 166nn9–10; in Bolivia, 151, 153, 156, 167n24; in Colombia, 145–46, 151–53, 155–65; and cultivators/farmers, 144, 148, 150, 153–54, 157–58, 160–61, 163–64, 168n24; and defoliation programs, 10, 143–53, 155, 157–61, 163–65; and dioxin, 146; and eradication programs, 144–45, 147, 149–53, 155–56, 158, 160–64, 168n24; and extortion, 154; and fumigation programs, 146, 151–52, 155, 157–65, 167n24; and glyphosate, 148–49, 152–53, 155, 159–62; and imazapyr, 155; and interdiction programs, 149, 156–57; in Jamaica, 10, 145, 147–49; and lynusol, 148; in Mexico, 10, 143–45, 147, 149–52; and paraquat, 144, 146, 148–52, 155, 163, 167n22; and Percy Amendment, 150, 152; in Peru, 151,

153, 168n24; and "source control," 156, 163–64, 170n45; and 2,4-D herbicide, 146, 148–50. *See also* drug trafficking/traffickers; drug war

Drug Enforcement (DEA publication), 167n17

Drug Enforcement Administration, U.S. (DEA), 10, 148–50, 167n17

drug trafficking/traffickers, 146–48, 150–60, 163–64; in Burma, 170n45; and Cali cartel, 152, 154, 157; and ELN (National Liberation Army), 153, 169n34; and extradition, 152, 154; and FARC (Revolutionary Armed Forces of Colombia), 153–54, 156–60, 164; and M-19 (Movimiento 19 de Abril), 153, 169n34; and Medellín cartel, 152, 154–55, 157; narcotraffickers, 152–54, 156; and protection money, 154

drug war, 10, 13–14, 144–45, 149–52, 155–61, 164–65; and drug czars, 144, 158; militarization of, 146, 150–51, 155–61, 164–65, 170n43. *See also* drug control; drug trafficking/traffickers

Dugway Proving Ground (Utah), 253

dumping, 125–26, 182, 248

Dunning, Gordon, 94–96, 98

Durango (Mex.), 144

Duval, Merlin, 132

DynCorp Aerospace Technologies, 159–61; lawsuit against, 160–61

E

eagles, 243, 270, 273; bald eagles, 270

Earth Day, 278

earthquakes, 64

Eberline Instrument Company, 101

ecocide, charges of, 14

ecology/ecologists, 3–4, 12–14, 46–48, 68n8, 68n10; "ecological degradations," 163; ecological risks, 11, 198; and endangered species, 243–44, 247, 251–52; and military-to-wildlife conversions, 266–69, 271–73, 276, 279–83;

and Superfund sites, 11, 177, 196, 198

economics, 4–6, 15; and Agent Orange, 119–20, 125, 132; in Brazil, 119; in Colombia, 153, 158; and drug control, 144, 153–54, 158, 160; in Ecuador, 160; and endangered species, 245–47, 249; and Japan, 232n6; local economies, 33; and longleaf pine ecosystem, 3; in Mexico, 144; and military-industrial complex, 81–82; and military-to-wildlife conversions, 267, 271–72, 276, 280; and nuclear testing, 81–82; and public lands, 33; and South Korea, 211–15, 217, 220, 231; and Superfund sites, 15, 189, 195–99, 206n25; and World War II, 25

ecosystems, 3, 14; and endangered species, 254; and military-to-wildlife conversions, 269–70; and Superfund sites, 177

Ecuador, 146, 151, 157, 160

Edgerton, Germeshausen, and Grier, Inc., 82–83

educational efforts: and endangered species, 255; and military-to-wildlife conversions, 275, 281; and nuclear testing, 86, 95; and public participation programs, 15, 186

Edwards Air Force Base, 82

Eglin Air Force Base (Fla.), 15, 119, 133

Eisenhower, Dwight D., 60, 62–63, 66, 70n18, 81

Elliot, Robert, 269–70

Elliott, Richard G., 98–99

ELN (National Liberation Army), 153, 169n34

El Paso (Tex.), 76, 78, 82

El Salvador, 151, 157

Embattled Garrisons: Comparative Base Politics and American Globalism (Calder), 5

emergency powers, 7, 20–23, 25–31; challenge of returning to normalcy, 21–22, 34–36, 37n13; difficult to retract, 26–27, 30–31; as temporary powers, 20–21, 27, 29–31, 35; unlimited emer-

7, 9–10, 113, 133, 136–37; environmental stewardship, 270, 277, 282; environmental studies, 4, 6–7; and greening/greenwashing, 268, 277–79, 282; military environmentalism, 3, 8–9, 12, 14–15, 113, 128, 137, 138n4, 255–56, 263n89, 270, 277–80, 282–83; and military-to-wildlife conversions, 15, 270, 277–80, 282–83; and "polluter pays principle," 221, 224; and public participation programs, 183, 189; and Sauget (Ill.), 117; and South Korea, 212–13, 215–31; and Superfund sites, 183, 189; and sustainability, 278–80

Environmental Joint Working Group (S. Korea, U.S.), 229

environmental justice, 15, 175–76, 182, 184, 187, 189, 194–97, 199; advocates for, 187, 189; and inequalities, 175–76, 196–97; and race/ethnicity, 15, 189, 194, 206n25; and South Korea, 230

environmental laws/regulations/regulators: and Agent Orange, 9, 14, 112–13, 115–17, 119–20, 125, 128–32, 129fig., 131fig., 134fig., 136; and drug control, 144–47, 149, 161, 163, 166n10, 167n22; and endangered species, 239–56, 258n16, 259n22; ENR (environmental and natural resources) laws, 222–23; and Germany, 225; and military-to-wildlife conversions, 277–78; and nuisance laws, 245, 248; and public lands, 33; and public participation programs, 184–93, 195–96, 198–203; and South Korea, 15, 220–25, 230, 233n32; and Superfund sites, 176–79, 184–93, 195–96, 198–203, 204n7. *See also* safety procedures; *titles of laws*

Environmental Protection Agency (EPA): and Agent Orange, 9, 112, 117–18, 120–22, 125, 127, 132–33, 135, 140n29; and certification of landfills, 135; and drug control, 147, 149, 161–63; and endangered species, 247; and nuclear

testing, 124; and public participation programs, 179–81, 185–86, 188, 190–94, 197–99, 201–2; and at-sea incineration permits, 125; state-level, 177, 184; and Superfund sites, 177, 179–81, 183–86, 188, 190–94, 197–99, 201–2, 204nn6–7, 205n9, 205n13

environmental science, 46–48, 50–53, 56, 62–67, 72n49; defined, 46–47

eradication programs: and drug control, 144–45, 147, 149–53, 155–56, 158, 160–64, 168n24; and feral goats, 250, 261nn55–56; manual, 147, 151; Operation Fulminante, 151

erosion, 10, 163

Escobar, Pablo, 154

European Union, 271

executive orders, 7, 26, 30; Executive Order 4467, 122; Executive Order 9066, 26; Johnston Atoll as wildlife refuge, 122; and military-to-wildlife conversions, 277; as Public Land Orders, 38n31

executive policy makers/making: defined, 46; and drug control, 144, 147, 149–52, 155–56, 163; and nuclear testing, 46–48, 52–56, 62–67; and public participation programs, 178–79, 181, 190–92, 194–96, 199, 203; and South Korea, 223; and Superfund sites, 178–79, 181, 190–92, 194–96, 199, 203

executive powers, 7, 20–31, 34; abuse of power, 21; cabinet-level approach to withdrawals, 31–34; challenge of returning to normalcy, 21–22, 34–36, 37n13; and conservation policies, 22–23; and emergency powers, 7, 20–23, 25–31; as "express power," 31, 40n53; implied, 23–27, 35; and independent powers, 20, 23–25, 27; inherent, 25, 27–28; Office of Drug Abuse Policy, 144; and stewardship presidency, 23–27, 37n16; as temporary powers, 20–21, 27, 29–31, 35; and war powers, 7,

272; and Johnston Atoll, 124; and mental maps, 8–9, 79, 81, 84; and military-to-wildlife conversions, 271–73, 282; and nuclear testing, 9, 46, 52–54, 79, 124

geology/geologists, 8, 46–47, 52, 54, 56, 64, 66–67, 68n8, 256; geologic faults, 64

Georgia, 3, 16nn1–2, 239–40. *See also names of Georgia cities, towns, and military bases*

Gerard, Sumner, 147–48

Geren, Pete, 278

Germany, 6, 225

"Global Defense Posture Review" (U.S.), 219–20

Globally Important Bird Areas, 265

global war, 21–22

global warming, 163

glyphosate, 148–49, 152–53, 155, 159–62; harmful side effects of, 161–62; as Roundup, 149, 152, 159, 161

goats, feral, 241, 249–51, 261nn55–56; and capture program, 250; and eradication program, 250, 261nn55–56

Gonzalez, Ricardo M., 47–48, 68n8

Government Accountability Office, 279

Grand Canyon, 90–91

Graves, Alvin C., 87–89, 96

grazing: and Agent Orange, 119; and nuclear testing, 8, 76, 99; and public lands, 31, 33–34, 40n65. *See also* cattle/cattle deaths; ranchers

Great Basin, 82

Great Bay National Wildlife Refuge, 273

greenhouse gases, 163

green turtle, 248–49

Green United Korea (GKU), 215–18, 225

Ground Renewable Expeditionary Energy System (GREENS), 279

Groundwater Act of Korea (S. Korea), 224

Guajira Peninsula (Colombia), 151

Guaviare (Colombia), 153, 155

Gulfport (Miss.), 112, 115–16, 120–22, 126–37, 131*fig.*; Chamber of Commerce, 127; documentation of, 130–31, 131*fig.*, 133, 136; drainage ditch at, 134–35; mayor of, 127; and re-drumming, 128–29, 129*fig.*; workers at, 128–29, 136–37

Gunsan (S. Korea), 221

H

habitat: and endangered species, 253–54, 258n21, 261n56, 277; habitat destruction, 277; and military-to-wildlife conversions, 266–71, 275–77

Hacker, Barton, 67n7

Hakina (East) Island, 123

Halloween, 66

Hamilton, Neil, 132

Han, Heejin, 11–12, 14–15, **211–37**, 303

hand grenades, 184

Han River (S. Korea), 218–19

Haraway, Donna, 142n56

Hato airport (Aruba), 157

Havlick, David G., 12–13, 14, 15, **265–87**, 303–4

Hawaii, 9, 49, 58*fig.*, 122, 127, 246–47, 261n56, 123*fig.*

Hawaiian stilt, 246–47

hawksbill turtle, 248–49

Haynes, Eugene D., 91

hazardous waste materials/sites, 175, 177–79, 202–3; and military-to-wildlife conversions, 277; and South Korea, 223, 225–26. *See also* Superfund sites

health, environmental: and Agent Orange, 125–26, 128; and drug control, 147–48, 151–52, 160–63; and military-to-wildlife conversions, 268; and nuclear testing, 47–48, 52–53, 56, 67n7; and public participation programs, 189, 192, 198; and Superfund sites, 15, 177, 189, 192, 198

health/well-being, human, 10, 12; and Agent Orange, 111, 113–16, 118, 125–33, 136, 141n42; and drug control, 144, 147, 149–50, 152, 160–62; and

Inouye, Daniel, 127

insurgent groups, 146, 153, 155–59, 164, 166n7, 171n55; and counterinsurgency, 155–59, 164–65, 170n41, 170n45. *See also* drug trafficking/traffickers

interdiction programs, 149, 156–57

interdisciplinary research, 4–7, 13

"International Counternarcotics Strategy" (George W. Bush directive), 156

International Security Assistance Act, 150; Percy Amendment, 150, 152

Iraq war, 3, 204n2, 279

Iron Curtain Trail, 271

Isacson, Adam, 158–59

Isbell, Jason, 16n2

J

Jackson, Robert H., 22, 24–30, 33, 35–36

Jamaica, 10, 145, 147–49, 151, 166n10; "antagonistic terrain" of, 147; Department of Agriculture, 148; drug trafficking in, 147–48; and Operation Buccaneer, 167n17

Jang Ha-na, 228

Japan, 6, 9; attack on Pearl Harbor, 25; Hiroshima and Nagasaki bombings, 48, 69n11, 69n13, 91; and international lawsuit, 65, 73n53; and *Lucky Dragon* incident, 60*fig.*, 61–62, 92–93; military bases in, 213, 232n6; peace treaty with, 30; and World War II, 25, 30, 123–24

Japanese Americans, 26

Jefferson Proving Ground (JPG, Ind.), 266, 273, 281–82

Jefferson Proving Ground Heritage Partnership, 281

Jet Propellant 8, 228

Jim Crow laws, 183

Johnson, Chalmers, 5

Johnson, Lyndon B., 146

Johnston Atoll, 9, 14, 115–16, 121–37, 123*fig.*, 140n29; and "burn zone," 125–26; documentation of, 130–31, 131*fig.*, 133, 136; guano cultivation on, 122;

long-term studies at, 135; militarization of, 122–24; and nuclear testing, 123–24, 140n30; workers on, 128–30, 136–37

Joint Chiefs of Staff, 51, 128

"Joint Environmental Information Exchange and Access Procedures" (TAB A, S. Korea, U.S.), 218–19

Jornada del Muerto, 75, 82

José Ortiz y Pino Ranch, 76, 104

Journal of Military History, 7

K

Kandahar (Afghanistan), 15–16

Katyal, Neal, 24

Katz, Eric, 270

Keirns, Katherine M., 12, 14, **239–63**, 304

Kennedy, John F., 66, 146

Kennedy Space Center (Fla.), 244

Keystone Report, 179, 194

kidnapping, 154

Kingston (Jamaica), 148–49

Kinkela, David, 166n10

Kirk, Robin, 159

Kirkbride, Rodney, 252

KISE ("known, imminent, and substantial endangerment"), 218, 221, 224

Korea Federation for Environmental Movement (KFEM, S. Korea), 215–16

Korean War, 24, 211

Korea Rural Community Corporation, 228

Kyungsu Park-Jung, 222

L

labor unions, 179, 194; and strikes, 24

Lacey Act (1900), 242

Laird, Melvin, 113

Lamar, L. Q. C., 27

Lancaster (Calif.), 82

landfills: and Agent Orange, 115, 133–35; fires at, 183, 198, 201; leachate from, 187; and military-to-wildlife conversions, 274; and nuclear testing, 124, 182; and Superfund sites, 182–84, 187, 198–99, 201

rhetoric of, 20; and South Korea, 217,
230–31
National Security Directive 18, 156
national wildlife refuges, 12, 265–68, 271.
   See also military-to-wildlife conversions; *names of national wildlife refuges*
Native peoples, 54, 179, 194, 266, 275
NATO countries, 212, 225
natural environment/world, 13; and
   Agent Orange, 116, 128, 130, 136; and
   military-to-wildlife conversions, 12,
   268–70, 272–74, 276; as "nature," 268,
   270, 272–74; and nuclear testing, 8,
   45–48, 51–54, 64–67; and presettlement historical condition, 12, 269–70
Nature Conservancy, 239, 241
Naval Construction Battalion Center
   (NCBC, Gulfport, Miss.), 112, 115–16,
   120–22, 126–37, 131*fig.*
Navy, U.S., 123–24; and drug control,
   157; and endangered species, 246–51;
   and feral goats, 249–51, 261nn55–56;
   lawsuits against, 183, 246–51, 253;
   and memorandum of understanding,
   249, 260n53; and military-to-wildlife
   conversions, 279; Naval Defensive
   Sea Areas, 123; Naval Radiological
   Defense Laboratory (NRDL), 182; and
   nuclear testing/weapons, 81; Office of
   Naval Research, 279; and public lands,
   31; and San Clemente Island (Calif.),
   249–51, 261n55; and Vieques Island
   (P.R.), 247–49, 260n53. *See also names
   of naval bases*
Nebraska, 252
nerve gas, 126, 176
Nevada, 8, 82–86, 89, 102; Desert Fish
   Council, 251–52; and endangered species, 251–52; and missile bunkers/silos,
   251–52; perfect weather in, 89. *See
   also* Nevada Proving Ground; *names of
   Nevada cities and towns*
Nevada Proving Ground, 56, 59, 64, 72n37,
   79; and mental maps, 81–85, 104–5; as

Nevada Test Site, 56, 64, 72n37; and
   Operation Teapot, 80*fig.*, 87, 89–94,
   97, 103–4
New Mexico, 43, 52, 75–79, 77*fig.*, 80*fig.*,
   83, 86, 94, 98, 100–105. *See also* Los
   Alamos Scientific Laboratory; *names of
   New Mexico cities and towns*
New Mexico Cattle Growers' Association,
   100, 102
New Mexico College of Agriculture and
   Mechanic Arts, 76, 100
New Mexico State University, 76
Newton, Michael, 119
New York City, 92
New Yorker, 68n10
New York State, 150
New York Times, 75, 87–90, 92, 95–97, 99,
   256n3
NGOs (nongovernmental organizations):
   and endangered species, 250; in South
   Korea, 11, 212, 216, 222, 224–27, 229
Nha Trang Air Base (S. Vietnam), 113,
   114*fig.*
9/11. *See* September 11, 2001, terrorist
   attacks
Nixon, Richard, 24, 111–12, 144, 243,
   259n22, 114*fig.*
Noise Control Act, 248
Noksapyeong Station (S. Korea), 227–28
Nomans Land Island (Mass.), 269
nonhuman elements/actors, 4, 6, 46, 266
North Carolina, 239–40. *See also names
   of North Carolina cities, towns, and
   military bases*
North Korea, 211, 213–14, 231; and
   Demilitarized Zone (DMZ), 226–27,
   260n49, 271; and Nordpolitik, 214,
   232n8; nuclear brinkmanship of, 231;
   and reunification, 214; and Sunshine
   policy, 214
North Kyungsang (S. Korea), 225
nuclear energy, 64
Nuclear Regulatory Commission, U.S.,
   124

nuclear testing/weapons, 8–9, 13–14,
43–67, 44*fig.*, 45*fig.*, 75–105; and
Amchitka Island, 8, 46, 53–56, 71n31,
71n34; atmospheric testing, 9, 49–51,
53, 62, 86–87, 124; and blast waves,
49–51, 58; and cattle deaths, 8–9,
13, 76, 78–79, 84, 86, 93, 97–105; and
endangered species, 241, 246–47,
251–52; and fission, 60, 64, 78, 86, 97,
182; and hunger strikes, 65, 73n53;
and hydrogen bombs, 59–62; and
international lawsuit, 65, 73n53; and
Johnston Atoll, 123–24, 140n30; and
laboratory animals, 8, 14, 46, 51–52,
69n15, 70n18, 95, 182; and mental
maps, 9, 79, 81–85, 104–5, 105n6; and
missiles with warheads, 93–94, 124,
241, 251–53, 262n70, 262n73; moratorium on, 105; MX missile, 251–53,
262n70, 262n73; and names of tests,
66, 74n59, 85; Operation Castle,
60*fig.*, 61–63, 92; Operation Crossroads, 46, 48–53, 70nn18–19, 182,
50*fig.*; Operation Cue (Miscue), 85,
95; Operation Dominic, 124; Operation Hardtack, 66, 74n59; Operation
Plumbbob, 63–65; Operation Ranch
Hand, 10; Operation Redwing, 63;
Operation Teapot, 78, 85–105, 88*fig.*,
89*fig.*; and public lands, 81, 253; and
sheep deaths, 85, 90, 94, 102, 104–5,
108n37; and ships, 49–52, 66, 69n15;
and Superfund sites, 177, 201; and
thermonuclear bombs, 59–61, 60*fig.*,
63, 75, 92, 94, 97; and tower shots,
86–87; and treaty ban, 66; at Trinity site, 44–45, 48, 63, 44*fig.*, 45*fig.*;
underground testing, 8, 53–54, 64–65,
91; underwater testing, 49–51, 53, 182;
Upshot-Knothole series (1953), 85–86,
89–90, 94; and weather, 8, 43–46,
51–54, 56–59, 57*fig.*, 58*fig.*, 61, 63–64,
66, 67n1, 71n35, 85–91, 88*fig.*, 94–99.
See also radiation; radioactive fallout

O

Oatsvall, Neil, 8, 14, **43–74**, 304
Obama, Barack, 25
Ohayon, Jennifer Liss, 10–11, 14–15,
175–209, 304
oil spills, 213, 217, 227–29, 233n32
Okinawa, 9, 124
*Okinawa and the U.S. Military: Identity
Making in the Age of Globalization*
(Inoue), 6
Oklahoma Agricultural and Mechanical
College, 100
"100 Cattle Killed by Radiation" (*Albu-
querque Journal* article), 98–99
Operation Buccaneer, 167n17
Operation Castle, 60*fig.*, 61–63, 92–93;
Bravo test, 60*fig.*, 61–63, 92–93; and
"natives," 62
Operation Crossroads, 46, 48–53,
70nn18–19, 50*fig.*; Able (nuclear test),
49–51; Baker (nuclear test), 49–51,
50*fig.*; and blast waves, 49–51; and
resident populations, 52–53; and ships,
49–52, 69n15, 182; and Superfund
sites, 182
Operation Cue (Miscue), 85, 95
Operation Dominic, 124
Operation Fulminante, 151
Operation Hardtack, 66, 74n59
Operation Pacer HO, 112–13, 123*fig.*,
124–37, 129*fig.*, 134*fig.*, 138n4, 138n6,
141n42; documentation of, 130–31,
131*fig.*, 133, 136
Operation Pacer IVY, 112–16, 114*fig.*, 120,
126, 129, 132–33, 136–37, 138n4, 138n6
Operation Plumbbob, 63–65; Rainier
Shot, 64–65; and underground testing,
64–65
Operation Ranch Hand, 10, 136, 138n4,
144–45, 147–49, 166n12
Operation Redwing, 63
Operation Teapot, 78, 85–105, 88*fig.*, 89*fig.*;
Apple-2 civil defense test, 85, 87, 89,
95; Bee test, 87, 91; and blue snow, 76,

poppies. *See* opium poppies (*Papaver somniferum*)

"Possible Effects of Nuclear Explosions on Weather" (AEC conference), 59

poverty, 15, 200

preservation/preservationists, 55–56, 240

press: and Agent Orange, 111, 116, 118, 127–28; and cattle deaths, 98–100, 102, 104–5; and drug control, 148–49, 158–59; and endangered species, 239–41, 246, 250, 255–56, 256n3, 261n55, 262n70; and nuclear testing, 43–45, 53, 59–63, 66, 69n14, 75–76, 78, 85–90, 92–100, 102, 104–5; and Operation Ranch Hand, 148; and Operation Teapot, 85–90, 92–100, 102, 104–5; press conferences, 60, 66, 87, 94, 111; press releases, 43–45, 53, 85–86, 93, 99; and public participation programs, 181, 183, 191, 201; in South Korea, 216–17, 219, 221, 230; and Superfund sites, 181, 183, 191, 201; television, 94

"Procedures for Environmental Survey and Consultation on Remediation for Facilities and Areas Designated to Be Granted or Returned" (S. Korea, U.S.), 219, 224

prospectors, 54, 76, 97

protests, 14, 69n15, 70n18; hunger strikes, 65, 73n53

Proxmire, William, 131–32

public lands, 7, 15, 19–36; cabinet-level approach to withdrawals, 31–34; and challenge of returning to normalcy, 21–22, 34–36; and executive powers, 7, 20–36; "infused with public not private rights," 22; and land claims, 7, 19–21, 29, 34–35; and land laws, 22–23, 26–27, 30, 37n13; militarization of, 7, 19–21, 25–36, 36n3, 39n46; and military-to-wildlife conversions, 277; and nuclear testing/weapons, 81, 253; president's duty to protect, 20, 22–23; private exploitation of, 22–25;

and stewardship presidency, 23, 25–27, 37n16; and war powers, 7, 25–31

public land users, 30–34, 38n31; compensation for, 34, 40n65; and opportunity to object, 31–32. *See also* grazing; mineral leasing; mining interests

public participation programs, 10–11, 15, 175–76, 178–204; and accountability/authority issues, 11, 176, 178, 180, 189–95, 199–203; and agency-to-public communication, 178, 185–87, 200; barriers to, 11, 181, 188; and CIPs (community involvement plans), 185–86; and citizen advisory boards, 11, 175–76, 179–80, 188, 190–94; and conflicts of interest, 178, 191; and deliberative processes, 180, 185–88, 192–93, 195, 203; and employment issues, 189, 195–200; and environmental justice, 15, 175–76, 182, 184, 187, 189, 194–97, 199, 206n25; evaluation of, 179–80; at Fort Ord (Calif.), 180–81, 184–93, 195–98, 200–203; and hotlines, 186, 200; at Hunters Point Naval Shipyard (Calif.), 180–83, 185–89, 193, 195–203; interviews concerning, 181, 185–86, 188–91, 194–95, 199; and lawsuits, 183–85, 189, 191–92; and local issues, 182–85, 195–99; and meetings/workshops, 11, 181, 185–92, 198, 207n34; and military-to-wildlife conversions, 277; and public challenges, 178, 181, 185; and RABs (restoration advisory boards), 179–81, 183–97; and site reuse, 11, 179, 183, 189, 194–98, 201; and site tours, 11, 180–81, 185–87, 200; and societal rights/values, 178–81, 189, 195–99, 202–3; in South Korea, 11, 14–15; and Superfund sites, 10–11, 15, 175–76, 178–204; and surveys, 181, 185, 187–88; and trust/distrust, 15, 175–76, 180, 188, 198, 199–204; and websites, 185, 194

public relations: and Agent Orange, 112, 116–18, 125–27; and anti-Americanism, 212, 214–17, 220, 222, 230–31; and Bravo test, 62–63, 92–93; and cattle deaths, 78, 81, 84–85, 93, 98, 102, 104–5; and comment periods, 117, 175, 178, 185; and drug control, 148–49; and endangered species, 241, 244, 246–47, 249–52, 255, 257n12, 260n53, 262n70; and *Hiroshima* (Hersey), 68n10; and mental maps, 9, 79, 81–85, 104–5, 105n6; and military-to-wildlife conversions, 274–76, 280–81, 283; and MX missile, 252; and nuclear testing/weapons, 54, 59, 62–63, 65–66, 68n10, 73n53, 78, 81, 84–96, 98, 102, 104–5, 252, 262n70; and "open" relations, 87, 90; and Operation Teapot, 85–96, 88*fig.*, 98, 102, 104–5; and outreach programs, 180; and public hearings, 125, 252; and public lands, 31–32; and public notices, 178; and sheep deaths, 85, 90, 94, 102, 104–5, 108n37; and South Korea, 11, 14–15, 212, 214–22, 224–25, 227, 230–31; and "tell-nothing" policy, 87. *See also* public participation programs

Puerto Rico, 6, 157, 247–49, 260n53, 269

Putumayo (Colombia), 153, 158, 160–61

Q

Queeny, John, 139n14

R

RABs (restoration advisory boards), 179–81, 183–203, 207n34; and accountability/authority issues, 180, 189–95, 199–203; base official as cochair of, 179, 191; disbanded, 180, 185, 189, 191–92, 195, 197, 199; and implementation issues, 188–89; and local issues, 195–98; minutes from meetings of, 181, 190; selection process for membership in, 190–91, 194; and trust/distrust, 199–203

radar investigations, 226

radiation, 9, 13, 49, 52, 55–57, 62–65, 68n10, 69n15; and cattle/cattle deaths, 76, 78, 84, 86, 98–105; elevated temperatures from, 64; Geiger counter readings of, 76; "hazard" from exposure to, 57, 67n7, 87, 90, 93–94; internal radiation, 98; and international lawsuit, 65, 73n53; and laboratory animals, 8, 14, 46, 51–52, 69n15, 70n18, 95, 182; low-level exposure to, 90, 93–95, 98–100, 105; and mental maps, 9, 79, 81–85, 104–5; monitoring equipment for, 101; and Operation Teapot, 86, 89–91, 93–105; permissible doses of, 49, 62, 85–86, 90–91, 94–100; and sheep deaths, 85, 90, 94, 102, 104–5, 108n37; and Superfund sites, 176, 182, 195, 199, 201; temporary sickness from, 95; victims of, 91. *See also* radioactive fallout

radio, 94–95, 225

radioactive fallout, 9, 13, 46–47, 49–51, 53, 57–66, 57*fig.*, 58*fig.*, 60*fig.*, 68n8, 75; and blue snow, 76, 98–99, 103, 105, 109n58; and Bravo test, 60*fig.*, 61–63, 92–93; and cattle/cattle deaths, 8–9, 13, 76, 78, 84–86, 97–105; and fallout shelters, 90, 92, 94–95; and food, 91, 93–95, 97; and international lawsuit, 65, 73n53; and Johnston Atoll, 124; and *Lucky Dragon* incident, 60*fig.*, 61–62, 92–93; and mental maps, 79, 81, 84–85, 104–5; and military-to-wildlife conversions, 270; and movies, 68n10; and mushroom clouds, 69n14, 87, 96–97; 150-mile limit for, 89; and Operation Teapot, 85–105, 88*fig.*; radioactive clouds, 57–59, 69n14, 86–87, 90, 94, 96–97; radioactive dust, 91, 93, 98; radioactive water, 49–51, 66, 73n57, 124; and safety measures, 52–54, 58, 63–66, 67n7, 85–87, 97; and sheep deaths, 85, 90, 94, 102, 104–5, 108n37; and Upshot-Knothole series (1953), 85–86, 94, 102; worldwide, 66

radionuclides, 176, 182

rain forests, 163

Rampton, Calvin, 116

ranchers: and Agent Orange, 118; and endangered species, 252–53, 262n70; and nuclear testing/weapons, 8–9, 13, 76, 78–79, 85, 98–105, 252–53, 262n70, 104*fig*. *See also names of ranchers*

Rand Corporation, 253, 255

rape, 212, 216

Rea, Ted, 99, 101–3

Reagan, Ronald, 156, 253, 262n74

recreational activities, 33, 127, 250; and military-to-wildlife conversions, 271, 275, 277; and off-road vehicle use, 277

red-cockaded woodpecker, 239–41, 253–55, 256n3; habitat of, 253–54; killing of, 254

re-drumming operation. *See* Operation Pacer IVY

Reeves, James E., 78, 84–85, 88–89, 89*fig*., 97–98, 101–2

regulations/regulators. *See* environmental laws/regulations/regulators

Reina Beatriz airport (Curacao), 157

remediation, environmental: and military-to-wildlife conversions, 274, 276–78, 280; and South Korea, 212, 218–21, 223–26, 228–30; and Superfund sites, 11, 15, 175, 177–80, 182–84, 186–87, 190–91, 195–200, 203, 277–78

renewable energy, 278

Republicans, 246, 253

Republic of Korea (ROK). *See* South Korea

Republic of Vietnam (RVN). *See* South Vietnam

"resistance" school, 4–6

Resource Conservation and Recovery Act (RCRA), 204n5, 277

respiratory disease, 183

restoration: and "big lie," 270; and erasure of history, 12–13, 15, 270, 273–74, 281–83; future-oriented, 270; and military-to-wildlife conversions, 12–13,

15, 266, 268–72, 274, 280–83; and presettlement historical condition, 12, 269–70, 283; and public participation programs, 179, 194; and South Korea, 212–13, 222–23. *See also* RABs (restoration advisory boards)

Reynolds Electrical and Engineering Company, 82–83, 101

Ridgecrest (Calif.), 82

risk assessments: and Agent Orange, 120, 127; and drug control, 149–50, 160–62; and endangered species, 252, 256, 261n56; and military-to-wildlife conversions, 265; and nuclear testing/weapons, 9, 67n7, 252; and public participation programs, 10–11, 15, 176, 178, 180, 183, 185, 187–88, 192, 196, 198, 202–4; and risk distribution, 202–3; in South Korea, 11; and Superfund sites, 10–11, 15, 176, 178, 180, 183, 185, 187–88, 192, 196, 198, 202–4

risk society, 142n56

river otter, 265

Rivers and Harbors Act, 248

Robert E. McKee company, 76, 78

Roberts, Richard, 160–61

Rocky Mountain Arsenal (Colo.), 269–70, 273–76, 285n26

Roh Moo-hyun, 215

Roh Taw-woo, 232n8

Rollins Environmental Services, 117

Romer, Roy R., 262n74

Roosevelt, Franklin Delano, 20, 25–30, 122–23

Roosevelt, Theodore, 22–23, 37n16, 242

Roosevelt Roads Naval Station (Vieques Island, P.R.), 247

Rosamond (Calif.), 82

Rosenthal, Debra, 67n7

Rossiter, Clinton, 21–22

Roundup, 149, 152, 159, 161. *See also* glyphosate

rule of law, 35

Rumsfeld, Donald, 220

S

safety procedures: and Agent Orange, 9, 113, 118, 120–22, 128–37, 129*fig.*; and agriculture discourse, 145–46, 148; and drug control, 145–46, 148–49, 161–62; and military-to-wildlife conversions, 276–77; and nuclear testing/weapons, 52–54, 58, 63–66, 67n7, 85–87, 97, 252; and protective clothing, 128–30, 129*fig.*, 133–34; and Superfund sites, 178, 193

Saint George (Utah), 85–86, 89, 94

Saint Louis (Miss.), 134

Saint Louis (Mo.), 117–18

Salt Lake City (Utah), 33, 96

Samper, Ernesto, 155, 159

San Antonio Air Materiel Area, 120

San Antonio Light, 118

San Clemente Island (Calif.), 249–51, 261n55

San Diego (Calif.), 139n13, 249

Sand Island, 123–24

San Francisco, 182–83, 196, 201; Department of Public Health, 183; District Attorney's Office, 182; grand jury, 201

San Francisco Bay, 182–83

San Francisco Bay Area, 182

Sangre de Christo Mountains, 76, 98

Santa Fe (N.M.), 76–78, 77*fig.*, 80*fig.*, 83, 89, 98, 100

Sauget (Ill.), 117–18, 122, 139n14, 139n16

"Sauget Wind" (song), 139n16

Schroeder, Patricia, 274, 285n26

Seamans, Robert, 117, 127

sea otter population, 8, 55–56, 66

security guards, 85, 91, 93, 260n53

Security Policy Initiative (S. Korea, U.S.), 221–22

Seoul (S. Korea), 218, 227–29; Central District Court, 228–29; and lawsuits, 228–29; Metropolitan City, 228–29

September 11, 2001, terrorist attacks, 119, 159–60, 171n55, 220

sheep/sheep deaths: and anthrax outbreak, 104; and endangered species,

261n56; and nuclear testing, 85, 90, 94, 102, 104–5, 108n37

Shell Oil processing plant, 117

Shipman, Thomas L., 78, 84–85, 97

ships, 49–52, 66, 69n15; and Agent Orange, 115, 125–26, 128, 130–31, 133, 140n32; Dutch cargo ships, 125; *Lucky Dragon*, 60*fig.*, 61–62, 92–93; M/T *TransPacific*, 115; M/T *Vulcanus*, 125, 128, 130–31, 133, 140n32; steamer lines, 52

shipyard. *See* Hunters Point Naval Shipyard (Calif.)

Shulman, Seth, 33

Shutting Down the Cold War: The Politics of Military Base Closure (Sorenson), 5

Sierra Club, 258n20

Sierra Nevada de Santa Maria, 151–52

Sikes, Robert, 119

Sikes Act (1960), 277

Silent Spring (Carson), 68n10

silica, 64

Silver City (N.M.), 90–91

Sinaloa (Mex.), 143–44

slaves, 266

smuggling/smugglers, 151–52

snail darter, 245–46, 259n33

Society for Ecological Restoration International (SER), 269

Society for Historians of American Foreign Relations, 7

SOFAs (status-of-forces agreements), 5, 11, 15, 211–13, 215–26, 228–30, 231n1, 233n32; and Article IV, 211, 223; Environmental Subcommittee, 219–20, 222, 226, 229; and supplementary agreements, 212–13, 218–19, 221–22, 225, 230

soil contamination: and coral soil, 135; and drug control, 147, 162–63; and military-to-wildlife conversions, 272, 274; and soil biodegradation, 116, 135; and soil depletion, 163; and soil infertility, 10; in South Korea, 212, 217–19, 221, 226–27, 229, 233n32; and Superfund sites, 176, 183, 187, 199

and National Priorities List (NPL), 177, 183–84, 204nn5–6; prescribed burns at, 184, 193, 196, 200; Proposed Plans for, 178; and public participation programs, 10–11, 15, 175–76, 178–204; remediation of, 11, 15, 175, 177–80, 182–84, 186–87, 190–91, 195–200, 203; in Sauget (Ill.), 117; and site reuse, 11, 179, 183, 189, 194–98, 201

Supreme Court, U.S.: and Endangered Species Act (ESA, 1973), 241, 243–46, 249, 259n35; and public lands, 22–24, 28, 31, 34. *See also names of justices; titles of cases*

sustainability, 278–80, 283

Szasz, Ferenc M., 44, 52, 67n1

T

Taft, William, 23–24

Tambs, Lewis, 166n7

Taos (N.M.), 98

TCDD (tetra-chlorodibenzo-para-dioxin), 133, 135–36, 137n3; permissible limit of, 135–36

technical assistance grants, 11

Tellico dam (Tenn.), 245–46, 259n35

Tennessee River, 245–46

Tennessee Valley Authority (TVA), 245–46, 259n33

Tennessee Valley Authority v. Hiram G. Hill, 245–46, 259n25, 259n33

terrorists, 25, 219–20. *See also* September 11, 2001, terrorist attacks

Texas, 139n13; and Agent Orange, 117, 122; Air Control Board, 117. *See also names of Texas cities and towns*

Thalken, C. E., 133–34, 141n51, 134fig.

Thee, Marek, 67n5

Them! (film), 68n10

thermonuclear bombs, 59–61, 60fig., 63, 75, 92, 94, 97

Thornberry, Douglas, 117

threatened species, 243–44, 248, 277

Three Mile Island (Pa.), 116

timber interests, 118–19, 239–40, 253

toluene, 228

Tonopah (Nev.), 83

tornadoes, 59, 127

tourism, 248; and military-to-wildlife conversions, 265–66, 268, 274–75, 280–81

Tres Esquinas (Colombia), 146, 159–60, 165

trichloroethylene, 204n7

trinitite, 75

trinitrotoluene, 176

Trinity site (Los Alamos), 44–45, 44fig., 45fig., 48, 63, 75, 82

Trum, Bernard F., 98–103

Truman, Harry, 24, 31, 40n53, 48–49, 52–53, 60, 69n11

triumphalism, 22–23

Tsutsui, William M., 68n10

tuna, 62

Turbay, Julio César, 151–52, 155

turkeys, 281

turtles, 248–49

Tuy Hoa Air Base (S. Vietnam), 114–15

2,4-D herbicide, 118–19, 127, 137n3, 146–50, 166n9

2,4,5-T herbicide, 111–12, 118–19, 127, 137n3, 166n9

2,3,7,8-TCDD, 133, 135–36, 137n3; permissible limit of, 135–36

U

uncertainty: and Agent Orange, 115–16; and nuclear testing, 85, 89, 92; and public participation programs, 15, 178, 183, 193; and Superfund sites, 15, 178, 183, 193, 204n8

Uncle Tupelo (band), 139n16

Underground Railroad, 266

unexploded military ordnance (UXO): and military-to-wildlife conversions, 265–67, 269, 280; and Superfund sites, 176, 184–85, 191, 201

United Kingdom, 66

University of California at Irvine, 244
University of California at Los Angeles, 59
University of Chicago, 91
University of Colorado, 92–93
University of Nevada, 251
University of Tennessee, 98, 245
University of Wisconsin, 16n1
Upshot-Knothole series (1953), 85–86,
    89–90; and sheep deaths, 85, 90, 94,
    102, 104–5, 108n37
uranium, 76, 97, 100, 266; Geiger counter
    readings, 76
Uribe, Alvaro, 159–60
USFK (U.S. Forces in Korea), 211–31,
    213fig.; and Camp Carroll, 225–27; and
    Camp Kim, 227–29; crimes/wrongdo-
    ings committed by, 11, 211–12, 214–18,
    222, 227; Eighth Army, 227; and
    environmental issues, 212–13, 215–31,
    233n32; internal environmental regu-
    lations of, 223–24; redeployment of,
    219–20, 229–31; and SOFAs (status-
    of-forces agreements), 11, 15, 211–13,
    215–26, 228–30, 231n1, 233n32; and
    whistleblowers, 217
Utah: and Agent Orange, 116, 227; Depart-
    ment of Health, 116; and endangered
    species, 251, 253; and missile bunkers/
    silos, 251; and nuclear testing/weap-
    ons, 86, 90, 102, 251, 253; and public
    lands, 19, 30, 33. See also names of Utah
    cities and towns

V

Vandenberg Air Force Base (Calif.),
    244–45
Venezuela, 120
veterinarians, 97–103
Vieques Island (P.R.), 247–49, 260n53, 269
Vietnam War: and Agent Orange, 9–10,
    14, 111–16, 119, 121, 128–31, 129fig.,
    131fig., 136–37, 227; and drug control,
    144–49, 155; and Operation Ranch
    Hand, 10, 136, 138n4, 144–45, 147–49,

166n12; and Superfund sites, 176;
    veterans of, 130, 136–37
Villagarzón (Colombia), 160, 165
vinyl chlorides, 183
Virilio, Paul, 35
volatile organic compounds, 176, 182, 199
VX, 126

W

Wake Island, 123
Walker, J. Samuel, 69n11
War and Society, 7
War Department, 20, 27, 31; and nuclear
    testing, 43–45. See also Department of
    Defense, U.S.
"war on drugs." See drug war
"war on terror," 15, 159–60
war powers, 7, 25–31, 40n53; preemptive,
    25; unlimited emergency ended (1952),
    30–31
Washington, D.C., 92, 101
water contamination, 8; and Agent
    Orange, 113, 115–16, 125–27, 131–32,
    135; and drinking water, 9, 113, 127,
    131–32, 218, 226–27; and drug control,
    147–48, 162; and endangered species,
    242, 251; and groundwater, 10, 64,
    95, 162, 176, 182, 184, 193, 199, 201,
    217–18, 227–28, 251, 269, 272, 274; and
    military-to-wildlife conversions, 269,
    272, 274; and ocean waters, 125–27; and
    radioactive water, 49–51, 66, 73n57,
    124; in South Korea, 212, 217–19, 221,
    226–29, 233n32; and Superfund sites,
    176, 182, 184, 193, 199, 201; and water
    supplies, 14, 127, 148
weapons of mass destruction, 22, 62, 220
weather: and Agent Orange, 115, 117–18,
    122, 126–27; and blue snow, 76, 98–99,
    103, 105, 109n58; clouds, 57–59,
    58fig., 69n14, 86–87, 90, 94, 96; and
    cold winters, 103; and drought, 99;
    and drug control, 153; and flooding,
    65, 73n53; fog, 54; and forecasts, 57,